Through Dust and Dreams

The Story of an African Adventure

Roxana Valea

Published in Great Britain by RV Publications

First published November 2014

British Library Cataloguing in Publication Data.
A catalogue record for this book is available from the British Library.

Cover design, copy-editing and typesetting by Oliphant Publishing Services

Proofreading by Nicole Oppler on behalf of Oliphant Publishing Services

The world belongs to those who dream

CHRIS NEL

CONTENTS

CHAPTER 1 – A GUIDE IN THE DESERT

(TWYFELFONTEIN, NAMIBIA, APRIL 2002)

WE were sitting by the fire, watching it die. We sat in silence, listening to the darkness all around. This is a special time in Africa, the moment after the sun has set yet before the moon has risen. A time when everything is silent and all is dark, and it is too early to sleep and too late to finish any of the many things one needs to do when a camp is set up. Too dark to look for anything, anywhere, and in those hours humans usually gather together and light a fire. Around its light and warmth, the silence of the darkness dissipates. It's the moment when, surrounded by so much darkness, you are almost forced to look for light in the depth of your own being.

"There is only one real problem in this world: men have lost their courage to follow dreams," said Chris, and his words sounded like a heavy and somewhat sad conclusion. He reached over, grabbed the bottle of brandy and filled his tin cup.

We had drunk a lot that evening. First some Coke and brandy, then the Coke was finished and we carried on with the brandy (although it tasted more like petrol). The bottle was almost empty and I could feel the sweet, pleasant weight of the alcohol running through my veins.

I looked at his hands, holding tight the small, half-empty cup. I could almost see the pulse of life in his veins, the same way I could feel it in his voice.

"You see, Roxana, that's your problem. You're so caught up in the storm of thoughts going through your head that you forget to look around. It's like looking at the surface of the sea and not knowing what lies underneath. Go diving, get your head underwater, go deep inside and then you'll understand what beauty really means."

This was not the first night Chris had posed as my spiritual guide. I was already tired and irritated by the never-ending discussions about "the courage to become who you are". Big words, vague sentences, alcohol, lots of alcohol... I had a headache already and I couldn't really understand what he wanted to tell me. I could only feel that I was attracted by this man, deeply and powerfully, and it was this attraction that made me stay here, by the fire, deep into the night, long after all the others had gone to sleep in their tents... I was out there, listening to him, feeling the sound of his words going deep into my stomach, his strong Afrikaans accent with its rolling Rs melting and mixing with the food I had eaten at dinner and the feelings I never dared to show.

I had come to Africa at the end of a strange chain of events. First, there was my lunch with a friend and my complaints about how empty life was. I had just moved to Lugano, Switzerland, and was working in marketing for a big company in the household manufacturing industry. According to my friends, I had "made it". I had a good job and a good life. I should have been happy. I wasn't. Something was missing and I didn't quite know what it was.

My life up until that point seemed to have been made up of a series of events with no clear connection to one another. Born in Romania, I had lived there until I was 25 and obtained a degree in Journalism before turning my hand to entrepreneurship, founding a translation agency that I later sold. I seemed incapable of settling down, moving from job to job, always restless and always dreaming of far-away places. Then I moved to Italy and took an MBA degree. Now at the end of my two-year course, I was moving once again. After accepting the job in Switzerland I was trying to settle down once more: my third country, my fourth home, my sixth job.

Deadlock. It was the first thing that came to my mind when I tried to describe my life. The guy I was in love with decided to look for happiness elsewhere. My job turned out to be far less exciting than the promises made during the interview. Oblivious to the pain inside, I was carrying on: day after day, business trip after business trip... I saw no way out.

Until one day when I woke up and fainted. I had reached the bottom. Something had to change and it had to change fast. "Extreme physical and mental fatigue," doctors said, and gave me a stress level questionnaire to fill in. I could tick most of the boxes: break up of a relationship, starting a new job, moving house, problems at work, changing country. You name it, I had it! "She needs a holiday" was the verdict.

So I ran away from it all. I went to Africa, with no enthusiasm, no thoughts and no expectations. Maybe just a small, hidden hope that ten days' holiday would somehow show me what I was supposed to do next. It hadn't.

This was my last night here and I felt I had made no progress. All my questions were still there. On top of everything, I had met this fascinating guide who liked talking in riddles, and whose words would bring about laughter and embarrassed looks if heard in a London pub over a pint of beer. But here, in the immensity of the empty savannah, words carried a different weight.

I looked back at Chris, who seemed lost in his thoughts as he sipped the dregs of his brandy from the tin cup. I remembered my first impression of him, ten days before, when we met at the airport. He looked like an African version of Crocodile Dundee, somewhat at odds with the "civilised" background of an airport arrivals lounge. He was white, and this was my first surprise. I somehow expected to find that all Africans would be black. He wore jeans and a khaki T-shirt, the same jeans and the same T-shirt that he was wearing now as he shrivelled by the fire.

I was looking at him in silence; he was looking at the fire. His eyes were wide open, frozen, staring at the flames. His back, with strong muscles stretching under the sweaty T-shirt, bent towards the fire, his whole being attracted by the flames. He was silent, as if his soul had gone far away and only his shell was left there: the healthy, agile body of a man used to outdoor living. Only the veins of his arms, pulsing rhythmically, betrayed that there was still life inside.

The passion in his words had gone as well, as if sucked out by the fire in front of us. I wanted to bring him back, to grab his gaze from the fire that was taking him away and turn it towards me, so that I could feel again his eyes in mine and the warmth of his smile. So I did it in the only way I allowed myself to get close to him: by talking.

"So, that's why you told me to run down that dune at

Sossusvlei? Because beauty is all around us, even when it's so difficult to see?" I asked, trying to impress him with my logic. Somehow, the dots started to connect in my mind as if what he was talking about could indeed make sense. I remembered my first day in Africa.

It was still dark outside when we left. Chris and Max, the group's Italian guide, told us that we had to see the sunrise beside "dune 45". The sun rose before we got to the dune, but the light of the morning was still fresh enough to take good pictures. It was a lonely dune rising straight from a rocky area, as if some mysterious hand had drawn a fine but firm line: on one side the plain, on the other the desert. In single file, we started to climb the dune. Chris took off his shoes and I did the same. Max told me I must be mad because there could be scorpions in the sand. I thought for a second about going back to grab my shoes, but climbing a dune is not easy, so I decided it was not worth the 20 metres I had conquered so far. We climbed in silence for a while.

I came to the top hoping the view would be worth the effort. It was beautiful, but was it really worth it? We were high up and the plain was lying under us, stretching to the horizon. Every now and then a lonely tree would break the monotony of the landscape. The plain itself was a sort of desert, with rocky, light grey soil that could barely support the few trees or the thorny bushes scattered around. Rising abruptly from this flatness, a sea of huge dunes: soft, red sand. It was a borderline world, the place where plains turn into desert and trees give up fighting the sand. And in the bright light of the morning the colours were even brighter than I had seen them the day before, the sky was deep blue, the sand was dark red and I had the feeling I had been thrown into a colouring book world where a diligent child had taken the time to fill in all the shapes of the picture with vivid colours.

We sat there in silence and we looked around, each of us lost in our own thoughts. Chris had probably seen the landscape many times before and I wondered if he had found anything new to look at. My hands and feet were buried in the soft sand and I noticed it was warming up. Soon we would not be able to walk barefoot, so I had to think about getting back to the shoes I had left at the base of the dune. Yes, maybe it was worth coming so far, I told myself. The landscape, the colours and the warmth, all were nice and I was kind of pleased to be there. I was not enthusiastic though. It is sometimes hard to find a reason within oneself to feel enthusiastic about anything.

"Have you ever run down a dune?" Chris suddenly asked.

I looked at him without answering. I could think of no reason why I should ever have run down a dune.

"Come on, why don't you try? It feels like flying." Chris was looking at the horizon and I wondered whether he was talking to me. "If you're not going to try out such things, why come all the way here?"

Here on top of the dune or here in Africa? I wasn't sure but it didn't really matter. It was a powerful argument and I decided to erase in a few seconds all the pain and the effort of climbing that dune and the unanswered question as to why I was there.

I started running down, at first with a sort of uneasiness, as if I didn't really want to let myself go; but then, as I felt the wind blow through my hair, I ran faster and faster. The dune was steep and I suddenly felt afraid that I might fall and roll down to the base. But as I gained speed, I eventually let my body weight dictate the direction of my run and it felt as if I was in free fall and my legs were just briefly touching the sand.

My face was down, my body at a 45-degree angle as I ran and ran, smiling with my eyes closed. Then, all of a sudden, I forgot about where I was and what I was doing and I felt I was flying and there was no longer any dune or sand either, just the free fall and the emptiness inside, and the silence and time seemed suspended somewhere where time had not yet been born and the space melted and I woke up suddenly at the base of the dune. I couldn't say anything, and as I tried to regain my breath, I noticed my arms and legs aching. My mind was still a void and I simply could not think of anything so I just carried on smiling. My body felt alive, deeply alive, in a way it had not been for a long time.

His voice brought me back from my thoughts.

"Your problem is that you've got twins living inside you. One belongs to civilisation and all those posh things... your job, your studies, your life in your big and busy city and all the social status you're after, the other one brings you here and shouts out its own story about adventure and exploration, about nature and wilderness. The problem is the first one was born just ten minutes before the second one and she claims her right as 'firstborn'. You live by the rules she dictates, and you go ahead and build your life in the direction she takes you and you try hard not to hear the second one, whose shout is now no more than a whisper. There will come a time when you will not be able to ignore that whisper any longer."

I already had a headache. It was the combined effect of alcohol and a long, heavy day. We had reached the camp as the sun was setting and begun the usual routine of putting up the tents, unloading the cars and lighting the fire. We hadn't quite got around to settling next to the fire when I saw something long and black climbing quickly up Chris's leg. I jumped, screaming, but Chris shook his foot and with a sudden move I saw the creature falling directly into the fire. It was a scorpion. I looked at the animal's body twisting into the flames, changing its colour from deep black into almost reddish, contorting in a last spasm. I felt I wanted to save it, to get it out of there, but it was too late... On the other hand, it was better that it had landed in the fire: at least that way it couldn't climb on someone else.

Afterwards we had dinner, with feet up on chairs and tables. Then the rest of the group disappeared into the comfort of their tents, where a zip would protect them from all such strange creatures. The two of us, Chris and I, remained outside with a bottle of brandy and the leftovers of dinner.

"You see," he said, with an absent look in his eyes, "life is like a row of closed doors waiting to be opened; you never know what you will find behind them. A nice room, or a cellar filled with spiders' webs. All that you can do is open them and have a look. Some people stop after they have opened the first door: they cannot handle the insecurity of opening another one. Others go on and try to find something closer to what they are looking for."

"What do you mean, that I should go back tomorrow and throw away all that I have and all that I have built, give it all up, resign, leave my life? So that I do what?"

At that point I just wanted answers. I was just too tired of questions and riddles.

"I don't say you should do anything out of a sparkle of enthusiasm, jump into the unknown. I am only saying you should be honest and ask yourself if the room you're in at present is the one you really want to be in."

It wasn't. That I already knew, as I knew I should open another door, but which one was it to be?

"Just trust yourself," Chris continued, somehow encouraging, as if he had sensed the tears of frustration burning at the back of my eyes. "Be honest with yourself. And one day, some weeks or months or years from now, you will find the answers. One condition though: that you keep on searching."

I didn't understand what he wanted to say. I was trying hard but I just didn't.

"That is why you told me about the Bushmen and their way of living? Do you think that one can be happy only if one returns to wilderness? I cannot do this. Civilisation is a part of me, as are my city and my friends and my life back there."

"There's nothing wrong with civilisation," he said. "And you don't have to give it all up. On the contrary: use it, but do not become absorbed by it. Do you think that we live here without any trace of civilisation? I rent DVDs, I use the Internet and I will send my kids to school. I'm not saying the answer is somewhere in the hut of a Bushman."

"Then what on earth are you saying? It's too confusing."

"You have to live with the world and not in the world, use it but do not belong to it, otherwise it will suck your blood until you've got nothing else left. We cannot escape our lives, our century and all those things around us. But we can use them and not be used by them. It's so easy to become a victim, you know. How many people are doing it every day? You only need several shots of espresso a day, a fancy restaurant in the evening and some crazy music at a disco, all anaesthetics to help you forget, to ease the pain of not living in accordance with who you are."

I was getting cold. The fire had almost gone out and the darkness all around had become even darker. I felt as if there was too little light to fight, too little hope to keep me going. Was there any sense in that conversation? We had probably drunk too much.

"The world belongs to those who dream," Chris concluded. I had heard him say that before, but that night those words sounded soft and final and they linked somehow with my old dream of going to Africa one day, a link that I didn't fully understand at the time.

Who was this man talking to me, and how did he know

about those things? Who had told him about my questions and who had asked him to shatter my peace? He had made his own choices and seemed happy with his way. He had told me that he had an Engineering diploma and had even tried to work in an office. It didn't last too long: he soon realised it wasn't meant for him. Then he started searching and tried all sorts of things: professional scuba diver, fisherman... eventually he became a safari guide. There in the desert, he got back in touch with himself and sucked up enough energy to return to the city life, to his wife and two kids. He had found a part of his soul, hidden there in the wilderness, and from that moment on he never felt lost again.

This was where his power came from, the attraction he spread all around him. He was complete, he had managed to put his various parts together – something that at that time was for me only a distant hope. I felt his power, I saw him self-confident and relaxed. I imagined he would be a passionate lover. If I wasn't careful, I would fall in love with him and that wasn't a good idea. Not only had he a wife and two children, but that night was the last of my African adventure. I would never see him again after we said goodbye at the airport the next day. No, I would not fall in love with that man. So what if I was attracted to him, so what if he fascinated me? So what if he seemed to have all the answers that I was seeking in vain? So what if... I would not fall in love with him, just because I had decided not to.

He was so close to me that I could have touched him and I felt like putting my hand over his hands, still holding his cup of brandy. Instead, I reached for the bottle and I poured the last drops into our cups. That was it, the brandy was finished and I knew this meant my time with him was finished as well.

"Listen, I think you should sleep inside a tent tonight." Chris brought me back to reality with some practical concerns. "This is a really bad place for snakes and scorpions, it's too risky to sleep outside".

For several nights now I had slept outside next to Chris, despite the funny smiles of our travel companions. But I was happy with the newly discovered feeling of freedom, sleeping there in the open. And I couldn't care less about what everyone else was thinking.

"Look, this is my last night here and I'd really like to spend it outside. I'll be fine, really: after all, I was born in

November under the Scorpio sign and they won't attack one of their own!"

Chris seemed unimpressed by my logic. He kept quiet, lost in his thoughts for a while, with an empty look in his eyes, holding the empty cup by the remains of the fire. Something was missing, I could tell, but I didn't know what.

"OK," he said after a while. "But there is something we could do to try and avoid nasty surprises tonight: sleep in the fairy circles."

I had noticed them as soon as we had stopped that afternoon. They were large circles, looking as if they had been drawn by an invisible hand, scattered across the plain. They were just large enough to park the car in the middle of one of them. Nothing, no grass or any other plant, would grow inside these circles. Apparently nobody had managed to explain how they came into existence and what spell protected them from being covered with vegetation, like the rest of the plain, and because no explanation could be found, people just called them the "fairy circles".

"If we sleep in the middle of one of those, we're less likely to wake up facing the tongue of a snake. They prefer the grass. Let's get the bed rolls. And then I have something for you – something that will help you sleep better." His eyes were smiling and I wondered what it was he was talking about. There couldn't be another bottle. We had just been looking all around, trying to see if any alcohol was left anywhere.

He opened his bed roll and threw it down in the middle of one of the circles. I opened mine with slow movements as the alcohol in my veins made me stumble a little. I felt uncertain and vulnerable, the way one feels after a bit too much to drink. Here I was, putting up my bed roll next to him. A distant thought travelled through my mind. The other people in the tents must think there's some kind of a romance going on between the two of us with all those midnight talks. The thought made me smile. No, there wasn't romance, but it was something better than that. I felt like I had found someone who understood, and who could help me understand as well. I felt safe with him. I felt good. I knew my friends would call me naïve again, but I felt I could trust this man that I was putting my bed roll next to in a mysterious and profound way. I could trust him, despite being drunk, despite having met him only a few days before, despite the emptiness of the space around us and despite the tension that inevitably builds up as a man and a woman open up their bed rolls one next to the other in the middle of a fairy circle.

The fairy circle was drawn perfectly into the ground and the earth was flat in the middle. Maybe it had been drawn by some large animals walking in circles, or maybe some of the locals had strange rituals that involved making circles in the savannah grass. There was nothing and nobody around and I remembered that we had not seen a human face outside our group for days. We were in a strange place with a strange name: Twyfelfontein – "The Doubtful Spring". Somewhere, not far away from where we were sleeping, there was a spring with no identifiable source coming to the surface.

Chris had reached out his hand, his fingers upwards, as if he was trying to catch the moon. Then unexpectedly he stretched it towards me and said, "Give me your hand!"

I didn't move. My heart was beating strongly. What did he mean?

"Come on, give me your hand. I want to see how big your palm is compared to mine..."

I gave him my hand, shaking, and I felt a shiver when my fingers touched his. We were lying about a metre apart, but now, with our arms outstretched and our fingers clenched, all the distance had suddenly gone.

I was breathing heavily... No, I didn't want to... or maybe I really wanted to... I felt another shiver in my stomach.

As if sensing my panic, he suddenly let go and his hand disappeared inside the sleeping bag, searching through his pockets.

"Here, do you want to try?" With a wide smile on his face, Chris had rolled himself a joint.

So that was what he had been saving for later, I told myself, with a sigh of relief that the scary intimacy was now over and the joint gave us both another, far less frightening, way of being together. I had seen him smoking before, at the end of a busy day or when he felt pushed to the edges of exasperation by some strange comment from the group.

He passed the joint to me and I felt another warm weight flowing into my veins. And this time it wasn't the alcohol. I had another smoke and gave it back to him. We were lying face up in the middle of a fairy circle, each of us buried deeply in his or her own bed roll. The moon had finally risen and it seemed to have a strangely intense colour: it could be anything from deep yellow to pink or maybe even purple...

"I told you the full moon is special in this place." Chris broke the silence.

I couldn't answer since the joint had been passed back to me again. To be honest, I didn't feel like talking any longer.

Far away I heard the screaming bark of a dog.

"Jackals," Chris observed. "They will not come too close though, they are fearful creatures."

The noise continued for a while, and in the silence of the night it seemed that the whole world was reduced to two people smoking a joint and a jackal searching for food somewhere in the savannah.

I looked at the moon and the moon looked back at me, and I wondered how the world would look from up there, seen through the eyes of the moon. And I wondered how two people would look down there, in the middle of a fairy circle, in the middle of a plain, buried in their bed rolls and in their questions and answers, trying to run away from it all with the help of a joint. How would they look in the eyes of such an old moon? The light started to get stronger and stronger and it seemed like another type of day had started, another type of world had opened.

I watched the last bit of the joint disappearing under the thirsty lips of my fairy circle mate; it was over, it was all gone, the bottle and the joint, and my holiday... and my questions and... and nothing mattered any longer and my senses were numb. The drug had already made its way to my brain and I didn't feel like talking any longer or even thinking. The moon was up and it was all that mattered and I felt a warm sensation of knowledge spreading through my veins, telling me that in fact it was all useless because in the immensity of the universe only things like the rise of a full moon mattered, and the moon had been there yesterday and the day before that and the month before that, and it would always be there. And a part of me was there yesterday too, and the year before, and would forever be there, lying on my back in the middle of a fairy circle drawn by an invisible hand in the grass of the savannah. Because I was one with the moon and the moon lived inside me and together we were neither moon nor human.

"You see, once in a blue moon, the moon can indeed turn blue," Chris whispered, lost in his own thoughts, which seemed to be even more nonsensical than my own.

And then, right under my sleepy eyes, the moon turned itself blue – because all it needs is a drop of faith and someone willing to believe that its light is blue and this is how we can make things happen because in fact reality does not exist outside ourselves: we contain it all and it contains us, and I understood, once again, that my questions were in fact not important. Neither was it important if that man, who tonight had drunk half a bottle of brandy with me, was right, or if what he spoke about made sense. It didn't matter that I had not yet found my path, because I had all the time in the world to find it, because once you become aware that you need to look for it, then the whole universe opens up and you can reach up to the moon.

"Think of something old, something buried deep down in you, some memory that you cherish and which could give you some insight into what could make you happy, into how you would like to live..." His voice faded away into the abyss of sleep.

And then and there, at the border between dream and reality, an older image started gaining form. I was a little girl again and I was running around the park next to my parents' house, where I used to spend my childhood days. I was hiding behind some bushes and then I walked a bit further and crossed the boundaries of what was "allowed playground", and I stepped into what then looked like a wilderness, and there, a most amazing sight unfolded in front of my eyes. It was a green meadow surrounded by tall trees and there was nobody around and I was hidden behind a big bush, afraid of but thrilled by the thought that I might spot some mysterious animal. The grass was high, I could feel it touch my elbows and I stood still and watched it, and breathed in the sight of a far-away place, hidden beyond the border of the trees I was forbidden to cross. That view had always lived in me. For years and years I had carried with me the image of that meadow in the light of the morning sun, and all the promise of discovery and excitement that awaited me when I would be old enough to start walking on it.

I think I must have smiled just before letting go of that image as I crossed the border of sleep and entered the world where dreams become reality. But I knew I had it in me and it would come back if I called on it and it would give me guidance. For I had found again the little girl who seemed lost for such a long time, and now that she was awake and aware she would ask for her right to go and discover the rest of the path she gazed at that morning. And the woman in me made a promise to the little girl that they would go together.

I woke up at sunrise. My guide was already up. His "day in the office", as he called it, started pretty early. He had to start preparing breakfast and coffee, clean up the remains of the feast from the night before, get things into boxes and boxes into cars.

"See you later," he had told me before disappearing in the direction of the camp, with his rolled bedding on one shoulder. "We're leaving early today so see that you're ready soon."

Yes, I knew we had a lot of distance to cover that day. All the centuries between wilderness and an airport terminal.

I lay there still and did not speak. From where I was lying I could see the colours of the sunrise dancing on the horizon, first some sort of grey that turned gradually into purple and then lighted up to bright pink. The sun was about to rise and with it a new breeze of hope would descend on the surface of this earth, with the promise of a new beginning.

The first rays came out and the light was deep orange. There was no longer any time to waste; there was no time not to be ready, the world was going round and willingly or not, I had to go with it. And there would be another sunrise tomorrow; only I would not be there, I would be in another country, far away from all this, where an alarm clock would shout at me the beginning of a new day, of a new rush. But today I was still here, alone in the vastness of the plain, and that day was unique and that sunrise was unique, because no two sunrises are alike and no two chances we are given are alike.

"I have to stop thinking otherwise I'll start crying," I told myself, and I tried hard to stop thinking.

I was lying there for a while until I decided it was time to stand up and roll up my sleeping bag. I started to walk towards the camp. The smell of coffee was already in the air and I could hear voices. Chris was already on the roof of the car, loading the tents.

I could remember all the details of the previous night and all the words that had been spoken were engraved in my memory. I was still trying not to think but I felt I had to stop walking. The panic had spread its poison into my blood and I looked around in despair, trying to contain it all: the smell of the grass and the purple light on the horizon, the shape of the mountains far away where the plain and sky were melting. The vastness and the silence and the breeze touching my skin: I wanted to grab all of them and take them home with me so that I could wake up with them again.

Then I realised I couldn't. Tears started rolling down my face and I stood still and I cried; I cried out my sadness at saying goodbye and my happiness at being there in that very moment; I cried for my loneliness and the grey life I had to return to; and I cried with hope that I would one day find my way. I cried silently and without desperation until I couldn't tell what exactly I was crying for. That moment, under the sunrise of that morning, I realised that something had been moved inside my soul and somewhere between the rise of the moon and the rise of the sun the transformation took place, as if I had been bitten by a scorpion that night and woken up in the skin of another being. And, having come to terms with myself, I cried a little bit more: for my memory of running down a dune; for the grass and the sun; for the silence and the dreams I had given up one day and which were now brought back to me by the sunrise of that morning. I made a pledge to myself: I would return here.

The way to the airport seemed to pass in a moment.

"Take care of yourself." Chris was smiling when he said goodbye. I knew he was happy to get rid of this heavy group. "Take care," he repeated, "and keep in touch, let me know how it's going."

The end of a holiday, the end of a tour. Was he saying this to all of his tourists or did he really care? Would I ever talk to him again?

"I will be back." And immediately after I said it, I regretted saying it.

It's always easier to leave when fooling yourself that you would return. It's not a proper goodbye because there will be another occasion. Yes, I was fooling myself because I felt sad to say goodbye.

But I knew it would come true somehow, sometime. I had to return there.

BACK TO EUROPE

"IT will start as soon as you board. The transformation, I mean. As soon as you get back in touch with your cold, impersonal world. A world with all those wonders of technology, and an airport is the best place for that. You will start to slowly doubt whether all that you have felt was true and all that you have seen was indeed that beautiful. A part of you will slowly die and another one will grow to take its place, and you will tell yourself that you have a house to return to and work to resume, and friends to see again and a lot of washing to do after this trip, and you'll show the photos to others and chat about your amazing trip. But guess what? Even the pictures will seem somehow faded and the colours won't look that bright any longer. For a while you will try to fight back and keep your memories alive, but then it will become a matter of survival and you will begin slowly but surely to let go and turn back to the self you were before the trip, just like an animal who changes its skin colour to match a new environment. And you will even doubt you have had questions and you ever searched for answers."

Chris had warned me that the transformation was about to take place and he was right. I could see it happening.

I tried fighting back and I tried to keep alive in me the purple of the sunrise of that morning and the smell of the grass, and my tears falling down my face in the middle of the fairy circle. But it was more and more difficult, and the marketing assistant with hopes of a management job took the place of the girl from the savannah and I no longer had to put up tents, I had to deal with marketing campaigns instead. And my alarm clock did the job of the first ray of the morning sun, and planes replaced the old Land Rover, and even the questions were forgotten.

I had come back to my old life.

CHAPTER 2 – HE WHO SPEAKS FIRST LOSES...

(LUGANO, SWITZERLAND, OCTOBER 2002)

I had returned from my Namibian safari. I tried hard to forget, to come back to my life and integrate, to grow up as people told me. My life resumed. I was living in a beautiful flat all alone, had no friends around and went to work each morning for a company I disliked.

I decided to change jobs but it wasn't the right time to be job hunting. Europe was in the middle of a recession. What else could I do to change my life? I had thought about taking some time off, about travelling. Africa came back to my mind again but I couldn't see a way to make it happen. Another safari? They were expensive and lasted a couple of weeks at most. Travelling on my own? Too scary.

October 15th was just another day, like all the days in the past months. I came to the office two hours earlier than usual, wrote a few application letters, attached my CV and sent them off. And then, maybe just to fight off the Monday morning blues, I clicked on the Lonely Planet site to allow myself a few minutes of dreaming before the day kicked in. I found an announcement posted by an English guy who was planning to drive from London to Cape Town and was looking for two others. "Application still open," I read, and went on to see more details.

I don't really remember what I thought when I saw the ad. I didn't jump off my chair, I'm sure. I didn't have any feeling that this was an answer to my questions or a sign of destiny. I just felt amused and intrigued, and a bit sad to see other people living the life I was just dreaming about –

envious of their freedom and possibilities.

I heard the voice of my boss and I realised my time was up. The day had started. I was about to close the page but then the words "application still open" caught my eye again. What did I have to lose? Click, click. I attached my CV to an email. Let's see if I would get this job.

I forgot all about it and my day carried on, with the same sense of lifelessness and monotony I was used to by then. The following day I got a short email. It was from him and it said, "If you're serious, we should meet."

That was the moment when I really panicked. "If I was serious" – I wasn't. In fact I was just joking. Seated at my desk, I stared blindly at the email. "If you are serious"... I wasn't... I couldn't be... I could... I would, in fact. I so wished that I would or I could or maybe just that I dared... "If you are serious"... Time stood still.

I felt numb. I stood up and drank a glass of water; looked around at the big hall with cubicles, at the people teeming busily around, at my business life that I had built over the years.

I opened the window and I inhaled the strong mountain air. It smelled of freshly cut grass. It was a late autumn day, the sun brimming over the city with its immaculate streets. I saw the lake in the distance, with a few yawls. All around, the mountain ridges covered with snow were shining. I thought about the winter that would soon come and about going skiing. I thought about the life I had here, in this world where trains came on time, where everything happened by the second – it wasn't for nothing that they made the best watches in the world.

I had got used to the postcard picture in which I lived. It had become my world, and even though I sometimes felt constrained by its strict rules, that was my life and I couldn't just drop everything on impulse. "If you are serious." I was struggling and struggling to swallow and forget and erase my memory and move on, but I just couldn't, and the phrase kept lingering on my computer screen and in my eyes and down into my stomach. "If you are serious." And what if I was, and if that was what I really wanted to do?

That was my first decision moment. I wrote back saying that I'd like to meet up.

LONDON, UK – THE FOLLOWING WEEKEND

THE first thing I noticed about Peter when I saw him smiling down from the third-floor window of his London apartment building was his eyes, deep and dark, very mobile and smiling with a hint of irony. He seemed polite and very controlled. Later on, when he told me he had spent several years in the army, I understood where his stiffness came from. An architecture graduate, a computer programmer in his day job and a dreamer of cross-African trips the rest of the time, he seemed an odd sort of a mixture. This made me feel at ease, since I'm an odd sort of a mixture myself.

To my surprise he was older than I thought. He confessed that he would turn 40 at some point during the trip. Just as I remembered from the pictures on his website, his face was long and bony. His gestures were quick and tense, his voice low and rapid. From the first sentence we exchanged, I struggled to understand his accent. I did not know it then, but this was to be one of my main frustrations in the eight months to follow.

There was someone else with him, a guy who had, just like me, responded to the ad. The two of them had first met the day before and had already decided that they would go together. And now they were both here to screen me and decide whether I was to be the third one.

"This is Richard," said Peter.

Another handshake and another pair of eyes stared deep into mine. These ones were big, steady and of an indefinite colour, somewhere between green and blue. They kept on looking deep down into mine as if he wanted to read all about me. He had fair hair and looked younger than Peter. I later found out that he had studied geography but wanted to become a stockbroker and was taking all sorts of financial exams.

He didn't say much for the first part of the evening. As an introduction he told me he had been backpacking for eight months in India, had travelled by public transport throughout Southeast Asia, then into Mexico and from there to Buenos Aires. He then flew over to South Africa and made his way north to Ethiopia. He was then 25 and had already travelled halfway round the world. He seemed very comfortable with the decision he had made 24 hours earlier to join a total stranger on this trip.

All three of us were facing the same problem. The job market was at its lowest point – it was nearly impossible to find any type of job, not to mention the "right" one. The right time to be away, they said. And then, when we come back in roughly a year's time, things might be better.

They asked me a lot of questions. They wanted to know if I had travelled before, if I could drive off-road, what I liked to eat, if I could dig a hole in the ground and use it as a toilet, if I could cook... I didn't ask them too many things. It felt like being interviewed.

They seemed polite and well-behaved. They seemed well-educated too, and this was important to me. If I was to spend eight months with total strangers I wanted at least to choose two people who I could learn new things from. They looked normal, almost scarily normal, and I realised that I had somehow been hoping to meet two lunatics and thus easily justify my decision to forget about it all.

I was still feeling tense. We went out for dinner and the wine we shared over some pizza helped me relax, although my senses were still alert and the questions I didn't dare to ask were still fighting to come out. Security was the main topic on my mind. I was to spend eight months with two total strangers. How would they behave? The horror movie my mind was playing involved being raped in the desert, killed and chopped into pieces!

"We are all in the same situation," Richard tried to answer. "We also don't know each other. It's a risk for everybody involved."

Yes, right, as if the main problem would be them fearing that I would get drunk and rape them in the middle of the desert.

It wasn't only this: the thought of a setup played around my mind. What if they were just two impostors, getting people to pay a £1600 deposit and then disappearing? Fear is a cunning being, always around, and when you least expect her she comes up with another idea.

That night, however, fear seemed to be reduced to silence. It may have been too much for her as well. But I knew she would take revenge soon, just as soon as the chat, the pizza and the wine were over, and then I would be alone with her and she would invade me, poisoning my brain: the job that I was trapped in, the rental contract for my apartment running for another year, the money that I did not have, these people that I knew nothing about...

But that evening, those thoughts lived only in the back of my mind. The other things were more real: things like the map of Africa and the car parked outside, the two of them talking about driving in the desert, their eyes sparkling, and the bottle of red wine we shared. It was a beautiful night. And when it was over and I went to sleep, I thought that if nothing came of this, at least I had allowed myself to dream for a few hours. I felt good.

The morning after, I felt sick. I had a hangover from too much dreaming (and red wine). I got out of bed because I had arranged to meet Peter again. There was one thought that wouldn't leave my mind and I had to get rid of it.

"Look, I have a problem," I told him. "There's one thing on my mind at the moment: that you and Richard are just setting this up for the sake of getting money off me and then you'll disappear and I'll never hear of you again."

Peter seemed quite amused by my bluntness.

"What can I do to convince you of the contrary? I could show you the registration certificate of the car, the green card, my passport."

"I guess I'm feeling uncomfortable about paying you beforehand."

"But you must understand, then, that you are shifting your risk on to me. If I accept that you pay me the day you turn up for the trip, I have to live with the risk of you changing your mind at the last minute and I have to start looking for someone again and it's too late."

"OK, but your risk is nothing compared to mine. This is really an issue for me. I would insist on paying you later."

Silence. Silence is always a sign that things will be decided soon.

I've been through negotiation classes. I've been taught not to break the silence that settles after a final offer. He who speaks first loses. My training worked well and I kept quiet, then easily enough the answer came:

"OK, fine, you give me the money when you arrive in London or Spain or Morocco, wherever you are able to join us. I'll take the risk. Are you happy?"

"Feeling better," I admitted, "but I still have to give you a final answer. Yes or no. I need to sleep on it and think about it for a few days."

"That's fine. You should know, however, that Richard

and I had a chat after our meeting last night and we'd want you to come along. Now it's up to you."

It felt like an interview where you've just been offered a job. Only that in this case I wasn't sure I wanted it.

"I'll let you know in three days maximum."

I was flying back home the following day and I knew that the mess I was in was so huge that it could take either three days and a miracle to solve it, or a whole year and no conclusion at all.

LUGANO, SWITZERLAND – THE FOLLOWING DAY

THE office was empty and I was the first person in, so no different from the usual start to the day. Only that this morning I wasn't there to send out CVs. I was there to think and to take a decision. I had spoken to my friends, I had rehearsed the pros and the cons, and I had gone to London and come back. I had met the guys, chatted and thought of everything again and again. My mind seemed incapable of reaching a decision.

Through the glass walls I saw my boss entering his office. This was the ideal moment; I couldn't allow myself to miss it. There was no more time to think, no more time not to be ready. I just went after him and I suddenly told him that I wanted to resign.

He leant back on his chair and his eyes looked steadily into mine. He was my boss, my mentor, the one who had hired me and bet his own reputation for me, a young woman with no experience but "lots of potential", fresh out of a big-brand MBA. I knew he wanted very much to see me promoted into a managerial position.

He spoke with a slow voice and even his harsh Dutch accent seemed softer. He asked me why I wanted to leave. I said I wasn't happy, that I wasn't feeling like I was walking my true path. For a while he looked at me quietly and then he exploded:

"Are we talking bullshit again? I thought you had come to your senses. What are you really looking for? What is this 'being happy'? Do you think these people working here are waking up every morning with these stupid thoughts in their heads? Do you think I can afford to think about that? Am *I* really happy?"

The violence in his voice surprised me. I kept quiet, not

sure what would come next.

"Listen to me and listen well. Nobody in this world, in this century, is truly happy. Nobody is walking his own path. This is something that does not exist. This is something we fabricate in our brains at some young age and it's something we grow out of when we become true adults. Come on! Wake up! Do you really know anybody who's 'walking his own path'?"

For a fraction of a second the image of Chris by the fire flashed through my eyes. I still kept quiet and he continued in a calmer voice.

"I told you things would change. I have a new assignment for you, a new position: it will be better this time. It's OK, you've gone through a bad period. But that's over now and you'll be a lot happier in your new role."

Then, silence. I kept mine and he kept his. He probably used the same silence technique I was so familiar with. He who speaks first loses.

I thought of what he said and I knew it might be true. I might be happier in my new position. I thought about the security I was about to leave and about the light of a full moon on an African plain. And I knew that this was my moment and mine alone. And nobody could do for me what I was about to do. I spoke first. But this time I meant to win.

"Look. I have taken a decision. I want to leave."

Silence again and then the last test.

"Are you absolutely sure?"

By then I felt lighter. The hard part was over. Actually, it was all over, there was no way back. Yes, I was sure. He told me to sort out the details with HR. There was nothing more to say.

"Thank you."

He didn't answer. I left. I went to my desk, sat down and froze there for a while, on my everyday chair, in front of my computer not yet turned on. I had just changed the course of my life and didn't know exactly what would come next.

BUCHAREST, ROMANIA – TWO WEEKS LATER

I went back to Romania to try and help my parents digest the news. The clock had already started ticking and I was busy trying to sort out all the details: shopping, packing,

jabs...
I had managed to sublet my apartment. Even my parents reacted better than I had expected. The only thing left was to get a flight to Spain, where I would meet the two guys: they had already left London.

It wasn't meant to be that simple, though, and one evening, a couple of days before leaving, I understood the full meaning of the word "trouble".

"There was an accident. The car is destroyed. I'm afraid it cannot be repaired. We need to cancel the trip." On the other end of the phone, Peter's voice was emotionless.

Silence. He must be joking, I thought. The British have a strange sense of humour! I felt my throat getting dry. I tried to speak.

"Peter, tell me that this is a joke."

A short pause, then I heard his voice again.

"I wish it were. But it's true I'm afraid."

I tried to swallow but the dryness in my throat stopped me. I tried to speak but nothing came out. I tried again. One more time.

"Peter, this is not possible. I've done it now: I left my job, I just told my parents, I gave up my apartment – there is no way back. You simply cannot tell me this now."

"I'm sorry."

Silence. There was nothing else to add. I hung up.

For a while I didn't move. I wanted to cry but nothing came out. There was simply nothing else to say.

Maybe all this was just an impossible dream and this accident was my wake-up call.

TARIFA, SPAIN – NOVEMBER 2002

I decided to go and meet them in Spain. I was curious and wanted to see the destroyed car to help me believe, as Peter confessed, that they had actually driven in Spain on the wrong side of the road. Even though the car had the steering wheel on the left, as in continental Europe, they had not managed to internalise the concept of driving on the right-hand side of the road. Less than an hour after they got off the ferry that had taken them all the way from England, they hit a Spaniard (who probably didn't understand what those crazy people were doing on the wrong side of the road).

I met Peter. He had managed to retrieve some of the equipment after the accident but the car was completely destroyed, waiting to be sent back to the UK so it could be claimed for on insurance. Richard had already gone, crossing into Morocco the morning I landed in Spain: he was trying to make his way south. After the accident he decided to go off on his own, backpacking. Peter told me he had an alternative in mind: an overland truck with six passengers that was crossing Spain and heading down to Cape Town on a route similar to the one we wanted to take. As for me, I had no idea what would come next.

In the middle of winter, Tarifa was a deserted city. The strong wind was stripping the wet sand from the empty beaches. It rained every single day and the water gathered in big puddles on the potholed streets. There was no one, no living soul, venturing outside. I was walking by myself on the grey beach, alone with the wild wind and the strong waves that threatened to escape from the sea and swallow me alive. The rain was whipping my cheeks and I felt the salty taste of tears in my mouth.

Where to go? There was no place to return to. I had packed my luggage, had the jabs: I was ready to leave. I had no home any more, no job, not even a residence permit in the country I used to call home. I had quit everything for another dream, an impossible one, which was ending there right before it started. On the other side of the sea I could see the coast of Africa. It made me feel even worse. It was so close, and yet so inaccessible.

I wanted to go on but I couldn't. I wanted to go back but I had no place to return to. Dangling in emptiness, between two worlds, between two dreams: Switzerland, which was already finished, and Africa, which refused to begin. I just stopped thinking. I had no choice but to put myself in the hands of fate. I emailed Richard, despite the fact that I had only met him for a dinner in London. I asked him where he was and what his plans were. He answered, saying that he was planning to travel for a couple of months and that if I wanted to join him in backpacking through West Africa, I could cross into Morocco, where I would get my Mauritanian visa. Then I could meet him and two others he had met in Morocco and the four of us would enter Mauritania. The meeting point would be Dakhla, deep in Western Sahara.

I decided to go for it. I was to cross into Morocco on my own and try to meet up with Richard in that unknown city. Suddenly the plan for this trip had changed again. However, it felt right. My enthusiasm for this adventure had returned and I felt like the whole situation deserved a good laugh. One moment I was travelling alone, then with Peter and Richard, then with Peter, now with Richard and two others!

"Peter, we need to speak," I announced early the next morning, and I told him about my decision.

"And when are you planning to cross into Tangier?" he asked, as if the practicalities were all that mattered.

"Today, by ferry in two hours' time!" I glanced at my watch and saw that I could make it in time to catch the two o'clock ferry. "I have to hurry."

Richard had told me that the three of them would be waiting for me in Dakhla, and that I had only one week to sort out my visa in Casablanca and then make my way south to the last Moroccan city before the Mauritanian border.

"How about your backpack? You'll have to carry it now." Peter reminded me of my main problem. My backpack was simply too heavy.

"Yes, I know, I'll just pass by the post office and send half of it to my parents' home. It's a pity most of my beauty creams will go!" I thought that there had to be a price for everything and that if my cream jars were to be sacrificed, then so be it!

"One last thing." Peter's voice was still inflexible. "I got a phone call from a mechanic I know in Gibraltar. He told me that someone brought in a Camel Trophy Land Rover for sale. He'll take a look at the car and let me know if it's in good condition. If it is, I may buy it. If I buy it, are you still interested in joining me? It will be the two of us in the car and then we'll get Richard on board at some point later."

No, he wasn't joking, he was quite serious. And I recalled he had told me a few days before that he had spoken with a friend of his, a mechanic from Gibraltar, about the possibility of buying another car for the trip.

"Do you really think that might happen? Are you really ready to buy another car?" It seemed too good a scenario to be true.

"I'm waiting for a phone call from him. But before I make a decision I need to know if I still have my travel partners. Will you join me if I get a new car?"

As incredible as that sounded, I thought that it would be nice to return to our initial plan for the trip. "If you get another car, I'm in. Let me know, but I'll cross into Morocco today, I can't wait. Who knows? Maybe you could pick us up on the way."

"OK, I'll let you know. Have a safe trip."

I left. It was already late and I knew I had to do an important task before I could rush to the ferry. I had to lose about 20 kilos, separate what I was to keep from what I had to leave and reduce my backpack to a weight I could carry.

It's incredible how many things one can live without, when one has to carry them on one's back. After an hour, I reached my target weight. My next trip was to the post office.

The phone rang just as I was leaving my room.

"I'm in Gibraltar. I got the car." Peter's voice sounded as immobile and emotionless as it had some two weeks before when he'd announced that he'd had an accident.

Silence. I couldn't answer. Fate was playing games with me again.

"Roxana, are you still there? The car I told you about this morning. I got a phone call from my friend in Gibraltar. He's looked at it and says I should buy it. I've already paid a deposit and now I'm on my way to sign all the papers. The car is in good shape, it's another Land Rover, a Camel Trophy Discovery, and well equipped for such a trip."

I still couldn't say a word.

"Hey, are you still interested?" He was probably worried by my silence.

I was. And I looked at the backpack I had finally managed to pack and at the box with half my things ready to be sent back. Maybe this trip will eventually teach me to be flexible, I thought.

THE two of us left Spain on a fine Sunday morning, crossing by ferry into Africa. The car was a Camel Trophy vehicle that had survived a race in Mongolia. It wasn't particularly well equipped for the desert, so we had to spend a few days getting some sand tyres and trying to adapt some of the equipment that had been recovered from the old vehicle.

Peter travelled in style. A roof tent, a real duvet and three pillows covered in blue bedsheets had to be fitted in and we spent a few more days ensuring all was in place. Then we fixed two jerrycans for water and five for gasoline, the fridge, the transformer, and the other 1001 objects that we were certain we would absolutely need. After that we said goodbye to Europe. Despite the delay, our adventure was about to begin at last.

CHAPTER 3 – FES BY NIGHT

(CHEFCHAOUEN TO FES, MOROCCO, DECEMBER 2002)

"DEAR Mr and Mrs Valea, it is with great sorrow that I have to inform you that your daughter has died in Morocco while choking on a huge goats' cheese sandwich..."

I watched him in shock and for a moment I forgot about the difficult business of chewing that much cheese. Then I burst out laughing, trying hard not to lose any pieces of the precious cheese. Peter could indeed be funny and I couldn't believe I had at last laughed at one of his jokes.

It was not only his sense of humour that seemed incomprehensible to me. Everything he said or attempted to communicate ended in questions. What did you say? Could you repeat? Sorry, I didn't understand...

I gave up eventually and he gave up too, and in these moments we just listened to music in silence. With the volume turned up to the max we had the perfect excuse not to attempt any further communication. It must be cultural incompatibilities, I told myself, hoping that we might get out of that phase soon. But we simply did not understand each other, and when it wasn't his accent there were other things. He talked about miles, I thought he meant kilometres. His jokes – and I learned to understand that they were jokes by the sort of questioning, inquisitive look he threw at me after every such remark – brought at best an indifferent expression to my face. It was all in vain, I did not understand.

After a while I simply I gave up. In short, we belonged to different worlds, we laughed at different kinds of jokes and my international English, which he called "a subset of the real language", seemed too poor to cope with the many different synonyms he used throughout the day. The solution was to interact as little as possible, in spite of the fact that we shared the same car every single day. We listened to music. He drove. I read the map.

Having established myself as a hazardous driver during a ten-minute test drive in Spain – this was as much as Peter could endure before asking to take the driver's seat – he decided that it was safer for both himself and his car if he did all the driving. Pretty good deal for me, since I was left with plenty of time to enjoy the beautiful landscape. This was when I was not busy with one of my many auxiliary tasks, clearly defined and communicated by the driver, which included making sure he drove on the right side of the road to ensure that the incident in Northern Spain wouldn't be repeated; checking the wing mirrors every time he reversed – "get into the reverse mode," he would shout; constantly checking the distance between the front wheel on my side and the rock on the side of the road; making sure we weren't too close to the crumbling edges of the road for high mountain roads; checking the street for potential cars coming in the opposite direction – "do shout if you see a car," he would say; checking if the road was free, as "you have a better angle to see the road"; steering the car when he took off a layer of his clothes; passing him various food and drink, and above all, watching the road to make sure we were still on it while he admired the landscape.

Roads in Morocco were of several types. The ones marked with red on the map usually meant overcrowded vehicles: ten people in a small car; sheep and cows stored one on top of the other with cages of chickens balanced on top of the whole thing; buses with people hanging outside and trucks carrying entire palm trees. Those marked with yellow were secondary ones and we had overtaken several of these while crossing the Middle Atlas and High Atlas mountain ranges.

The roads bordered with green had beautiful scenery and it was then that I mostly feared accidents, since Peter was usually admiring the view. White ones were tiny roads, winding across the tops of mountains through ruined mud fortresses – *kasbah* – with beautiful views of villages and lots of people hanging by the road, hoping a car might just stop by and they would get something. Men asked for cigarettes or money, but kids had longer lists: one *dirham* (the local currency), *bonbon* (sweet), *stylo* (pen), *tricot* (T-shirt), or simply "*donnez-moi quelque chose*" ("give me something"). I wondered whether these were the first words they learned in school during their French lessons.

Anywhere we stopped, even in complete darkness in the middle of nowhere, somebody would always appear suddenly, as if they had been hidden behind a rock waiting for us to stop. Men usually gave up after a polite refusal, but children were more insistent and usually a strange race started, with four or five of them running by the car grabbing at the mirrors or door handles. Then my list of tasks got a new addition: making sure we didn't drive over any of them. Women were the only ones who didn't want anything, either because they couldn't speak any French or because they had given up expecting anything from anybody.

Northern Morocco, and particularly the Rif Mountains, are well known for one crop only: marijuana. It's the most important source of income for the locals. By law they are allowed to grow and to sell it, but if you buy it, you can be arrested.

Hoping to stay out of trouble, we drove by countless locals trying to stop the car and sell us "*quelque chose de bien*"[1], as they call it in those parts. Everybody seemed to live on this trade. The children spot each foreigner and run to tell their parents. Teenagers and grown men then come into play, and they approach you with a wise smile. Are we looking for something? No we're not, but they don't usually give up that easily and will follow up with a long speech on why their "goods" are better or fresher or cheaper than any other goods we might find, and in addition we absolutely have to stop by and see their farm, it would be a real honour.

After rushing back to the car in panic a few times to escape these ardent businessmen, we chose to drive on and stop as little as possible. But it was afternoon already and hunger started building up, so after we had carefully looked in all directions to make sure we would not be disturbed, we pulled up at the side of the road. It looked as if we were in the middle of nowhere.

We were at the top of a mountain, more like a hill in fact,

---

[1] "Something good" (in French)

but the height allowed us to see the road in both directions. A small dot on the horizon grabbed my attention: it was growing bigger by the second and I started to feel worried. Was my lunch about to be cut short by yet another insistent seller?

In fact it was just a motorbike, and when it came closer it slowed down and eventually stopped beside our car. I remembered the guy who got off: he was a strange biker, dressed all in red, whom we had passed some time before on the road. "He's English," Peter had told me at the time, "I saw his plate number." We waved as we passed him, most probably covering him with a layer of dust. But here he was, slowly approaching us while trying to get rid of the enormous helmet covering his face.

He was indeed British: I could tell immediately by the odd pattern of communication that instantly sprang up between Peter and our unexpected guest. Here they were, in the middle of nowhere, two English guys trying to handle a conversation despite the embarrassment of not having been properly introduced to each other. They were positioned so as to be turned away from one another, with about two metres between them, and they looked down or up to the hills – never in each other's eyes. Words seemed to flow out of their mouths in spite of their efforts to retain them. Voices were flat and, needless to say, there was no sign of emotion.

We shared some bread and cheese and found out that his name was Karl: he was from near Leeds and had just started crossing Africa on his motorbike. He had carefully planned his trip for around two years, bought and fixed the motorbike and put up with the jokes of his friends. One morning he set off from London with one destination in mind: Cape Town.

We had a chat and opened some maps to have a look at alternative roads. We forgot to watch the road and soon enough we heard two cars pulling over next to ours: most probably drug dealers. By then we understood that they were not really dangerous, but the thought of the hassle we were about to go through made us cut our talk short and we began to wrap up our things.

Instead of coming directly towards us, as we expected, the two groups seemed to be more concerned with each other. Judging from the shouts and gestures, they were fighting to get the big prize: we three foreigners as potential clients. We speeded up loading the car and were almost ready to go when we realised Karl was having trouble starting his bike. "It must be really scary being alone on a bike," I thought; a lot more so than driving with an unknown guy but protected by a car. We waited for him to go first and this brought us into the hands of the winning group of drug dealers. The others had left the scene with angry faces.

"*Bonjour, bienvenue au Maroc*"[2] – it was the classic start of a sales pitch.

"No; we're not interested." It's better to make one's position clear from the beginning.

Karl was already on his bike and he looked ready to go. Luckily for him, all four men came towards Peter and me: they calculated that the two foreigners in the car would probably have more money to spend than the lonely one on the bike.

"*S'il vous plait*... can you come and visit my farm? I live just on the other side of the hill."

Karl's bike took off in a big cloud of dust.

"I have something good, something you like," he goes on, just as all the others before him had done and all the ones who would come after him would also do. He should read something about sales differentiation, I thought.

But it was hardly the place to give sales coaching to a Berber drug dealer and after a last look to make sure Karl was at a safe distance, Peter hit the accelerator and off we went. I couldn't stop laughing at the blank face of the group leader left in the middle of an empty hill, looking after a big cloud of dust: his big sale had just been blown off!

We met Karl again later that evening in the campsite outside Fes. We hadn't had time to agree on a meeting place earlier that day due to our precipitate departure, but it seemed that in Africa all roads become one and everybody travels it. This was a principle which we would become accustomed to in the weeks and months that followed.

Karl was putting up his tent and I wondered how safe he felt sleeping in there all by himself.

"Yeah, not too safe," he admitted. "Think I'd rather not use it when I'm on my own on the road; it can bring too

---

[2] "Hello and welcome to Morocco" (in French)

much unwanted attention. But for campsites it's fine, it gives me a bit of privacy. And then on the road I sleep outside so I keep an eye on Mave."

Mave, short for Mavis, was his bike: some sort of travel mate or even capricious girlfriend.

"You see, she is like a woman. She eats all my money, wants a lot of care and attention and stuff and may let you down when you least expect it. She's doin' fine just now, we'll see how she copes later on, with the Big Sand..."

The Big Sand was the Sahara and we found out he was planning to take more or less the same route we had in mind: down south through Mauritania, into Senegal and Mali. There are three main routes for crossing the Sahara desert, and with two of them going through Algeria, not particularly safe at that time, the third route through Mauritania became the only way south for all the cross-Africa travellers.

"How come you decided to set off on your own? It's a long journey down south."

"Yeah, kinda weird feeling being on my own," he admitted. "But then there wasn't anybody else who wanted to come along. Probably will meet some nice folks on the way."

And then, with a smile:

"I ain't alone though. Mave's here and we'll take care of each other."

If he managed to have a kind of communication going on with his Mave then I shouldn't complain about my lack of interaction with Peter, I thought.

We heard that Fes was supposed to be one of the most interesting old Moroccan cities and despite the late hour and the darkness all around, we decided to venture into the town for a visit and dinner. After all, it was only six o'clock in the afternoon and soon the fast for the day would be broken and the cafés and restaurants would open up and serve food again. It was Ramadan, the holy month of Islam, and everybody fasted through the day. We couldn't miss our chance to have a proper meal in the evening.

It wasn't destined to be a quiet evening though. Our taxi driver politely warned us as he left us at the gates of the old town:

"You need a guide to go into the medina by night, otherwise you may get lost."

But we didn't care. After all, we had come to Africa in search of adventures and an evening visit to the old town seemed the perfect place to start. Besides, in a group of three we felt rather cheerful: Peter had finally found someone he could share his jokes with, Karl was happy to have some company after the day's lonely drive and I felt quite protected walking beside the two of them, although looking rather strange with Karl wearing his knee-high bike boots and Peter in a weird full-length woollen *djellaba*, a sort of local dress for men that he bought the previous night from a bazaar.

"*Bonsoir*. I'll be your guide for the evening." Four steps from the taxi and the hassle had already begun. Being a "guide" was the easiest way to extort money from tourists, and Morocco seemed to have quite a long history of tourist-hassling. But we were not tourists, we were travellers, and the tall, cheeky teenager with a tiny moustache dressed in a very Western T-shirt and jeans seemed not to understand the difference.

"He's really good, let him be your guide for the evening," his friend joined in, hoping to facilitate the transaction.

"No, *merci*." Peter was always polite. "We don't need a guide, we're quite happy to walk on our own."

"You don't understand: you will get lost."

"We have a map. We will manage, *merci*." Peter was the one to conduct the defence.

"Listen to me and listen well. Nobody, I said nobody, goes into the medina by night without a guide."

We ignored them, hoping they would go away, but they knew better than that. They walked along with us. One of them started to recite the history of the city.

Peter stopped and looked at him.

"We don't need a guide, I said. Please leave us, we'll be fine on our own."

The guy's eyes suddenly started shining with anger.

"Go back to your fucking countries, bastards! If we cannot make a profit from you we don't want you here!"

We didn't answer. We tried walking faster but they were still walking besides us.

"Listen to me, you bastard. If you don't have me as a guide you will cry tonight, do you understand me? You will cry and there will be nobody to save you!" he directed his threats to Peter but I knew they were meant for all of us.

He started to push Peter, frustrated at the lack of any answer.

"Do you hear me? Do you want to cry tonight? Do you?" By then we had been walking for about 10 minutes and I didn't know where we were going. We were deep into the old medieval city with its narrow dark streets. Everything seemed deserted: even the old buildings had the shutters closed and looked uninhabited. There were no shops or restaurants or anything that might resemble a suitable place for a human gathering. There were no lights in the streets and I remembered that in the hour before the breaking of the fast everything is closed and dark, as if all the people would be hidden somewhere waiting for the time to pass so that they could eat and drink and laugh again. How long now? How long before the shops and restaurants open up?

I felt a push on my back and then I got smashed against a wall. It wasn't too hard and I went back to walking beside Peter and Karl without reacting, but I started to panic. If they dared to do that, they meant trouble. We hurried on.

Another push and I hit another wall. I realised that they were expecting a reaction from us, any reaction, no matter how small. If we had fought back, they would have jumped all over us. I looked at Peter: his face was motionless. He grabbed my arm and I immediately felt better. In a calm voice, he said:

"If it gets to a fight let's stay together, don't let them separate us!"

We kept on going, taking the kicks and punches without fighting back. I knew that it was only a matter of time before they would really attack us. I was already thinking of a secret weapon. I was going to scream as loud as I could if a fight were to start. Someone in that dark and empty town would hear the scream of a woman and hurry to the rescue!

We were walking fast and turning corners and they were following us closely. Another blow and Peter grabbed the guy's hand. This was it, I thought, and I looked around in a desperate search for shelter as we turned another corner.

The light seemed almost surreal, and so did the voices inside. A small café finally open! We pushed the guys away and ran inside without looking back, feeling barely safe enough to stop and catch our breath by the bar.

The place was rather dark, but compared to the darkness outside it was like the midday sun to us. In a corner a TV was turned on, showing some Moroccan movie, and lots of the men around were lined up watching it attentively before turning to watch us with the same intensity. Inside, it smelled like spices mixed with sweat and mint. They always put fresh mint leaves in the tea they drank and most of them had a small glass of tea on their table. The bar was long and rather dirty. A busy, round-faced owner smiled at us, seeming pleased to have us there.

"Three mint teas please." Peter tried to behave as if nothing had happened but I felt more threatened inside that place than in the middle of the street.

There was silence around us. Everybody had stopped speaking and was looking at us. About 50 Moroccan men with beards and the traditional long robe with a triangular hood called a *djellaba* were looking at us – or rather at me. I was the only woman in there.

"Peter, I think they are all in this game. Maybe the two guys from the street only wanted to push us in here and it will be here that they will all attack us." It seemed incredible, but I felt more frightened by those looks than by the two guys outside.

"Let's sit down and see what happens. I think they are looking shocked only because they didn't expect to see any foreigner in here, not to mention a woman," he said.

We sat down at a small table and sipped our teas. The conversation around us started to slowly rise, as if the men were getting back to minding their own business. They seemed to have digested their surprise and now we were holding only second place in their hierarchy of interests, after the TV.

"The guys are still out there." Karl showed me two shadows by the entrance door. Our so-called guides were waiting patiently for us to finish our tea.

"At least it looks like they aren't going to attack us in here." I felt relieved. "I'll try to speak to the bar owner: I'll ask him to call the police."

"Let's just wait and see; maybe they'll leave." Peter's voice was as inflexible as always but I could tell he was tense.

I was tense too, and I noticed my hand shaking while holding the small tea glass. My breathing was fast and shallow and I realised it would take me a while to calm down.

We drank in silence and time went by. They were still

there by the door and threw us occasional smiles, as if we were the best of friends.

"I don't think they will leave. We need to ask someone for help!" I was more terrified by the presence of the guys by the door than I had been in the middle of the road.

As if they guessed my intention, one of them came slowly towards us. "They cannot do anything inside here," I told myself, trying to keep calm.

He stopped in front of our table, smiled and threw us a dark look.

"You will drink your tea and then you will have to leave eventually. And no matter how long it will take, we will be outside waiting for you. Do you hear me, bastards? You will cry tonight, as I promised you," he said with a grin.

If he only wanted to hear me cry, I thought, I could do so immediately. Tears were already fighting to get out: one more threat like that and he would quite easily see me cry.

"Come on, we can be in here an hour or two if we need to and they'll get fed up and leave, you'll see," Karl whispered, trying to encourage me. He had probably noticed my desperate look.

"Don't worry; they stupid boys. No good people." I heard another encouraging voice speaking in broken French and this time it came from behind our table.

I turned and threw him a quick look. He was one of the many bearded men dressed in *djellabas* around. I looked at him for a while and didn't say a word.

"Some men good; some men bad," he carried on, rolling himself a cigarette. "But not all men bad," he concluded, looking at the final product with a smile.

How very philosophical, I thought. And how was I to say who was good and who was bad?

"Here. You smoke?" He offered me the cigarette he had just finished to roll up.

"No *merci*, I don't smoke."

"I no smoke too," he smiled, and I saw that his teeth were surprisingly white: they did not look like the teeth of a smoker.

"Only this, special smoke sometimes," he added.

So this was what it was. We were still in the land of pot and our next-table neighbour seemed to have chosen to break his fast of the day with mint tea and a joint.

"Are you married?" he continued from under a cloud of

smoke.

Men in this country are very direct, I thought. I looked right to Karl and left to Peter and wondered if either of them would mind being introduced as my husband.

I gave up. "No. Are you?"

"Woman very expensive here. No money, no married. Lots of money, find nice wife. I no lots of money."

So he wasn't married, I concluded.

"Do you live here?" I don't know why, but this strange dialogue with a local made me feel safer. Maybe I could find out how we could reach a police station and get some help.

"Me from mountains: Berber." He proudly pointed to himself. Berbers were the original inhabitants of the country and had been pushed up into the mountains by the settled Arab population. They still lived in rural areas, most of them nomads, and the guy in front of me was one of them.

His name was Hamid and he came into the city to look for work. He had found it eventually and was making carpets in a shop. He worked every day except Friday, had seven brothers and sisters and an old mother and was sharing a small room in town with all of them. He was the breadwinner in the family.

"You come see carpets in my shop? Very very nice. Very very cheap," the offer came.

Another sales pitch, I thought, but strangely enough I didn't mind it. After all, it was better to be shown carpets than hassled by unknown "guides".

We had already been in there for more than an hour and had drunk three cups of tea each. We knew we had to leave eventually and I was trying to delay the moment as much as possible. I didn't even want to think about venturing out. Maybe we did need a guide in the old city by night after all.

"I'd love to see your carpets. Will you be our guide for the evening?" I never thought we would come to ask but there we were, the three of us, desperately waiting to hear him say yes.

He looked at us, a bit surprised. "Your guide? And to see what, go where?" He didn't seem to have a very business-oriented mind. What did it matter what we wanted to see if we were to pay him?

"Look, we're lost." I tried to be honest. "We were followed by two nasty guys, you saw them. They entered here and threatened us. I don't know if they're still outside.

When we go out we need someone who knows the way and can get us out of here."

"And you come see my shop?" His puzzled look was now replaced by a large grin.

"Yes, we'll go see your shop on the way." I looked back in triumph to Peter and Karl, who seemed amused by my improvised solution.

"It looks like we got ourselves a guide after all," I told them.

We left and did not see our aggressors outside. Maybe they had given up waiting after a while, or maybe they were still there but would not try to attack us in the presence of a local. This was to become one of our main survival rules in Africa: "get a local by your side and you'll be safe". If only we had known it before!

Hamid seemed to know his way, navigating with sure steps through the labyrinth of dark and narrow streets. The first stop we made was, of course, his carpet shop.

They hurried to welcome us with another mint tea, the fourth one for me that evening. Seating us on some small chairs, they smiled to us and while bidding us "*bienvenue*" ("welcome") and bowing, they immediately took out several carpets and graciously let the show begin.

The owner was a round-faced, middle-aged man with a huge moustache who seemed to be the twin brother of the bar owner. Although it was rather late in the evening, the shop was filled with boys of different ages who ran around bringing us whatever their boss commanded. First, more tea. Then, more carpets.

The shop seemed a labyrinth, selling almost everything that could be made from fur, leather or wool. There were long slippers with rounded tops; pillow cases and blankets; shirts, dresses and *djellabas*; belly-dancing costumes, and a huge collection of wallets, suitcases and belts. Not to mention the countless souvenirs in the most diverse forms: stuffed camels, lamps, drums... you name it. Obviously their most valuable items were carpets and this was what the sales pitch focused on. With three customers in, they felt quite sure they would score at least one sale for the evening.

Carpets came out and were displayed in front of us in an amazing variety of shapes and colours. Which one did we like? The smiley, round face of the middle-aged owner was hoping for an encouraging sign.

We didn't want any of them but Peter made the fatal mistake of asking "how much?" Once these words left his lips there was no way back. The endless game of haggling had started and it lasted for about one hour while we were fed more tea, more carpets and bits and bobs of history about the city. Eventually Peter tried to escape the pressure being steadily applied to him and told the owner that we couldn't buy any carpet because we were living in a car; we didn't really have the space for a carpet...

"No problem! Ahmed, bring out the small ones..."

...and we were heading to South Africa...

"No problem! You must have a mother, a sister who can use a gift..."

...and we were short of money...

"Just tell me a price you want to pay and I'll do my best for you..."

...and... and...

We had finished the list of reasons why not so just decided to walk away, ignoring the desperate looks of the owner. I was feeling guilty at having drunk their tea for about one hour for nothing, but I told myself that was all part of the game. In the door the owner's face lighted up with a smile and he seemed to have come to terms with the loss of the big sale.

"Go in peace and, *Insha'Allah*, you may return to my shop one day."

Insha'Allah. God willing. This was when I heard it first. I didn't know it then, but this was to be our magic formula for the days and months to come.

CHAPTER 4 –THE SLAVE OF THE MERCIFUL

(KENIFRA TO WESTERN SAHARA, MOROCCO, DECEMBER 2002)

We travelled further on our road south, with frequent stops in various towns on the way. After a few days we arrived in Kenifra, a little town in the middle of the Atlas Mountains. We stopped in front of the first hotel we saw, probably the only one in town. *Mademoiselle* at the reception was friendly and spoke impeccable French. She was dressed in colourful pink and yellow pyjamas and I wondered whether she was getting ready to go to bed. Peter decided not to leave anything in the car so there we were, in the middle of an overcrowded street, trying to empty the car.

So for the next half-hour we carried everything into the room: first the big plastic boxes with our personal stuff, then our small day packs which usually sat on the back seat of the car and where we kept all sorts of little things we thought we might need during the day. Then we opened the safe which was fitted in place of one of the back seats and started to take out all our valuables: wallets with cash, credit cards and cheques, Peter's laptop, our cameras.

We kept our clothes packed in plastic boxes in the boot. It was a lot easier to load and reload the boxes, and it was fairly easy to search for what we needed in them. I didn't quite know what to expect, so I had packed all sorts of things: three pairs of khaki safari trousers, a long skirt (for the Muslim countries, I thought), several T-shirts, blue pyjamas (which Peter had a good laugh at, but which turned out to be very useful), a pair of boots (which I was wearing every day), and, most important of all, a huge reserve of creams: hand cream, face cream, eye cream, sun cream, after-sun cream.

Peter, on the other hand, seemed to be in the army. His clothes, nicely packed, were carefully selected: seven pairs of silver-grey T-shirts, all with matching underwear. He wore one pair per day for five days; on the sixth day he washed them and on the seventh day they dried. Two shirts and two pairs of khaki trousers, a thick fleece and a safari hat with large brim were the rest of his equipment. Not to mention the large collection of technology: laptop, camera, binoculars, MP3 player, GPS device and so on.

Back at the hotel with the car emptied and all stuff locked in the room, we were now looking for food.

We usually ate whatever we could find, but as a vegetarian I wasn't too enthused by the sight of half a cow hanging by its feet in front of a meat shop with hundreds of flies around it: a common sight in the small towns we passed by. I had already had some bread and cheese, the French version of the "Laughing Cow" brand called "La Vache Qui Rit", which was available in every little shop in every corner of that country. I didn't know then that it was to become my staple diet throughout Africa. For one reason or another it pervaded the continent, and I could buy it in Morocco in a supermarket and later on in some small barracks on the bank of the river Congo. Everybody sold it and it seemed made to resist the harsh climate of Africa: it didn't melt even in temperatures above 50°C, as if made out of plastic.

I wasn't hungry but Peter ordered some *brochettes* (small pieces of meat grilled on skewers) on the terrace that stretched in front of the hotel. I was waiting patiently to witness the long show that was to follow. In this country everything was negotiable and haggling was a simple game if you stuck to the rules.

- Rule number 1: you shall always haggle.
- Rule number 2: you will always be overcharged no matter how desperate you look, how nice they look, how high the demand or how small the amount.
- Rule number 3: always ask the price first.

Haggling was a slow and painful process to learn. Forewarned before we entered the country, we were still unprepared for the big battle ahead. In a bread shop the price – although written down – was changed to double that amount in front of our eyes. After this initial encounter, we were overcharged for everything we ever bought or ate. We soon discovered that it was not the overcharging we should worry about – it would have happened anyway – but the amount the price would increase.

Haggling made me feel highly uncomfortable. Peter was more skilful and the more he practised, the better he got. Among his absolute bests: haggling over an alarm clock featuring a call to prayer sound, an event that took place in the presence of about 20 locals intently watching the debate between the local vendor and the greedy foreigner, and a sudden attack of panic in Marrakech – "don't touch the tea before we ask how much it is!" We had asked the price of everything on the table before the mint tea mysteriously arrived and he figured out it would be the tea they would try to catch us with. But as time went by we got a pretty good grasp on what the real prices were like, usually somewhere between a quarter and a third of what was initially quoted.

We had waited for about an hour already and the waiter seemed to be in no hurry with our food. I think we looked so desperate that we attracted the interest of the only other person on the terrace, our soon-to-be friend by the name of Ab Rahman – or "the slave of the merciful", as he introduced himself. He was a lad of about 25, looking healthy and bored with life, and as soon as he moved on to our table he started to chat as if we were his best buddies.

It was an interesting conversation and it started with illegal emigration to Italy, where Moroccans are employed by locals to "steal" their cars in exchange for a reasonable amount of money. Everybody made a profit: the illegal immigrant who managed somehow to take the car into Morocco; the Italian owner who declared the car stolen and financed his new acquisition with the insurance money; the car industry itself, which boosted sales. Less so, of course, the insurance companies, who had started to be wary of the trick.

He told us about life in Morocco, about geography and about Casablanca, his native town. But soon he settled into his favourite subjects: sex and religion. Back and forth between the two: we learned about his adventures with some prostitutes in Poland and some other "nice girls" in Holland (he seemed to be a well-travelled Moroccan despite his young age). He then told us about the troubles of Moroccan men who couldn't possibly find a woman before marriage, and here his voice became nostalgic.

"Yeah, for you people in the West sex is like eating meat." He looked at Peter, who was gulping his *brochettes*. "It's just a normal thing, but for us it's so difficult; only here you learn to appreciate it." His eyes were half closed; he seemed lost in a far-away world and for a moment I wondered whether the intensity of his memories would bring about an orgasmic explosion.

I resisted, of course, the temptation to ask him when his last time was and luckily he suddenly woke up from his trance and abruptly changed the subject. Then we got a bit of Qur'anic teaching, learning the history of why Christians converted to Islam, and some background on the common prophets of Judaism, Christianity and Islam. .

Then, back to sex. He argued that it was because of the purity expected before marriage that Moroccan couples had more children than Europeans. He seemed to struggle to find meaning in his repressed sex life and nodded with gravity:

"Yeah, we have to go through all these troubles here, but when we finally get a woman, just look around what happens."

I looked around: there was nothing but the empty terrace. I doubted that could have anything to do with the sex life of Moroccans.

"We have seven or eight children here, not like in Europe where it is one or two. It's because over there, you people waste your strength. But we preserve ours, you see, we keep all our strength, and this is how it comes out."

I tried hard not to burst out laughing at the image of Ab Rahman's preserved strength. I could see on Peter's face that somewhere deep inside, he too was laughing, in spite of his careful attempts to concentrate on the meat in front of him.

"But for people young and healthy like you two, this is not a problem." He carried on looking at us with hungry eyes and his gestures became animated again.

"You're so lucky, really, you can do it wherever you like, whenever you like, and nobody can throw you in the prison because you are not married. Not like us, who have to go weeks and months without a woman..."

With Peter still saying nothing, I felt like correcting the

views of this young Moroccan. "You're wrong, my friend: we're not having wild sex every time we think about it and if I'm quite honest my last time was a long, long time ago. And as for Peter, I don't have the slightest idea when his last time was." I didn't say a word though: I almost felt like I shouldn't destroy the image of paradise he carried in his mind.

He decided eventually that religion should have priority in his teachings to his foreign friends and ended the evening with a huge, unstoppable sermon which could be summarised in two words: *Allahu Akbar*, or God is great. We agreed, of course, shook his hand, and having finished dinner we wished him goodnight and headed upstairs to our room.

The room was small and reasonably clean, with twin beds. It was the first night that I was to sleep some half a metre away from a guy I had met over the Internet one month before. So far I had slept either in my own tent or in my own room, but this place only had a twin room for us. All the horror stories my friends had told me, usually involving rape, torture and murder and invariably ending with me being chopped into pieces by this dangerous maniac, came to my mind. The moment of truth: was I going to get chopped that night?

I opened my sleeping bag and arranged my bed in silence, while Peter seemed to bother more about his laptop and burning some songs on to a CD than about my unspoken worries. The room was freezing and Peter decided to go back to the reception and ask if we could get a heater.

"He suggested we should generate our own heat," was the answer he came back with. The suggestion came from Ab Rahman, who had rented the little room next to ours and was about to spend the night with his ear stuck to the separating wall so he would not miss any of the entertainment he was sure would take place next door. He may even have thought of making a hole in the wall. Yeah, he surely had something to see – two frozen people covered in their sleeping bags under a heap of spare blankets.

Peter had left his sleeping bag in the car and couldn't bring himself to go down and fetch it, preferring to fight hypothermia the whole night instead. I was feeling quite comfortable though. I was wearing two jumpers inside my sleeping bag and had about three blankets on top of it, and if it wasn't for my murder worries I could have quite a peaceful sleep.

In the middle of the night and at the deepest point in my sleep cycle, the light was suddenly turned on. "Maybe it's happening now: I will get chopped into pieces after all." My half-asleep brain registered a threatening movement from Peter towards my bed.

"May I pinch a blanket?"

I didn't really understand, but I figured it had to do with him being frozen and one of my many blankets so I just fell back into the abyss of dreams. I survived: my last conscious thought of the day.

The distance between us started to melt after that first hotel room we shared. Waking up alive next to a half-frozen travel mate made me laugh at my worries and start seeing him as a bit more human. We were both still going through sudden mood swings though, and for the rest of that week travelling towards Casablanca and then on to Rabat we had days of driving and not sharing any thoughts with each other.

Then we ventured into the high Atlas Mountains, where the landscape became wilder and the roads more dangerous, and I thought that finally this trip was starting to look more like the adventure it was supposed to be. I still found Peter's jokes a mystery but we started to have some bits of conversation between the seemingly endless music. Then, when he got out of the car in the middle of the crowded city of Casablanca while trying to read the right direction from the stars in the sky, I burst out laughing and thought that it was actually fun to be part of a strange trip next to this strange guy.

Then we entered Western Sahara and the landscape started to change into empty and endless flat desert. I felt thrilled to be in the Sahara at last. The days of driving were long and tiring and I started feeling closer to Peter.

On Christmas Eve we had to bribe a policeman to let us enter the military-controlled city of Dakhla, and after we reached the empty campsite and tried in vain to find something to eat, we realised we had to change a tyre in total darkness. Then we got into the car with empty stomachs and dirty hands, and we poured two glasses of his treasured malt whisky and we toasted, and I thought of my family, who would be gathering around a big table somewhere in

Romania precisely at that moment, and maybe Peter thought of his family too.

The next morning I had my best ever Christmas gift: a real bed and a nice bath in a mysterious 4-star hotel rising from the middle of the city. Peter decided to be generous and got a room, and we both spent the whole of Christmas Day sleeping for some 20 hours in a row. I came out of the bathroom after two hours all refreshed and creamed up, and I was even able to use the small epilator I had brought with me. I felt truly a lady for the first time in several weeks.

Peter was sleeping in the double bed we shared. I was starting to feel slightly embarrassed and it had to do with feeling like a lady again. Sharing a room with a guy is a lot easier when packaged under the "adventure hardship" category. But this luxurious room suddenly made me return to the world of "back home", where one shares double beds in romantic hotel rooms with one's boyfriend.

"What was that strange noise in the bathroom?" Peter asked from under the blanket.

"My epilator," I answered, not feeling quite sure if I had to share with my travel mate my intimate activities in the bathroom.

"I was wondering what it was. I thought you'd brought along a vibrator," he added in a dry voice, and turned on to his other side to continue his sleep, leaving me speechless and furious.

Another one of his jokes. Sometimes I simply hated him.

CHAPTER 5 – A JOURNEY BY TRAIN

(NOUADHIBOU TO OUADANE, MAURITANIA,
DECEMBER 2002)

A fly made a big circle, as if undecided where to land, and finally settled on the edge of a small glass of tea on the wooden table. The soldier ignored it, too absorbed in the laborious task at hand: copying all my passport details into a notebook.

He wrote with the speed of an eight-year-boy forced to go to school. I had already stood there for quarter of an hour and it looked like there would be more waiting yet. Apart from the fly that had moved on to exploring the back of the barracks, there was no other movement. The sun was high: it must have been over 50°C outside and a lot more than that inside, since the roof of the small barrack room was made up of iron sheets taken from old barrels. I could see drops of sweat forming on the forehead of the soldier. He wiped them off with the back of his hand, then wiped his hand on his shirt and went back to his monotonous task.

We were at the Moroccan–Mauritanian border point, and by no means did I want to start a confrontation with all these soldiers who stared at me as if they had never seen a woman before.

We had woken up early that morning and left the Moroccan border point, barracks similar to this one some 30 km back on the sand track. They stamped our passports, smiled and wished us good luck. They also told us that no way should we stop until we arrived at the Mauritanian border post. The No Man's Land between the two countries was in fact a huge minefield, and the countless carcasses of burned-out cars and camel bones on the side of the road were not an encouraging sight. We knew, though, that the road itself was clear and since the border crossing was legal – it had just reopened earlier that year – we did not expect major problems.

Nevertheless, the moment we spotted the barracks with the Mauritanian flag on them we felt relieved. Peter spent about an hour trying to sort out the legal issues and I thought it was all done, but when he came back to the car he told me they wanted to see me too. And for the next quarter of an hour there I was, standing in front of a wooden table with a soldier carefully trying to write down every single detail on my passport.

The fly came back and this time it landed under the table on the barrack room floor, made of a mixture of sand and earth. Next to it I could see the big black toenails of the soldier at the table. He didn't wear any shoes and his toenails looked like they could use a pedicure.

The barracks were quite small: in addition to one bed and a table there was only one chair, the one used by the soldier. In the back of the room hung a piece of dried meat with lots of flies on it. In a corner, a pot containing what was probably tea: some greenish substance with yet more flies drowned in it.

"Madam, madam! Come, sit." The four other soldiers crammed in one bed were smiling and inviting me to sit with them.

"No, *merci.*"

Peter was back at the car already, probably reading again. He was absent, as usual. I wanted him to be there with me. I didn't feel comfortable at all, crowded in that hut with four soldiers staring at me.

"You have a different name than the other one. Different passport as well. He cannot be your husband." The guard seemed to make sense of all these things at once.

"No, he's not my husband," I admitted.

"So you are not family," he concluded. "You cannot travel together then."

As simple as that, and I wondered what I was to say next. It looked like the rules in the Islamic Republic of Mauritania were pretty strict for locals and tourists alike. In that country a woman could travel with her husband, father, brother or son. Never alone. And never with another man she wasn't related to. So, how come I was travelling with Peter?

"We're cousins," I said.

They all started laughing at once and I wasn't sure what to say next. I was getting scared. The image of the two bottles of alcohol, one of gin and one of whisky, that we had carefully hidden inside the duvet in Peter's tent crossed my mind. Alcohol was forbidden by law in that country. The second law we had broken.

I didn't know if they believed me, but after a long and insistent look the chief inspector decided to carry on.

"What is your profession?"

"Marketing assistant," I instantly responded, but on seeing his eyes go wide I decided to change my profile to a more feminine version.

"Teacher," I smiled. "I teach writing and reading to young children at school."

This was the right answer and he smiled and handed over my passport. I took it with a sigh and went back to the car where Peter was reading his book, silently, without suspecting what I had gone through.

EXCEPT for goats on each and every street in Nouadhibou, the second largest town in Mauritania, there was no sign of any inhabitants. We soon understood the reason. Everybody came to life later in the day, once the exhausting heat withdrew and the cool wind of the evening started to blow. People would appear out of nowhere, all wearing large white or blue African robes. They had Arab facial features but quite dark skin, sometimes as dark as the Sub-Saharan Africans.

People of Mauritania are divided into Moors and black Africans. The Moors, of Arab descent, are the rulers and up to a few years ago, the Sub-Saharan Africans were their slaves. Although slavery was officially abolished in 1990, men are reportedly still being bought and sold in Mauritania. There were signs of it everywhere: the subdued Sub-Saharan Africans walking a few steps behind their masters, the arrogance of the Moors and, most shocking of all, the sight of an old man kneeling in the middle of the street and kissing the hand of a young Moor. To me, that seemed like big-time slavery!

The town had two paved roads and together they formed

a sort of city centre. Everybody was out for an evening walk on Boulevard Median, the main north-south "avenue". The street was lined with supermarkets selling expensive, imported tinned food and several street foot stalls.

To my surprise I saw an Internet café, a small room where young Moors would arrive on camels, bind the animals in front of the entrance and then spend hours in front of a computer screen reading web pages in Arabic. Since there was no fixed-line phone connection anywhere, I deduced that this whole Internet boom must have been supported by the equally booming mobile phone industry. Once again, Africa was skipping the development stages: from camel to mobile phone and Internet in the blink of an eye. Everybody in this small city in the middle of nowhere had a mobile phone. Batteries and top-up cards were sold at every corner.

Women walked by in groups and wore colourful *mehlafas*: ample pieces of fabric that covered them from head to toe, and occasionally their faces as well. Most of them were fat, since fatness was considered a sign of beauty, and many Moor mothers fed their daughters a diet of milk and dates to get them fat and make them more desirable marriage prospects.

There was no road leaving the town. The only way to move forward was by train. We were to load the car on a train platform for a trip that took roughly 12 hours and would take us close to the desert oasis that we'd decided we had to see.

We woke at sunrise the next morning and went to the "train station", a simple building in the middle of nowhere some 5 km south of the town. There was a train leaving that day – nobody could tell us when – but we weren't sure we could take it, since we had no tickets and didn't know who sold them.

With us were some Swiss guys in their 4x4, Roger and Bernard, who we had previously met and camped with at the Moroccan border. At the train station we met others: three French cars with a group of friends who had decided to take advantage of the good market for second-hand cars in Sub-Saharan Africa. The game was simple: buy a second-hand car for next to nothing in Europe; drive it down to Sub-Saharan Africa, crossing the Sahara; have some fun on the way; and at the end of the holiday, sell it off in Senegal,

Mali or Niger and get a lot more than you paid for it – enough to cover all the costs of your holiday and your flight back home. It wasn't a bad deal!

The day went by slowly; morning became noon and the sun was hot. We were reading our books, waiting for the train. Suddenly, out of nowhere, a platform was pulled in front of the small building and we all loaded the cars and tightened the wheels with thick wire. Then nothing happened for a while: we were left there waiting, overwhelmed by the numbness of the place, by the stillness of the landscape; put to sleep by the heat of the air. We were waiting with no hope that anyone would come, that anything would happen, that the train would finally move.

By 7 pm, to celebrate sunset and thus a whole day of waiting by the railway, the French took out some wine and we all toasted together: French, Swiss, British, German and Romanian, united by a common question: "Will a train show up eventually?"

We were a strange group of people gathered there in the station, waiting for that mysterious train. The French guys were trying to escape into another dimension for three weeks; they did it every year during their holidays. Even Gerhard, a German grandfather of about 65 years old travelling on his bike, was running away. A scientist in his "normal" life with a doctorate in physics, he couldn't help but plan to run away for a while every two or three years to some strange and uninhabited place. Now he was riding his bike through Mauritania and hoping to cross the Sahara in six weeks. "Once you have tasted this wilderness and the empty spaces, you never give up," he told me when we met him later on in Senegal. "It's like a curse you carry with you. And even if you build yourself a normal life, with family and kids and a mortgage and all of that, you still need to come back to this from time to time, just to remind yourself of who you truly are."

Was that running away, or maybe finding a way to put it all together? Hard to know, but spoken by an old man on a bike these words seemed deep and serious and I felt I could understand what he meant.

Bernard and Roger, the middle-aged Swiss from the other car, were talking about the same thing. Each of them had a "normal" career in sales and engineering, but they had bought an old 4x4 and taken four weeks off to run away from family and work. They wanted to cross the Sahara to celebrate another journey they had taken 30 years ago when they were much younger. "Once you felt the taste of wilderness..." Maybe Gerhard was right after all...

Night fell and nothing happened. All the cars were blocked on the platforms and we were still waiting inside ours. There was nothing we could say, nobody to get angry with. The train station was deserted now and the night was falling heavy and windy.

At 10 pm the train suddenly appeared, just as we were in the middle of our bread and cheese dinner inside the car. It was already dark outside so we couldn't see anything, but we felt a sudden movement. Without any warning, the platforms had been attached to the train and off we went: a journey of at least 12 hours had started.

It was a strange feeling to be inside a still car and yet moving. Outside, in the light of the moon, the desert landscape went by: first the outskirts of the city we had just left with some huge ore deposits, then the dunes and the wide spaces. The light was surprisingly good and we could see far into the distance, deep into the surreal, empty, moonlit spaces of the desert.

"Let's sort out some sleeping arrangements. Do you prefer the front seats or the back ones?" Peter broke the silence, sounding like an air hostess in first class.

What could we possibly do to turn the car into a sleeping place? The front seats were divided by a high console in between and I reckoned it would be difficult to bring everything to the same level. The back ones looked even more uncomfortable. One of the back seats had been taken out to make space for the safe box and the fridge on top of it. The other two were crammed with all sorts of things: our day packs, the remains of dinner, our water bottles, maps, books, and other items we thought we would need during the day. How could we make sense of this chaos? In addition, we couldn't open the doors of the car, we couldn't get outside and a grid separated us from the boot.

"I'll take the back ones," Peter said, tired of waiting for me to make up my mind.

We pushed our imagination to the limit for the next half-hour. Tons of equipment got moved from front to back and the other way round. The water jerrycans came to the front seats in an attempt to somehow bring the surface to the height of the console; my self-inflating mattress was spread over the whole thing and my sleeping bag on top of it. On the back seats, Peter managed to push all the stuff down into the leg space of the seats and so books, clothes, day packs and bottles of water made the whole surface level with the seats. On top of this newly created flat surface, he was lying in his sleeping bag, his legs up and around the fridge. I thought he didn't look particularly comfortable and I felt lucky to have mine over the wheel of the car instead.

"See? It's not that bad. I think we can even have a reasonably good night's sleep in here." Peter could be encouraging when he tried, although he didn't try very often. He could also be inventive, I thought, looking around at the way our car had been transformed into a dormitory.

Silence settled in and we both looked out of the windows, lost in our own thoughts. In the yellow light of the moon, the dunes danced in silence. I wished I could find something we could talk about but the silence was long and heavy, uninterrupted despite my being awake on the front seats and he being equally awake on the back ones.

Peter was still a mystery to me. He had outbursts of kindness and then sudden retreats into silence and distance. He was pretty unpredictable, just as his remarks could be sometimes. He was like an onion, with many layers of skin, and each time one layer was shed there was a different reality underneath and a different layer to be peeled off. Where was the real Peter? I knew how he looked in his underwear and I knew he didn't snore when he slept. I knew he liked monkeys and was passionate about anything related to army life. And I didn't know much more apart from that; the most familiar stranger in my life.

I must have fallen asleep in the middle of all these thoughts and the sound of the door opening suddenly woke me up. We were not meant to open the doors for as long as we were on the train.

"Peter, what's going on?" I could see him trying to get of the car.

"The train has been stopped for some time now. I need a pee; I'll just quickly jump outside."

I was half asleep and didn't understand how much time had passed before I felt the train moving again. I looked around in panic and saw that Peter was still out. I looked out of the windows and realised that the train was moving. I didn't see anybody around, anybody running after the train. I desperately hoped Peter had been able to climb up into the moving train, but then I remembered the platform was quite high above the ground.

What could I do? My mind travelled fast, discarding alternatives. In a normal train I would have pulled the emergency signal. But here, in the middle of nowhere, I couldn't even open the door of the car: there was too much stuff leaning against it. Open the window and shout? Who was to hear me? This train was about a mile and a half long, the longest train in the world.

Thoughts kept on running through my mind but I saw no solution. If Peter couldn't hang on to the platform he must have been left in the middle of the desert. Maybe if he followed the tracks, he would come to a human settlement...

The image of Peter walking alone in the desert following some lonely train tracks was not a pretty one though. This was not an *English Patient*-type movie. This was real. If he didn't find a village, he would be dead before he reached Choum. It was simply too long a way away.

Time went by in silence and it felt just as peaceful as it had some ten minutes before, only that I was now alone in the car. What was I to do when we arrived in Choum in the morning? Alert the police? Was there such a thing as a police force in this country? I recalled the image of the border soldiers and I shivered. I wasn't even sure I could get the car off the platform all by myself.

A sudden knock on the windows made me freeze. I could see a hand through the glass and before I made a move the door had opened. He was back!

"What happened?" I couldn't articulate anything more.

"It started to move just as I had found my spot. It's not easy to run after this train trying to pull up your trousers at the same time!" He seemed to take it pretty lightly, I thought.

"I managed to pull myself up," he added in response to my silence. "Did you think you had to continue all by yourself?"

"Sort of," I admitted. "I was just thinking about how I could get this car off the platform myself; it must have been quite tricky to get it on. And I also made a plan to send the army to hunt for you in the desert," I added sarcastically.

I wanted to tell him that I was so happy he was back and

that he had been so stupid to get off in the first place; that I really didn't want to be alone with this huge car in the middle of nowhere; that despite the fact he was a stranger to me, he was the only person in my life at the moment and I was really happy to feel a human presence next to me. That I did care about what had happened and I had been frozen with worry.

But none of these things came out. We had never talked about this kind of thing before and it seemed almost improper to do so now. It was as if the whole relationship between us was subject to the cold and impersonal rules of communication that governed the people of Northern Europe, who don't usually talk about their feelings. So I chose to deal with it the British way instead, and I just smiled and kept quiet and fell back on the seats trying to sleep, despite the train moving on and shaking the jerrycans under my mattress, despite my legs hitting the wheel and my head banging against the door.

OUADANE

Ouadane is an oasis in the middle of the Sahara, with stone houses built some hundreds of years ago. Under the scorching heat of the day, the empty little streets were buried in sand. There was sand everywhere: on the streets, on the houses, in the backyards, around some huddled palm trees that happened to survive in the sand sea. The sand paved the streets, gathered in piles in front of the small, laboriously engraved wooden doors and danced ceaselessly in the cruel wind that whipped our cheeks.

There was no trace of human life on the streets. It seemed like the sand had won the battle and taken over, slowly but surely, the stone houses, swallowing their inhabitants. The only living thing in that town was the desert, with the constant buzzing of the Harmattan[3] wind and the endless dunes all around.

We were climbing heavily the empty streets, slowly cutting our way through the sand drifts. It was as hard as climbing a dune. Somewhere further down, we could see the

---

[3] Harmattan: hot, dry wind that blows from the northeast or east in the western Sahara and is strongest in late autumn and winter

houses crushed under the heaviness of the silence and the heat.

The call of the *muezzin*[4] suddenly broke the numbness of the afternoon. I was expecting to finally see some people in that phantom town, but no: no one was daring to show up. Only a silhouette moved rhythmically, bowing and kneeling in the sand that paved his courtyard. In his silence and almost swallowed by the sand drifts, a Moor was meeting Allah in his daily prayer.

But there was life in that town and we discovered it abruptly and with surprise, just as we turned the corner of a little street. A group of girls, with their long and colourful shawls, were sitting in the sand, gathered in a circle around a piece of rug where they had bracelets and jewellery for sale. I stopped, struck by the absurdity of the sight. There was nobody in this town: no tourists, no natives, only the wind and the desert and the silence of the afternoon. To whom were they selling? I stopped in front of them with a mixed feeling of doubtfulness and joy. I had found a human soul.

I was fascinated by their enormous shawls, *mahlafa* as they called them: some rectangle pieces of thin cloth, very long – probably more than 10 metres. I had bought one myself, back south of Morocco, and I still hadn't found the moment to wear it.

My only attempt to wrap it up, on top of my trousers and boots, ended suddenly when I got out of the car at a gas station. A car full of angry men shouting stopped next to us. At first I didn't mind them, but when I saw that they were getting out of the car and starting to run towards us, I panicked. I couldn't understand what had got into them: I just stood there, paralysed, feeling the mad beat of my heart, looking at them with wide eyes. I don't know what would have happened if the owner of the gas station hadn't come out in the street shouting, "Tourist, tourist!" They stopped immediately. They had thought that I was a native girl in a car with a European man – a deadly sin. Peter immediately put an end to my desire for playing the Moorish girl.

"Take that thing off before we get lynched! Are you mad?"

I took it off and I have never tried it again since.

---

[4] Muezzin: person appointed at the mosque to recite the Islamic call to prayer

THE girls invited me to drink tea with them in the house and I accepted right away. I entered by the small wooden door and we all sat down on the floor of a small, empty room. All kinds of things were hanging on ropes above me: I recognised the strong colours of women's *mahlafa* and the white and blue of men's robes. That rope was their wardrobe. On the floor were some mats and nothing else. In a corner, a small teapot was already sizzling on a few burning coals. It was tea time.

The girls entered the room all together after me and sat down in a circle on the mats. The one who had invited me, who had introduced herself as Fatima Mint Omar (that meant Fatima daughter of Omar) went directly to the teapot and started the ceremony of mixing the tea with the sugar, a long ritual in which the liquid was poured from one pot into another. Fatima did the job with long, rhythmic moves. One hand up, and the tea was poured into the pot on her lap. The other hand up, and it was poured back into the teapot...

The *mahlafa*, which usually covered her face as well, fell down on one side, uncovering her long and fine features. The black skin contrasted in a strange way with her long face, thin lips and pointed chin, and I asked myself once more what strange blood mixture ran through the veins of those Moors, with European facial features but dark African skin colour. When she lifted up the teapot, I could hear the bracelets on her arm tinkling, the same bracelets she had for sale on the rug in front of her door.

She brought me a cup of the thoroughly mixed liquid and sat next to me. She smiled, uncovering her little sparkling white teeth, and asked me directly, "Are you married?" Marriage was the one and only subject for young girls there: as anywhere, in fact.

"No. Are you?" I asked in return.

To my surprise she wasn't, although she was already 18. "Here we marry when we're over 20," she explained with a serious face, and went on to enquire how this happened for us back in Europe and whether I, too, was waiting for my father to choose the right man for me as she was.

No, I wasn't, and I told her our fathers don't choose husbands for us. This was a novelty for her and after lots of enquiries she decided I was to be pitied.

"How can that be? It can't be that way... you mean you will have to choose by yourself?" She seemed scared by that thought. She gave me another long look and continued, still amazed by what she had heard.

"How can you be sure you choose the right one? Who will protect you from a bad choice, from a bad man? Who will ensure he will treat you right? That he will not abandon you? How can you do all these things alone if your father does not do them for you?"

I looked back at her and decided not to answer. Indeed, who was to protect me from my wrong choices, I thought, and I suddenly wished life could be that simple and I could be born again in that small oasis in the middle of the desert and I would be Roxana Mint Someone and that Someone would take care to find a proper husband for me. But, as things stood right now, my father would never dream of interfering in my private life, and in the name of independence and adulthood I had to go on and look for the right guy all by myself and carry on making mistakes and maybe, again, fall in love with the wrong kind of guy.

I went to the car and I came back with the blue *mahlafa* I had bought in Morocco. If I couldn't be like them, at least I could pretend. I asked her to show me how to put it on.

They laughed and pulled me out by the hand. Behind the house the desert started, with its heaps of golden sand built in dunes, stretching as far as the eye could see. The wind blew strongly and I immediately shut my eyes. While I had drunk tea in the dark little room, I had forgotten about the continuous sensation of sand in the eyes.

Fatima let her *mahlafa* fall down to her feet: it remained hanging in one knot only, around the shoulder, like a piece of bedsheet used by a child playing at being a Roman soldier. Her round shoulders shone naked in the strong afternoon sun. Her heavy and soft breasts, with pointed nipples, pushed the cloth away and underneath the thin material I could see the large hips of a well-fed Moorish woman.

I was surprised to see her undress in front of me with such ease, but the more closed those women were towards men, the more open they were towards other women. The sweet smell of her skin hit my nostrils: she smelled like milk and honey, probably because of her milk and dates diet.

I watched her in silence, her half-naked body not yet uncovered in front of any man. I felt like an intruder, with my safari trousers and trekking boots, even though I was a woman too. I felt as if my manly clothes were sacrilegious near that girl who had let her veil fall to her feet.

With a sudden move she shook the heap of cloth, and the wind unexpectedly took it and blew it first above her head like an enormous parachute up into the sky; then the girl handled it with precise moves, the wind obeyed her and the long piece of material suddenly froze in a straight line behind her, perfectly stretched by the strong wind.

She smiled at me and started her dance with the wind; with slow waving moves that seemed to come out of her belly, she covered herself with the *mahlafa*; spinning, bending, under the hands, under the chin, on her back, on her hips, she twisted slowly, and the piece of material sat quietly on her young body, barely covering her shapes, drawing her graceful silhouette. She was dancing, with her hands held out as if she wanted to fly and the wind immediately tailored the sleeves. She twisted in a pirouette, with her head bent on her back, and now the *mahlafa* covered her hair... she waved once more in the wind and the material settled over her hips... easily and smoothly the piece of veil disappeared, covering her body, and her shapes hid behind the layers of material and I suddenly understood that every morning she was in fact dancing with the wind, fulfilling some sort of strange ritual for which they needed one another – the wind that dressed her every time in a new gown while she kept it prisoner in the waving layers of the fine material, until a new date, until a new dance, when she would again set it free in the middle of the endless dunes...

A CAMP IN THE DESERT

IT was the first day of the New Year. Last night we celebrated with gin and tonic thanks to Andreas and Sophie, a Swiss couple we met at the campsite. We carried a gin bottle, carefully hidden between the many pillows and large duvet in Peter's roof tent, and they had tonic water. With my favourite cocktail in hand, things didn't seem too bad.

We had toasted and drunk for the Romanian New Year at 10 pm, for the Swiss one at 11 and for the British one at 12. Shortly after we went to sleep: the Swiss couple in their car, Peter in his comfortable, luxurious three-pillow-and-duvet roof tent, and me in the hut we had to rent so as to be allowed to camp here.

I tried to move my head but it felt too sore. It was not a

hangover. I was feeling sick and I felt so throughout the night. A sensation of freezing and four trips to the loo were all I could remember. The toilet was a hole in the ground in another barracks some 50 metres from the gates of the camp.

After the diarrhoea came the fever and I remembered I had to almost crawl back after my last trip outside. I felt weak and incapable of moving, shaking under the shine of the moon, even incapable of shouting for help. Would I fall down there and have to hope someone would find me tomorrow morning? Only the fear of lying down outside the camp gates made me gather enough strength to crawl back into my hut. Then, a vague sensation of dizziness and my hut seemed to start moving, and I soon realised I was just having a fever.

Morning came and Peter found me in the same state. After taking my temperature, close to 40°C, he went away to prepare some rehydration solution. Shortly after he came back with a cup:

"Drink this. I know it has a horrible taste, but you have to drink it all."

Of course it tasted horrible: water mixed with sugar and salt always does. I drank it, and after that he put the thermometer back in my mouth.

I lay there all morning. Peter came a few times and brought me boiled rice and more cups of water with sugar and salt. We had to leave that morning, but seeing the state I was in, he didn't say anything and I was very grateful to him for letting me be ill in peace and for coming from time to time to ask how I was.

It wasn't open compassion that I felt from Peter, but some sort of reserved and serious concern, with very few words. How is it? Still bad... drink this... put the thermometer in your mouth...

But he was there with me and the simple fact of being able to hear him outside gave me comfort.

I was sick, my head hurt, my belly hurt, my bones hurt and I felt awfully weak. In the afternoon I felt like I needed the loo again. I rose slowly and headed along the same path I knew so well by then. I slowly slid inside the barracks and tried to keep my balance. The diarrhoea came again, as watery and sudden as I remembered from last night, and I felt again that I was about to faint. It felt sickening to think about how I would look if someone was to find me here, passed out on top of the horrible smelly hole in the ground with my trousers round my ankles, so I hung on to the walls and decided that I wouldn't faint, no matter what. Then I suddenly realised what was happening, and this made me freeze in terror.

I slowly made my way out of there and found Peter, talking with the camp owner.

"Peter, I need to speak to you. Now," I added, since he wasn't moving.

"What's happening? I see you're out now. Are you feeling any better?"

"Peter, this is embarrassing, but I need to tell you something." I stopped, not sure how to put it. "I'm shitting blood," I continued, feeling too exhausted to try and package reality. "I've just been to the loo now and it's all thick, brownish blood. It must have been the same thing last night."

Silence. He was not a doctor, after all.

"You sure? Is it not..." He didn't finish, but I knew what he was thinking of.

"No, it's not my period. It's not like anything else I've ever seen before. It happened four times last night and now again. It's blood diarrhoea."

"Wow, I don't know what it is; maybe malaria. We're out of the risky area though. What can it be? Maybe you have to take some antibiotics; maybe we can find a hospital somewhere." He looked puzzled. I really doubted there would be a hospital close by.

"Look, our mobile phones are still working here," he continued, as if suddenly struck by a great idea. "Why don't you give your parents a call and describe your symptoms, then ask them to talk to a doctor and tell you what to take?"

I wasn't sure if he was serious but I decided to ignore the suggestion. The first plane back was what they would have told me to take.

I went back to lie on my mattress: there was nothing else to do. But Africa taught me that as soon as you give up trying to find a solution, it usually finds you. A Moor from the camp came to bring me tea, just like that, out of the blue, because he had heard that I was sick. I still don't know what that tea was made of, but I know one thing: I have never drunk something that tasted more horrible. But by dawn I was back on my feet.

CHAPTER 6 – AUBERGE D'OR, A DECENT PLACE

(DAKAR, SENEGAL, JANUARY 2003)

"HELLO! Mum? Can you hear me?" The line was bad, with interruptions and noise. The voice on the other end seemed to come from another planet.

"Yes, I'm fine; all is well; sorry I couldn't phone before, we've been crossing the desert." Parents are sometimes notoriously difficult to reassure and for the next ten minutes, despite the line that broke every now and then, I tried to present to my mum an improved version of reality.

"Oh, I'm enjoying myself so much, Mum! Everything is beautiful and there is absolutely no danger here. We're in Dakar, the capital of Senegal." The capital of crime in West Africa as well, I was not about to add.

"No, we had no problem whatsoever so far; yes, the car goes well..."

Actually the car was shortly to be taken to a garage for a clutch replacement, but sometimes it's better to leave the details out of the big picture.

"I'm in a beautiful place by the sea. It's a great hotel, called Auberge D'Or. I'm just at the bar in front of the beach as we speak."

This was entirely correct. I had learned by then that whenever telling not entirely true stories to parents, it helped if as much truth was mixed in as possible. It made your voice sound more confident and your conscience less guilty.

I was indeed at the bar and I tried to make my mother imagine the tourist brochure picture I saw in front of my eyes: the sea was deep blue and stretched straight ahead from the private beach nicely arranged with sunbeds. I told her all about the palm trees round about, the heat outside, and since back home it must have been snowing I even managed to feel lucky to be there. I omitted from the picture, however, the khaki-uniformed bodyguards walking in pairs all around, as if we were in a military conflict area. I also omitted to mention the small group of lovely young ladies who chatted in a carefree manner as they came close to the bar.

"Yeah, don't worry, Mum. We only stay in the best places. I need to go now. I'll call again as soon as I get a chance!"

I managed to keep the optimism in my voice for as long as my mother was on the line. But when I hung up, I felt free to let my face drop as I heard the comment of the guy sitting at the bar next to me.

"*Voilà! La poupée Barbie!* But what is happening to my darling Barbie? *La poupée Barbie, elle est fatiguée*[5]?"

The girls laughed and I watched the Barbie doll arriving. She was beautiful, as most of them are. Barbie did indeed seem not to have slept a lot the night before. She wore a short, black raincoat that looked pretty out of place in a bar next to a hot beach. Her long, chocolate-brown legs seemed even longer because of the high-heeled shoes, and they ended under the black raincoat that barely covered her bum. A belt highlighted her thin waist and her small breasts were almost popping out from under the lapel of the raincoat. She didn't wear anything underneath. Her face was serious, with long features. Her hair was plaited, caught in a ponytail that elongated her thin cheekbones even further. Surprisingly, she didn't wear any make-up and she looked very tired – she had just come off her shift. I was face to face with the incarnation of the sexual tourism that had made Senegal famous ever since French Colonial times.

"*Viens ici, ma petite, viens boire un verre; tu as beaucoup travaillé.*[6]"

He, a Frenchman over 65 years old, grabbed her arm and sat her on his knee. He had a wide smile on a face swollen by alcohol and when he laughed his belly layers shook,

---

[5] "Look! The Barbie doll! Is the Barbie doll tired?" (in French)

[6] "Come here, my little one, come have a drink; you have worked a lot." (in French)

brimming over his belt. He was content with himself and the girls who smiled obediently every time the hotel owner put his hand on their bums.

As in most places in Africa, this was a strangely mixed world. We were staying at one of the decent hotels in Dakar. But prostitution was a common thing there, and the distinction between hotels and brothels didn't exist most of the time.

I felt embarrassed to come from Europe, the same Europe as the bully sitting in front of me; from Europe, the land of conquerors, of colonialists, of white people with money in their pockets who could buy anything, even a soul trapped in the hope of a better future.

Those girls were probably dreaming of the white prince who would take them away from their grey world. But instead they only got the sly smile of their "daddy" and several clients a night. I walked away, trying to ignore what was going on. Behind me, the man with the big belly almost managed to get on top of Barbie, who, caught between him and the counter, could barely breathe. The other girls were cheering, the owner was breathing heavily. What next? Sex on the counter?

For the people around, it seemed like an ordinary show. Two other girls seated on the high chairs by the bar were drinking some yellowish juice with an absent look. One of them was chewing gum, totally ignoring the hot scene at the bar. In the meantime, the owner opened Barbie's raincoat and grabbed her breasts. Half naked, Barbie pulled back a little, trying to fasten her belt up again.

OK, enough: it wasn't my business, I thought. If that was what they wanted to do with their lives... but the thought that maybe they didn't have a choice haunted me.

While Monsieur had fun with his Barbie doll, we asked Madame for a room. Madame was probably Monsieur's wife and she served behind the counter. French, old, her flesh hanging loosely, she was smoking a cigarette and didn't seem bothered by the flock of twittering girls around Monsieur. It was, after all, a family business.

We took the only available room. I had shared a few different hotel rooms with Peter and we had already set a routine for such occasions. A few dry jokes, then he would politely withdraw and let me change, then I would politely do the same for him, and eventually we would end up each in our own bed, most of the time wrapped in our sleeping bags. Many times, however, we would take a room somewhere and I alone would use it: he would sleep in his comfortable roof tent, on top of the car. He felt more secure guarding the car during the night and I was usually quite happy to have the room all to myself.

It was a system that worked well and despite a few embarrassing moments, for instance when he walked into the bathroom as I was about to get dressed, it seemed that we had found a shared set of rules to govern our lives.

Peter was still the onion I had discovered in Morocco and after six weeks of travelling together and seeing many different layers of him, I had sort of given up trying to understand where the layers ended and the real Peter began. He seemed to move through a complex pattern of being pleasant and close and then distant and inexorable, and during those days he would usually listen to the music in the car and barely say two words from dawn to dusk. We would eat in silence, load and unload the car in silence and drive along in silence. Other days he would talk and laugh, and he would tell me stories of his past and I would tell him of mine.

He was set in constant joke mode and he would always find something to pick on. Last night the subject was the "not-so-feminine" type of underwear that was hanging up to dry. I looked at my dark blue cotton sporty knickers and I remembered how I bought them with two of my friends, who both declared that it was a very wise decision, since they were so unattractive and unsexy that they might prevent any type of unwanted sexual encounter. Since that day, I referred to them as my anti-rape knickers.

Despite the anti-rape underwear, I was still a woman and many times I felt alone. Peter was the only man around me. He did not seem interested and that kind of bothered me: I would have liked to feel that my presence had some sort of effect on him. But on the other hand, I felt relieved there was nothing... and still...

That night at Auberge D'Or – a place built on the concept of desire – the woman in me felt suddenly embarrassed by the forced intimacy of our lives. I glanced at the small bed in the room that I was about to share with Peter and I gave up the thought of going to reception and asking to change to a twin room. The concept of separate beds had nothing to do with the business that was going on in that hotel...

Very well, I would sleep with Peter in the same bed: it wasn't the first time and it probably wouldn't be the last, I told myself with a knot in my throat. Sexuality, a subject we had never discussed, was suddenly uppermost in my thoughts: even more so with the moans we could hear from the room next door. The girls were working.

"It's bit too small for the two of us. I'll be sleeping in my tent," Peter decided out of the blue. I looked at him and said nothing. I felt relieved.

"I'll get out of here in a moment, but I need the loo first. Do you mind waiting outside?"

The toilet was practically in the room, with no wall in between. I left. I felt cold outside and sleepy too, so I opened the car door and fell down on the back seat. I must have been there a while. His voice woke me up.

"This is where you've been! I've been looking everywhere for you for the last half-hour!"

I thought I'd only closed my eyes a minute ago.

"I looked for you all over, even on the beach, under the car and on top of it. I even thought you went into my tent!"

"Into your tent? Why would I go there?"

"Well, after all this time travelling together, I thought you couldn't control yourself any longer."

Maybe one day I'll get his sense of humour... still, did he really think he would find me in his tent?

NEXT morning we got to know Madame better. The division of labour worked well in that household: Monsieur had the girls, she had the money. And I immediately understood that she knew her business quite well.

The pay cheque arrived and was three times bigger than what we had agreed to pay the day before.

"You must be joking," Peter said with a calm voice and immobile face. "This sum is much more than we have agreed."

"This is what you owe me. For the room and for the parking."

"I don't really think so. We had a deal at half this price for a luxury twin bedroom and, instead of that, you gave us a small single bedroom. You told us we would have hot water and we didn't. I'm sorry, but this bill is outrageous. I'm not going to pay it!"

Madame didn't say anything for a couple of seconds. She stood there with her arms crossed over her enormous breasts, which hung loose under the pink top. The greasy, dirty white hair was tied at the back with a plastic hook. She looked at us for a while in silence, no muscle moving on her flat face, then she turned towards the kitchen to leave, but not before she said:

"*Pas de problème.* If you don't pay, I'll call the police."

She disappeared behind a dirty curtain at the back of the bar. We looked at each other, confused.

"Listen Peter, the police here are not gonna give us any justice! Let's not get in trouble over some CFAs[7]. If she really calls the police we'll have to pay the bill anyway, plus pay them to go away..."

"I can't do it. It's a matter of principle."

Peter was as inflexible as he could sometimes be. I hoped he was joking but he looked quite serious.

"Are you mad? A question of principle? Here?"

"Yes. If I don't accept being robbed, I stand up for the principles I believe in. Eventually they'll have to respect this."

"Peter, are you mad? This isn't central London, remember? And if they call the police it will be very different than dealing with your 'bobbies'!"

"I refuse to let myself be mistreated by a bunch of thieves."

I felt I was about to lose my temper. Great, we were going to be arrested because Peter wanted to teach a morality lesson to an old French pimp and his Madame.

I looked at the bodyguards all around and I felt my mouth go dry. Peter counted a few banknotes and left them on the counter next to the bill. He went to the car and I followed him.

"Let's try to get out of here. I left her the money that I agreed to give her. Let's see if they dare to stop us."

Of course they did. As soon as we tried to move the car they surrounded us, all dressed in their khaki uniforms, and soon we weren't sure any more whether they were the police or the hotel bodyguards, or whether the two were one and the same guys after all.

"You are not going anywhere," one of them said, and I

---

[7] CFA: Communauté Financière Africaine – the local currency in Senegal and in most of West Africa

could see a glint of satisfaction in his eyes.

They didn't attack though. They were waiting, all around the car: it looked like they were waiting for orders. It was obvious we couldn't go anywhere.

"Peter," I screamed furiously. "Are you stupid or what? What are you waiting for? For them to jump on us? I don't know about you, but I care about my own life. I'm going back to pay Madame the rest of money."

He seemed calm. I remembered him when we were attacked on the streets of Fes. Just as then, he seemed to somehow enjoy the danger: probably a skill he acquired in his army life. His calmness drove me even more hysterical.

"Do you hear me? I'm going back to pay her! They could kill us here and nobody would ever care!" I tried to get out of the car, but the angry looks of the bodyguards outside my window frightened me. I stopped, not sure what to do next. Behind the gorillas who surrounded us I could see the big iron gate, locked with a bolt.

"They can't harm us. We're two white tourists in the capital," Peter tried to encourage me.

I didn't believe him. I felt the panic growing inside me. It wasn't so much the fear of being attacked but the terror of being locked there, in that brothel... the picture of Barbie with her naked breasts, caught in between the counter and Monsieur's belly layers, was playing in my head and freaking me out – I could see myself in her place if we didn't get out of there immediately. The drawn bolt on the iron gate was giving me the shivers. I wanted to get out of there at all costs!

It was Peter's fault. His fault for not seeing that I was scared, his fault for not getting me out of there... his fault for putting me in danger for the sake of those damn principles... his fault for being so indifferent and incapable of understanding my emotions... his fault...

We argued: me aggressively, almost yelling, he with cold and sharp answers. The bodyguards seemed more amused by our fight than worried about keeping us prisoners.

Peter gave up unexpectedly. He got out of the car, went back to the reception and paid Madame the full price. To this day he still claims he got a discount as a result of the show, and I'm still not convinced that was the case. But that day, when the bodyguards opened the gates and we saw the open road again in front of the car, I wasn't thinking of money or Peter's stubbornness or Madame and her little army of gorillas, or anything at all. I was simply happy to be out of there.

Adieu, Auberge D'Or. I hope never to be back.

CHAPTER 7 – THE GREEN TRUCK

(TAMBACOUNDA, SENEGAL, TO MALI-VILLE, GUINEA, JANUARY 2003)

17 JANUARY, 8.30 AM

"TWO omelettes and three coffees, please." My French was getting better by the day.

I was experiencing real black Africa for the first time and it all started in a breakfast place, in some dirty and crowded street food stall off the Gare Routière in a small city called Tambacounda in eastern Senegal.

The Gare Routière was a suffocating place, with hundreds of cars arriving, leaving or just moving around. It was the main bus stop of the town and the heart of its street commerce as well. It was a struggle to walk by: hundreds of people were trying to get into the right car or just find it, or maybe see someone off. Women carried heavy loads bundled over their heads and babies strapped on to their backs with coloured pieces of clothing, men tried to sell things and kids begged and grabbed you by the arm or trousers or bag, even tried to stretch their hands into your pockets. Everybody was out to make a profit, especially so the young lads who tried to make a living by pushing potential passengers into the right car for their destination; all for a small commission from the drivers for getting clients.

There was no timetable; there was no concept of time at all. "Leave when full" was the name of the game and this could take anything from thirty minutes to seven hours, so we had nothing better to do than head towards a small hut with wooden benches for breakfast. The place was full, but nevertheless three places immediately became free on the benches. After all, white people are always a source of extra income in Africa. The owner's smile was large and welcoming and I guessed his mind had already started to work out how much he could overcharge us.

For the first time on this trip, Peter, Richard and I sat down to breakfast together. We had finally met up the previous night after a month and a half of trying to catch up with each other, setting meeting points by email and then missing them due to unforeseen delays. Peter and I had arrived the night before, using public transport. The car had broken down in Kaolack, a town some 150 km away, and since Richard was waiting here with no email and phone access it was the only way to let him know what had happened.

"It must be me," Richard concluded after hearing the story of the car with the broken clutch. "It's not meant to be that I travel in a car. First the old one rolls in Spain. Now, after almost two months of hearing all these stories about this beautiful new car, it goes as well: it must be me bringing bad luck to all these cars!"

It wasn't him, it was the clutch, or maybe the sand, or simply crossing the desert. But for one reason or another, the car needed urgent repairs back in Dakar and Peter's plan was that we all went back with it.

It was a nice evening when the three of us finally reunited in front of three bottles of beer in the courtyard of the Auberge du Désert in Tambacounda. Exactly three months before, we had met for dinner and a glass of red wine in London and this entire trip had seemed pure fantasy. Now we were living it: we had made it happen, each of us in our own way with our own choices and path to follow; each of us having lived our own fears and treasured our own successes. We were together again and for the first time this trip seemed to get back to what it was originally meant to be: the three of us and a car.

The car wasn't there, though, and upon hearing Peter's plan, Richard decided that he wouldn't go back to Dakar to wait for two weeks in a hotel while the car was being repaired.

"I've spent too much time waiting for the two of you. I've been here for a whole week doing nothing, just hoping you might turn up. I've waited for you in southern Morocco, then in Mauritania, then on a beach in Senegal over Christmas. I can't do it again. I can't wait any longer. I'll go crazy if I don't get going. I'll go on and do a tour of Guinea on public transport and meet up afterwards, let's say in Bamako, Mali."

I knew he was right and I tried to imagine how it would feel to be trapped in a hotel in Dakar for two weeks waiting for the car to be repaired; in a place like Auberge D'Or, for instance.

I think he must have grasped the silent desperation in my eyes:

"What will you do?"

I didn't have an answer yet.

"If you want you can come with me. We'll meet up with Peter and the car in two weeks' time and we get to see another country while the car is being done up."

He watched me and so did Peter, and they both expected an answer and as with all significant decisions in my life, this one seemed to take shape in a place I barely had access to, somewhere far away from the conscious borders of my mind.

"OK. I'll go with you."

I don't really know why I said yes: maybe because of the fresh memories of Auberge d'Or, or maybe because I was tired at the thought of waiting for this car to be carried from one garage to the other. Maybe because, travelling with Peter in our shiny car, I felt somehow removed from the reality outside. We had entered Sub-Saharan Africa some two weeks before and ever since had seen more Europeans than locals.

We spent time in posh camping places for overlanders, nice Western-style restaurants, hotels and bars for expatriates in Dakar, and hung around with other travellers we'd met on the way. We had spent a lot of money on imported luxuries and tried everything to keep away from the streets.

I lived in constant fear of being attacked, overcharged or otherwise scammed. I was a bit disappointed. Was this the Africa I came to see? Occasionally I would glance through the windows of our car at the overloaded minibuses with people hanging outside, at kids eating some strange green fruit in the streets (which I later discovered were just oranges), at street food stalls with fat black mammas cooking in huge pots, at people sucking plastic bags with some strange red stuff in them, at all this life that was going on outside and in which we had no part.

"It would be nice to experience that," I said one day, pointing to an overcrowded minibus. "After all, it's the real thing!"

"Feel free to step out of the car." Peter's answer wasn't encouraging and I wasn't, after all, prepared to voluntarily leave all the comfort I had got so used to. But now I felt this was finally my chance to have a taste of that and I wouldn't miss it.

Richard seemed happy with my answer; Peter not so much but he graciously accepted that it made sense for the two of us to try and get the best out of the two weeks we had. We agreed to meet in Bamako, the capital of Mali, in two weeks' time.

"Do you need anything from the car?" Richard seemed concerned with practicalities and I knew that I had to decide whether we would waste the whole next day on the journey back and forth from Kaolack.

I had a small overnight bag with me and I tried to make a mental inventory of my possessions: except for what I was wearing that evening I had one spare T-shirt and one change of socks and underwear. Did I need anything else?

"My medical kit."

"You can use mine and I can give you some Lariam pills as well," Richard offered.

So that was malaria taken care of, and that was the most important thing.

"My sleeping bag and tent."

"We'll use my tent if we have to. But we'll try to get a room whenever possible."

"I don't have anything thick enough if I'm cold."

"You can wear some of my clothes, I've got plenty."

"I've got my camera but I have no spare film."

"You can use some of mine and give me some of yours when we get back to the car."

"Money. I don't think I have enough cash with me."

"I can lend you some," he said, as if we had known each other for ages.

Richard seemed to have an answer for everything and I suddenly realised that I didn't in fact need anything other than my passport. And I had it.

There was one thing, though, that I had left in the car and that I knew I couldn't borrow from him: my birth control pills.

Although my sex life was non-existent at the moment and I expected it to stay that way for a while, I took birth control pills. My gynaecologist advised me that it was preferable not to have periods in strange and dirty circumstances, and taking birth control pills without a break for nine months would do the trick. I'd never done something like that before and I wasn't aware it might work, but since a doctor recommended it I took her advice. I bought lots of pills and stuffed them in my first aid kit, and pretended to ignore Peter's wide smile when he saw them. "You know, it's safer to use condoms in Africa, if you're interested. One in four guys is likely to have AIDS."

"I take them for health issues," I told him, trying not to blush thinking of what he must have imagined.

Now my pills were in the car, but I didn't feel like explaining the problem to my two travel mates. I calculated in my mind that I had five pills left; my period would arrive some three to four days after I took the last one and then Peter and the car and my pill supply would arrive in Bamako, just in time for me to start another pack.

"No, there's nothing else I need from the car."

It was all settled. We were to leave early next day.

I had a restless night. I tossed and turned in the small double bed I was sharing with Peter in the one and only room available. Richard was sleeping in the courtyard in his tent. I regretted not having the car with us so that Peter could have slept in his roof tent and I could have stretched my legs out in the whole bed. Last time we shared a bed was in the luxury hotel in Morocco on Christmas Day, and although by now I had become accustomed to being around Peter he was still a stranger to me.

And now I was about to leave this stranger to go on with another stranger, the one peacefully sleeping in his tent right now. In the darkness of the night I was staring at this man sleeping next to me, his chest going up and down with the rhythm of his breath. What am I doing here? What am I doing on this trip?

Morning came, and I gathered my few things and forgot about my unanswered questions. With or without answers, it was time to leave. In the courtyard Richard's tent was silent: he must have still been asleep. I gave his tent a good shake.

"Come on, wake up! I thought we said we would leave early!"

He unzipped the tent and stuck out his head, with eyes swollen from sleeping and a heap of blonde hair pulling in all directions.

"Good morning, World!" he said, yawning and looking around with sleepy eyes. I was under the impression he was speaking to some invisible spirits behind me. "I'll be ready in a few minutes!"

Behind him you could see the mess in the tent. The mattress, lying diagonally, with the sleeping bag pushed on to one side; objects all around, clothes, some water bottles, a torch, shoes, a few plastic bags. It simply looked like he had pushed all the things aside to create some space to sleep. A big pillow in a blue case was right in the middle of the mess.

Where on earth was I going with this crazy guy?

LATER that morning, the three of us were having breakfast for the first and last time.

"Go away, do you hear me? Go away, I said!" Richard shouted at one of the unwanted helpers around us.

As soon as we stepped into the Gare Routière, we were the target of one of the many guys hanging around in hope there was some easy money to be made. They offered to arrange transport, to help us talk to the drivers, to get us a coffee: anything that might prompt us to pay a few CFA. We didn't need any help but they didn't go away. Luckily, by then Richard had three months of bush taxiing experience and knew that we didn't need a guide – that would probably have made the price of our journey three times as much so the guide could get a reasonable share of the fare.

We sat down on a wooden bench and got coffee. There was no jam, and since I didn't eat eggs I decided I could survive on the brownish Nescafé with condensed milk and lots of extra sugar that they generally called coffee.

Our unwanted helper was still around. He had followed us to our breakfast benches, sat himself by our side and was now deeply engaged in a long conversation with our waiter. They spoke Wolof or Fula, or another one of the many languages that you can hear around and that I collectively referred to as "local language". We didn't understand a word, of course, but luckily for us they didn't have words for numbers and used the French instead. So after hearing 200, 500, 1000 and 1500 a couple of times we got it easily: they were discussing how much the price would increase for us.

"We'll have fun now," Richard said, and I wondered what would happen next.

Peter and I were confused: compared to the expensive, posh places we used to have breakfast in, this place was cheap even for the 1500 CFA price we were quoted.

"*Combien*? 1500? Here you have 200 for the coffee and 300 for the omelette. Goodbye." Richard walked out and we followed him. What we were quoted was three times the normal price. They screamed and talked in their language, gesticulated and were obviously angry. This wasn't the plan. We weren't supposed to know how much a breakfast really cost.

"Cheeky buggers: they don't know I had the same breakfast yesterday and I know how much it is! I've been here for a week now and in Africa for two months already, and I wasn't born yesterday." Richard was confident enough to walk away, with the angry waiters still following us down the streets.

A strange dialogue started: they shouted and Richard shouted back, and in between some "Ay ay ay!", "Oh la la!" and "No no no!", I wondered how all this was going to end. It went on for a while and I imagined Peter and I must have looked like two aliens dropped in the streets, watching the show in astonishment. Welcome to the other world, the real world, the world of black Africans who ate in the street, the world where a cup of coffee cost 200 CFA and not 1000 CFA as we paid in posh white expat places, the world where one haggles and fights back, the world where survival equals the art of saying "No".

By then a large crowd had gathered. The three waiter-owners were still screaming for their money, our former kind helper was still around, shouting louder than anyone else – after all, it was his share of money that was being questioned – people watched and I started feeling insecure. Would we have a fight?

"Let's get a local on our side, it's the best way." Richard explained the story to the driver of our bush taxi, who listened, agreed and chased away the shouting waiters; after all, we had paid a fair price.

Our minibus was waiting, and I realised that somehow all things worked out for the best. I wouldn't voluntarily have left the car to try out those bush taxis even though I wanted to experience something more "authentic". But now I was about to start my two weeks of authenticity, and the small, rotting and crowded car loaded with lots of plastic chairs on top seemed to be the right place to begin.

LATER THAT DAY

GREEN trucks bring bad luck. Now I know this, but that afternoon the green truck looked exotic, peaceful and even funny. A journey by truck? Why not? After all, I was still thrilled to be discovering all these new things: life as a backpacker! That morning we had said goodbye to Peter and left Tambacounda, and I had survived my first bush taxi – "wasn't that bad," I thought. We were in Kédougou, the border town, and about to head for the border crossing into Guinea on a route that the *Lonely Planet* guide did not recommend. We only read that paragraph some ten days afterwards.

We had travelled the whole day in the small minibus loaded with dozens of people, two people sharing one seat normally, plus countless kids. In Africa children don't count as passengers, since they don't pay a fare, so they could be loaded up and considered as individual luggage as long as their mothers or anybody else managed to keep them on their laps. There were many such kids in the van and I wondered how they could be so quiet considering the crowded environment. Richard and I got the last seats at the back, and despite the exhaust fumes making their way through the rotten floor, I found the trip quite bearable.

We had frequent stops on the way and they served all sorts of purposes. People would get off and move around, trying to get their joints back into their original positions; men would smoke; some would eat, and children would run around. Then everybody would somehow mysteriously fit back into the car, silence would fall and we would all wait for another stop.

We arrived at our destination eventually, by sunset and we went into a small wooden hut to eat something. I was stressed and tense not knowing what would come next and asked Richard several times what we were to do.

"Relax," he said, lighting himself a cigarette after finishing the meat and bread he had bought. "Just relax," he repeated. "We'll find something."

He looked like he knew what he was talking about and the confidence in his voice and the slowness of his movements made me somehow feel at ease. I trusted him when he said that we would find something.

We did, and it was that green truck that was to take us to the other side of the border into Guinea and that was currently loaded with countless sacks of merchandise. The driver told us they would take some people on top of everything else in the open back of the truck, and that the journey would last for the whole night. I thought it wouldn't be too bad, given that we could lie down on the sacks and perhaps even take the sleeping bag out. Almost a first-class ticket! But Richard looked at the truck in silence and concluded with a flash of intuition what was to come.

"This is going to be a hard ride," he said, and went to find some cigarettes to help him survive the trip. "Just in case I really need one."

I soon learned that Richard had given up smoking – or better to say he was in the process of giving up smoking, constantly. He still needed a cigarette occasionally: after a tiring journey for instance, or during a tiring journey, or after a good meal, or when he was happy, or when he was bored and had nothing better to do, or just because he would give up smoking another day. Because he had given up, he usually bought just one cigarette or just two, and then one again, and this technique worked well for not being truly aware of how many cigarettes he really smoked in a day.

We checked the map again: 120 km was the distance we needed to cover to the town on the other side of the border. In Europe this would have been one hour on the highway; here it was a bit longer but it didn't look that bad. In the meantime, the green truck was loaded with all sorts of things while we hung around: white sacks with oranges, rice, some mattresses (soft to sit on, I thought), cooking pots (sharp edges and therefore to be avoided): they were all meant to reach a market in Mali-ville at the end of our journey.

When all these goods were on we had a final look at the space left: a bit tight but not too bad considering there were only about 20 others to share it with.

By nightfall we were already moving and it looked like everything would be fine. For the last two hours we had had a pretty comfy ride, and we even managed to arrange the sleeping bags on top of some soft sacks. I was looking forward to getting some sleep, but my hopes disappeared as soon as the truck stopped outside a village and we saw a huge crowd running towards us.

"Oh no," I thought. "I hope they don't imagine they can all fit in."

They did. People climbed up and everybody fought for a place. We tried to preserve our space and the soft sacks we had arranged for the night. We fought fiercely, stubbornly refusing to move our feet and confine ourselves to a smaller space while every free inch around was filled in an instant. People squatted everywhere: there was not enough space to sit or lie down.

After the whole surface was covered and the white of the sacks underneath could no longer be seen, more people were still climbing in. There was simply no more space, I thought, looking around at the crammed, squatting figures. We soon discovered that the concept of space is arbitrary, though, and a 15 m^2 surface could look crowded with 20 people lying on it as well as with 150 squatting, and there was always some more space that could be grabbed.

After everybody had found a spot it was the kids' turn to be loaded. They were passed from hand to hand, lifted on top of the truck where the driver held a torch (it was already dark outside) and tried to find more places: ayyyy! He had found a place where he could squeeze in another one, just between the feet of that man and the elbows of the fat mamma at his side. Yes, a crying two-year-old baby could be fitted there, and the baby disappeared. Another one; kids cried but miraculously shut up as soon as they were found a place. Women tried to have their own kids nearby but sometimes they ended up caring for someone else's baby. It wasn't a problem there. We were all one big family with a common purpose: to cross the border into Guinea.

Despite the struggle and Richard shouting, "No, you won't fit a crying kid between my knees, move the torch away from me," we had lost most of our space and found ourselves squatting like everyone else. The crowd around us was like a huge anaconda, and every time you breathed out you found that another inch of the space you had was lost: the crowd had conquered it and what was taken would never be given back.

I felt the pressure of a woman's back on my chest as she squatted in front of me and I felt I couldn't breathe.

"You OK?" Richard had probably seen the imminent faint in my eyes. "Let's try to rearrange and find another position."

I managed to push her a bit but my leg was trapped somewhere far away from the rest of my body. I waited until the pain told me my bone was about to be broken. My leg was lost somewhere under two sacks of rice, some kids and a fat mamma, and it was now being pressed against a sharp edge.

"Now! Let's try to move!"

In a joint effort we pushed away the bodies that covered us everywhere. "Ayyyyyyyy!" the crowd protested. After all, in the last half-hour everybody had found a survival position for themselves. The truck's movements had somehow equally distributed the load, as when you shake a box with lots of things inside and each one naturally finds its own place and fills its own space; you cannot disturb the naturally created order just because your leg was about to be broken.

We managed to push the angry faces a bit and found ourselves in a slightly different position, as uncomfortable as the first one but at least we had changed the pressure points. My leg was now free so our aim was achieved. Richard felt he needed a cigarette. He had only one arm free, so he managed to find it but I had to help him out with lighting it: his other arm was caught somewhere, under something; unreachable. Arms and legs and heads and faces all melted together. The night had fallen, the kids had stopped crying and the burning spot of a cigarette end stood out on top of an overloaded green truck.

Some hours later we had to change position again. I had already given up worrying about the small bag containing my camera and sunglasses, buried under feet and sacks. I didn't know where it was but it didn't matter any more: there was no hope I could get it back with the contents unbroken. Richard had somehow managed to pull out from under the feet of an old man sitting beside him the meat sandwich he had saved for dinner, and was happily enjoying what was left of it.

We attempted another joint effort to move: the pain had become unbearable again. We changed the pressure points once more, and this time we found ourselves sitting on the edge of the truck, half outside, and the sharp metal edge wasn't that comfortable. But a new position was always better. For a while. Until bones started aching again. And then it was time for another move. There was nowhere we could go next, however. Jump out? It was as if the huge anaconda made of human bodies had rejected us: two white faces who didn't belong there, who should have travelled in luxury cars as all other white tourists do, and so it pushed us slowly but surely away.

I felt a hand gently touching my hair. I looked up and a little girl of about five or six with big, round eyes smiled at me. With the only arm she could move, she was petting my hair. She was squeezed between Richard and a fat mamma, could obviously hardly breathe but she was smiling. Maybe we were the first white people she had ever seen. She kept on smiling for hours in a row and her big, round eyes were shining into the night. When I pulled her on to my knee, she put her arms around me and closed her eyes. She was happy and I could smell the baby scent of her hair, neatly done up in small braids. Despite the dust and dirt of the roads and the lack of water or bathrooms, people are surprisingly clean here, I thought, and looking around, even in the darkness of the night, I could see that my clothes and Richard's were the dirtiest.

"Ayyyy!" Richard's head bounced back suddenly. A branch had hit him in the face. The road was narrow, bordered by trees. It wasn't a problem when we were squatting like everybody else, but now that we were sitting on the edge of the truck we were somehow higher up than the rest of the people and more exposed – and therefore more inclined to hit branches or anything else in our way.

"It's bleeding," he said after a while. I didn't think it would be too bad, but nevertheless I switched on my torch and checked his face: to my shock it was flooded with blood and it looked like half his nose had gone! The light of the torch helped us see how much blood he had lost in the last 10 minutes: blood on his T-shirt, trousers, my T-shirt, the people around; blood everywhere.

There wasn't much we could do about it. I tried in vain

to reach for the first aid kit, buried in the backpack somewhere in some corner of this overcrowded truck, but there was no chance we could get to it. More blood spilled out, on to his clothes and my clothes, while we desperately attempted to keep our balance as we sat on the sharp metal edge of the truck.

Luckily the wound stopped bleeding after some time, just as we reached the border post. Down from the truck, I checked his face once again: there was a big stain of blood in the middle of his face that had started to dry. The dust had probably helped stop the bleeding and a crust was starting to form: what could we do about it? Break it open again and try to clean it?

There was chaos around us: people jumped down from the truck and we understood it was pointless to try and find our bags or Richard's lost sandal. Barefoot and stained with blood, he limped in total darkness towards the barracks of the officials, heading to the place where a huge queue of people was already forming.

Eventually our passports were stamped: we were officially in No Man's Land. We decided not to get back into the truck. Richard had lost a lot of blood and was exhausted. I couldn't even think about the sharp, uncomfortable edge any longer. We decided to try and put up the tent for the night and then deal with the whole situation the next day. If need be it would be better to walk for a few days, all the way to Mali-ville!

We found the driver and explained that we wanted to get out, but he didn't consent to leave us there.

"Come with me, quickly!" he whispered, and he took us by the hand and walked us through crowds of people waiting to have their cards stamped, a bunch of soldiers, and some other trucks parked just outside the border point. He stopped in front of another truck that we could barely see in the darkness.

"This one will be better," he added, and before he left he spoke to the driver for a while, pointing to the two of us.

"This truck does not go to where you want to go. The driver will leave you in a village and I will come back for you, do you understand? I will come to pick you up, just wait there!" he repeated in a confident voice before he disappeared.

I understood his French but I couldn't make sense of

what he was saying. It was clear that he had got rid of us and passed us on to this second truck. That one seemed a bit less crowded. We looked at each other and we decided to take the chance: it couldn't possibly get any worse.

The new truck was still crowded but we could lie down now. We managed to get the sleeping bag out to create a sort of cover. This new spot was a pretty comfortable one – comfort suddenly had a different meaning for us; we could lie down and we were lucky enough to have some soft sacks underneath us. We got some other sacks as pillows, wrapped the sleeping bag around the two of us and Richard's wound was looking a lot better. We were lying down with our legs stretched out and it felt great after hours and hours of squatting.

Suddenly I felt someone was trying to move my feet and I wondered whether they wanted to steal my boots. If they did, there was nothing I could do to prevent them: my feet weren't within reach, twisted somewhere far away. But no, it was just an attempt by someone to get themselves more comfortably seated. Richard's feet were also moved and somebody placed a pot with sharp edges on our legs. "Ayyy!"

They gave up eventually and we were back to the newly discovered notion of comfort. Richard felt better and told me about his other travels, about other hard truck rides. Twenty-four hours had passed since I met him the night before, and if I didn't count the dinner we had had in London some time ago, I felt it was the fastest friendship I had ever formed. On top of that truck, we were lying one next to the other and my head rested on his arm. We talked and he smoked and it felt like we had known each other for ages.

A lad squatting next to us was sound asleep, judging by his snoring. His hands were grabbing the metal edge of the truck somewhere above our heads. He lost control over his arm and dropped it exactly on Richard's newly cut nose. "Ayyyy!" That must have been painful. Blood again. The guy woke up, swung back his arm and fell asleep again. "Ayyyy!" again. Richard's wound had reopened and it started bleeding again.

He tried to figure out whether he should laugh or cry. The third time he got angry. There was nothing he could do though, nowhere he could move, and he couldn't prevent the man from falling asleep again with his arms grabbing the edge of the truck. We spent the next hour watching a hand that slowly slid away and, finally, invariably hit the wound on Richard's nose no matter how much he tried to figure out another position for his head.

Just before dawn, the truck stopped in the middle of nowhere. It was still night and we hadn't reached our destination. We didn't know where we were but the driver asked us to get out. He then threw our bags into the middle of the road and waved for to us to get off:

"The other truck will arrive to pick you up."

"When?"

"*Tout de suite.*"

Tout de suite or *maintenant* were two favourite words of the Africans. They could mean anything from half an hour to several days.

Some other people got off as well, then some of the sacks were unloaded and the truck left.

We looked around and couldn't figure out what to do next. It was dark, as dark as it usually gets just before sunrise, but we could tell we were in a village, with small huts around the main road.

Too tired to put up the tent, we just opened it, threw it to the ground and tried to pull it as far away from the road as we could. The last thing we wanted was to be run over by another truck in the middle of the night.

"Do you want the sleeping bag or the liner?"

I would have preferred the sleeping bag but it was his, after all, so I decided the liner would do. All I was feeling was a sensation of weakness spreading to my bones – I was less bothered by the cold outside than by the total lack of strength I felt, and to this day I don't know whether I fainted or simply fell instantaneously asleep as soon as I lay down on the ground.

I did freeze in the end, though, and about two hours later I started trembling and eventually had to open my eyes. The sun had risen in the meantime but it was still early morning.

As soon as my sleepy eyes grew accustomed to the light, the first thing I saw was a chicken. It was watching me carefully and it didn't move. It was standing on my leg. I moved and the chicken jumped off and went away to mind its own business; it joined its mates and stuck its beak in the dusty ground, looking for some food. There was a bunch of them in the middle of the courtyard in which we were lying.

Next to me, Richard opened his eyes as well. My sudden argument with the chicken must have woken him up.

"Are you cold?" He could probably see it on my face.

I nodded. I had two liners but they were hardly doing the job, and my thin T-shirt underneath didn't help either.

"OK, you take the sleeping bag and I'll take the liners: let's switch."

I nodded again and said nothing. I was desperately grateful though. We switched, and I slid into the sleeping bag that still carried the warmth of his body. I gave him my liners and tried not to feel guilty for the totally unfavourable switch; it was he who suggested it, after all.

I was warm again and it felt good, but I couldn't sleep for much longer. The scene around me soon became too animated.

The head of the family – we found out later – was a tailor. He had an old, noisy iron-cast sewing machine and he had already taken up his chair and started to sew in one corner of the courtyard, under a huge mango tree: this was his shop. Three women, probably all his wives, were lighting a giant fire to prepare breakfast and all the subsequent meals of the day, and his kids were running around half-naked. They seemed unimpressed by the two white bodies lying in the middle of their courtyard.

Richard got up and I did too. We went to him, said hello and introduced ourselves. He smiled and answered in French and told us we were welcome in his house. Nobody asked us what we were doing there, but we felt we had to explain that we were waiting for a truck. A green truck that was supposed to come and pick us up *tout de suite*. The master of the house smiled and nodded.

"If they said they will come, you must wait."

We waited and watched the family go on with their daily life, and the sun came up and we had a tour of the small village: we even went up to the local school. The building had no windows and a bunch of kids inside suddenly stopped their lessons and surrounded us, smiling. The teacher smiled as well and told us he was honoured to show us around. The kids were writing on small wooden boards using chalk. No paper, no pens, no books. The only thing they had was a teacher and a wooden room with no door or windows and a roof made of straw.

By noon we had found a small shop and bought some

bread, then we sat down under the same tree in the courtyard of our host and started reading our books – actually Richard's books, who, in addition to his *Lonely Planet* bible, carried two or three reading books that he periodically exchanged with other travellers.

The truck did arrive in the end, as mysterious and unexpected as when it had left the previous night. It stopped just outside the gates of the courtyard we were in, then a guy jumped down, came to us and told us they had come to pick us up. And even though we had no idea if it was the same truck we had left or another one that just looked the same, it seemed like a good idea to trust them. We loaded our bags and as we climbed up, realised with surprise that more than half the people were gone. The others were crammed in at the sides and all the space in the middle was taken by two bodies lying down: two injured men. As the truck started moving, a woman next to me told me that they had had an accident last night after they had left us – they had hit a tree and several people were injured. Some others got off in other villages on the way and now we were heading on to Mali-ville, our final destination and the biggest town around, in search of a hospital for the two injured guys.

The truck went up and down, clouds of dust settled all over us, people moved and bumped into each other and the two guys screamed every now and then during the hours that followed. Eventually we reached the town and pulled up into the main square. The injured were unloaded, and as they passed by I could see the open wound and the broken leg bone of one of them.

Finally out of the truck, I felt I had to throw up and I moved slowly towards the wall of the hospital bordering the street. I tried to regain my balance but I felt I must sit down at once otherwise I would just fall.

"Get away from there!" Richard shouted as I slid down the wall. "They always piss on walls here!"

With my last ounce of strength, I moved away and sat down in the middle of the road, surrounded by dust. Richard sat as well and we looked at each other. In the light of the late afternoon, the stains of blood on his T-shirt seemed to fade under the dust that the last two hours on the back of that truck had covered us with; new dust on top of old dust from last night on top of blood and dust from yesterday, all melting together and sinking deep into the fabric.

"We have arrived," he smiled. "It's not so bad, is it?"

No, it was not so bad. The trip took 24 hours, his nose was half gone, the truck we had travelled with hit a tree and injured a dozen people and I had just had a close view of the broken bones of one of them. But we were fine and alive and had made it to the other side of the border. Maybe it wasn't bad at all.

NEXT DAY

THE town was made up of one long dirt road with houses on both sides and several other small, dusty side streets. Some shops offering everything from small plastic bags of washing powder to bread and rice were scattered here and there, several women sold fruit and vegetables sitting on both sides of the road, and goats and children were everywhere. We went inside one of the houses that looked like a restaurant or some sort of eating place, judging from the tables and the chairs outside, and we smiled at the woman who came to greet us.

"Can we eat here?"

"Of course you can," she answered in very good French. I was always amazed how well those people spoke a language that was not their native one. "You will honour my place with your presence," she added.

It was more of a hut than a real house: a large bench in front of the door and then one room with one big table, covered with a sort of plastic sheet. There were no pots or plates; I spotted another small door to one side and I figured out that must have been the kitchen.

We decided to eat pasta. Two little girls hung around her skirts and they both looked at us with big, round eyes. The woman explained that she would need to buy some coal to make the fire and cook some pasta, since she didn't have any. Then she said she was not sure how to cook it.

"I'll do it," Richard said. "Just get some pasta, onions, oil and tomatoes, and some sardines." That was the complete range of food on offer in the shops around.

One of the little girls got ready to go but then she stopped in front of us with her palm outstretched.

"Money..." she whispered.

We looked at each other. What a strange restaurant: they

were charging us before the meal and they didn't even have any provisions! We gave them some coins and soon we had a fire. Richard chopped the tomatoes and threw them into the boiling pasta. I tried not to think that any decent Italian would have had a heart attack to see his national dish cooked in this way. After all, we were hungry and that was all that mattered!

The mother and her daughters watched carefully and tried to help Richard by handing over a knife or cleaning the rest of the chopped tomatoes. They all smiled and seemed fascinated, and even though it all seemed a bit strange I felt welcome and safe with them.

We ate and we shared some pasta with the woman and the two girls, and in the meantime two other girls came back from school and they all looked like a happy family. They talked a lot and asked us questions, and one of the girls who sat next to me had already asked me twice to take her over to Europe with me. The mother agreed.

"Yes, take her to a better life, we've got nothing over here. What will she do in her life if she stays here?"

I looked at the pretty girl sitting next to me. She was 13 or maybe 14 and she smiled at the idea of being taken to Europe, and in that moment I hated to think what a child trafficker's answer would have been under similar circumstances. Could it possibly be so easy to lure a mother into giving her daughter away just for the promise of a better future?

I told them that we couldn't take the girl with us: that we were travelling for some time, and that if she stayed at home she could give some help to her mother with running their small restaurant.

They all burst into laughter and laughed for a while before we understood our error. We were not in a restaurant; we were in that woman's house. We had entered her door and arrogantly demanded that she lit her fire and cooked pasta for us, thinking this was good business for her. And she said nothing and did everything we wanted with a big smile on her face and told us she was honoured to have us visit her place. She only asked us for a few coins to buy the coal and the food. They laughed again and they told us once more that they were very happy to have us there, but I felt embarrassed and, maybe for the first time during that trip, grateful. Maybe the difficult drive in the green truck the day before had had one purpose only: to bring me to the Africa I came to see, and if I wanted to see it and live it, I might have to learn to be a bit more humble.

NEXT evening we decided to explore a bit further, but a sudden threatening movement as we were walking in the darkness made my heart stop.

"Shit! I thought it was some sort of horrible animal." Richard breathed fast, his arm still up protecting his face from the sudden leap of the strange creature. I was hiding behind him, with both my hands grabbing his other arm.

It was indeed an animal, a very big dog actually, but it wasn't horrible at all. It had jumped on us from the side of the road and in the darkness of the night it could have been anything.

"You there, could you not be gentler? You scared the shit out of us!"

I soon learned that Richard talked to different things: animals, little African kids who didn't understand a word, the moon and stars, and sometimes to the sun. Now he was talking to this dog, which obviously had no aggressive intentions.

The dog wasn't listening though; he seemed happy to be with us and rubbed his back against our legs. He then walked with us on the long dirt road and stayed with us as we were waiting for Jamel, the teenage lad who rented us the room, listened to music with us all afternoon and had promised to take us out tonight: we were going to the local disco.

The disco was hosted in a house outside the town and even though it was still full moon and the light was pretty good, we struggled to walk through the huge holes in the road. No wonder they could only use trucks there, I thought, remembering our green truck.

The dog was still with us as we arrived at the door and despite the loud music coming from inside the building, he walked with us to the entrance. The house was the only one with a generator in the whole town. Once night had fallen, gas lamps had started to appear and the whole town seemed sunk in darkness and silence. But there, somewhere far away on the outskirts of the town, the atmosphere was quite different and we could tell it was the hotspot for all youngsters in the area.

We paid the fee, got rid of the dog finally since he wasn't allowed to come in with us, and walked through the entrance where a bunch of teenage guys were collecting the money. Inside it looked like a large house with two main rooms. An old stereo in one corner delivered music from the '70s. In another corner, some green and pink lights attempted to create the atmosphere of a dancefloor, and through the missing windows I could see the outstretched hands of the many kids who remained outside because they could not afford to pay the entrance fee. Fortunately the windows had bars; otherwise it would have been impossible to stop the crowd from coming in.

The rooms were half empty. Girls wearing large trousers and rubber boots sat in one corner and giggled among themselves. Boys, on the other hand, were all crowded into the opposite corner. The average age must have been somewhere between 15 and 17. When the music started, both groups rushed towards each other and started dancing in suddenly-formed pairs. When the song ended, they parted as suddenly as they had come together, and the girls returned to their corner and giggled and the boys returned to the opposite part of the room and stared at the girls in silence.

Richard and I sat on a wooden bench by the wall and watched the show. We were the only two white faces inside and soon we attracted attention. I was invited to dance by a daring local who must have thought his dreams would become reality that night, but I refused and moved closer to Richard. The guy didn't give up.

"Can't you hear? She doesn't want to dance!" Richard shouted to cover the noise of the music, and the grumpy look on his face was suddenly back. How does one command such looks when one needs them?

This time the guy disappeared without further insistence.

"Do you want something to drink?" Jamel asked. He had come in with us, was sitting with us on the wooden bench and in exchange for the entrance ticket we had bought for him, was eager to take care of us for the evening.

I looked around but there was no bar, nowhere you could get a drink. I had noticed several guys by the entrance with some big bottles of juice; you could pay for a glass of that liquid but it looked more chemical than anything I had seen before so I doubted it would taste good.

"A real drink, I mean," Jamel smiled, and invited us to

follow him.

He took us along a side corridor where the pink and green light of the dancefloor faded away. At the end of it, in total darkness, he opened a door and pushed us inside. Several candles were scattered around the walls and in the dim light I could see a big room, very similar to the other two where the dancefloor was. There was no dancing here though, only about 20 guys sitting around the walls on small wooden benches with glasses or bottles in their hands. In the middle of the room there was just one big piece of furniture: a huge double bed with a rotten cover on it. Everybody seemed to look at it. I froze. There were no girls in the room. The men around looked like they were waiting for some kind of a show to start and the bed looked like a stage. Behind us the door closed with a sharp noise and the first thought that crossed my mind was that even if I screamed for help, nobody could hear anything outside because of the pounding sound of music from the other room.

I looked at Richard in horror and he looked back, and I knew we were both thinking the same thing. Suddenly all my fears of being raped somewhere along this trip seemed nothing compared to the reality of that big double bed in the middle of the room and all those guys around with hungry eyes.

My mind froze, trying to deal with the reality around me, and I knew I had to act quickly: if only I could manage to think of something. I felt we were pushed towards the bed; then a guy to my left smiled and said hello, and before we could get ready to fight he bent down and grabbed something from under the bed: a case of beers. He smiled again and asked what we would like. It was the bar and the bed served as a hiding place for alcoholic drinks. After all, we were in a Muslim country where drinking was not the norm and all those guys were just hiding their beers in one of the back rooms of the deserted house used as a disco.

I took a deep breath, Richard smiled and I tried hard to push down the adrenaline in my body and make space in my mind for the new version of reality that had just unfolded. One minute earlier it had looked like I would have to fight my way out of there at all costs; now I just smiled back, grabbed my beer and tried to catch my breath. Slowly things were getting back to normal, and we said a few words about what a strange place that disco was and why on earth they had thought to hide beers under a bed, and we sat by the walls together with everyone else, joked about our fears and tried to get over it.

By my side, Richard drank his beer and chatted to Jamel, and on the crowded bench my shoulder was pressed against his and there was a feeling of confidence coming from his arm and his tone of voice. Somehow, without any words or any reassurance, I knew he would have done anything to get me out of there if he had to, he would have fought his way out and mine too, and even though I had known him for only slightly more than two days, there was a knowledge spreading in my stomach and it was mixed with the beer I was drinking and it said I would be safe with him and he would take care of me.

LAST DAY IN MALI-VILLE

WE had lost our sense of time. Ever since I left Tambacounda, only three days ago but it felt like a century, I had decided to stop wearing my watch. In fact it was Richard's idea. He told me it looked too shiny on my wrist and it risked attracting too much unwanted attention.
I took it off and life seemed to suddenly slow down. Hours weren't important any longer but the moment of the day was, and I started to think in terms of sunrise and noon and early evening, when a sensation of hunger made its way into my stomach and we knew we had to look for something to eat, and then sunset, and darkness meant it was time to sleep. Just three days had passed but I felt like these rhythms governing the world around us were all that mattered, and from that moment on I never wore a watch, not for the rest of my time in Africa.

Richard seemed to know about these things as he seemed to know about washing clothes in a bucket, and he taught me how to do that using a small sachet of powder bought from the local shop. He seemed to know how to talk to people too, jumping from total grumpiness one moment to a large smile the next. He could shout "No!" when someone tried to overcharge him and then he could smile back the very next second. He talked to a teenage boy about music, to a fat mamma about how to cook pasta and to the dog that kept on following us wherever we went these days with the same ease, and his voice rose with happiness and he spread around him a sensation of openness and total immersion in what he was living. He could spot immediately where the right place to eat was and where we could find shelter and transport, and he would treat people around him with a mixture of suspicion and trust that I found very hard to replicate.

I felt safe around him and it was hard to know whether the feeling started instantly that evening when I decided to go with him to Guinea or during the long hours of silently suffering together on that truck; or maybe he won my gratitude when he offered to switch my frozen liner for his sleeping bag that morning when we woke up on the doorstep of someone's house. I wore his clothes, listened to his directions and followed him around much like the dog that was following both of us.

We were having dinner, and the newly discovered notion of street food was as delicious to me as the salad I was eating. The sun had set and the town was sunk in darkness. Here and there, some gas lamps scattered small lights around; these lights were yellowish and they looked like small fires or candles, or simply an oasis of light and warmth. One such light was coming from a small wooden table covered with different pots containing lettuce, boiled potatoes, boiled eggs, tomatoes, onions and the like. Others contained some strange white substance. A woman with gentle eyes was serving salads and you could sit on one of the chairs around and ask her to build your salad, choosing anything from the pots around, much like at a salad bar except that we were in the middle of the dusty street.

We were difficult clients: I didn't like onions and Richard didn't want tomatoes. She remembered from the previous day and we didn't have to explain again; she picked up two plastic plates, threw them in and out of a pot filled with greyish water and once she decided they were clean enough we got our respective mixtures. That time we wanted to be innovative, though, and Richard picked up some of the white stuff from one of the pots and tried to mix it in the salad.

"Ayyy!" she yelled suddenly, and we understood it was not the right thing to do. Then she smiled and waved her head. This international language was clear enough: the white substance was not supposed to go into the salad. Richard decided he would be happy with some *brochettes*, grilled meat chopped in small pieces that someone was frying on the other side of the street, and we ate in silence.

The dog was still with us. The night when we went to the disco he waited patiently for hours in front of the building and then he escorted us to our room. He would appear mysteriously any time we wanted to go for a walk and would come and rub his back against our legs and jump up and down around us. It was as if he had decided he wanted us as his masters, and tonight he was lying in the dust some distance away from our food place watching our every move.

The woman smiled and leant back on her small chair. A small boy of about four or five came by and she took him into her arms. He soon fell asleep and she watched him in silence, his head on her breasts, one of her hands on his head. She smiled as she watched him and seemed lost in a faraway world.

"*Mon fils*," she explained, catching my look. Then she smiled again and I knew I was watching someone who was simply happy.

"Do you have others?" I asked, just to encourage the conversation. Of course she did: here women had five or six children at least.

"No," she answered quietly. "Only him."

I swallowed my next question. There was no need to ask why. In nearby Senegal, one in every four children died before the age of five, usually from malaria. This was Guinea, even poorer and where no statistics were available.

I didn't feel like talking or asking anything more. The darkness around grew thicker, but in the light of the small lamp I could still see the sparkle in her eyes as she contemplated her son asleep. Today, like yesterday and like any day before that, she put her child to sleep with a smile, with the same smile that she served us salads. Tomorrow she would be on the streets again with her pots and lettuce, waiting for other customers, earning a living for herself and the boy. And, God willing, maybe that one would survive.

WE left Mali-ville the next morning in a small, rotten pick-up pompously called a car. Dog had come all the way with us and watched us loading our bags on to the roof of the car next to two goats, strapped down as inert luggage despite the fact they were alive and protesting quite loudly. In Africa there was no other way to transport meat. Since there was no refrigeration, animals had to be kept alive and they were killed only immediately before they were eaten. And so they were carried around as luggage and strapped on the roofs of the cars or on to bicycles, or thrown in a big pot and carried around on someone's head if the animal happened to be small enough, like a chicken for instance.

"We can't take you along, we really can't." Richard was having one of his usual talks with the dog. "Look at those goats; do you think you'll be happy up there?"

As if he understood, the dog looked up and then back to Richard. His eyes were sad and I knew that he knew we were leaving.

"You really won't like it, I tell you. It'd hurt like hell to be strapped up there next to the goats and I don't think I can get you a ticket inside the car. You're better off staying here and picking up someone else after we're gone. You're good at choosing your victims, I tell you."

We sat down and had a coffee, waiting for the car to be loaded. Dog was still with us in spite of Richard's convincing speech. I felt sad to leave him; or maybe it wasn't only the dog but all that small town with its smiley people. It was maybe the salad woman who would probably be waiting to see us again that evening, or the girls of the household we mistook for a restaurant who had done up my hair in little African braids that had taken about two hours and a lot of Richard's patience to get rid of; or the newly discovered notion of having beers from under a bed or the feeling that, for the first time in that trip, I was living the real Africa and it was not at all as scary as it seemed.

One way or another, Mali-ville had sunk deep into my stomach and it was there that I had started learning about living, whether that meant surviving a hard ride in a green truck or watching someone smiling at the last child she had left; and the food of the streets and the smell of the dust were part of it and Richard's talking to the dog was another part, and I looked at the road ahead, the dusty road that was supposed to take us all the way south, and I knew that, from that moment on, I would see it in a different light.

The coffee was a mixture of Nescafé with lots of sugar and condensed milk and it was so sweet that you needed no other breakfast; the calories were enough to keep you going for the day.

We got into the car, immediately squashed on the back seat between a fat mamma with a baby on her lap and three other guys. Richard asked me if I was OK; I remembered the green truck experience and decided that by my new standards this was quite comfortable, and then off we went with a sudden movement and a cloud of dust.

Dog tried to run and catch up with us for a while and I could see him in the window jumping up every now and then to check if we were still inside. Eventually he gave up, stopping in the middle of the road, and his silhouette – blurred by the cloud of dust – appeared far away, growing smaller and smaller, until it got as small as a dot. And even if I couldn't see the sadness in his eyes any longer, I knew it would still be there, and that he would feel lost and empty, as someone feels when trying to move on while a part of him is gone. And I knew it was true because we had taken a part of his heart with us, but it was a fair exchange for the part of mine that was left for good there, in that dusty little border town that only heavy trucks could reach...

CHAPTER 8 – TOO MANY PEOPLE ON THE ROOF

(MALLI-VILLE TO SÉRÉDOU, GUINEA, FEBRUARY 2003)

THE sheep was running, feeling the terror of approaching death. We all watched it, hoping it would make it. But no: a small bump, as if it were just another hole in the road, and a sharp noise coming from the front of the car told us that it was all over. The sheep must have been dead by then and the driver wouldn't dream of stopping.

I was squashed on the back seat of the car with five other adults and a couple of babies. I closed my eyes and tried to ignore the thought that we had just killed a sheep that had happened to be on that road. But the image of the white wool desperately running for a few minutes before eventually being dragged under the wheels would not leave my mind. I felt sick and I wondered whether I would throw up, just like the little kid on my right did this morning.

To my left, Richard was squeezed into the door; to my right, a fat African lady breastfed her baby. Because she also had to care for the other kid, the one who was sick earlier, and because in Africa kids never pay for transport as long as they travel on the adults' knees, she ended up pushing the baby she was breastfeeding on to my knees. I felt really sick and I knew that if I was to throw up, it would probably be right on the head of the baby in my lap.

We were bush-taxiing in Guinea and it seemed an appropriate name for that form of transport, judging by the vegetation that had already started to change from the semi-desert lands where baobab trees grew, to thicker bushes. The word "taxi" was a bit of a forced comparison, though. We were in a very old car, the kind that would be found in some car cemetery back home. The norm was filling it with double the number of people that it was originally designed for: not counting kids, of course. The front two seats were taken by four men – two on the driver's seat – of which one was the driver and the other one a passenger who was in the unfortunate situation of having to accommodate the gear stick between his legs. Seeing the driver reaching out to change gears, Richard had commented earlier that we were quite lucky to be on the back seat.

We were crossing Guinea and the plan was to go far south and get a feel for the tropical forest, spend some days there and then try to make our way into nearby Mali. After the green truck experience and the few days of rest we had had in Mali-ville, we'd both been feeling quite recharged and ready to rough it again. But now, a few hours into the first bush taxi of the day, I was already starting to change my mind.

We drove on for the remainder of the morning, with some short breaks for food, and the woman on my right continued to breastfeed her baby and then push him back on to my knees. I was starting to feel a severe back pain pushing down into the muscles of my left leg and just as I desperately tried to move around to get some more space, I heard Richard's offer.

"Do you want to swap places? I think she feels a bit too comfortable with you on her side. Let's see if she gives the baby to me as well."

She didn't like it and protested quite loudly when we changed places. She had to keep both her babies on her lap now and went on and on saying something about her preference to sit next to a woman but I couldn't really be bothered to listen to anything. Pressed in between Richard and the door, for the first time that day with no baby on my lap, I fell quietly and peacefully asleep. Happiness sometimes really is within our reach.

LATER THAT DAY – DALABA

DALABA used to be the communist elite's retreat in Guinea. Just like my native country of Romania, Guinea also comes with a heavy legacy of communism. The former Guinean dictator Ahmed Sékou Touré, who died of heart failure in 1984, was replaced during a military coup by the then-current president General Lansana Conté. Guinea and its over seven million inhabitants passed from communism to a military dictatorship in the blink of an eye. Which of the two was better for them? People would agree that the thousands of political prisoners and widespread torture of Touré's era were things of the past, but the Guinean life expectancy of 46 and adult literacy rate of 36% did not show much sign of improvement.

It was clear to us, though, that we were in a military-controlled country: the countless roadblocks and the many stops, when our bush taxi drivers had to produce several banknotes each time, were proof that things were not quite running smoothly.

The people were smiling, though, and – unaccustomed yet to mass tourism – they were not begging. Although two white tourists must have been quite an attraction for the locals, we were greeted with a smile everywhere we went, and in spite of the military presence all around, we felt safe. It was as if once in a bush taxi we became part of a group, and the group would look after us and make sure that we arrived safely at our destination.

The next day we decided to rest. We figured out pretty quickly that the way to survive those exhausting bush taxi rides was to throw a day of rest in between two journeys. Wake up late, have a stroll around town, have a bite to eat, usually street food, and I would feel quite happy doing nothing else for the rest of the day.

We discovered a ruined hotel with a stunning round terrace built around a huge mango tree. We had been sat there for a while, Richard writing postcards to his grandmother and me reading the guide book, when it all happened: a couple of German travellers came to sit on the terrace with us and told us that the way south through Angola was now open.

Crossing Angola? It was just a crazy idea but it set our imaginations on fire and we spent the next few hours thinking about it. How about if we went south on the west coast through Cameroon, Congo, the former Zaire and Angola instead of attempting to cross over to the east side through Sudan? Our *Lonely Planet* guide didn't give us much info; after all, it was made for tourists who weren't supposed to cross some of the most notorious no-go countries in Africa.

We talked about it for a while; Richard buried his head deep into the map and I saw a smile taking shape on his face.

Richard was born smiling, I thought. He could produce one almost instantly, even a second after a stormy quarrel with some hassling local or following a heavy negotiation where staying grumpy meant securing a good deal. He smiled as he woke up in the morning and he smiled when he said goodnight, and in between these two moments he smiled a lot more as the day unfolded, all slotted in between fits of grumpiness. But it almost seemed as if he was smiling even when he was grumpy, as if trying to say something like, "Don't take me too seriously, this is just a mask: I'll get back to smiling soon." And sure enough he was smiling in his passport picture, a big, cheeky, ear-to-ear smile that brought him a number of astonished looks from puzzled officials at various border points.

I knew that his smile meant he'd started to figure out which route to take to emerge safely from Angola. Night had fallen and as we got up to leave, Richard folded the map slowly and thoughtfully.

"Angola, hey? If we ever go there, we'll remember we were sitting on this terrace when we first talked about it."

We walked away in the growing darkness and I thought the whole new route sounded more like a crazy dream. But three months later, when it became reality, I wished it had remained a dream.

WE left next day in the early morning on board another bush taxi: a minibus this time. All seats inside were occupied to the count of two adults per seat plus countless kids, babies, sacks, animals and other belongings. We were greeted politely and given as a ticket a piece of paper on which was written *Monsieur Richard et Madame.* The seats we were assigned were the last two at the back of the minibus. By then I had already learned enough of bush taxiing to understand that these were the worst seats and I had already developed a kind of wordless communication with Richard that allowed us to open our mouths simultaneously.

"No!"

"*Que dites-vous? Je ne comprends pas*[8]. These are your seats, Monsieur et Madame, very nice seats."

I controlled my smile and we went again in one united voice.

"No, no, no, no, no!"

Then Richard carried on alone.

"Five times no. Now you understand?"

He didn't, but when we insisted that our luggage be taken off the roof and told them we would just wait for another car, our seats were miraculously changed for two others in the middle of the crowd.

We sat down, and I barely had time to meditate about how liberating it felt to be able to say "no" without feeling guilty when I heard a horrible deep, suffocated sound. I thought someone was drawing his last breath.

People were looking around but it was impossible to see anything in the middle of the crowd. The same sound came again and this time Richard figured it out.

"That's not a crying baby, that's not a dying old man: that sound came from a goat, and it must be somewhere in here."

The poor creature was struggling for a mouthful of fresh air and the horrible sound could be heard again and again as we set off, and for a while afterwards before it eventually stopped. I tried hard not to think but I was afraid that the animal would be dead by then, suffocated somewhere on the floor in a corner of this overcrowded minibus with tons of luggage bundles fitted everywhere.

There were countless roadblocks on the way and men dressed in old military uniforms were standing by these improvised barriers, collecting money from every car that passed by. To this day I don't know whether it was some form of official road tax or just a plain bribe that allowed them to make a decent living.

It seemed an old practice, though, and every time we approached one of these roadblocks our driver had a handful of banknotes already prepared. Most policemen would grab them, throw a quick look inside the bus and then we would drive on without any further explanation. We soon realised that the policemen were counting the people inside. As incredible as it may sound, there was a maximum number of

---

[8] "What are you saying? I don't understand." (in French)

passengers allowed per vehicle (somewhere in the area of two people per seat), and if the driver took any additional passengers he was supposed to pay a fine.

We passed through a lot of villages that day and the car stopped and picked up more and more people, and before long the space inside became even more crowded: we must have exceeded the maximum allowed number. At the next road stop, the driver pulled out some 20 metres before the policemen and in plain sight of the officers asked about ten people to get off and walk until we had passed the roadblock. Then, feeling satisfied with his trick and seemingly not bothered that the whole show had unfolded under the eyes of the officials at the roadblock, he drove on. I couldn't believe my eyes and Richard was already laughing aloud, preparing for a good piece of comedy.

"Look at them. Now they'll all walk by the roadblock pretending to have appeared out of nowhere, and of course saying they've never seen this minibus before!"

Sure enough, we were stopped at the roadblock and an intense dialogue started between the driver and the policemen. They counted the people, the driver gesticulated and seemed very involved with what he was explaining, apparently trying to persuade the officials that he had only the permitted number of people in the minibus. The passengers discarded 20 metres before had reached the barrier by then, and the incredible happened in front of the driver's unbelieving eyes: one policeman asked a woman walking by for her identity card. The woman searched her pockets and all the many layers of colourful skirts and eventually gave up: she had forgotten her purse in the car. She jumped on the minibus, recovered her purse, produced her ID and then went on gesturing towards the road, presumably explaining that she was just walking on the road and by some miracle her purse had happened to be in this overcrowded minibus that she had never seen before.

By now Richard and I were almost falling out of our seats with laughter and this attracted the attention of the policeman, who forgot all about the driver's story and the ten people walking by and directed his attention towards us.

"*Vos cartes d'identité nationales, s'il vous plait.*[9]"

He wanted our national identity cards. With a very

---

[9] "Your national ID cards, please." (in French)

serious face and in spite of the laughter that had built up in his throat, Richard started explaining that the UK did not issue its citizens with identity cards but he was happy to produce his passport. The policeman, though, seemed as though he had never heard of the purpose and concept of a passport and got quite angry, demanding to see our national identity cards (which he expected to look identical to the Guinean ones).

The driver was smiling widely and seemed quite happy that the policeman's attention had been diverted on to the two white tourists, and while we went back and forth arguing with the policeman, showing him our passports and trying to explain that these were our documents and they were at least as valid as a Guinean identity card, all the other passengers got back into the bus and took their seats. Eventually the policeman was satisfied with our passports, the driver produced a handful of banknotes considerably larger than any handful he had produced at any previous roadblocks and off we went. There is nothing a good bribe can't take care of.

Later on we stopped for lunch and everybody seemed quite relieved to be out again. People started smiling and talking, and it seemed that everybody was having a good laugh about the events at the roadblock while grabbing something to eat. At noon, women would come out of the villages along the road with pots and pans and would offer food to passers-by, and the bush taxis would normally stop and have a break of about one hour.

Richard had gone to find some of his *brochettes* (grilled meat on a stick) and I spotted a woman carrying a large bowl on her head, who smiled and waved at me. When I got closer, she showed me the contents of her bowl: yoghurt. Africans are not really good at processing milk, and things like cheese were almost impossible to find. Yoghurt was rare as well and I felt like having some. The concept of pasteurisation, though, was as foreign to this land as that of refrigeration, and I couldn't stop thinking that this was exactly the type of food every decent travel guide would advise against.

"We'll be as sick as dogs tonight if we eat this, but it does look nice, doesn't it?"

Richard was tempted and so was I, and before we knew it we were given two plastic bags full of yoghurt. We ate like everybody around did: using our teeth to break one of the corners open and then sucking the contents from the plastic bag without using a spoon or glass. It tasted great and I told myself that it was worth any illness that might come of it.

Richard went for a wander and returned with some green oranges, then used his huge Gerber camping knife to cut them into halves before using the same knife to clean his nails. Richard had quite clean nails, I must say, and he was obsessed with cleaning them at least a couple of times a day. Having finished the oranges and the manicure, it was time to drive on.

Everybody somehow got back into the overloaded minibus; I had given up thinking about the goat and I got myself ready for a nice siesta. The car started moving in a cloud of dust and the road stretched ahead, as potholed and dusty as always. Richard opened a lollipop, his favourite substitute for cigarettes, stuck it in his mouth, closed his eyes, and with a wide smile on his face seemed the image of happiness incarnate. It had been a funny day after all.

SÉRÉDOU

I had fallen asleep with a mixed feeling of relief – we were in a bed after all – and fear – there was no window in that room. Instead, a huge hole in the wall was barely covered by a dark cloth used as a curtain. Fear was around me, I could sense her, and she whispered in her usual dark and quiet voice: "You know you'll be attacked here, don't you? They can come in so easily through the window." I started to answer back but then I remembered my winning tactic and tried hard to ignore her voice.

We were in a pretty safe place, I thought. After a few days of bone-cracking bush taxiing, we had arrived south in a corner of the country with borders to Sierra Leone, Liberia and Côte d'Ivoire. Guinea somehow managed to care for about half a million refugees from these countries and you could see these people scattered in the villages around. They didn't seem dangerous at all, and even if we knew we were close to these conflict areas, nothing suggested we would be in danger in that small town.

When we arrived late that afternoon, the first thing we discovered was that there was no hotel/*auberge*/guesthouse/ campsite. We were offered a dodgy room on top of a hut doubling as a bar, or the courtyard to put up our tent.

Luckily, a nicer alternative soon emerged and we were taken by an enthusiastic teenager to a house which he called in a respectful whisper "*Chez François*".

François must have been the absent owner of the house. His wife was at home, though, and she readily welcomed us. In exchange for 7000 Guinean francs a night (about £3), we got the family's master bedroom.

We very soon realised that it was the nicest building in the village, one of the few made of bricks and pretty well arranged inside. The bedroom we were given was next to a bathroom, and even though it didn't have any running water, it did boast a toilet with a seat. On top of all that, the bed actually had quite clean linen! Pure luxury, I thought, and if it wasn't for the missing window I would have felt in paradise.

Our evenings had a newly discovered routine. For the last week we'd shared rooms and beds and it felt like I had known Richard for centuries. We had settled into a set of unspoken rules, somehow, like the set of rules I'd had with Peter except that this time everything seemed to happen more naturally and – something I greatly appreciated – with no strange, sarcastic jokes. The routine worked well: he left the room so that I could change my clothes and he did this as soon as we arrived, even before I had time to ask. Then, changed and hopefully bucket-showered, I left the room to him. At night I was wearing a T-shirt and my pyjama trousers in bed, while he was stripped naked except for his boxer shorts. Each of us stayed on our side of the bed: we were both careful never to touch each other during the night, which usually meant we were both about to fall out of bed. He used his liner as a cover while I used whatever was on the bed. There was no romantic talk in the middle of the night: not much talk at all in fact. He read before sleeping and every now and then let me know when he didn't agree with some passage of his book. I wrote most evenings, putting the events of the day into my journal.

Tonight I started writing about my travel mate and his reading routine. In the dim light of the room, I was staring at Richard's shoulders as he read his book, his back towards me. He was half-naked, his long legs covered by the silk liner he always carried with him. I was staring at his wide shoulders with clearly defined muscles; at his wide back with fine baby-like skin, and it suddenly came to mind that he had the body of a professional swimmer. One thing was clear: he was a really attractive guy, Richard, and he didn't seem to be aware of it.

"OK enough with all this silliness," I told myself, and I closed my eyes to sleep. And yet, the image of his well-built shoulders was still dancing in front of my eyes. "No, stop thinking," I told myself, chasing the image away. But it kept coming back, and I fell asleep in fear that I might just reach out for his shoulders and cuddle up to him in the middle of the night and in terror of the awkwardness that this could have brought between us.

One's obsession always finds a way to come to surface, though, and I did grab his shoulders in the middle of the night, although it happened in a totally different context than the one lingering in my mind as I fell asleep.

A shout, a quick movement and I woke up with freezing certainty: someone was trying to enter the room. The curtain covering the hole in the wall was moving and I could see someone's arm already in the room. Without even having time to acknowledge that sometimes Fear speaks the truth, I got my nails into Richard's arm, shook him desperately and whispered in horror:

"We're being attacked! Someone is entering the room!"

Richard was up in two seconds and saw the man as well.

"Oyyy!" The grumpy variation of the international sound was enough to stop the intruder.

"*François, j'ai besoin de te parler.*[10]"

"*Qu'est-ce que tu veux*[11]?" Richard's French was surprisingly fluent for someone who had just woken up...

"*François, viens vite, j'ai besoin de toi*[12]!" By then it became clear that the intruder believed he was speaking to the owner of the house.

"There's no bloody François here!" Richard was now more irritated than grumpy and as a result switched to English.

"François?" The guy still did not understand, and to help him grasp the situation Richard jumped out of bed, went to the window, pulled away the curtains and shouted into the guy's face:

---

[10] "François, I need to talk to you." (in French)

[11] "What do you want?" (in French)

[12] "François, come quickly, I need you!" (in French)

"I told you, there's no bloody François here! Now let me sleep!"

All I could hear was a loud cry and the man running away. Richard's half-naked white body and his boxer shorts must have shown up quite clearly in the light of the moon, and to this day I still don't know whether the poor man has found an explanation or if he still believes that he saw a white ghost in the bedroom of his friend.

Back in bed, Richard mumbled something about the guy now being more scared than I was and about the marks from my nails in his arm, and then turned over and continued his interrupted sleep. As for me, my breathing went slowly back to normal and, as usual, it took some time to digest my fears.

It must have been the effect of adrenaline, but as I fell asleep again the image of Richard's shoulders had disappeared from my mind and I was back where I belonged: in the reality of a jungle village in Guinea, sharing a bed with my travel mate in a house with no windows.

A JOURNEY TO KANKAN

I had fallen asleep I think. I remembered Richard's right arm had somehow twisted around my shoulders and hung out of the window. There was not enough space to fit between the two of us or anywhere else. I thought of the nice, comfy pillow I could make out of his shoulder and then closed my eyes: just for a second, I thought. But I must have been asleep for a while.

I opened them as I noticed that the usual business of bone shaking as a result of the car going over potholes had seriously increased. The first thing I saw was nothing really: just high grass and small trees. We had left the road and were in the middle of the bush. Eventually the car came to a stop. Nobody was injured but everybody was shouting; they got out of the car then Richard went straight to his backpack and took out his emergency kit, where he found a cigarette. He had given up smoking, actually, but this one didn't count. We had almost had an accident.

Not only that, but we had broken down again. This time it looked as though the brakes had gone, which would have explained our wander through the bushes. While the driver was crawling under the car, Richard leant against the bonnet with a look of satisfaction on his face, enjoying his cigarette with as much passion as would be expected from a newly declared non-smoker.

It was the fourth or maybe fifth breakdown since the morning. By then we knew that there was not much we could do. Just wait and be patient, like all the other passengers who had got out of the car and found some siesta spot under a tree. Maybe the driver would find a way to sort it out, as he had the previous four or five times. If he didn't we would just put up the tent and sleep in the middle of the field that night.

"Be careful. If you spoil it, you must pay for it." It was an attempt to speak English in a former French colony – unheard of before – and it came from one of the lads who had got off the back seat of the car.

"What?" Richard looked astonished, and I wasn't sure if it was because he heard English being spoken or because the warning was the last thing he expected.

"If you spoil it you must pay for it," the lad patiently repeated. "The car I mean."

"Which car? This one?" Richard was smiling, experiencing something between amusement and irritation. "I wish I could spoil it. This is gone, my friend. It is fucked. Completely, trust me. There is nothing you or your friend who's just crawled under it can do to it. In my country, you would get less for it than you would get for that chicken."

The chicken in question was tied up on top of several bundles securely roped on the roof of the car. And it was probably more dead than alive by then, after a five-hour journey.

Richard's expression had changed from enjoying his cigarette to having fun: real fun. He felt like he had found an interlocutor and went on in English, turning towards the driver who most probably didn't understand a word.

"I told you this would happen if you took too many people on the roof. I told you that you shouldn't have taken the last two, remember?"

I was not sure the driver remembered, but I did. The car was already overly full, ten souls crammed on five seats, and if we were to count the chicken on top of the roof we were 11 altogether. Then the driver stopped and picked up another guy from the road, who climbed up on the roof. Then, some half-hour later, he stopped again and, seeing two other guys about to jump on the roof as well, Richard screamed out in frustration: "No no no! It will break down now, do you hear me?"

He heard but didn't understand – or didn't care. The two guys jumped on and by then we were 14 souls crammed into a 20-year-old, five-seater Renault.

We did break down pretty soon and after the driver mended the first problem – we had lost the exhaust pipe due to a far too heavy burden and far too potholed road – we carried on, with the burning hot exhaust pipe now roped on to the roof as well, just beside the chicken which, miraculously, managed to move its head away and avoid having its throat cut as the driver threw the broken piece on to the roof.

Five hours and four breakdowns later, the brakes had given in.

"Yeah: now I want to see what you do!" Richard continued his conversation, which had now turned into a monologue. "How are you going to fix this one, I wonder?"

With a piece of his shirt, was the answer. Needing a rope and not finding one – it had all gone into securing various bundles of things, as well as the chicken on the roof – the driver decided to use a piece of his own shirt. He ripped off the lower part and disappeared under the car again, trying to tie who knows what to who knows how much damaged brake wire.

It had been a day of waiting. In the morning, we started the journey after some two hours of waiting inside the car. The only way to secure the very best seats we could hope for was to actually sit on them until the car left. And since all timetables in Africa are subject to the "leave when full" rule, the waiting could be anything from half an hour to half a day. But by doing this we got our reward: only two hours later we set off, with Richard and me sharing the front seat.

I was feeling lucky. With the driver on the other seat and no extra passenger, it meant quite a lot of leg room – certainly more than on the back seats, where four adults were trying to juggle three kids on their knees. And with the kids being slightly older this time – the oldest one seemed about 12 – that was difficult.

We had set off in the morning for the town of Kankan, one of the few major Guinean towns on the road towards the eastern border with Mali. It was getting late though: the sun was quite low and it looked like we had no more than two hours before sunset, and as no cars travelled during the night there we started thinking about putting up the tent by the road for a good night's sleep. There was one major problem though: how to avoid being caught up in the fire.

The rainforest was constantly ablaze and we saw it burning pretty much during the whole day. As incredible as it may sound, the people living in it were the ones setting it alight. For one reason or another they frequently burned down their forest: whether it was to catch a dangerous snake that lived too close to their houses, to hunt a deer, to clear space for land that might one day be cultivated, or just for fun or because the neighbours did it and they wanted to do so too, or for no apparent reason but to fight boredom.

As we drove, the landscape started to change slowly and the rainforest – quite thick around the town of Macenta, the starting point of our trip that day – gradually opened up and the trees became smaller and the bush less dense. We drove through villages and we stopped in some. We drove past women carrying firewood and I thought that those living around forests or bushland were quite fortunate compared to the women of the desert or semi-desert, who sometimes had to travel for half a day hoping to find firewood.

Like fetching water from the wells and transporting it in large bowls on their heads, gathering firewood also fell under the category of "woman's work". They seemed to have a very broad definition of "woman's work". It started with giving birth and caring for children, and most of the women of fertile age we had seen were carrying a small bundle – a toddler – safely strapped to their backs. Cooking was also amongst their tasks and it meant finding and carrying firewood, fetching water – which sometimes led to a longer walk than that for firewood – and above all, finding something to cook in the large bowls hanging above the fire. Cultivating a small piece of land around the house, wandering through the forest in search of fruit and sometimes carrying back home a whole, small tree on their heads was part of their duties, as was going to the markets, sometimes several days' walk away from home, in the hope of making some money out of the few products they had managed to grow, pick or make.

Women were the engine that kept the society alive: they were the ones placing their pots in the middle of the villages at lunchtime and selling food to the bruised passengers of some bush taxi, or washing their clothes in rivers in groups of five or ten with their feet in the shallow, muddy water, their bodies bent completely and their arms banging wet clothes against rocks. They were the ones keeping and serving in small eating places with wooden benches and tables covered in plastic by the roads; they were the sellers and buyers of the markets.

They were everywhere and were constantly doing something, as if each part of their body was meant to fulfil a different role: the head that carried huge bowls of water, or anything else they could place in them; their hands in constant movement, cooking, serving, carrying, holding; their backs hunched under the heavy weight of a strapped baby; their skirts on to which older children hung. Their eyes were smiling, though, and they did not seem to question whether it was right or wrong that they had to work so hard.

It was simply the way life was: for those women other things were more important than justice in the world, and those things usually had to do with feeding the children and making it to dusk with all their jobs done. One would become a woman very early in this society and I often saw little girls as young as five or six with some younger sibling strapped to their backs, trying to play with other kids even though they couldn't run as fast because of the heavy load. Older girls would join their mothers at the river and bash clothes against the rocks, and then giggle and undress and go for a swim at the end of the washing day. Young girls would light fires and could carry on their heads a weight at least double that of their thin bodies. And when girls reached puberty they would quickly be married and would start bearing children, one after the other, and although some of these children would die young, others would survive, and then they would have to make sure they had something to boil in their pots for the kids' dinner.

As time went by and children grew up, these young women would become a bit fatter and a bit wiser and send the kids to complete tasks they used to do themselves: finding the firewood, fetching the water. And they would sit longer and longer and get heavier and heavier and a bit closer to the ideal they had been working towards for their whole life: that one day they would be fat enough to be considered a well-off woman (fatness there was the symbol of wealth, since one got fat when one had more than enough to eat).

One would ask what men were doing. They were lying in the shade, a favourite pastime in Africa. In a culture with a history of tribal wars and hunting, men were not traditionally expected to do anything around the house and therefore they usually waited for something to happen. Some of them worked as tailors or shoemakers or some other respectable profession, but most of them would just hang out in the middle of the village under the shade of a big tree. There was nothing to read so they didn't read. There was nothing to drink: alcoholic drinks were almost non-existent, with the exception of the beer that could be found in the cities, and water was too precious, so they didn't drink. They would talk amongst themselves, but they had probably exhausted all subjects long ago; they were usually quietly waiting for something to happen so that they could talk about it. They would squat under the shade of the biggest tree in the centre of the village, close their eyes or stare at the horizon, and wait. For someone to tell them dinner was ready; for someone to pass by and maybe give them a job to do; for something to happen, or simply for the day to pass.

The days would pass one after the other and it seemed not to bother them too much. It may have been because of the different way they understood time. Time for them was not something to be planned, contained, scheduled; something to be played with and dominated. Above all, time was not some external concept and it did not govern them. Time was within their bodies and their hearts; it was within their breath; it contained them. Time was when one felt hungry, since then it was time to eat. Time was when night fell, since then it was time to sleep. In the same way, there was no time schedule for anything, for how could one decide in advance when the right time was for a bush taxi to depart? It will go when it is full; in other words, it will go when the moment has come.

Because they do not attempt to contain it, time is long in these places; it is not cut down into units or pulled or pushed or extended artificially; it is as it should be, some form of mystery, some form of magic that contains life itself. For an African, the future is a very abstract thought: how can one plan for the future when the future itself is such a mystery? How can one know when the time is right to do this or that? Only time itself will tell.

One could argue that they were happier that way. Not planning to live but simply living. Not waiting to fulfil a plan but existing without one. And as we slowly sank into this concept and started borrowing their habit of checking the position of the sun to decide whether it was the right time to set up camp for the night or to slow down and have a bite to eat under the shade of a tree, as we gave up expecting things to be "on time" or planning the future in detail, we felt a lot more at peace with ourselves and with the world around us. We felt that maybe there was a higher logic that commanded it all and that our efforts to push and squeeze actions and thoughts and movements so that they would fit into a particular window of "time" was useless, if not harmful. This was when we started to add the phrase *Insha'Allah* (God willing) at the end of each sentence in the future tense, and we became a bit less stressed and a bit more humble having acknowledged that the future was a mystery and things would be as they were meant to be.

Applied to the journey of a bush taxi, the African concept of time meant that "it will take as long as it lasts". Just as it was impossible to predict when a particular car would leave – it all depended on how quickly it filled – it was equally difficult to understand how long it would take. Who could foresee how many breakdowns we would have along the way and how serious these would be? Who could have foretold that a river had flooded the road? Who could have assured us that the forest fire would not cross our road at the wrong time?

Just as the time of arrival was unknown, the very fact of whether we would arrive at all was unknown and this explained why local people usually started a journey praying to arrive safely. Our airports and train stations in Europe, with departures scheduled minutes apart, seemed totally alien, as did our practice of complaining and maybe getting compensation for our flight being late or our luggage being lost. And maybe we lived more stressful lives just because we assumed that if there was a schedule and an anticipated journey duration, we had the right to get upset if things went differently, as if by having scheduled everything we assumed we had tamed time.

But there, in a land of no schedules, no insurance and no

reassurance, one could not simply get angry and we learned to accept everything that happened along the way with a newly developed sense of patience and acceptance. The breakdowns, the accidents and the killing of sheep, the crowd and the delays; it was all as it was meant to be. But occasionally, our dormant instinct for controlling journeys through time or distance came back and we would try to ask how far away we were from our destination.

It must have been linked to their concept of time: physics shows, after all, a relationship between time and distance, but the answers we usually got regarding distance were equally confusing. For time, it was usually *"maintenant"*, the "now" being the only solid concept in the mindset of the everlasting present tense, and for distance it was "just around the corner", meaning after the bend of the street, or after the next hill you saw on the horizon; and just as *"maintenant"* could usually mean anything from half an hour to six hours, "just around the corner" was stretched to cover distances starting with a few metres to a few hundred kilometres.

But despite the highly volatile concept of time and space, there was one way out: relying on some external natural event like nightfall. No car travelled in darkness there, therefore all journeys ended by sunset. It mattered not whether the passengers had arrived, or where exactly they had arrived at, or whether the town they had arrived in was the same as the one they were supposed to be in. The sun was down and night was falling, therefore the journey had to end.

For us, having set off in the morning from Macenta with the destination Kankan, a city halfway to the Malian border, we found ourselves stopped at nightfall in a small town in the middle of nowhere. We didn't find it on our maps but we asked around and learned that we were in Kérouané, somewhere on the way to Kankan, which was "just around the corner".

The car stopped in the main square with no explanation, and as we untied our luggage from the roof (where three guys were happily using it as comfy seating), we understood that we were in a totally unknown town. The darkness was thick and candles had been placed around the square, marking the spots where one could find food.

We didn't want food though. As always after first arriving in an unknown town, we wanted to secure a place to sleep, leave our bags somewhere reasonably safe and only afterwards venture out to find a bite to eat.

We walked around for a bit but it was all confusing. It was hard to move since a lot of people, were gathered in that square: bush taxis were parked randomly in the middle of the roads, wooden benches and hot pots were out again and people around were eating. We knew we had to sort things out quickly, since meals there didn't last long and once pots were emptied, that was it for the night. If we waited too long, it meant we could go to sleep with an empty stomach.

It was dark, very dark, and we soon realised that there was no electricity in the town and the only light came from small candles or gas lamps. We tried to ask for a guesthouse/*auberge* but there were none. We tried to ask where we could put up a tent and the main square was vaguely indicated: wherever we wanted. There were a few roads leading up to that main square and we wandered around in darkness for a while, trying to find a spot to put up the tent. It was a complex decision. One didn't want to put up a tent in a too isolated place, like at the outskirts of a town for instance, because one was likely to get robbed there. The outskirts were close enough to the town that our presence would be known, but not close enough to be protected by the proximity of other houses and people. One also did not want to put up the tent in the middle of the road or in the middle of the main square because, besides the discomfort generated by the total lack of privacy involved in sleeping in sight of the whole community, one couldn't be sure that a car wouldn't run over the tent at some point in the early morning. One could thus be tempted to go far out of the town and walk in darkness until one arrives at a place that could be considered a safe distance from any trace of civilisation, and where one could hope the tent would go unnoticed for the night – and this was what we usually did when camping with the Land Rover. But in this particular country, where setting fire to the bush was the favourite local sport, one could not be sure one would wake up unburned. So the only other solution was to try and find someone kind enough to let us put up the tent in their garden or courtyard, away from cars and hopefully away from fires as well, and a bit more protected from local robbers. Being in someone's garden was equal to being under the protection of the owner of the house and we had learned by then that the best way to get help in Africa was to get a local on your side.

We spoke to an old woman with no teeth left and she said we could camp in front of her door. It was dark and we could barely see around us, but what we could see was rather depressing. Several houses were stuck to each other – unlike other villages with lots of space between the huts, this one seemed to be built with houses close together as if people were trying to hold together against some mysterious enemy. In front of the huts, a few square metres of muddy ground – no toilets, no water, no bushes around; nowhere I could hide if I needed a pee. Some kids went running by and I knew they would suddenly become very interested in us, and in our tent as soon as we put it up. In short we had to be content with putting up the tent in the middle of the walking path, but at least this one was narrow enough to ensure no car would run over us.

I looked at Richard and he looked back, and in the darkness of the night I saw the whites of his eyes. He wasn't smiling this time: he had a tired but at the same time calm expression. We both knew we had to take this, the only opportunity we would have to put up the tent, and then somehow try and get some sleep until the morning when we would hope to reach the next town jammed into another rotten car.

We decided to go back to the square and have a bite to eat before putting the tent up. It simply wasn't safe to leave all our things in the middle of that walking path.

We ate and tried to exchange a few words of encouragement; maybe it wasn't too bad after all. We'd put up the tent and we'd try to get some sleep and tomorrow would be another day, and maybe we'd be luckier. The food wasn't particularly tasty: the same old "La Vache Qui Rit" for me and the same *brochettes* for Richard. But it was better than nothing and with half-full bellies we felt ready to head back on to the dark path, ready to deal with putting up the tent and making it through the night.

Then the miracle happened. It happened right there, in the middle of that crowded square, in the middle of the food stalls, while I was still chewing on the bread and cheese. Totally unexpected, there came one of the lessons that Africa would keep on teaching us: good things happen when you have given up expecting them. Why is it that one must always go through a harsh reality and simply accept it before this reality magically changes and unfolds into a far better version? Why is it that sometimes events unfold in a way that you would never have expected and it usually happens when you have given up wanting something better, desperately trying for something better or simply once you have given up feeling frustrated because life is not as nice as it was supposed to be?

A very tall lad came up to us.

"I can help you," he whispered. "Trust me."

In the small towns we passed through, we were usually the target of young lads who hoped they could somehow harness the earning potential of our passing through their village, whether it was by carrying our bags, giving us unwanted directions or escorting us to the only guesthouse in town (which we would have found anyway), or into what was obviously the only bush taxi leaving from the main square. We usually ignored them, which worked a lot better than telling them we didn't need their services, and after trying in vain to get some money out of us they usually gave up. It was the best strategy and we stuck to it that evening, walking in silence towards the small, muddy piece of land we had previously decided was the best place for putting up a tent.

The lad still walked by and seeing he couldn't persuade us to talk to him, changed strategy and uttered a few words in English. That worked and by then we were intrigued; it was not easy to find someone who knew even a few words of English in those parts.

"I can help you," he repeated with a strange conviction. "I know people who can help you. English people."

"Where are these people?" Richard was now interested and so was I.

"Just come with me; trust me." And he pointed in another direction, towards a narrow little road even darker than the one we were walking on.

Yeah, right, trust him. He could get us to some mysterious English people who could "help" us, even though we were quite sure we didn't need any help, or he could just get us around the corner where he and probably some of his mates would rob us of all our possessions. We were not naïve but there was something in his voice that sounded somehow, unbelievably and impossibly, true.

"Trust me," he said once more. "I take you to English people. Just there."

Richard and I looked at each other and then back to him. We didn't talk but we didn't need to. Somehow we had both felt that, despite our wisdom and our experience of how to stay alive in a small African town in the middle of nowhere, we should go with him.

We went and walked in silence for a few minutes. Roads were dark and all we could see were shadows of some huts we were passing by, and then some bushes and we realised we were almost walking out of town, which didn't seem very wise. But just as we were about to let our reason question our trusting impulses, the guy stopped in front of a very tall gate made of iron, the type of gate that it was very difficult to find in those places. He started knocking, using both his fists and his feet, and soon the gate opened slowly and another dark face stuck its neck out of the narrow opening, starting an intense dialogue with our lad. It was all in Fula or Malinke or Susu, or maybe another language of the place, and as usual we didn't understand much, with the exception of the word "English" that came by a few times. Then the gate closed and the guy turned to us and said:

"We must wait; they will come now."

Who were "they"?

The gate opened again and this time a bright light blinded us. *Oh God, they must have electric light in there and someone has just turned it on.*

Our eyes were still closed but our ears were open and we heard a true British accent somewhere very close.

"Oh dear, this is a bit unexpected but please do come in."

We walked through the gate with our eyes still closed, since the light was too strong. I couldn't help but think that all descriptions of paradise started with a very bright light.

The voice continued:

"We'd gone to sleep, you know: we sleep early in these places. And then the security guy came to tell us there were two Brits outside. I thought it was a joke but look at you, who would have thought..."

Slowly we opened our eyes and the owner of the voice started taking shape: he was white, middle-aged, very, very clean, and British judging by his accent. He stretched his hand out and said:

"Really pleased to meet you. I'm Paul."

"Richard."

"Roxana."

We couldn't say much more than that.

"You're most welcome to our small compound. We're a group of engineers working for Rio Tinto Mining Company. We're based here and we haven't really had any guests so far."

Yes, it was true. Sometimes the skies open and angels do descend to Earth, and they take the form of a dark-faced, tall lad who says "I can help you". And then they change into the clean, nice-smelling clothes of a Western expat who was right now shouting at some sleepy-looking maid: "Hey you, put up the table and prepare the guest room please. Go wake up John and the others: we have guests!"

Before we knew it, we were seated at the table. It was tall and homely and had a white tablecloth. We tried to avoid sitting on their armchairs for fear our trousers were too dirty, and we didn't want to leave stains of red dust on their white cushions. But Paul said it wasn't a problem and had us seated, and before we had time to argue the others came out: John and Bill and a couple of other guys, all Brits and all really happy to have us there. They asked us if we had eaten and we said we had, and they then said they would like to offer us some drinks. And some bottles of red wine with the labels printed in French were brought to the table, along with some cold beers, and John asked us if we would prefer some gin and tonic instead. We just sat there, staring round and then at each other with eyes wide open: we couldn't stop asking ourselves if we were dreaming.

After a couple of hours' chatting and drinking some fine wines and beers, I remember being shown into a bathroom, and I mean a real bathroom, and being given some clean towels, and I almost collapsed and struggled hard not to fall asleep under the shower, the only hot shower I had had ever since leaving the four-star hotel in Morocco some two months before. And when I finally emerged from the bathroom, about an hour later, feeling incredibly clean and equally drunk (it turned out that one hour under a hot shower can't erase the effects of the wine previously consumed) I barely heard Richard's remark, something about people thinking they should come and rescue me from under the shower, and I couldn't respond to the invitation of having just another glass with all of them on the terrace; I just followed a little woman dressed in a white maid's uniform and collapsed into a large, comfy double bed with fresh-smelling sheets. It was simply too good to be true.

It wasn't a dream and as we woke up in the morning – Richard sore with a hangover, as it turned out he'd had a lot more drinks after I went to sleep – we stared at each other, trying to make sense of that strange evening. As we emerged from the room, another maid took us to a nicely laid table, asked Richard how he preferred his eggs and returned some 10 minutes later with a tray containing a classic English breakfast for him plus the continental version of bread, butter, jam and orange juice for me. Then we had some real coffee, and it was the only time in Africa that we were spared the ever-present Nescafé. Finally, we were asked if there was anything else they could do for us.

There wasn't: there couldn't possibly be anything else they could do for us and as we went around to their offices, all hosted in the same large compound surrounded by tall walls, we realised that we had touched a piece of heaven and for a moment we had been spared from the harsh reality of the world outside those gates. We had been offered a bit of help to cope with life, just when we expected it least and just when we were quite prepared to deal with the hard situation we had got ourselves into.

"Good luck," they said as they left us in the same dusty square we had arrived in the night before. As our next rotten bush taxi exited the town of Kérouané that morning, I felt that despite all the hardships and the dirt and the dust, we had been very lucky people indeed. We had just witnessed a miracle.

Yes, there are times when angels come searching for two hungry, dirty and exhausted travellers, and when they finish their mission they go back as quickly and quietly as they had come, not even leaving space for much thanks.

A NIGHT AT THE MISSION CATHOLIQUE

I cannot be bothered was a state one entered into easily after spending a few hours crammed in a bush taxi. It was as if your brain had decided to protect you from the ever-present pain of the squeezed and stretched muscles and injected a sort of anaesthetic into your consciousness. You felt like you were somehow floating above the car, above the people you shared your seat with, and you went into a sort of a daydreaming state where your brain slowly registered what happened around you without responding. The red dust was everywhere, entering the car and settling on your face and clothes. You were closer to the window and you probably looked a bit worse than your neighbour, who was already so covered in dust that only the whites of their eyes showed clearly. You couldn't be bothered to try and cover your face. The car didn't stop for lunch even though you were starving. You couldn't be bothered to say anything. It was all fine and it was all OK. It was as if your desires had been suspended, your needs had been placed on hold. Whatever happened, it was fine. You couldn't be bothered to think otherwise. And when the car finally stopped to fill up with petrol in one of the towns you passed by and a young kid of five or six came begging at your window, you smiled faintly and couldn't even find the strength to tell him that you couldn't be bothered.

Another day and another long trip and another retreat into the *I cannot be bothered* state, and we arrived at last in the long-awaited city of Kan bloody kan. But by then we were so deep into the *I cannot be bothered* state that except for the nice nickname we found for it, we couldn't even be bothered to be happy that we had arrived in the city at last. In fact one didn't arrive anywhere, it was just another point on a journey, and Kankan was for us both a destination and a starting point. The next day we were leaving for the Malian border.

But the next day was far away and the present was more important. Once we were out of the bush taxi and had stretched our arms and legs and looked around the crowded, smelly and noisy Gare Routière, we slowly came back from the *I cannot be bothered* state and started looking for a place to spend the night.

La Mission Catholique was a tall, white building designed like a fortified compound, with a nice, square inner courtyard and heavy iron gates that closed for the night. It was just around the corner from Place de l'Indépendance, we were told. All major towns in West Africa had some sort of Place de l'Indépendance. To our surprise, "just around the corner" turned out to be the exact description and the next moment we were standing in front of a middle-aged Sister with a dark, shiny face. We had asked for a double room for the night and she was trying to figure out what she should do with us.

"How many nights do you want to stay?" she asked, with her head buried in what looked like a heavy register.

"Just tonight." We would be leaving early the next morning, I was about to add.

"Hmmm," she said, and then she paused. There was a little problem, I could tell, and I could guess what it was.

"Hmm." she said again. "We have one room free for tonight. But only one room."

As expected, men and women were not supposed to share rooms under the respectable roof of the Mission Catholique.

"Can we take it?" I asked, pretending not to understand what the problem was.

"Hmmm," she said again. "I could give you the room but we have a problem. Only one of you can stay here. It is our policy that men and women cannot share rooms."

As plain as that. So what could we do?

"Look, Sister," I began in a convincing tone. "This is our last chance to find somewhere for the night. We have tried to find a room at Chez Marie and Hôtel de Gare and they don't have any rooms for us. They sent us here saying you'd be able to help us. We have nowhere to go."

This was true; the other two so-called hotels had sent us away immediately. We might have found something else in town but it was getting late and dark and a common-sense principle says that you don't want to wander outside after dark in search of a hotel while carrying all your belongings with you.

Sister was still studying the register, her eyes down, and she was silent. Richard was outside, waiting with the bags. I was standing in front of that reception desk where our fate for the evening was about to be decided and I felt so tired, so dirty and so hungry that I was about to slide back into the *I cannot be bothered* state and tell her that if she didn't give us the room we would just put up our tent and sleep in front of their gates and we'd be fine.

"You know, this is a sacred place. *Dieu* has given us commandments, and we simply obey them; men and women are not to sleep together in this place of worship."

Actually the place of worship was somewhere down the road and we were in the hostel they ran for travellers just like us who desperately needed a place to sleep for the night:

just to sleep, I promise.

A longer silence followed. She was in the middle of a moral quandary. I was also in the middle of something: I was between the *I cannot be bothered* state and some form of irritation which told me that deep down inside, I could, in fact, still be bothered.

"We sometimes make exceptions. In circumstances like this one, for instance, when someone needs a room very badly." She watched me with a look of pity on her face that made me wonder whether I was looking *that* dirty.

"But always, always, if we make an exception, we must be sure that the man and the woman in question are married in the eyes of God," she continued, and she lifted her eyes from her register and looked directly into mine.

I felt her look and I felt a bit guilty for what I was about to say, but there was no other way out.

"Then we do not have a problem. We are married."

I had no ring and neither did Richard, and if she asked for some kind of a marriage certificate we were in trouble. But it was worth trying to get that room.

"Then *Dieu* will understand," she said, her eyes still fixed on mine.

"Yes, I hope God will understand," I thought, still feeling kind of wicked at lying with such conviction to a nun under the roof of a church. But I got the key and she didn't ask for any proof, somehow assuming no one could possibly utter such a lie. And as I walked out to Richard with a smile of triumph and told him about our newly married status, and after we had laughed about it for a while, I tried to forget that uncomfortable feeling of looking into that Sister's eyes. And later on, having had a nice (if cold) shower and a bite to eat and stretched my bones into the double bed next to Richard, I thought some more about it and hoped God would understand. For yes, I had lied, but it wasn't too big a lie for there would be no sin that night under the roof of the Mission Catholique.

SIGUIRI, THE BORDER TOWN

We were standing in line at the only bank in the main square of the town. The main square also doubled as the Gare Routière and we desperately needed to change some money, as little as $5 to pay our way on to the next bush taxi that was to take us across the border.

"Sorry, we cannot change that here." The clerk gave me my five-dollar bill back.

"What do you mean?"

"It's too small. We cannot deal with such small amounts." And he waved on the next person standing in the queue.

"Try on the streets," he said, seeing my puzzled look. "Someone may change that for you."

On the street meant going to the black market, the illegal money changers.

We tried again and this time we had a middle-aged shop owner telling us the same thing with a pitying look in his eyes.

"We can only change 50 or 100 US dollar bills in here. Sorry. Try somewhere else."

The incredible had happened again. Nobody wanted our five-dollar bill and we needed to change two of those to get enough money for the journey. As all guide books seemed to recommend travellers should keep their money in bills of small denomination, this was how we were keeping ours. But there was a different law governing this place.

"You see, the problem is we don't know how much this is worth," another guy, younger this time, told us.

"But if you can change a 100-dollar bill you should also be able to change two five-dollar bills. It's worth one-tenth of a 100-dollar bill," I said as I tried to make him see there was no problem.

"No, it's not that simple. Nobody wants a five- or ten-dollar bill here, so they are worth less per dollar. The problem is, how much less? Sorry, *ma soeur*, but I don't know how much your bill is worth."

Ma soeur was a respectful form of address in African society. It made me think of the Sister at the Mission Catholique and my undigested feelings of guilt. *Maman* was another expression they used and it was supposed to show even more respect, but it sounded kind of weird when someone at least 10 years older than you called you "mother".

We walked around and found out that a five-dollar bill was absolutely worthless in Siguiri. I had no other money, since I was living on money borrowed from Richard which I hoped to repay once we met Peter and the car again in Bamako. Then I would have access to the cash I had deposited in the safe box of the car, or I could use my Visa card to get some cash out at an ATM. There were always ATMs in the capitals we passed by. But we were not in a capital yet, we were in a dusty little border town where nobody wanted our five-dollar bill and, worse even, the bush taxi that was supposed to take us to the other side of the border seemed ready to leave.

"We'll use my banknote collection," said Richard.

He was collecting banknotes – one of each kind – from every country we passed by. He had collected banknotes ever since he started travelling; he had banknotes from South America and Asia and now he was collecting banknotes from Africa. It was like a ritual and as soon as we entered a country and changed money, he would immediately put away a few banknotes for his collection. He would keep all those collected banknotes wrapped up in several envelopes and plastic sheets. After his camera and film, they were his most treasured possession. If we used his banknotes then and crossed the border, there was no way to be sure we would find others to replace them. Mali had a different currency.

"We'll use these banknotes," he said again and I looked at him and said nothing, not even "thank you".

Call it the British culture of understatement, or simple generosity, or the way Richard was built. For two weeks he had been sharing with me his clothes and his tent, his mattress and his Lariam pills. He shared with me the oranges he bought on the streets, the book he read, his camera film and his mosquito spray. And today he would share with me his treasured banknote collection and he would take this decision and go ahead with it as if it were the most natural thing in the world, with no fuss at all.

He took them out and we paid for our tickets, and as we got into the last two seats of the minibus and just before I fell into the *I cannot be bothered* state again I thought that I had still not thanked him. For being simply, deeply, and naturally generous.

CHAPTER 9 – TOUBABS IN THE HEAT

(BAMAKO, MALI, FEBRUARY 2003)

Toubab means "White Man" in West Africa: we figured that out pretty quickly. We'd also figured out that it was a scary name and it had some evil connotations as well, although it wasn't entirely clear how bad they were. It was something that African mothers would scare their children with: "If you're not behaving, the *toubab* will come and eat you". I wasn't sure if *toubab* was an insult or if it was just a sort of funny concept for older kids, the way something that scared you when you were little becomes something funny later on. One way or another, African kids liked the word a lot and did not miss a chance to gather around us or run by our side, laughing and shouting again and again, "*Toubab! Toubab!*"

They were all around us again, and we, poor *toubabs*, had nowhere to hide. We were looking for a hostel.

We had come to the fourth hostel, or hotel or whatever they called it, where we had tried to get a room and they had none. I couldn't believe it but it seemed this was the high season of "tourism" in Bamako. We glanced at another room containing four double beds where some exhausted white faces lay motionless, like all the other rooms we had seen. It was simply too hot: too hot to breathe, too hot to move; much too hot to be wandering the streets aimlessly looking for a hostel.

Auberge Laffie was a hostel like many others. It was on a street with no tarmac and a goat tied to the gate – or maybe it was a sheep. I was too tired to notice the difference, and besides, it was getting dark outside. Incredibly, this one had a free room: actually, one double bed in a big communal bedroom. We looked at each other, Richard probably seeing the same mask of red dust on my face that I could see on his, then looked again at the hot, smelly and sweaty room with several bodies stretched on beds. We decided to take it. It was too hot and we were too tired to keep on looking.

Trying not to feel too bothered about sharing my room with 10 other *toubabs*, all guys, I fell down on the bed, noticing the sweaty smell of bedsheets and trying not to think how many other sweaty travellers must have slept in them since they were last washed. Then back to some nicer thoughts: I tried to cheer myself up by thinking that this was Bamako. We had arrived in Mali and Peter and the car and all my luxuries and toiletries, and above all my birth control pills, should be here any day now.

After a cold shower and with the red dust mask on my face gone, we headed out into the cool breeze of the night with only one target: to find an Internet café (or more likely, a place that had an oh-so-slow Internet connection). For more than two weeks we had not communicated with Peter or anybody else: there were no telephones and no Internet in Guinea. But now we were in the capital of Mali and felt pretty sure that the Internet and mobile phone boom that was sweeping through Africa would be felt there too.

We quickly found an Internet café, and as we each sat down in front of a computer and I went through the emails that had gathered in my Yahoo inbox, I felt I had entered another world where I was again just a click away from friends and family and all the other life that was going on, somewhere in another universe.

There was one email, though, that both Richard and I looked for with hungry, desperate eyes. Peter was supposed to be in town by then and emailing was our only form of contact with him. He should have let us know where he was – maybe we could see him tonight; maybe I could finally change into something other than this T-shirt and trousers I had been wearing for the last two weeks. Where was he?

He simply wasn't there, it turned out. More specifically he was still in Senegal, having treated himself to a short tour of Gambia while waiting for a new clutch to be DHL-ed from the UK (since it was cheaper than buying the parts from the Land Rover garage in Senegal). He had sent us a short email saying he would be late for the meeting. How late? Maybe a week, maybe more: and he was hoping we would wait for him there in Bamako.

I felt like I was exploding! The long-dreamed-of comfort of travelling in a Land Rover again rather than a rotten bush taxi was quickly disappearing; my cream collection, all those luxuries the car was packed with, were suddenly unreachable. Worse than all, my next supply of birth control pills that I desperately needed to continue was also not available.

"Did you see this? The bloody car still needs the bloody clutch and bloody more time. He's bloody useless, Peter!"

Richard was more amused than irritated by Peter's delay.

"Oh, oh, young lady! What bad language!"

"Oh Richard, give me a break. I'm about to explode. Don't you see that he's not here?"

"Well, that's his problem."

"No, it's not his, it's mine and yours. We'll get crazy waiting a week or two for him in this horribly hot town."

The image of the smelly, sweaty bed in Auberge Laffie was making me feel sick.

"We won't." Richard seemed quite sure.

"But he's not here."

"Look, I don't know about you but I won't wait here for Peter. Not here or anywhere any longer, actually. I'm going on and you can come with me if you want. Or you can wait for Peter here."

There was no way I would wait for Peter there on my own, I thought.

"It's easy," Richard carried on. "We can get our Burkina Faso visa, spend another day or so here and then carry on. We go to Djenné and Mopti and then on to Timbuktu. He can catch up with us where he wants to."

"But he will want to see Mopti and Djenné and Timbuktu and he'll always be behind us; we'll have to wait for him somewhere," I said, still depressed.

"He'll have to skip some of them, or he'll simply move faster."

"And what if he doesn't?"

"Look, I've been waiting for the two of you for two months in Morocco, Mauritania and Senegal. Waiting for Peter and the car has become too much of a common theme lately. I'm moving on."

"Up to where?"

"Up to South Africa if need be."

Richard wasn't smiling now. I knew he was also irritated, although he tried to present a type of *I cannot be bothered* image.

"Sure, it's frustrating," he said after a while. "But you see, you did well in Guinea and you had nothing from the car. You can do well for the rest of the trip with or without the car."

"But you don't understand: my birth control pills, my creams," I was about to add, but I remained silent. Maybe I could do well without all those things. The alternative of moving on south with Richard in some form of local transport was, after all, not so bad.

"OK, I'll write to him saying we're going on."

And because sometimes I'm a vengeful little being, I wrote a pretty harsh email saying, among other things, that he had just lost his travel companions and we wished him good luck in travelling on his own, ending with "See you in South Africa". And I signed it R&R.

It made me feel better that I had put my frustrations into writing, even though I also felt a bit like a child overreacting. I didn't know if my hormone levels were exploding just because I'd learned that having to discontinue my birth control pills meant I would need to deal with my periods somewhere on the dusty roads of Africa, or if I was simply too tired, too exhausted and too sick of thinking about the smelly, sweaty and burning hot room where I would spend the night with ten others, but it all seemed too much. The hope I was hanging on to, the nice image of Peter and the car, was vanishing slowly, and in the empty space it left behind something else was taking shape, still a bit too unclear to see but it looked like something with roots in the *I cannot be bothered* state, grown into a sort of certainty that I would make it one way or another with or without the car, with or without creams, with or without...

I was still feeling angry, though, and I thought that maybe a bite to eat would help us both feel better. Richard was trying to seem OK but I knew he wasn't fully, although he was the one to pick up on my harsh email and sweeten it with another one to Peter which started with "Let me be the diplomat in all this. You can understand why Roxana feels upset..." He did it naturally, not suspecting that that short email was to be the first of many occasions to come when he would play the referee and try hard to defuse tensions between Peter and me. But that happened a long time after Bamako, when Peter did eventually catch up with us and the original vision of the three of us in a car became reality.

Back into the streets to look for some food and we noticed the usual fat mammas with huge pots were out already: dinner time. Richard had got back his usual ear-to-ear smile and was conversing with each of these mammas, and each time the same dialogue was repeated like a ritual:

"*Bonsoir!*"

"*Bonsoir, Monsieur!*"

"*Qu'est-ce que vous avez pour manger ce soir?*[13]" Richard's French got better when he was hungry.

"*C'est très bon. Viens, viens voir!*[14]"said the owner of the pots with a large white smile.

And then, following their encouraging signs, he became nosy and lifted all the lids off the big pots, had a look into each of them and asked some more questions:

"*Qu'est -ce que c'est ça?*"

"*Manioc.*"

"*Et ici?*"

Cassava or *poulet* or *poisson*, or some other word describing some other type of soupy, greasy mixture.

What he hoped for was to hear *brochettes*, and what I hoped for was *salade*. But that night there was neither of those.

We found some fried potatoes, or rather fried yams – a type of root commonly fried just like potatoes and the common substitute for potatoes here.

"*Yam pour 100 CFA,*" he said, and we watched how the mamma counted the chips one by one. Eventually she decided that 35 chips was a fair amount for 100 CFA (or 10p back home) and we got a pretty big pile of them.

Richard was being nosy again and lifted another lid. Underneath, countless chicken heads laid nicely arranged on a tray, their beaks up, their feathers still on, their eyes seeming alive and looking vividly up at us despite the oil in which they had been deep fried, which dripped over the edges of the tray.

"Urghhh – that was an ugly view. Let's try another." Richard didn't give up easily and lifted the next lid: countless chicken feet were under this one, deep fried as well with the claws still intact. I suspected they must have belonged to the

---

[13] "Good evening. Good evening, sir. What have you got to eat this evening?" (in French)

[14] "It's very good. Come, come see!" (in French)

heads in the previous pot.

"Yams will do for this evening," said Richard, who had suddenly lost his appetite for chicken or meat, and we sat down on two little wooden chairs provided by the mamma with the chicken heads and toes and ate our chips. Although the image of the fried eyes and beaks stayed with me, it didn't manage to spoil my appetite.

It was cooler now, and in the darkness of the night the street seemed less dusty, we looked less dirty and the yams tasted less over-fried. And as we headed back in silence to the Auberge Laffie and its sweaty rooms, my mind wandered away and it went beyond the quiet streets, the Internet café, and Peter, and the car that wasn't there, and even beyond the chicken heads. It went somewhere far away and it travelled on a dusty road south, and I knew that somehow, with or without my creams, the road was there and it was waiting for us. We would leave that city soon.

WE did not leave too soon, though. We had a number of practicalities to deal with and the process of arriving in a capital involved a number of compulsory steps: Internet (that was done), wash clothes (easy since I didn't have too many), have pizza as a nice treat and get visas for the next country: in this case Burkina Faso. On top of everything, we had a very important trip to make to the only DHL office in Mali, where two mysterious packets would hopefully have arrived from two different corners of the world and would be waiting for us: Richard's Visa card and my new passport.

So we got up early, ready to start our errands. I was wrecked though. I had hardly slept the whole night. Not because of the heat and the smell of putrefaction that was filling the room, not because of the many others snoring, and not because of the mosquitoes. We couldn't open the windows for fear of them attacking, and although we desperately tried to wrap ourselves in the old mosquito net full of holes hanging on top of the bed, they were everywhere and feasted on us until dawn. Not even because the bed was too small and too uncomfortable, but because of the horrible sound that came from the sheep tied by a short rope to the gate in front of the house. It kept on making despairing sounds throughout the night, again and again, with a sort of steady desperation in its voice that only the certainty of death could bring. It would die soon and it knew it, and it kept on calling, again and again, as if trying to beg for forgiveness or some miraculous pardon from the death sentence.

I knew it had a few more days to live, like all the others, all the sheep tied in front of the gates to the right and the left of that house, on other streets as well, in all of Bamako. We were approaching Tabaski (as Eid al-Adha is called in the Wolof language), the biggest annual Muslim holiday, and ritual demanded that every well-off family would kill a sheep and give a third of the meat to the poor. Since Bamako was full of families rich enough to afford the ritual, each of them had a sheep they had purchased for the occasion tied to their gates, the trees or to whatever they could find, waiting for the fated day.

I woke up after a nearly sleepless night and as I walked through the courtyard towards the bathroom, carefully trying to ignore the sheep that was still shouting its lungs out, I noticed something else: a bunch of kids were playing football, their faces wide open with smiles, their eyes vivid and their excited shouts covering even the noise of the poor sheep. When I looked at the ball I froze. It was a big rat, probably half dead by then but still trying to escape between kicks. Another player kicked it and the animal shook and was thrown into the air, his paws moving or maybe just trembling, and then fell to the ground and tried to move again, but another foot was near and there came another kick. It went on and on, and the laughter of the boys covered the tiny screams of the animal, and it was hard to know which kick it was that finally brought about death and the end of all that torture. I was in the toilet by then and I was throwing up.

"Come on, we have things to do, people to see!" Richard's optimism was hardly shaken by the sheep or the rat or the mosquitoes or anything else. He handed me a cup of *café au lait*: it was breakfast time at Auberge Laffie.

In the courtyard, under a big tree and not far away from the unhappy sheep, two *toubabs* were sitting on a small wooden bench. They were a couple, Alice and Toby, and they came from Sweden. Their backpacks were clean and shiny and still bore their flight luggage tags. They were both blonde, with white faces, clean shirts and very new trekking boots. They had arrived by plane the day before and spent the night in the *auberge* just like us, and it turned out they were among the occupants of one of the other beds in the big room. They looked like they had slept as little as me, but they were smiling and seemed happy to be there. We had a chat as we drank our brownish Nescafé with lots of sugar and condensed milk and they told us that they had just started a six-month trip through Africa: that they had worked a lot and saved a lot for this trip, but that they were finally there and it was all good.

"We are going on to Dogon country! Have you been there?" Alice asked with a radiant smile.

"Not yet, but we're heading on to it after Timbuktu and the desert."

Everybody passing through Mali went to see the so-called Dogon country and its fascinating villages. It was the jewel of Mali, its number one tourist offering, competing very closely with Timbuktu and the magic of the desert.

"I'm so excited!" she carried on. "After so much dreaming we're going to be there at last. And you know, we're so lucky: everything is a lot easier than we expected here. We only arrived yesterday but we've sorted out everything already; got a guide and all that. Now we're all set for this trip. And it didn't even cost as much as we thought."

"Where did you find this guide?" asked Richard, and I noticed his voice was tense. He did not need to say more. I knew what he was thinking.

"Actually he found us. He was a very nice lad and he started to speak to us, you know, he even spoke a bit of English; we're really lucky to have found him."

OK, so that was rule number 1 broken: never accept help from someone who approaches you. If you needed help it was always better to ask someone else. But it was too late to say anything to them.

"And after all those things we read about bargaining, it wasn't too bad either. We discussed a bit and he seemed OK with the price we set. And he was happy with only half of that for advance payment!" Alice carried on, blissfully innocent.

"Oh my God," I thought. The picture started getting clearer: so clear that I almost didn't need to hear anything else.

"So we made a deal and we shook his hand and we're set. Actually we're waiting for him to come and pick us up this morning. By afternoon we'll be trekking in Dogon country."

I noticed Richard looking deeply into the remains of his Nescafé, as if he had found an extremely interesting little thing on the bottom of his mug. I looked around without saying anything. It was useless to ask if they had paid the guy in advance. Of course they had. That was why they were waiting here with their shiny bags and new trekking shoes on.

"We need to go, we've got a lot to sort out today: you know, visas and all the rest." Richard suddenly decided he had heard enough.

"Well, it was nice to meet you guys. I don't think we'll meet again but good luck to you. We'll probably be gone by the time you're back today," Toby said.

We got up and we shook hands and we wished them good luck. But we knew perfectly well that we would see them again. Because a guide who approached two nicely dressed foreigners with shiny backpacks bearing their flight labels on the streets of Bamako and asked for a lot of money, to be paid in advance for a seven-day hiking trip into Dogon country, would never turn up. He simply wouldn't, and it was all because those nice guys there had broken the first two rules. And rule number 2 said: never, ever pay in advance for anything.

CHAPTER 10 – "I AM HERE TO HASSLE YOU..."

(NIGER RIVER, FEBRUARY 2003)

DJENNÉ is today a small town on the shores of the Niger River. It has the same dust roads as any other village and town, the same narrow streets with a sewage channel in the middle, the same small mud houses, and it is as hot as anywhere else. It is the oldest known Sub-Saharan town and it used to be one of the great centres of Islamic learning and pilgrimage.

Like Ouadane and Chinguetti in nearby Mauritania, the town is a faint shadow of its former self. The Great Mosque, which was declared a UNESCO World Heritage Site in 1988, still dominates the central square and is the main reminder of its glorious past. Built entirely from sun-dried mud bricks, held together by mud mortar and plastered with mud, it is the biggest mud construction in the world. The current building was constructed at some point in the early 20th century, although tradition says the first mosque to have been built there dates from as early as the 13th century. We couldn't go inside since it was forbidden to non-Muslims, but the view from the outside was impressive enough.

In a country so dry that every drop of sweat dries instantly, a mud building has every chance to survive. And since mud is the most easily available and cheapest resource around, Djenné's masons have become incredibly skilled in using it. Everything in the town is made of mud: the houses and the shops, the *auberge* that hosted us for the night and the religious school near the mosque. Hordes of tourists rush here to take photos of these mud buildings, the Grand

Mosque most of all.

Like other small towns in Africa disrupted by the sudden flow of foreign money brought in by tourism, Djenné saw an array of consequences both good and bad. The city grew in importance, transport became more frequent and owners of small shops and *auberges* became richer. But children got used to begging, and irresponsible tourists who came to see Africa in a week and couldn't contain their feelings of guilt at the thought of coming from and soon returning to a much richer part of the world started throwing all sorts of objects to them: T-shirts, pens, money, sweets. After a while, kids grow to understand that a *toubab* is a potential source of endless wonders and they started begging "*donne-moi un bic*", "*donnez-moi quelque chose*": the old chant of Morocco was back.

Young lads, on the other hand, had figured out other ways to exploit the boom of tourism and insisted they could be your guide and point you to the huge Grand Mosque that dominated the whole town (which you would have found anyway). Unpleasant memories of Morocco started coming back and I realised what a blessed heaven Guinea had been. Because no tourists went there, the disruption they brought to local people's lives was less clear. There, people did not beg because they had not been taught to. People did not expect to be paid for a picture or a small service; they did it instinctively and naturally, with a big smile on their face and no hope of any reward. But that was Guinea and this was Mali, another world where tourism had already arrived.

We had spent two days there and were getting ready to leave. In fact we got up that morning with the intention of getting into the first available bush taxi and heading over to Mopti, another touristy heaven of Mali situated at the meeting point of the rivers Bani and Niger. From there we were to carry on towards Timbuktu. We were in a hurry to reach Timbuktu because Tabaski, the important religious festival that I called "the killing of the sheep", was getting closer and we hoped to be able to join the celebrations in Timbuktu, the hometown of the Tuareg people.

Djenné was a mixed experience. The evening before, we had accepted the invitation of a local lad to go and visit a small village of Fula people nearby. It seemed like the right thing to do. We took our cameras and he gave us a ride in his little wrecked cart pulled by two oxen, and when we arrived we thanked him and paid him a few coins for his services. The chief of the village came by, an old man dressed in a white robe and with a good command of French, and to our surprise he took us around himself and showed us the buildings, all made of mud, and their mosque, a smaller version of the Grand Mosque. Children were begging all around us and he asked them to leave us alone. But before that, he turned to us and asked us if we wanted to take a picture. Girls were walking around the village topless and he told us that they did so until they were married and when they got engaged they would paint their lips with smoke from their kitchens. Then he took us to the house of one woman, who had the biggest pair of earrings I could ever imagine, and asked her to put them on and allow us to take a picture. Big gold earrings were a sign of wealth there and they were supposed to be offered by the husband on the day of the wedding.

"You may get something like that on the day of your wedding, too, from your husband." The old man smiled at me and I wasn't sure if he was joking or being serious.

By the end of the tour I was feeling sick and I had only one desire left: to get out of there. We left some money as a goodbye gift for the village and we went back, having taken some pictures. We now had to deal with the bitter taste that this experience filled us with: we had just visited a human zoo.

Why did it feel so wrong? They were happy to have us there and make some money out of tourists; the way everybody does in every little corner of Europe as well. But still we felt somehow wrong, as if walking in the middle of that village with our expensive cameras was in itself an insult to their way of life and to their civilisation. What felt wrong was that we were not there to live with them for a while, as we did, for instance, at Chez François in the small jungle city of Sérédou in Guinea, or to talk to them and share their company: we were just there to take a couple of pictures and disappear, and all the arrogance of the Western world meeting the developing world could be summarised in this concept: take a picture and run away.

A CHILD WITH HUNGRY EYES

IT was dark outside and Richard and I were having some street food on a small wooden bench in Mopti. Rice with sauce, the type of food that was cooked in the huge bowls and that you could get on a tin plate in exchange for 100 CFA. We ate in silence. Around us, six or seven kids squatted down and looked at us with hungry eyes.

After months of travelling through some of the poorest countries in the world, one develops a sort of immunity to scenes like this one. There were always children around and in most cases they begged. And in most cases they looked helpless and charming and you wished you could give them something. But firstly, it is not feasible to keep on giving something when you've set off travelling for nine months, otherwise you will end up not owning anything pretty soon. And secondly, you tell yourself that it's better to stick to the "don't give anything" principle as it will stop them from becoming beggars.

But there were also nights like that one, when you ate a huge bowl of rice and sauce in front of the hungry eyes of some six or seven squatting kids and simply didn't know any more what was right and what was wrong.

They were dirty, very dirty. Those kids looked white with dirt, a sort of white film of dust covering them from head to toe. Their clothes were powdered white as well: ripped T-shirts and buttonless shorts. They were barefoot. They were silent.

Most of them wore an empty tin, kept in place with a wire that went around their necks. The tin was a receptacle in which they could store food and it served as a distinctive symbol. They were street children: children with no parents or relatives to care for them. They had had parents at some point but they were given away by their families, who probably lived in some poor village a long way from there. They were given to some nomad Islamic teacher, and there were many of those who wandered from village to village, taking several of such boys under their "care" and promising to teach them the Islamic law. The boys were responsible for their own food, meaning they would walk around towns and villages from dusk until dawn with the tins hanging on to their small chests, begging for a bite to eat. And knowing that they were *talibe*, religious students without a family to care for them, people would be generous most of the time and would throw some food into their tins.

Sometimes they were lucky. Other times they were less so. But one way or another they always had that desperate look of hunger in their eyes, and they were usually silent. Unlike most of the other kids who ran around us, calling us *toubabs* and trying to extort something from us, be it a pen or a coin, these ones were silent and just looked desperate. These ones were simply hungry.

We finished eating in silence and we somehow felt that our unspoken rule of not giving anything to anybody was wrong that evening. Richard started first – he held his half-full plate towards the children. They stood up in a second and came all around us and we found ourselves spooning the rice and sauce directly into their outstretched, dirty hands. They ate as soon as the food touched their hands and again stretched them towards us, their eyes as big and round and silent as they were while squatting down.

We left and walked in silence towards the *auberge*, leaving the kids to feast on some other portions of rice and sauce we had purchased from the same fat mamma in exchange for the equivalent of 10p back home. Was it right or was it wrong? Did we just encourage those kids to become beggars in the future? Or was it that maybe principles just seemed too small and pale when placed next to a pair of big, black, hungry eyes?

We did stick to our principles as we moved on and we did not give any *stylo*, *bonbon* or *tricot* to children when we passed through many more countries and saw much more poverty. But we learned something that night, and from then on we always bought more food than we needed in the evenings and gave our plates to be cleaned by some street children with tins around their necks who would always patiently wait, squatting somewhere nearby.

ON THE NIGER RIVER

IT must have been well past midnight. The river seemed a huge, dark monster flowing in silence, not caring about anything or anybody. There was no moon that night and that made the darkness even heavier. I could barely see the long, dark shape of the *pinasse*: the small, flat-bottomed boat that had brought us there. It was anchored by the bank and all the other passengers seemed to be sleeping already. Unlike us, two *toubabs* who were still struggling to put up the tent by the light of a small torch.

Among other things, the boat carried several mattresses.

Like the rest of the goods, as well as all the passengers – us included – they headed towards Timbuktu. The easiest way to reach the city of the desert was, paradoxically, on the river.

We had put up the tent but we only had one mattress and Richard went back to the boat to try and get another one from the pile, but he was stopped by one of the many *capitains*.

"*Qu'est-ce que tu veux*[15]?"

"I want a mattress."

"There is no mattress here."

"Yes there is, I've seen it. There are a few of them over there."

"I told you there is no mattress."

Silence.

"Look." Richard's voice sounded incredibly patient. Maybe he, too, was tired. "We have one tent but only one mattress; we are two people. We cannot sleep on one mattress. So I need to borrow another bloody mattress for the night."

"I cannot give it to you. It needs to go to Timbuktu."

We were in the middle of nowhere, just camping for the night. The next morning we would be back on that boat, which would take us all the way to Timbuktu. We were all going there: us, the boat, all the other passengers and all the mattresses.

"Yes, I know it will go to Timbuktu. Tomorrow. But tonight I need it to sleep on."

"Why is it that you white people believe you can have everything, whenever you demand it? Why do I have to give you that mattress?"

Maybe he had a point there, but Richard didn't want to argue. He wanted the mattress. Actually the mattress was for me, since he already had his own.

"Because you don't need it and I do need it. That's why," Richard said, as patiently as before, and knowing his sudden attacks of grumpiness I wondered how long he would manage to keep his polite tone.

Silence. They seemed to be deadlocked.

"*Bien, alors*. I will give you the mattress."

It had taken some time but it was worth it.

---

[15] "What do you want?" (in French)

"So give me the mattress then."

"I will give it to you."

"Give it to me now!" I finally detected a tone of impatience and it was not hard to understand why. It was well past midnight, we were all dying to sleep and that dialogue seemed more absurd than ever.

"Do you hear me? The mattress!"

"I told you I will give you the mattress. Wait," the captain said.

"No, my friend. I'm not waiting. It's well past my bedtime and I need this mattress. I am here to hassle you until you give me that mattress and none of us will sleep until then. Do you get it?" Richard's patient tone had changed into a grumpy one. What was next: a fight in the middle of the night over some useless mattress that was tied somewhere on the roof of that boat?

But no, the dialogue went on for a while and soon Richard returned with the prize.

"Some might say it should not have been so bloody difficult!"

Sometimes things in this world were complicated. For no apparent reason, something that seemed initially very straightforward could suddenly fall into some sort of deep and mysterious complexity. And one must find one's way out of that labyrinth with a mixture of patience and grumpiness.

THE Niger River is one of the biggest rivers in Africa. Not quite so thoroughly explored as the other mighty river of North Africa, the Nile, and not quite so blessed with ancient temples on its banks, it is nevertheless an impressive sight. On its shores, Sub-Saharan Africa meets the people from the desert, or Tuaregs. It is a natural frontier separating two civilisations: the one of the farmers and the one of the animal breeders, the sedentary black Africans and the nomad Arabs. On its shores, people have come trading since ancient times. Black people from the forests of Ghana and Guinea used to come here and leave their gold in exchange – ounce for ounce – for the precious salt the Tuaregs used to dig out of the mines deep in the Sahara. Trade flourished and cities were founded, empires were built and burned, but the river has always been there and boats like the *pinasse* we were on have always travelled along it.

We got on this boat in Mopti: it was a passenger boat and the captain said it would reach Timbuktu at the end of three days on the river. We had Karl and his bike with us. He had turned up as if by a miracle at the same *auberge* we had lodged in in Mopti, and hearing we were all set for a boat trip to Timbuktu he decided to join us.

It took some five lads and lots of effort to get Mavis on to the boat, though, but after some fuss and shouting the bike was tightly secured at the front of the boat, just where the Vikings of old used to sculpt the head of a female goddess: hardly a better place for Mavis.

Karl was worried, though, and he spent three days in utter despair, suffering for the danger the bike was in. If she should fall into the river, nothing and nobody could ever take her out!

The boat was pretty small, not more than 15 metres long and about 1.5 metres wide: quite comfortable with about eight or ten wooden benches. Karl, Richard and I were sharing one of these, and while one was seated one could let one's hands touch the water. It had a curved roof made of straw mats, on top of which the nice mattresses we had fought for the night before were bound. At the back of the boat, a small toilet seemed to complete the feeling of luxury. Actually it was more like a hole on the deck above the water, surrounded by more straw mats, but it was all one needed. One could have privacy only when seated: when standing one was in plain view of the others. With the Malian flag at the end of the boat and the motorbike safely strapped on top, we must have looked like a warship.

The days were long and peaceful. We got stuck a few times, as the waters were low and even a small, flat-bottomed boat like that one occasionally hit the high sands. When that happened, three of the four self-proclaimed "captains" who commanded the boat as a sort of a joint team effort would jump into the water and push the boat, and even though we were in the middle of the river the water would barely touch their waists. Then we would go peacefully on until we would stop to carefully avoid a few hippos stationed on another sandbank.

On the shores of the river, life went on as it had for centuries. Small boats with sails made of rice sacks sewn together sailed past us; women washed clothes by the bank; kids swam; birds fished.

We spotted several villages on the banks and the boat stopped at a few of them. In one such village we happened to arrive on market day, the last day that families could acquire their ritual sheep. Tabaski was coming closer, with only three more days to go, and trade in the last of the sheep seemed to be flourishing. The market was filled with the people of the desert, the Tuaregs, and seeing these nomads with their blue robes and their heads and faces covered by indigo turbans I could not help but feel I was in a movie. Some of them had swords, real swords, and I was later told that they were not used as weapons but as a reminder of the time they had made a living as salt cutters.

One such nomad, dressed in a long, red robe with a dark indigo turban, was walking on the bank of the river towards the village market when the call to prayer suddenly broke out from a faraway mosque. The Muslim call to prayer comes five times a day and the faithful are supposed to answer it wherever they are. He went straight to the river, washed his face, his hands and feet, then placed his sword on the sand in front of him and started alternately kneeling and standing. On the shores of the Niger River, he was praying the way his ancestors had prayed for centuries and centuries, with the sword, his most treasured possession, in front of him. Up and down, his lips moving slowly with the verses of the Qu'ran, his head touching the sword and the sand, oblivious to the rest of the world, to we three stunned foreigners watching him; oblivious to the river and the market and the kids running around. And watching him, I felt that he was transmitting a part of his trance to me, and I felt I was slowly stepping with him into another world.

It was a beautiful, peaceful day and when the sun went down again I felt I had entered into another type of an *I cannot be bothered* state. But it was different from the one induced by the bush taxis, for there was no noise or hassle or aching bones here. Just the river, the immensity of it, and the deep, red reflection of the sunset colours on its waters, and my fingers touching the surface of the water and the birds on the bank. And it must have been that the trance the nomad had transmitted to me as I watched him pray stayed with me for a while and I was feeling that I had just been born right then and there, in the middle of that mighty river, and even though I knew the night was coming closer and we'd probably have to fight for another mattress soon, I simply couldn't be bothered to think of it. For I was in another world, a much warmer and simpler one, where all that mattered was the calm flow of the river: much like a long time ago, when all that mattered in the fairy circle at Twyfelfontein in Namibia was the rise of a full moon. I was back with the vision I carried in me and for the first time on this trip I felt as happy and at peace with myself as I had felt that night in Namibia. I felt I had come home at last.

Good things come to those who give up demanding them. And as I soaked deep in the happiness of that sunset and felt ready to deal with another tiring night with another quarrel for a mattress, the boat pulled into the bank surprisingly early, just after sunset. And as Richard and I were putting up the tent in silence, we saw the *capitaine* of last night walking towards us. Only this time he was holding two of those mattresses under his arms.

"I thought you may need them tonight," he said, in a low and friendly voice. "Two are better than one; it will help you sleep better."

"*Merci.*" We were shocked.

He vanished before we said anything else.

Yes, good things happen when one has given up demanding them and one is ready to live the future like a blank, empty page, with no preconceived thoughts, with no demands and no expectations.

MY LAST BUSH TAXI

I didn't know it then, but that rotten, blue pick-up truck that waited for passengers by the river as we approached Timbuktu was to be my last bush taxi of west Africa. At that time I thought there would be many more to come. Having come to terms with the fact that Peter and the car might not, in fact, catch up with us at all and having had a frank discussion with Richard, I was feeling quite comfortable thinking I would bush taxi my way down to South Africa. I felt surprisingly confident that I could make it, and even though I was glad to hear Richard offering to travel together all the way south, I knew that if need be, I would be able to make it on my own. It was as if the scared little girl who had climbed on to a green truck somewhere on the Guinean border only three weeks before had grown overnight into a woman who knew she could easily make it on her own. When did this happen? Even today, when I look back at those days, I find it hard to say what happened and when exactly the transformation took place. What was the poison that made its way into my blood, and when did I stop taking the antidote? Which night was it that I became infected, and under the light of which moon had a part of me died? And exactly when was it that the other part was reborn, within the sunrise of which morning?

One way or the other, I felt I had grown in those three weeks more than I would have in three normal years, and above all I felt fine. And this was the next step on from the *I cannot be bothered* state, and it was beyond being or not being bothered. It was, simply, about being fine.

The bush taxi was not yet full and as usual we were hanging around waiting for other passengers to turn up. Our *pinasse* was anchored not far away. Having discarded its passengers and goods after three peaceful days on the river, it was now getting ready to go back to Mopti.

"Hey, heyyyy!" the call came from one of the other boats.

And as we approached, we found that to our surprise, the couple we had met in Bamako, Toby and Alice, were smiling at us.

"Hey guys, how are you?"

They got off the boat, came to the bank and we went through the classic ritual of asking what had happened since we had met last. It turned out that their so-called guide had indeed let them down, and after waiting for two more days in the Auberge Laffie in Bamako they decided to accept they that had been cheated. Then they jumped into a truck and arrived in Timbuktu, where they spent a few days with no further incidents. Now they had just done a deal with the boat they were in to go down to Mopti, the very city we had come from.

I looked at their boat. It was a cargo boat, dirty and ugly. It did not have benches; it did not have a toilet. You couldn't touch the water while you were seated. And you couldn't hear one another when you talked because of the noise of the engine.

"How much did you pay for this?" Richard asked them.

"10,000 CFA each. They say they will reach Mopti in three days."

"Look guys, we just came from Mopti on this other one,"

Richard said, showing them the silhouette of our elegant *pinasse*. "And it's only 7,000 each and they also give you some food for the money. It's really better. I think you should take this one."

"I don't really know," Alice said. "We have a deal now with this other boat…"

We tried in vain to persuade them, to tell them that they simply couldn't survive on a boat without a toilet for three full days. We tried in vain to make them grab their backpacks and change boats. In vain. They had struck a deal. Again. And of course, they had already paid half the sum. In advance. Again. There was nothing else to do.

We said goodbye, wished them luck and jumped into the rotten bush taxi that was supposed to take us to Timbuktu. It was now full and ready to go, and besides, the best thing you can do sometimes is to mind your own business.

To my right, a smiley, cheeky guy who looked quite wealthy attempted a dialogue.

"*Donnez-moi* 5,000 CFA[16]."

Many of them asked for things and most of the time I ignored them. But this one was particularly cheeky; he didn't say "please" and he wanted ten times more than the others.

"Why should I give you money?"

"Because I am hungry."

I looked at the shiny wristwatch he was displaying and at his dark sunglasses, on top of which he wore his traditional shawl, and I really doubted he was hungry.

"You have to give me because you are white and I am black," he went on, and his words summarised the whole problem of Africa.

You have to give me something because you are white and I am black. A *stylo*, a *bonbon*, a *tricot*, money, food, weapons, military troops, government aid; something.

"Why don't you give me some money?" I decided to answer back.

He was shocked. This was not how the discussion was supposed to go.

"Why would I give you money?" he asked, puzzled

"Because you have a nice watch and I haven't," I said, happy I had at last managed to twist his logic around. "How

---

[16] "Give me 5000 CFA." (in French)

about that?"

I did not get his watch or his money, but at least I got silence. Obviously he wasn't happy to continue the argument. In the meantime, we all got in, about 15 of us squatting on a pick-up truck platform of about 4 m². The roof consisted of straw mats, on top of which were loaded all sorts of things – amongst which was a huge plastic bag filled with smelly fish, which I believed were in an advanced state of putrefaction. On top of everything they placed two sheep, upside down with their legs tied. They then tied the whole bundle securely to the roof and off we went.

Ten minutes into the journey, some liquid started to pour through the thin roof. There were two possibilities: either the sheep were peeing or the water in which the smelly fish were kept in the plastic bag was dripping. I really didn't want to know which of the two alternatives was the correct one.

We were so squeezed against each other that we couldn't move an inch. The first drips landed on the head of a baby that a woman next to me was holding in her arms. The baby cried, the woman shouted and the dripping stopped for a while. The car went on. There was no way the driver could know what was happening or hear the shouts of the woman. And even if he did, was there anything he could do about? Then it happened again. And again. The baby was spared this time but his mother was not, and before long the poor woman held her baby with one arm and a pot that she found in her many bags with the other, and she held it as close to the roof as she could in a desperate attempt to prevent the horrible liquid – smelly fish water or sheep pee, whatever it was – dripping on her head. A bend in the road and the load on the roof moved, and this time it was the lad next to her who got the drip in his face. I couldn't stop a small, vengeful smile. It was the bloke with the shiny watch. He got some more drips and so did one of his neighbours, and before long Richard and I looked at each other in terror, waiting for our turn to come. If it did, there was absolutely nothing we could do, nowhere we could move: we would just have to take it the way all the others took it.

By a miracle it didn't happen, and as we got out of the car some one hour later in the central square of Timbuktu amongst people protesting and screaming and the ever-present horrible smell all around us, I thought that maybe there was some truth in the saying that Timbuktu had to be reached at the end of a long and tiring journey. Once upon a time that meant a long caravan through the desert. Today it was just a sheep peeing through a thin straw mat, but I wasn't sure which of the two was hardest to bear.

CHAPTER 11 – MADE IN TIMBUKTU

(TIMBUKTU, MALI, FEBRUARY 2003)

THE town was a labyrinth, with small, unpaved roads and a sewage channel in the middle. Sand everywhere. People everywhere. Shops with open doors, kids running. Mud-brick houses. Hot, very hot.

We didn't have to look too long for accommodation. We were picked up from the car directly. "Do you need somewhere to stay?" Yes, we did, but it was not wise to deal with the first guy who approached you. It was better to ask someone who was just lying in the shade nearby: "Do you know of a house where we may stay for a few days?"

Everybody wanted to make some cash and everybody had a room on offer. Before long we were escorted along the narrow roads. A corner, another corner and another mud-brick house: this was it. Welcome.

The courtyard was small, maybe not more than 5 m². It was all surrounded by tall walls, with a small opening for the gate. A woman, covered from head to toe in a white and red robe, sat on a mattress in a corner. A little girl slept on the woman's lap. Next to her, two metallic doors were open: one leading to a small kitchen with no windows, the second one leading to the proper house. We were shown in through this second door and ushered into the main room. There was only one room anyway. Several mattresses were piled up in a corner. An old, wooden wardrobe in another one; some more pillows and blankets. A few chairs and – to our surprise – a proper table.

"You can have this room," the woman said. Toilets were near the kitchen: another small, dark room with a smelly hole in the ground and no windows.

We learnt that the head of the family was a tailor. We seemed to mostly come into the houses of tailors. He was not at home but there were many guys around, children or maybe other relatives. There were always a lot of people around. I wondered where they all slept. The room they had just given us seemed to be everybody's bedroom.

In the small courtyard, tied securely to the door leading to our bedroom, another sheep struggled for life. We named him Hector and, like all the other sheep in this country, he too was waiting for the fateful day when a third of his meat would be given to the poor. Tabaski was tomorrow.

Unlike his fellow at the Auberge Laffie in Bamako, Hector was silent. His eyes were big and the colour of hot chocolate. He looked at me intensely. I patted him and he seemed to like it, closed his eyes and stretched his neck. He should have been born a dog, I thought. Sheep aren't too lucky in this world.

We decided to take the room and went for a wander in the city.

Timbuktu is such a legend that as you arrive you feel inevitably disappointed. One of the seven holy cities of Islam, just like Chinguetti in Mauritania, it is now threatened by the advancing sand dunes. But the narrow streets and the half-sunken building are still hiding one of the most precious treasures of mankind: over 300,000 ancient Islamic manuscripts are thought to exist in private libraries in the city. Like the other oasis in the Sahara, Timbuktu had the perfect conditions for conserving manuscripts. For centuries they were carried on the backs of camels, read and treasured by scholars, and have since been kept like well-guarded family possessions.

Legend says that Timbuktu was founded some time around the year 1000 by the nomads of the desert, and its name comes from that of a Tuareg woman (Bouctou) and her well (Tim). Today the well is still to be seen if one can find one's way through the maze of little streets.

The city was later incorporated into the Songhai Empire. Then the Moroccans came, then the French, and today it is a Malian city.

Although far from its former glory, it is still an important hub in the trade routes of southern Sahara, and the main trade that happens there is the same as it was in the old days: salt. It comes on the backs of camels from the far north, from the mines of Taoudenni, and is traded by Tuaregs and Arabs to the Bambara people, who take it down the river to Mopti where it changes hands again.

Besides, the city has a good reputation on the map of international tourism, and with a couple of decent hotels and an airstrip used by Air Mali flights from the capital, it is in a pretty good position to welcome them. But apart from the expensive flight from Bamako, the city was still notoriously hard to get to and maybe this explained why we saw few white faces around.

We met a few travellers who we had met before. They were planning to buy a sheep (alive) and drive somewhere near the town to feast on the poor creature among the surrounding dunes. A pretty shocking show for a vegetarian, and I decided I would not join them for the night.

With Richard gone to the feast, I was wandering aimlessly around on my own. The sight of a woman alone was a pretty one for the many hungry eyes around the town and I soon started to hear the usual chorus: hissing, whistling, *bonsoir madame* and the like; but by then I knew they wouldn't get more daring than this and ignored them. It seemed that every man was interested, from boys older than 12 to their grandfathers. The young ones were the most aggressive, though, and as I tried to make my way through the endless hissing I decided to take refuge on the terrace of one of the hotels.

Travelling with either Peter or Richard for most of the time so far, I was spared the insistent attentions of men in the countries we passed by. But this ended as soon as I was on my own, and I suddenly realised why travelling alone as a girl is a lot more difficult. It did not matter too much that I was "covered" enough, with long trousers, my old trekking boots and a long-sleeved shirt. It did not matter that most of the time I was dusty and dirty and looked more like a teenage lad than a woman who would arouse their desires. They knew I was a woman and it was enough for them. Guys would follow me on the street, trying to talk to me, desperately trying to get my attention. Their heads must have been full of stories about all those available European women and obviously they were trying their best. One French girl I met on the way who, very unusually, was travelling alone, told me that all this attention was more of a show and it almost never got to be a real threat. She told me, laughing, how she had left for a five-day desert trek back in Mauritania with two local guys: the owner of the camels and a Moor guide, and how the guide desperately spent his whole afternoon before the trip searching for condoms in town. "You won't need them, don't worry," the girl told him, and off they went – and, as incredible as it may sound, she was fine after five days in the wilderness with the two men.

"They will not insist once they are refused," she told me, and her story gave me some comfort. I was starting to think that despite being more difficult, if would not be impossible for me to continue on my own without Richard.

I was travelling well with Richard and it was almost one month now that we had shared the highs and lows of the road. Maybe it was just pure luck, or maybe we were very much alike, but I felt we could understand each other naturally somehow, almost without words. He was not only instinctively generous but he also had an easy way to deal with whatever came along that almost always made every problem seem smaller and more manageable. This philosophy of life appeared to have its roots in the *I cannot be bothered* state but it went a long way beyond that, passing through a sort of "whatever happens, I'll be fine" aura that he managed to transmit to me and ending in a constant willingness to do things for the person next to him. It was always me who had the best seat in a bush taxi, the best mattress, the first access to a shower; he would usually just smile and say, "I'll be fine, you go ahead". I got used to the way things were and inevitably sort of lost my feeling of gratitude and started taking things almost for granted. But during the last two weeks, ever since our Guinea experience ended, I could feel some tension building between the two of us. Was he fed up? Was I being a burden to him?

Maybe he needed some time to himself and to be honest I did as well, and for a few days I was contemplating the thought of maybe going on by myself for a while and perhaps meeting him later on. Peter and the car were somewhere in Africa, but it was very unsure when and whether they would meet us again. Was this the moment to give up on the original idea of the three of us on this trip?

I felt kind of alone with my thoughts and a beer on that terrace as the night was getting deeper, and so I didn't mind too much the young lad who pulled up a chair and took a seat on the next table with the evident hope of starting a conversation.

"You know, if I look at you, I really don't know where you come from," he said after a while.

It must be really hard, I thought, for guys to think of an opening line. But I was feeling alone that night and since he did not hiss or whistle but actually thought hard of something intelligent to say I decided to answer back.

"Yeah, it is sort of difficult," I said. "Let's say somewhere in Europe. Most of the people can't figure out more than this." This was entirely correct. Not many people would think of Romania, a small country somewhere in Eastern Europe.

He smiled and said, "I could try and see if I'm better than most people!"

"I don't think you want to get yourself into that. It's pretty difficult, I can tell you."

"Just let me try. Three guesses. If I can find out in three goes where you come from it means I'm better than most people, right?" He smiled now and seemed pretty confident.

He was very young, a lot younger than me: I guessed somewhere at that indefinite point where young teenage boys turn into men. Eighteen? Twenty? I didn't think he was older than that. His skin was deep black and this made me think he wasn't a Tuareg. They were usually lighter. He must have belonged to some other tribe: the Songhai or the Bambara or who knew which other. The ethnic groups in this country were a puzzle to me.

He was wearing a pair of jeans and a T-shirt, both very clean: a lot cleaner than my dusty trousers. His jeans looked new. He had a big smile on his face and seemed very confident he could guess right.

"OK," I said. "You have three guesses."

"But what do I get if I am right?" he said, his white smile larger than before.

Now he gets cheeky, I thought.

"Can I buy you a beer if I win?" he offered.

"OK," I said pretty confident this wouldn't be the case.

He looked at me with thoughtful eyes and said after a while, "You're not French: this is clear. You speak well but it's clear it's not your mother tongue."

Now I felt almost humiliated. We had been speaking French up to that point and although I had been studying the language for over 10 years in school, inevitably I found out that all of the locals spoke it a lot better than me. And I doubted they had studied it for more than 10 years in school.

"If you prefer we can continue in English," he offered, and to my surprise switched languages instantly.

"Where did you learn English?" I asked

"Here and there; from tourists mostly," he answered. "But I don't think you're English. It's your look, you know; it's sort of different."

He was doing well so far, I had to admit, but now he would bury himself in the usual Spanish/Belgian/Italian mumbo jumbo of all the others who have tried before.

"Somehow more southern, I would say. *Parli Italiano?*" he tried.

Yes, I spoke Italian. I did a postgraduate degree in Milan and spent about three years in Italy. And I was really curious now to see how well he spoke that other language.

We switched to Italian and I told him I was really surprised to hear he spoke this one as well.

"I learned it from tourists; you see, people from all over the world come here. But let's go back to where you are from. I don't think you're Italian either, is this true?"

"No, I'm not. Let's say this was your first guess." By now I felt more frustrated than amused. I usually think of myself as fluent in Italian. How could he tell it wasn't my mother tongue?

"You speak it really well, though. It must be that your mother tongue is somehow similar to Italian." He still looked at me intently and I could tell he was concentrating.

"You are not Spanish though. I take Spanish tourists around all the time; you don't say *rrrr* like they do... no, you don't sound like them."

We were still speaking Italian at that point and I wondered if we should have switched back to English. Would he be able to recognise a Romanian accent? But still, how could he? He had probably never met any Romanian tourists in this corner of the world.

"I think I'm getting close," he said with a triumphant look in his eyes. "Your mother tongue must be of Latin origin but you are not Italian nor Spanish, and definitely not French. You must be Portuguese."

He was dangerously close. I was not Portuguese but this was the closest language to my own. I felt like I was about to lose a chess game. I had already told him I was from Europe. They were not many Latin languages left, and if this black boy happened to learn at school that Romania was the only Latin-origin language in Eastern Europe he might even have guessed where I came from.

"No, I'm not Portuguese," I said, trying to paint a look of indifference on my face.

He smiled – a wide, white smile – and looking into his eyes I knew I had lost.

"You're Romanian."

I was shocked: utterly, completely shocked.

"I'm right, aren't I? You must be Romanian! I told you I would figure you out."

He was either one of the most intelligent people I had ever met or one of the best actors. In a split second I thought that maybe he knew it all along. Maybe I had told the people at the house that I came from Romania. I couldn't remember but I would generally say so when asked by owners of *auberges* or houses we would stay in, and they might have asked. And maybe he knew those people and maybe he followed me here and maybe it was all just a pretext to start a conversation. But if that was the case, he had done it so skilfully and so naturally and had conducted the discussion in three languages with such ease that it seemed an even more impressive hypothesis. One way or another, he was a really smart guy.

"Can I bring you another beer now?" he said

I nodded and he went to the bar, and I thought that I couldn't remember ever before having been approached in such a smart way.

"I'm Isa," he said, as he returned with his palm outstretched.

"Roxana."

We were still speaking Italian and I could see he was really at ease with the language.

"How many languages do you speak?"

"I am quite good in Italian and English. And I can survive in German. Plus French, of course," he said, and it didn't sound like he was showing off. I didn't need to hear him speaking German to know that it was true. This kid could indeed speak four European languages.

"But none of these is your mother tongue, is it?"

"Oh no," he smiled, probably thinking I was as ignorant

as all the white people. "My language is Tamasheq, the language of the Tuaregs."

"But you're not a Tuareg, are you?" I asked.

He was clearly black, and even though we had only just arrived in this town of the Tuaregs I knew they were people of Arab descent, and despite their colour, which could be quite dark at times, they had the bone structure of white Europeans.

"No, I'm not a Tuareg," he said. "I'm a Tamasheq."

This was quite confusing, and after some more questioning I found out that he belonged to the tribes of the so-called Bella people, the black Southern tribes (Hausa, Songhai, etc.) who were the former slaves of the Tuaregs. And because these tribes were enslaved by the Tuaregs for hundreds of years, they, too, were speaking the language of the nomads, the language commonly referred to as Tamasheq. It must have been because the term Bella had a negative connotation that my friend here preferred to refer to himself as Tamasheq, which was sometimes used to describe the language and at other times used as a synonym for Tuareg.

Having clarified this hazy issue and having understood by now that the young lad in front of me must be some sort of a language guru, I asked him if he spoke anything else.

"We all speak Bambara and Songhai here."

These were the other two major ethnic groups in Mali, with the Bambara being the leading one.

"And then I've been taking tourists quite often to the Dogon country, and I had to learn a bit of their language too."

Dogons are another distinctive group of people, and their language is as similar to the other two as back in Europe Portuguese and Dutch would be to each other.

So this meant my friend, who was enjoying his beer next to me, could speak a grand total of eight languages: four from his own region and four European ones, and I had just tested him in three of those.

He next told me that he earned a living taking tourists around and he seemed to be one of the genuine guides. He was earning good money and had been doing this for quite a while, and he enjoyed talking to foreigners, he said, since he learned a lot of things from them.

"Tell me about your country," he asked, and for the next

half-hour he sucked all possible information about Romania out of me.

He told me he dropped out of school at the age of ten, and I suspected that much of his awareness of the world came through this type of discussion. He had never been outside his home country.

"How old are you?" I asked him.

"Twenty-five."

He was lying and I knew it. He couldn't be more than 20, but maybe he didn't want to seem too young for a potential date.

We chatted for a bit longer and he told me his name meant Jesus. Isa (in Arabic) is a very common Muslim name and we went into talks about religion, and he seemed very educated about various similarities and differences in religions worldwide. He could talk about history and world affairs, about religion and geography. He had learned all that from tourists, he said.

It was getting late and he offered to walk me home. And before he went away, he asked me if he could take me to a rap concert the next day.

"A rap concert? Where?"

"Here in town," he said.

It sounded too incredible to be true and I told him that yes, I'd be delighted to go to a rap concert with him tomorrow.

RICHARD came back late that evening but I wasn't asleep. Lying on my mattress for hours, I was trying to find a solution that would get rid of all the mosquitoes the room was filled with, but I hadn't been very successful.

I heard him coming in and throwing himself on another mattress in the other corner of the room, and then tossing and turning as he became aware of the mosquito ordeal.

"Hey," I whispered after some time.

"Oh, I thought you were asleep."

"There's no way to sleep in this bloody room. It's full of mosquitoes!"

It was too dark to see anything but I heard them, the constant attack of mosquitoes. And Richard heard them too.

"I think it would be worse outside," he said

"At least outside we can put up the tent."

It sounded a bit ridiculous to be lodged in the nicest

room of that house and be thinking about getting up and putting up a tent.

Silence. I could hear Richard's breath in the other corner of the room.

"What do you think?"

"I think it's too complicated. There's no space outside," he said.

He was right; there was no space in the small courtyard next to Hector the sheep, and we certainly didn't want to put the tent up in the middle of the narrow street.

Silence again.

"Let's not bother; maybe we can get some sleep," Richard said after a while.

Yeah right, maybe or maybe not, I thought, but I said nothing. I, too, wasn't sure that putting the tent up was such a good idea.

Some more tossing and turning. I could hear Richard slapping his head, trying to get rid of the invaders.

"What did you do tonight?" he asked after a while, probably giving up on sleep.

"Just went for a wander." I omitted to tell him I was feeling sort of alone. "I got myself a date with a local for tomorrow evening."

"Uh-huh, young lady," Richard answered "I leave you alone for once and look what things you get yourself into!"

I could tell he was amused. I was, too, when I thought of Isa's wide smile.

"Yeah, nice lad; about 10 years younger than me but he promised to take me to a concert," I said, smiling in the darkness.

No answer. Richard must have thought I had gone insane.

Silence again and after a while:

"Hey?"

"What?"

"Let's put up the tent!"

I knew I was insistent but there was no other way.

"Where? This room is all we have."

"Let's put it up in the room then."

I didn't know where that thought had come from but Richard liked the idea. He was up in a second and turned on the light.

We looked around and tried to figure out what we could

do. There was a lot of stuff in the room: a table, some bags, more mattresses. We started moving the things around until we created some empty space in the middle and then we put up the tent: only the inner part of it but it was enough to protect us from the mosquitoes. Then we pulled both our mattresses inside, zipped it up and tried to stretch our bones. With two mattresses in it was rather tight, but at least all the mosquitoes had been locked outside.

"Ah, great," said Richard with a sigh. "Just when I thought I could finally have a sleep on my own!"

For a long time now we seemed to have been condemned to sharing a bed or a tent and this room was the first one where they had offered us two mattresses instead of the usual double bed.

"Yeah, you have to put up with me again; but at least it's better than sleeping with the mosquitoes."

"Yeeaaahhh."

Sometimes one's choices aren't so easy, I thought as I was trying to fall asleep. I felt good though. Richard and I needed some distance, that was clear, but at least it was good we could joke about it. And it was a lot better putting up with each other than with the mosquitoes.

THE KILLING OF THE SHEEP

IT was the big day: it was Tabaski, and as we woke up early in our tent in the middle of the room we felt excited and ready to go. There would be celebrations in the city throughout the day.

Before we went out we were invited by the family to have breakfast in the little courtyard. They had woken up long before us and they had already eaten, but hospitality was still a strong part of the culture in Timbuktu and they insisted they wanted to give us something to eat. As we had taken their only room, all of them were now sleeping in the small courtyard next to Hector, the same place we had considered putting up the tent last night. Seeing all the mats on the sand, I thought that maybe we should switch places for the following night: give them back their mosquito-invaded room and put our tent in the courtyard instead. The woman had entered the room in the morning and couldn't contain a small shout of surprise, and judging from the look of horror in her eyes at the sight of our tent in the middle of her room it seemed that we had not done a very polite thing. But we could get some sleep in the end and that was all that mattered.

We sat down and had some eggs. Actually Richard had some eggs that he cooked himself in a small tin plate on burning coals, while I had some bread and Nescafé. Hector was still there, watching us with his beautiful docile eyes the colour of my Nescafé. I patted him again and I thought again that he looked more like a dog. It was the big day and still he was alive; maybe they would keep him alive, I thought, wanting badly for this to happen. He was eating some grass in his corner, his eyes a bit sad but sort of wise, and as he looked at us eating our own breakfast next to him he seemed more human than sheep.

We had arranged for one of the guys of the household to take us to the big central square where the communal prayer would take place that morning. He sat on a little stool and waited for us to finish breakfast, but we failed to read his signs of impatience. He didn't say a word, maybe because it was against their sense of hospitality to interrupt us when eating. The net result was that, as we got up to the square all excited and all prepared to take some incredible pictures of those robed nomads bending together for the biggest communal prayer of the year, we understood that it was over. We had arrived too late.

"Why didn't you tell us?" We turned to our guide filled with frustration.

"How could I? You were still eating!" the guy was equally disappointed.

To us it was a disaster that we were not told to hurry; to him, it would have been rude to interrupt our breakfast. Call it cultural misunderstanding but there was nothing else we could do: we had missed it all, the prayer; the ritual killing of the first sheep done by their imam immediately following the prayer and the dance of the kids around the dying animal; the yell of the women at the sight of the first drop of blood; the painting of kids' faces with the blood of the animal. We had missed all that.

As we arrived, only some stains of blood in the sand indicated the place where it had all happened. Maybe it was better that way, I thought, wandering aimlessly through the market: I would not have liked to see a sheep being killed in front of my eyes anyway.

People were going home now, each of them with a mission: as the first sheep of the day had been killed, they were now free to kill their own sheep and they did so one after the other. It all happened behind closed gates and strangely enough we did not hear much noise. It was as if the poor sheep already knew of their fate and did not put up any resistance. It was only later on that morning as we wandered through the streets that I started to notice the deep sewage channels which were cut into the middle of the street, usually filled with dirty water and garbage, turning red with the blood of the countless sheep and goats killed that morning. It seemed the city itself was bleeding.

We came back to the house eventually and the first thing I noticed was that Hector wasn't there. The grass he had chewed on that morning was still there, though, as was the rope he had been tied with. And just above the place where I had patted him that morning a big piece of meat hung, tied, with the legs upside down: what was left of his corpse. He was already skinned and the fleece nowhere to be seen, and I felt immensely grateful that I did not have to see it somewhere on display. I couldn't have borne the memory of having patted the same animal in the morning. The front legs were gone already, straight into the family soup I guess, and the piece of meat, all that was left of him, looked a lot smaller than the way I remembered him. Was it worth it? Was it worth taking a life for such a small piece of meat?

And as I passed through the door on which the meat was hanging, I tried hard to contain my feelings of guilt. I could have bought him this morning. I could have paid some money to this family and Hector would have become mine and he would still be alive now. But then I would have had to leave him here as we moved on, and sooner or later he would have still been reduced to that piece of meat that was hanging outside the door.

I entered our room and lay down on my mattress. Outside, people were celebrating and laughing and I heard the owner of the house asking Richard if he wanted to share their meal, most probably made with various parts of Hector. I didn't want to be part of all this. I simply didn't.

By evening I still felt sick but I had a date to go on. Isa turned up at dusk and even though I didn't really feel like it, I went with him to the rap concert. It happened at the local school and the kids on the stage, all dressed in jeans and T-shirts, mustn't have been older than 16. To my surprise Isa jumped on the stage as well and started singing some sort of Tuareg or Tamasheq rap. Kids all around were clapping and dancing. Girls were dressed in large robes, with silver coins plaited into their hair. Some of them were darker, some lighter. These kids represented all the tribes that lived in the city.

"There must be someone you fancy in here," I said to Isa.

"Yes, sort of," he admitted. And then, in a low voice, "The one over there in blue. But she doesn't really care about me."

Aha, so my date took me here to make his darling jealous. It was quite amusing to step back into the high school era.

The girl he pointed out had fairer skin than his. She was dressed in a bright blue robe that touched the ground and covered her head as well. She chatted vivaciously with two other local beauties.

"Why doesn't she like you?"

"You know, she's a Songhai, they only like their own people," he said, and I noticed some sadness. Timbuktu must still be a very caste-segregated city.

"But you can sing," I reminded him. "It sounded good. What where you singing about, anyway?"

"Oh, different things: life in the city. This is my band, we get together here and we sing from time to time."

"What's your band called?"

His eyes shone again and his mouth opened into a big smile.

"Made in Timbuktu," he said proudly, pointing at himself. "We are Made in Timbuktu!"

MORNING came and it brought another confirmation of the principle that good things happen to those who have given up demanding them. We decided to pay a visit to the only Internet café in town. It was very expensive and very slow, but we did our tasks and I felt good to be in touch with friends and family again. We also found a guide for a camel trek we were trying to arrange for the next day, and to my delight Richard said he was interested in coming along as well. I thought I was going on my own. It really felt good to be back doing things with Richard again, I thought, and as we haggled for the price with the guide I couldn't contain my smile at seeing the well-known show again. He said

10,000 per day; Richard's face went grumpy. What? 9,000: the guy made another tentative offer. "Oyyyy," came the answer. The guy then figured out he could maybe do it for less. And it went on and on and on. In a grand finale, Richard dismissed the guy with a gesture and said that the price was mad and he couldn't even be bothered to talk about it, and went back to the computer to check some more emails. Then I entered the game and told the astonished guy that I couldn't do anything for him, since Richard was angry now. Silence. Then the camel trek guide was back and came to me directly: maybe we would reconsider... 7,000. I sent him to speak with Richard but he didn't want to: he said *"Monsieur il est dur[17]."* Ten more minutes and the price had now come down to 6,000 and eventually we had a deal for 5,000 a day including camel, guide and food. Exactly half of what he had initially asked for.

And as we prepared to leave and get ready for our trek, the door opened and there Peter stood: a bit dirtier and sweatier than I remembered him and with an overgrown beard but he was there! Somewhere behind him I could spot the car: the yellow camel as we called it.

I jumped for joy and embraced him, and suddenly all my anger was gone and I forgot about the missed encounter in Bamako and the lack of my birth control pills and my creams. Everything was gone and the only thing that mattered was that he was there, as if another miracle had just taken place. Fate was playing games with us again, but this time it had decided that the trip was finally to become what was planned a long time ago: the three of us and a Land Rover. And it started right there, in that tiny room stacked with old, slow computers, in the middle of an ancient desert town...

A DAY WITH THE NOMADS

THERE was silence inside the tent and the heavy heat of the afternoon made bones feel heavy and inert. Bodies lay down wherever they could: on blankets, straw mats or simply in the sand. The dim light that crept through the roof of straw mats seemed to make the air cooler, though. There was no

---

[17] "Mister is tough." (in French)

movement: even the flies had disappeared. I fell asleep with one hand deeply buried in the sand, my head resting on a leather pillow, my eyelids heavy as stones. There was a strange taste in the air: somehow salty, as if we were on the shores of the ocean.

We were as far away from water as one could be, in the middle of the desert, the desert of all deserts: the Sahara. We had left our car and our belongings in Timbuktu, got a deal with a camel owner and now, two days deep into the desert, we were to finally understand how these nomads lived.

I woke up hearing a lonely voice singing a monotonous melody. It was more of a whisper and it came from a faraway corner of the tent where the woman of the house was preparing tea. We had drunk more tea in those two days than in the three months before, and another pot was on its way.

The charcoal was ready and she put the small pot on the fire. On a round tray she placed a few short glasses, and next to these a grey plastic bag containing sugar. Sugar was their most treasured possession.

She waited patiently for the water to boil, her knees bent under her and covered with the indigo robe, her eyes gazing somewhere outside. The whole structure of the tent was supported by wooden pillars stuck deep into the sand. On top of those, the thin mats were tied with ropes. They never reached the ground, though, and the opening that was left in the walls served as both window and door.

Her child knelt down in front of her. He was a healthy-looking toddler of about two. He was completely naked: children here were kept completely naked until they were five or six. Then one day they were suddenly dressed in the same way as their parents, in big blue robes, and they passed from childhood to adulthood in the blink of an eye.

The water was boiling and she removed the pot from the charcoal. Next she poured sugar from the bag: a lot of sugar. The tea leaves must have already been boiling with the water. The child stuck one of his fingers into his nose and followed her movements attentively. With one hand she lifted up the pot, as high as she could, and the brownish substance started to pour down into the glasses. But the tea was not ready to drink and the long dance of pouring had only just started. From the glass, the tea was then poured back into the pot and then back into the glass, then into the pot again. By now she had stopped singing.

Her movements were quiet and smooth, her body immobile. Only her arms seemed caught in a strange ritual: left one up, pouring tea into the glass; right one up, pouring tea into the pot. She was completely focused on catching every drop and her robe fell on her shoulders, revealing her straight, black, neatly arranged hair.

Women must have spent a long time doing their hair up in this place, I thought, and I later found out they used butter to grease the hair as it was the only way to keep it clean. Water was far too precious. From the top of her head, her hair was parted into several braids, the ones going towards the ears having small silver rings woven into them. Her eyes were dark, her face long. Her skin was sort of dark, but more like a deep tan rather than black, and her colour reminded me of a Native American. But this was Africa and she was neither Arab nor black. She was a Tuareg woman.

She poured the tea once more into the glass, which was filled more with greenish foam than liquid. It was the sign that it had been mixed enough, so she filled the other glasses and put the tray in front of us: it was teatime. There was no way one could escape the tea "treat" so we drank in silence.

The glasses were dirty, very dirty. Water here was too precious to be wasted on washing dishes. The drink tasted bitter and very strong; I wondered where all the sugar she had poured in it had gone.

She collected the glasses without a word and put the pot back on the fire. A second round would follow soon, done with the same leaves, in the same pot, mixed using the same endless pouring technique. And when we were done with it, she would put the pot back on the fire for a third time. There were always three tea rounds here and we always had to drink all three glasses we were offered. Doing otherwise would have been very bad manners.

The first tea is as bitter as life, the second is as strong as love and the last is as sweet as death, say the Tuaregs. To me all three of them were bitter, which might have shown I was more inclined to live than love or die.

She was now waiting again for the water to boil, her eyes fixed back on some mysterious point at the horizon. The child stood up and walked uneasily towards her. She sat him on her lap and seemed not to mind when he pulled her robe away, found her nipple and started sucking. I never knew one could breastfeed a kid of about two. She sat there as immobile as a stone with her eyes turned towards the desert, a light smile on her lips, and she seemed just fine.

There were several men in the tent and they ignored her as they ignored everybody else, lying on one mattress or another, trying to sleep or just remain still. We were doing the same, and after the brief tea interruption we were back to sleeping or dozing or simply doing nothing. There was no TV there, there was no radio, nothing to read and in the heavy heat of the afternoon people didn't chat to each other. They were, quite simply, resting.

Life in the desert was fairly straightforward and it was built around the concept of survival. And lying in the shade of a tent under the melting afternoon sun was also about survival, and these people, the Tuaregs, the lords of the desert, knew that better than anybody else.

Nobody knew exactly where they came from, or, more importantly, where they went or what happened to them. They were the people of the desert, the Tuaregs, the masters of the Sahara. They were different from the Arabs of the Maghreb. They were different from the black peoples of the savannah and the forests. They were related to the Moors of Mauritania but they were not Moors. There were about one and half million of them left and they roamed a territory as big as Western Europe, across the borders of five countries: Mali, Niger, Libya, Algeria and Burkina Faso.

They came and they went as the wind of the desert blew, herding their camels and goats in search of water and pastures, once upon a time burning the villages of the black people who lived south of the Niger River and stealing their animals, but in this century simply asking for permission to water their camels at a well. They called themselves the "free men" and were often referred to as the blue men of the desert, and this name didn't come so much from the colour of their robes, mostly blue, but from the bluish shade the indigo robes left on their skin. There were several Tuareg tribes, named after the places they lived – or rather the places they roamed into – or the clans they belonged to. Several tribes formed a confederation, but things were not always easy within such confederations and most of them preferred to keep their allegiance to their family, clan and tribe only. They did, however, have a strong sense of identity and it must have been due to their ancient language, the Tamasheq, which they fiercely preserved to the point of refusing to send their children to schools where they would have been taught in other languages. The language had its own alphabet, the Tifinagh, which was passed from one generation to the next.

Warriors by tradition, they were in continuous conflict with the settled agricultural tribes of black Africans, who they used to raid and enslave. Today, however, both Mali and Niger, countries where most of the Tuaregs lived, were ruled by black tribes who tried to take revenge for years of Tuareg assaults on their villages. A Tuareg rebellion followed in the mid-1990s and many lives were lost.

Opinions were varied and each of the factions involved in the conflict had their own story. To the central Government, the Tuaregs were outrageously uncivilised and wild, incapable of settling and incapable of parting with their banditry and slave trade past.

The nomads, on the other hand, lived under the oppression suffered by many minorities, in a country where they made up only 10% of the population. They saw all the wealth and advantages being split among the members of the ruling tribes and they struggled to survive in a world where it became harder and harder to pursue a nomadic way of life.

Mali and Niger had gone through these conflicts, and a lot of travellers were trapped in these countries in the mid-1990s. Rumours abounded that Tuaregs used to attack European travellers and highjack their 4x4 vehicles. Some people were killed and soon the region became a no-go area. These days, although memories of recent events were still fresh in the minds of both travellers and locals, one could go around reasonably safely.

The huge monument in the heart of Timbuktu, marking the end of the Tuareg insurgence of the 90s, was supposed to act as proof that war was now over. It didn't look particularly reassuring though. It was called the Flame of Peace and it was a huge, triumphant arch – even though there was no triumph to celebrate. Under the arch, the burned carcasses of hundreds of automatic machine guns marked the place where they had burned their weapons as a sign of surrender. Peace was back again, but for how long?

The Tuaregs had always struggled and yet somehow managed to maintain their way of life, despite the droughts and the harsh desert winds, despite colonial powers that had drawn artificial frontiers dividing the territories in which they had once roamed freely, and despite their troubles with the central governments of the countries they belonged to these days. But recently their youngsters had started leaving their families and going away with the hope of making a living in the big towns, giving up their robes and swords and trying to blend in. The Tuareg society began to lose its people.

Then tourists came, and some of the young now chose to stay and try to become "guides" like the lad who had brought us here; to dress up once again in their traditional robes (although completed nowadays with metallic wristwatches and dark sunglasses) and make a living out of taking tourists for a few days' trekking in the desert. Like everywhere in Africa, tourism was a mixed blessing here. On the one hand it allowed them to make some money, sell their souvenirs and survive in the same way as they had survived for centuries. Yet on the other, sooner or later it would erode their society, and soon enough all their costumes and their swords and their way of life would lose their authenticity and would become – as in so many other parts of the world – just a show put on for tourists.

But today they were still an authentic tribe. And this woman, breastfeeding her baby in the middle of her tent, was as foreign to the concept of putting on a show for tourists as her baby was. They lived as they had for centuries and the fact that three white faces were lying on their pillows in their tent did not make any difference to them.

The tribes were Muslim, but practices were liberal and women were given a lot of independence and status. They were monogamous and women kept ownership of most of the things in the household, even after they were married. The tent we were in belonged to that woman, not to her absent husband who had gone somewhere for business. If they divorced, she would keep all their possessions and the children, a striking difference from other Islamic communities in Africa where children always belonged to the father's tribe.

The women were not veiled and their faces were always shown. The border of their robes, much like the *mehlafas* of Mauritania, covered their heads but it was a loose covering. Men, on the other hand, were traditionally forbidden from showing their faces, especially their mouths. They wore long shawls, sometimes more than five metres long, in a variety of blue shades but most often made of indigo linen. The end of the shawl always covered the lower part of their faces, with only their eyes left uncovered. Once upon a time they would not even remove it to eat, although today they were more relaxed.

Their most important symbol, which occurred again and again in the design of their jewellery, was the cross. It must have been through the knights of the crusades that the cross had arrived with these nomadic tribes, or maybe they took it from the cross of life, the Egyptian Ankh, but one way or the other they had kept it as a precious symbol. They had developed several particular shapes, each tribe owning a specific one.

We did nothing for the remainder of the afternoon. More tea was served later on, before the fall of night, and we knew that another big pot filled with rice and some goat meat would follow soon as dinner. Then we would sleep, inside the tent if we wanted to, or outside in our own tents. And when morning came, the camels would be gathered and saddled again and they would kneel for us and we would get up for another morning of marching until we would stop in another tent, arising mysteriously from behind another dune in another village of three to four tents, just like this one.

Time passed differently here, and although in general time in Africa flows a lot more slowly than anywhere else, it felt as if it sort of dragged, in fact almost stopped, here in the tent of these nomads on a long, hot afternoon. I don't think we would have been able to cope if we had just arrived from Europe on one of those flights landing in Timbuktu the day before. But we were already trained and had already learned a lot about patience, and I found it possible to slow down even more and that afternoon I felt again the strange sensation that time did not exist here. Did it matter that I had been lying on a leather pillow for the whole afternoon? Was there anything else to do?

Did I need to do anything, in fact? Back home our lives are all about rushing to do things. Go to work, go to a party, see a film, go shopping, plan your holiday. Here such things did not exist: there was nothing one could do and so one was simply free from doing anything. Here all that mattered was surviving, or simply living. And this was why, in the hot afternoon, nobody would dream of doing things: they would simply live.

A girl of about six or seven came up to me and played with my hand. She was dressed in a long indigo robe, just like a grown woman. Her skin was dark but her hair had chestnut, dark golden highlights. It was hard to tell how many types of blood were mixed into the veins of those nomads.

Soon others started to come by, sit and drink tea. They were relatives, or maybe neighbours, or maybe travellers on some mysterious path through the dunes who had decided to stop here for the night. We were told that there would be a big celebration that night. It was the third night of the Tabaski holiday and everybody was in a party mood. We were told that we could come along if we wanted.

We did join them later on that evening, and it felt like time wasn't suspended any more but going backwards and taking us with it, and we somehow arrived in another time, in the same place but centuries ago. Under the bright light of the full moon, a group of Tuaregs were celebrating in a circle on the top of a dune, the women seated, drumming with henna-painted fingers and chanting a monotonous melody, very much like the one I had heard the lady of our tent singing earlier that day. Men were clapping and occasionally joining in parts of the song, and some children were running around naked, trying to take part in the celebration of the adults, although they were harshly sent away by their parents.

This was a party with no food, no drink and no musicians. Only the rhythmic sound of the goat-skin drums played by the women, and their voices travelling far away into the desert. Men were dancing: a warrior dance they performed with their swords in their hands to the rhythm of the women's chant. And the silver jewellery in the hair of the women was shining as they kept on drumming and smiling, oblivious to the reality around them: oblivious to us, three white tourists accidentally dropped into the middle of their celebration. It went on long into the night, the men with sparkling eyes and their faces covered by indigo turbans, the women with bright, white teeth lost in a sense of timeless joy. They had gathered there tonight much like their ancestors had been gathering at similar events for centuries and centuries, on top of some dune somewhere in their country with no borders.

I didn't put up my tent that evening, but opened it and covered my sleeping bag with the flysheet instead. I felt I no longer needed to have a roof over my head, as if the nomads with powerful voices who I had seen dancing that night had managed to transmit some of the meaning of the sparkle that lightened their eyes.

Their song must have been in Tamasheq and I didn't know that language, but I didn't need to understand their words. Somehow I knew that the sound of their melody and the mysterious words and the chants and the drums were all talking about one and the same thing, and there was a part of me that could make sense of it all, and it was beyond the understanding of languages. I knew they spoke of wind and sand, of the beauty of their women and the bitterness of their lives... of their goats and camels... of war and death... and above all I knew they spoke of freedom and of the joy of being, simply, alive.

CHAPTER 12 – UNDER THE SHADE OF A TREE

(DOGON COUNTRY, MALI, FEBRUARY 2003)

AT the beginning of the universe, Amma created the Earth in the shape of a woman and then married her. Out of their union the Pale Fox was born. The Fox was born without a placenta and thus robbed of his female counterpart, and he brought about chaos in the world. Since he could not find a female companion, the Pale Fox committed incest with his mother, the Earth. But this was a disastrous union and as a result the Earth bled the first menstrual blood as a sign of impurity. Amma did not give up, though. This time he was luckier and after having refertilised the Earth with a shower of rain, the Nommo twins were born: fish-like Gods who lived in the water and later helped humans acquire knowledge.

Upset by the betrayal of the Earth, Amma decided to withdraw and continue the creation on his own. But, before this, he made a pair of humans – a male and a female – who were circumcised by the Nommos and later gave birth to four pairs of twins. These twins were the ancestors of the Dogons and were represented each by a holy animal: snake, tortoise, scorpion, crocodile, frog, lizard, rabbit and hyena.

These Nommos somehow came from and returned to the Sirius star, which the Dogons believed to be the centre of the Universe. In fact they said it was not one star but three, and they had said this for hundreds of years – despite the fact that Sirius B, the second Sirius star, was only discovered by the modern world in 1862. The existence of a third star, the one that Dogons referred to as Emme Ya, has not yet been scientifically proven.

But other things they believed have been proven through the centuries, and little by little the world's anthropologists have turned their attention to this small community of around 100,000 people who lived around the Bandiagara Escarpment in Southern Mali.

Centuries-old songs and masks, and the oral traditions passed down by their priests, all talked of things peculiar to this place lost in the middle of the African savannah: they said the moon was barren and dry, that the Earth moved around the Sun, that Jupiter had four moons, and they drew Saturn with a ring around it. And they said that all this knowledge about the skies had been passed to them by the androgynous Nommos, who had descended from their vehicles in thunder and fire after having poured a huge reservoir of water on to the Earth. Since they were fish-like creatures, they could only live in water.

Having left behind the Tuareg lands, we were now back in the savannah. We had been trekking for a few days in the Dogon country and the talk of our guide Michel seemed straight from the hallucinations of a heavy drug user. We heard bits and bobs, and sometimes the stories contradicted each other. "Hang on: didn't you say that the Nommo was the brother of the Pale Fox? Then how did he arrive later on from the sky?" At other times, resting under the shade of a tree away from the hot sun of the afternoon, it was just too complicated to make sense of it all and we gave up trying to understand.

We were walking from village to village, all of them scattered around an escarpment that rose sharply from the plain and separated the two worlds of the high plateau villages and the low plain ones. In the middle of these two worlds, the steep cliffs rose high into the sky, as if an invisible hand had sunk the earth underneath.

The *falaise* was steep but filled with ancient dwellings. These holes in the cliff were so high up that one could not imagine how they were used. Maybe they had ladders made of ropes. Or maybe wetter weather had once covered the escarpment with vines and plants, allowing people to climb on them. Or, as our guide Michel believed, they built their shelters so high because they could fly. The Tellems were the original inhabitants of these places: the Dogons described them as small, red-skinned beings. For a while they had coexisted peacefully with the incoming Dogons, continuing their existence high on the cliffs while the Dogons settled more into the plain or the plateau, but inevitably conflict emerged. The Tellems were defeated and had to run away further south. Nobody knew who they were and where they went, but their description suggested striking similarities with the pygmies who today inhabit parts of the rainforest in central Africa.

Their villages were a maze, impossible to navigate without a guide, and Michel, the lad we found in a street food stall in Bandiagara, seemed the right person to help us survive this total immersion in the customs of that place. There were sacred rocks one was not allowed to touch, sacred areas of the village – next to some holes in the cliff where they buried their dead, for instance, or next to some strange symbols painted at the base of the huge *falaise* – that one was not allowed to enter. There were strange formations of small rocks or mud piles on the side of the path that one was not supposed to step on.

One of these places was the toguna, the shelter and meeting place for the elders of the village that no woman, not even a tourist, could enter. It was built from stone and mud, with a very low roof made of dried millet and branches, and it served as a meeting place to debate village issues. It had a low-built roof that deliberately did not allow men to stand up while talking, and thus it calmed them down – when one couldn't stand up, one couldn't shout, Michel explained with a serious face.

Their places were all about fetishes, interdictions and the spirits of ancestors, and their symbols were intricate and ornate, and they told their legends again and again, carved them on the doors of their granaries or sculpted them on the pillars of their meeting houses. Above all, they tried to say it all in the design of their masks.

The mask was a central part of the life of a Dogon. There were small masks and huge masks, ordinary masks that could be shown to tourists and sold for souvenirs, and holy masks, sometimes as high as 10 metres, that were kept secret and taken out only on the occasion of their important festivals like the Sigui (a major Dogon celebration that happened every 60 years, when they called in the spirits of their ancestors to help them pass on their beliefs and traditions to the next generation). Somehow this major festival was calculated, taking into account the time it takes for the star Sirius to navigate its orbit, and their calculation was more exact than the one used by modern astronomers.

Their lives were governed by their rituals and traditions, and it was a system that had an answer or a ritual for everything. From interpreting the future using the footsteps of the Pale Fox to hanging red-and-white-painted, breast-shaped rocks in trees to invoke fertility, they had a way of doing things that was theirs only. When an old man died, the whole village danced on the roof of his hut until it collapsed, because the death of an old man was like the destruction of a library. They had priests, the hogons, who performed mainly agricultural rituals, ensuring that the land remained sacred and blessing each culture. They had elders who ran their villages and took decisions, and fortune tellers who had an answer for everything. They seemed capable of bringing together three religions – Animism, Islam and Christianity – sometimes within the boundaries of the same village.

Like everywhere in Africa women worked hard, but here they had a holiday every month when they went to their menstruation houses built somewhere outside the villages. There they stayed until their period ended, doing nothing, probably chatting to each other. In the meantime their husbands took over all the wives' duties: looking after the children, fetching water, working in the fields.

They were very skilled in agriculture, which they claimed was the result of the teachings of their Nommos. They managed to tend small plots of land, sometimes as small as a few square metres hanging from the top of the cliffs, and they carried water on their heads to irrigate these plots of land, where they managed to grow vegetables and rice. They also grew millet and made beer out of it. But onion was their main crop, as well as the main ingredient of their meals, and it gave a distinctive scent to their villages.

Everything about them was just different. Their week was five days long instead of seven and they held a market day on the fifth, in a different village each time, which led to some pretty complex calculations in order to understand when and where the next one was due. They stored their hay high up in the baobab trees so that it was not eaten up by animals and they produced all sorts of medicines from the bark or fruit of these baobab trees, which they believed had a cure for everything.

They had special adult initiation rites, with circumcision houses filled with kids from about 10 to 12 years old. They went through weeks of training before the big moment arrived and it seemed they practised circumcision on both boys and girls, although this latter practice, also known as female genital mutilation, was officially banned by the central Government in Bamako.

But in those villages, life went on as it had for centuries and for a Dogon, his Nommo ancestor was a presence felt a lot more vividly than some faraway minister in a faraway capital. Women walked around topless and wore beautifully dyed indigo cloth around their waists. They worked hard and were most often seen carrying water in huge bowls on their heads. Men, as everywhere else in Africa, mostly lay in the shade, but these men were also active in weaving, smithing, and the production and sale of all sorts of wooden sculptures and other souvenirs. Tourism had arrived here as well as everywhere else. The first wave had stripped the Dogon houses of precious, centuries-old wooden sculptures and objects, and now the Dogons had woken up. Only newly manufactured items were to be sold to tourists.

Peter had managed to break this rule the day before when he had started an afternoon-long negotiation with the village hunter to buy his gun, which must have been made some time at the turn of the last century. The hunter's hut was very ornate, with monkey skulls, bird feathers and animal furs, and by now we knew all about these fetishes[18]. Some were not to be touched; others were not to be looked at or walked in front of.

Peter got his gun and as we later bought some indigo cloth, nicely sculpted granary doors and various other bits and bobs, we felt we had irremediably lost our aura of "traveller" and sunk into the more humble condition of "tourist". One couldn't escape being simply a tourist sometimes, but it was quite rewarding judging from the wide smile on Richard's face as he contemplated his last purchase: a goat skin complete with legs and head made into a small backpack, with legs that could be tied around the owner's

---

[18] Fetish: an inanimate object worshipped for its supposed magical powers or because it is considered to be inhabited by a spirit.

waist.

A week had passed since the three of us met in Timbuktu and it looked like we would need more than that to become a team. For the first time we were travelling together, the three of us. Up to that point each of us had travelled with each of us, and we had managed to somehow establish a balance and function in those situations: Peter and Richard in Spain, Peter and me in Morocco and Mauritania, Richard and me for the last month. We had managed to find a way of interacting with each other and set some rules, and it had been fairly easy. But now, for the first time, we were all three together and the rules that govern the interactions of two people change dramatically in the context of a group. I knew that we had to go through the usual stages: forming, storming, norming, performing. We had formed back in the UK some three months before. Now we were storming, and as uncomfortable as it felt I knew it was necessary. My only worry was that it would take forever.

Peter fell back into his "one joke sorts it all" attitude. His jokes would get on my nerves each and every time he would try one, especially since he seemed to pick on me for his various comments. Richard seemed to be bored with life – or maybe just with the two of us – and looked like he'd be much better on his own for a while. I, on the other hand, was living through one of my worst episodes of premenstrual syndrome ever – my interrupted cycle of birth control pills must have got my hormones to an explosive level. Nothing seemed to work well, nothing seemed to function and I could barely take refuge in the beautiful scenery that surrounded us.

We had left the car in Bandiagara, a border town where the Dogon country started. The villages could only be explored on foot. We were walking for at least four to five hours every day, but not even the hard walk under the sun managed to calm me down. I used to walk on my own, behind the group, taking refuge in my thoughts, trying to understand why I was so irritated, so intolerant of my travel mates, and especially of Peter.

That morning I was walking behind the two of them again, lost in my thoughts, and I didn't notice that the distance between me and them was getting bigger. Peter waited for me and walked with me for a while in silence. I knew he wanted to talk. But I had nothing to tell him. I was angry, angry with the world, angry with this trip that started as a dream only to fade into a monotonous day-to-day routine, angry with myself for not enjoying it fully, angry with my own anger. Angry with my travel mates just because they happened to be around. Above all, angry with him: his jokes, his impossible sense of humour.

"You know, if you'd roll up your trousers you'd be able to walk faster," he said after a while.

Maybe he was simply trying to start a conversation. Maybe he was trying to be helpful but to me it sounded more like arrogance.

"Thank you, Peter. I'll ask for your advice when I need it."

"Just trying to be helpful," he said with an indifferent look.

"You'd better try to mind your own business," I replied in an irritated voice.

Silence. And then suddenly he opened up in a way he had not done before and told me in a serious and soft voice, "Roxana, what's going on with the two of us? Where's all this intolerance coming from? Have I done anything wrong?"

I felt him to be sincere, open. For the first time I felt he had opened up a bit of himself and showed me that somewhere inside he really cared. Maybe that was the heart of the onion finally, the heart I had tried to get to with no success so far, the heart that was usually buried under a thick layer of sarcasm.

But I wasn't ready to handle this openness. And the more I felt he opened up, the more I closed myself off. What was going on? I didn't have an answer. I was tired, lonely and fed up. I travelled with these two guys, I shared all of my days and nights with them, and yet I felt lonely, so lonely, and yet so incapable of finding any moment of privacy. How could I explain all that? Two men and a woman living in forced intimacy, trying their best to avoid any intimacy at all.

I didn't tell him any of those things. I didn't even answer his question. I kept silent and hurried along until we caught up with Richard, who threw us both a grumpy look.

"The two of you, can you walk any slower than that?"

"Peter was trying to teach me how to wear my trousers," I said, choosing to ignore everything else.

"Did you tell him to fuck off?" Richard asked with a

smile, but his voice was still grumpy.

"I did, but he didn't quite understand it," I said turning towards Peter. I felt I had had my revenge. I was answering his attempt to open up with a joke, just like he had done so many times before...

"Let's try again. Fuck off," Richard repeated. "Now do you understand?"

I wasn't quite sure if it was for Peter or for me or for both, or simply a joke. But Richard smiled and Peter too, and I thought that maybe it was only a joke after all. We were back to talking about anything else except our feelings, but I still had a sour taste in my mouth.

We carried on walking in silence. The sun was about to set and we had almost reached Ireli, the village with the most amazing views of the escarpment. We wanted to spend the night there but our guide had other plans. He hurried past the village. We let him go on but turned towards the village. When he realised we were not following him any longer, he came back shouting. No, we could not stop there for the night. Yes we could, we said. People started to gather around us, watching him shouting at us and us shouting back. It was quite a show!

It turned out that Michel had arranged for a family in the next village to put us up for the night. We couldn't care less about his arrangements. All we wanted was to spend the night in Ireli so that we could take nice pictures the following morning.

"You can't make me lose face. See, they are all laughing at me now!"

But we didn't understand his problem. All we cared about was the pictures we would take in the morning, and the principle of expecting the best possible service for the money we had paid. For a moment we were back to being three arrogant Europeans, stepping upon the unwritten laws of a traditional society.

Michel did not give up and nor did we, and the quarrel went on for some time. But when he raised his walking staff to hit Peter, I froze under the certainty that we would have a fight.

"Stop! Stop for a moment!" I cried from the bottom of my lungs.

The proximity of danger had opened my communication channels. I still didn't understand what had made him so mad, and I didn't care. I had found a possible solution to get us out of trouble. I was going to play the helpless woman.

"It is my fault and I must apologise."

Michel threw me a sceptical look and my travel mates another, which read more like "you must be insane".

"It was because I couldn't walk any longer that we decided to stop here. I was tired, you see, so tired that I needed to stop urgently."

Men are the same everywhere. Tell them that you are too weak to keep up with them and they won't question this.

"So why did you not come and tell me?" Michel still looked sceptical but the staff had returned to the ground.

"You were walking too fast; I couldn't catch up with you. I had to stop immediately otherwise I would have fainted. You see, I can barely stand now. I'm really sorry we have to stop in this village, even though I know you have arranged for us to be hosted by this other family."

Richard and Peter looked at me strangely but they didn't say a word. But Michel believed me, and we stayed there that night and took all the pictures we wanted the next morning.

We found another family to host us, on the roof of another hut. They took out three mattresses and shared their millet beer with us. I was drinking in silence, looking at the mattresses nicely arranged one next to the other. Three people, three personalities and three different points of view, trying hard to melt into a team. Would we succeed? I had no trouble playing the game with Michel earlier and saying sorry for an imaginary fault. But accepting my real faults and saying sorry to my travel mates, that was an entirely different story...

MORNING came and we carried on our walking routine with Michel, who looked like he had forgotten all about last night's incident. He stopped by a wooden door engraved with some strange symbols and started explaining.

"You see, the lizard is a very important animal for these people. It is made up of three lines pointing upwards, the head and the front legs, and three lines pointing downwards, the back legs and the tail. In between, the line connecting them is the body. What it means is that the world of the heaven, made of God, angels and spirits, is linked to the world of the earth, made of stone, plants and animals. It is all linked through the centre line, the human being, who is the only one to put together the world of the heaven and the world of the earth."

In this small Dogon village in the middle of the African savannah, I couldn't believe what I was hearing. It was an old Christian concept, with its root in the Jewish symbol of the candelabra with seven arms, transformed into a stylised lizard on a centuries-old wooden mask in the Dogon country.

For a second the image of the Tuareg cross in the shape of a lizard, worn and respected by Muslims, flashed through my mind, and as the guide went on talking about the holy lizard living in the same water that once upon a time the Nommos came from, I felt my breath slowly coming back and I knew, once more, that what he meant to tell us was in fact something else. It was about people being similar everywhere, with the same emotions and feelings and the same representations of the world. And it was about all religions being one and all of them sending out the same message, which was a concept hard to digest in our modern world with all those worldwide conflicts between Christians, Muslims and Jews. But here in the Dogon country, an old and mysterious civilisation had this message inscribed on their masks and woven into their dances and ceremonies, and for them it seemed to be the simplest and most obvious truth in the world.

CHAPTER 13 – WELL PAST MY BEDTIME…

(IN THE BUSH, BURKINA FASO AND GHANA, MARCH 2003)

I knew it was Richard. I didn't need to turn my head to check if it was really him as I heard the branches cracking under someone's steps. I kept my chin on my knees, my arms around my legs and my eyes gazing at the narrow stream flowing in front of me. My back was resting on the trunk of a tree and I felt leaning against it gave me some comfort. I wasn't crying any longer but didn't feel like talking either. The night smelled of grass and water, and the monotonous flow of the small river seemed to add some life to a bleak picture. The moon had risen and I could see pretty well. I knew the light was bright enough that if I wanted to, I could turn my head and check on whoever was sitting next to me.

We had arrived late at this private game-watching lodge – more like barracks actually, but we were still hoping that we would see some elephants the next day. There were elephants in this part of Burkina Faso and back into the capital we had learned that this was the best place to see them. But I wasn't thinking about elephants that evening. I was just thinking of my misery.

I felt sad, deeply sad. Maybe tired as well. Maybe irritated, fed up, homesick and alone. It could have been because the tensions in our group were rising instead of settling. We were learning to live together and it wasn't easy. Or it could have been because, four months into this trip, I was still thinking about what I had come here to find. Was it worth it? All the dust and the heat and the feeling of exhaustion; the tension in our group, and the quarrels; were they all worth it?

It all seemed too much somehow, and as we finished putting up our tents for the night I felt I could no longer suppress my tears. We had finished eating in silence and as Peter was climbing up the ladder into his tent on top of the car and Richard was brushing his teeth, juggling a bottle of water and a torch in one hand, I felt I needed to go away: find a place where I could simply hide and cry.

I didn't move for a while but I knew he was still there, in the silence. I knew he knew that I'd been crying and I knew he had come to sit with me because he wanted to give me some comfort. And I knew he wasn't going to come close and put an arm around my shoulders and hold me tight as I so desperately wished. But I knew he was there and, strangely enough, the simple fact of his presence on the bank of that river, some five metres away from me, seemed to be telling me that it wasn't all that bad.

"I couldn't sleep," he said after a while. "I've got this stupid story going through my mind. You know sometimes, something pops up in your brain and you just can't get rid of it."

I didn't say anything. I just kept quiet and he went on.

"There's this old man who checks into a hotel one night in the beautiful town of Brighton in England. Have you ever been to Brighton?"

Silence again and he gave up expecting an answer.

"Anyway, this is a weird old man and as he enters his room the first thing he does is notice there are several little soap bars into the bathroom," he carried on, and then he paused again. Was he making up the story?

"Oh Richard, why is it so difficult sometimes?" I said in a whisper. I wasn't even sure he heard it.

"Because it simply is," he answered and I knew he had heard me. "It all gets too much... being tired, being dirty; missing home," he said after a while.

So he knew about that feeling.

"Does it happen to you too?" I asked.

"Sometimes," he admitted.

I couldn't remember ever having seen Richard depressed. I remembered having seen him grumpy or impatient or desperately wanting to go off on his own for a wander. But I hadn't seen him depressed.

"I'm sad sometimes too," he carried on. "Everybody is and it's just the way things are."

"And how do you deal with it?" I asked, hoping for a miraculous solution.

"Well, I let it come and I'm sad for a while and I know it will go away. I feel sad but I also feel fine. It's fine to be sad, you know..."

This was a bit too complex for me. One feels fine and sad at the same time.

"It's OK to miss home and friends and all that. It's OK to ask what you're doing here. And it's OK not to have an answer. We're all a bit here a bit there. When we're here, we miss the other world; when we're there we want to be here," Richard said.

A bit here and a bit there; people belonging to two different worlds, carrying both of them inside, and sometimes not knowing where they would rather be. Like Larry, the Danish lad we met in Djenné. Like Gerhard, the German grandfather who set off to conquer the Sahara on a bike. Like Karl, the other biker that we kept on crossing paths with. Like Richard, who now sat next to me in silence. Like myself. There was a big tribe of us out there.

Silence again. I wanted to tell him that my friends must have been gathering somewhere in Italy for a ski weekend and that I so badly wished I could have been with them. That I missed their jokes and their humour and I missed wherever I called home: Romania where my parents lived, Switzerland where I still had an apartment, Italy with all my memories of great student parties and my friends going skiing. I wanted to tell him that I felt lonely and depressed. And I so badly wanted him to hold me in his arms and tell me that it wasn't so bad.

Silence. I didn't say any of those things.

"Anyway," Richard continued after a while. "Back to my story. You see, this man was a bit puzzled. He can't understand why he was given so many bars of soap. So he puts them into a drawer and writes a small note to the housekeeper, telling her that the hotel has a strange policy on soap."

What was I doing there, in the middle of the bush, camping in front of a small river in the company of two weird British guys? What was I doing with my life? Tears came into my eyes again.

Richard stopped. I wasn't sure he could see my tears. He got up and for a second I thought he would sit next to me and put his arms around me, and then I would hide my face on his shoulder and cry and cry until I got all the sadness out of me. But he didn't. He just came a bit closer and sat down again.

"The housekeeper comes and finds the note but doesn't find the bars of soap, since they were hidden in the drawer, and guesses that the gentlemen in question wants some more bars of soap. She leaves three more bars in the room."

Sometimes it's difficult to express what we want. Is this what he was trying to tell me? Was he trying to tell me anything, in fact? It didn't really matter. What mattered was that I was sad in the middle of the wilderness and I would somehow need to get out of this depressed state and crawl into my tent, which waited empty and dirty back where we were camping, and I would somehow have to put up with another night alone. Having met the car and recovered all my hidden treasures, I had gone back to using my own tent and sharing Richard's tent, mattress and sleeping bag had become a thing of the past. The peace and understanding we had shared while travelling together also seemed a thing of the past. Now we were trying to settle into this new routine – the three of us and a car – and it wasn't easy at all.

Peter was doing much of the driving and he occasionally asked Richard if he wanted to drive. He never asked me, though, and I felt unjustly discriminated against. In fact, this was the trigger of all my depression tonight.

"The old man comes back from his stroll and he opens the door of his room and finds three more bars of soap. He now has six bars of soap and feels like he is being mocked. He writes another note and this time it's a stronger one; he says he doesn't need any more soap! The next day he goes out again and the housekeeper comes back, and she sees the note and the six bars of soap placed on top of the note, and she takes all of them away: the note and the bars! Now our gentleman is left with no soap and when he comes back to the room he's really angry."

I wasn't listening, but I was hearing whether I wanted to or not, and what I heard seemed such a nonsense that somehow it brought a smile. And as Richard carried on and the old man in his story wrote some more notes to the housekeeper, who went on taking back all the soap bars or supplying too many, the incredible happened and I burst into laughter.

"Anyway, this was a silly story," Richard concluded. "And I'd better get to my tent and get some sleep. It's well past my bedtime. And I've talked enough nonsense for the evening."

I was still smiling, and it was not so much because of the old man and his soaps but because of Richard and his way of expressing care.

"Thank you, Richard."

It was the first time I had thanked him so formally. The culture I come from is not about formal thanks: in fact, it would be strange to express things in such a way to a friend. And it would be equally strange for a friend to tell a story about some old man and his soaps instead of giving you a hug. But in a way, Richard's approach worked and we walked back to the camp together. And as I slipped into my cold, lonely tent I thought that perhaps things were not so bad after all, and maybe everybody at some point faces the challenge of getting the exact number of soap bars one needs.

BUSH CAMPING ROUTINES

IT was half past six and the sun was up already. This meant I had about five minutes to get out of my tent, which would become as hot as a greenhouse in the ten minutes that followed. There was no escape from the sun in this place, and once it was up the day had started. Good morning Burkina Faso, the land of the incorruptible as the translated name reads in English. I was about to start another day in paradise.

The fire from last night was already smoking, and as far as I could see through my half-closed eyes, Richard was kneeling down by the fire blowing his lungs out. "Coffee," I thought. "He must be in desperate need of a coffee if he can blow this much, this early."

I looked around and the setting of last night's camp became clear. We were in the middle of nowhere, just as I remembered from the night before; the car was still there, as covered in red dust as the day before, and no movement seemed to come from Peter's tent on top of it.

We soon understood that a fire was the main feature of a

camp. As soon as we stopped, usually around half past five in the afternoon, we started looking for firewood. Then, hopefully having returned successfully from our wanderings, we would light the fire and forget about it for a while. Richard's wisdom usually came to the surface in such moments. "It will be ready for you when you're ready for it," he said, watching his piece of art with a glimmer of satisfaction in his eyes. We let the fire burn away while we set up the camp and, sure enough, once we were ready to cook it had slowed down and was ready for us.

We were applying the same principle in the mornings. Before anything else one needed to get the fire going, and whoever got up first would immediately start blowing his lungs out into the remains of last night's fire. Richard managed quite well that morning.

I brushed my teeth outside my tent, then I poured some drops of water on to my face – this was the morning washing routine – and I felt ready to start the day. I was already dressed: I slept half-dressed anyway, and besides, I wore the same pair of trousers and T-shirt for days in a row.

Some movement in the roof tent on the car – Peter's sleeping paradise, as I liked to call it – and it seemed that the heat had managed to pull all three of us out of our sleeping bags. Peter's tent had a duvet, three pillows and bedsheets, and every time I wrapped myself in my sleeping bag at night and tried to ignore the uncomfortable sensation of the hard ground through the thin mattress underneath, I thought of Peter's paradise and I envied him for it.

The morning routine went on in silence. We unpacked the car again, since as a precaution everything we had used the previous evening – table, chairs, cooking pots, food – had been stored back in the car for the night. We rolled up our tents, Peter closed his and we got ready to have a bite to eat before setting off.

We were not very talkative in the morning. We drank coffee in silence and moved on to repacking the car. We had a lot of things in that car and they were usually placed in plastic boxes that were frequently moved into and out of the boot. The pots and pans were washed with some of the water we carried in two jerrycans, the food box was packed up, our tents were rolled up and we were almost ready to go. I had discovered a new way of rolling up my tent that made life quite easy. Instead of packing my mattress, sleeping bag and various pieces of clothing I used for the evening separately, I left everything in the tent; I then rolled everything up in the flysheet and rolled it into a plastic bag, hoping to keep the dust away. This way it only took a couple of minutes to have my sleeping corner set for the night.

The washing machine went on top of the roof. It was a waterproof bag in which we put our dirty laundry, added some detergent and water and then let it shake on the roof of the car for the whole day. In the evening we took the clothes out, and they looked pretty well washed except for the occasional colour run caused by dark socks on white T-shirts. But it didn't really matter.

We got into the car in silence and I still felt relieved thinking about the fair rotation system we had managed to agree on for sharing the driving. The driver changed every day and all of us rotated between seats in a pre-agreed direction. The map reader next to the driver became the new driver, and the one who had been sitting on the back seat went up in front and did the map reading for the day. As for the driver of the previous day, he could enjoy a day of no responsibilities and admire the landscape from the back seat. It was working well and it made me think that we had finally moved out of the storming phase and started to set some group rules.

It was half past seven in the morning and we were starting a new day of driving. In front of us the long, red, dusty road stretched into the horizon. In Africa the earth is always red. They say it's because it's full of minerals. The dirt road was red. The dust was red and it settled everywhere: in a thick layer on the car, on my face, on Richard's previously white T-shirt.

We were driving in silence: Richard at the wheel, Peter on the back seat and me trying to make sense of the maps I was supposed to be reading for the day. The one who drove got to choose the music for the day and so we were listening to a Coldplay song, coming out of the hi-tech MP3 player the car was fitted with. It was one of the few parts of the car that didn't give in.

We usually stopped just once during the day for a brief lunch break. The rest of the time we drove on, with the red earth road stretching in front of us and a huge cloud of dust – red too – at the back of the car. The sun set early, around half past six, and darkness came shortly after that so we always stopped at least one hour before sunset. We left the main road and drove for a while through the bushes until we felt we were reasonably safe and well-hidden. We always tried to keep the camp as hidden as possible. Then as soon as we stopped, the same routine kicked in: gather firewood, tents up, unload the car. Sometimes, like tonight, an extremely important event occurred: we were showering.

I got into my tent, changed into my swimsuit and emerged, only to see about ten kids of all ages looking at me with eyes wide open. Of course our small camp had not gone unnoticed. It never did. Somewhere far away, or maybe close by, there was a village, and even if we were not aware of their presence they were aware of ours, and these kids sitting respectfully some 20 metres away from the camp had come to check us out. Trying hard to ignore their looks, I moved to the back of the car, put my shampoo on the spare wheel and heard Peter's remark.

"A woman in a bikini! They must think their Friday prayers have come true..."

"I'm ready, Peter. Get the water going."

Richard was ready too. He stood next to me wearing his shorts, and was ready to swap places with me once I was all soaped up; not a drop of water would be wasted.

Peter turned on the water and it felt warm and good, and we were soon putting the shower on each other and laughing like small children would do in a bath. Peter thought this was too funny and grabbed his camera.

"Peter, what are you doing?" I had soap in my eyes but I could see him taking some indecent pictures.

"Just carry on!"

"Peter, I will have my revenge: your turn comes soon!"

Richard moved the shower on to Peter and we were spared from pictures for a while.

"Hey, water off!"

"Peter, leave the damn camera: water off!"

The water was turned off finally. I was still half soaped, though, but it wouldn't get any better.

"Here, hold this." Richard passed me the shower and started soaping up with frenetic movements.

"Water on, Peter."

"Are you two not done yet? I'll get my camera out again."

We switched places and Peter held the shower for

Richard while I ran to turn the ignition key on and off with water still pouring down.

"Shit! It's too hot."

Unlike a real bath, a shower from the jerrycans was either cold or hot. The jerrycans had been under the sun for the whole day and this was the result.

Some more laughter, and I failed to take some pictures of Peter in his underpants. The kids watching all this must have thought we were insane, but before the water ran out completely we were showered and somehow clean.

Clean and changed, we now proceeded to the next part of our routine: cooking.

It was usually a simple decision: pasta or mashed potato. The latter usually came out better, maybe because it was an English dish, but pasta soon turned into something that no decent Italian would touch.

That night it was pasta and we soon started the never-ending discussion about how long it had to be boiled for: *al dente* for me or totally overcooked for them. Richard was a very resourceful cook so we usually let him do the job. He washed the pot, where he had previously chopped the tomatoes and onions and poured the water on to the boiling pasta.

"It's OK, I didn't use detergent. It's just tomato remains," he said in answer to the disgusted look in my eyes.

Another pot, smaller this time, went on the fire and this was where a can of beef mince was mixed with all the spices in the world. The two of them would then add it on top of their pasta, while I only added two cubes of "La Vache Qui Rit". Dinner was served!

It was almost like a two-course meal: we used the spoon to eat the sauce first, and then the fork to eat the pasta left on the plate. Next a couple of drinks: gin and tonic usually and a sip of single malt whisky for Peter, and we felt at peace with the world.

We didn't usually talk much during these meals. It almost felt like once all the duties were performed, the camp was set up and our bellies were full, there wasn't much left to say.

Another pot went on the fire: this time it was cocoa, our last ritual before bedtime. It must have been no later than half past seven, but for us this was the end of the evening.

The kids were still around, squatting silently on the

ground some 20 metres away from us, in the same spot as when I first saw them. They didn't come closer and they didn't beg. They simply watched us in silence and we tried hard to ignore them. Peter took the pot with the remains of the pasta, placed it on the ground halfway between us and them and left it there. In the morning we found it in the exact same spot, only that it was spotlessly clean.

LATER that night my fears came true: it was not meant to be a peaceful night. I was woken up by the sound of a bicycle with a broken tyre. It came closer and closer. Maybe the kids of last night had brought a whole village to our camp and now we were about to be attacked!

"Richard! Peter! What's that noise?" I cried out in terror, without moving from my tent.

A grumpy voice answered, and I knew it was Richard in his tent more than 15 metres away, on the other side of the car.

"There's nothing. Go back to sleep!"

"Richard! What do you mean there's nothing? Can't you hear? It must be a bicycle! What if they attack us?"

"There's nothing, mad woman! Go to sleep!"

Peter woke up too, and soon we were shouting all three at each other, each buried in our own tent while the noise continued undeterred.

In the end I gave up trying to make sense of it and I fell asleep with a pillow on my ear so that I couldn't hear the noise any longer.

The following morning at breakfast, I froze with the cup of coffee in my hand as I heard it again.

"Look, there's your bicycle." Richard was smiling but I barely noticed.

A very big bird, the size of an ostrich, was walking slowly past our camp. It had very long legs and a long beak as well, and it gave out some strange sounds remarkably like an old, rusty bicycle with a broken tyre.

BANFORA

THE waterfall was not very tall, some 10 metres only, but the current was quite strong. As I took another step and felt the slippery rock on the bottom, I wished I hadn't listened to Peter's encouraging words.

"It's a great bath up there. It's like a natural pool. I felt like I wanted to stay in it forever."

I went up there as well, and now that I was in the water I didn't feel at all like I wanted to stay in there forever. It was more like, I would give anything to get out of there alive.

Another step and the inevitable happened: I slid, fell, was pulled along by the current and saw I was quickly approaching the edge of the waterfall...

"Oh please, God, please, NO!"

This was a silent cry but it worked. My nails grabbed at another slippery rock and I managed to get my fingers around a tiny edge. At least I wasn't advancing any more, but I was too terrified to move. Some two metres away from me I could see the edge of the waterfall, and the beginning of free fall for whoever was so unfortunate as to be dragged into the current.

"OK, slow, think. Just move slowly and think!" I told myself.

There was no point in crying for help. There was nobody around. Peter and Richard were setting the camp at the base of the waterfall, at the end of the free fall. Even if they heard me, it would take them at least 15 minutes to climb up to where I was following the path through the forest. Not to mention that I was completely naked and didn't particularly look forward to having them pull me out of the water in this state. I had felt so secure that there was nobody around that I had confidently left all my clothes on the bank and gone into the water looking for that small, beautiful, naturally formed pool Peter was talking about.

I knew I had to move, even if this would mean risking getting closer to the edge. My other hand tried to find another point on the rock to grip. It was all slippery and my nails scratched its surface in vain. Here was a small rock. This was better. I slowly moved my right foot. The water was cold and it came up to my waist. I figured out that if I managed to get higher up on another cliff, the current would have less force. One step, another one. I breathed deeply and let out a small sigh. It felt like I had found some solid ground under my feet.

In about half an hour I finally emerged from the waterfall. My elbow was bleeding and so was my knee, and my nails were broken from trying to scratch the surface of too many slippery rocks. But I was alive. "It wasn't really worth the effort," I thought as I came down towards our camp.

At the other end of the waterfall, my travel mates welcomed me with the usual comments about how long a woman can stay in the bathroom.

"Peter, next time I follow your advice I'll think twice beforehand." I didn't know why, but somewhere in my mind it was entirely his fault. If he hadn't told me about that nice pool...

"I was about to come flying down over the waterfall," I added, feeling like I owed them an explanation.

No comments. We left it there and went on with the cooking. Richard was boiling water, the same water he had taken from the bottom of the waterfall as I was washing on top of it. It didn't really matter. Nothing really mattered any longer. I was clean and it felt good.

LATER that night I was lying awake in my tent. It must have been well past midnight. Outside the darkness was deep: as deep as it could be under thick trees on a night with no moon. I knew it because I had unzipped my tent a couple of times that night trying to look around, trying to make sense of all those frightening sounds. Nothing. I could see nothing. I could only hear strange sounds, again and again and again. Back in the tent with a pillow on my ear, I hoped, I desperately hoped, I could sleep. But I couldn't, and this time the trigger for my panic attack was a sudden noise I heard just on top of my tent. If sounded like someone was laughing at me and the laughter was just there, just outside my tent.

I pulled the zip down again. I gathered all my courage and I looked around, my left hand holding tight the useless self-defence spray I insisted on placing just next to my pillow every evening before I went to sleep. I didn't even know if I could use it against a large animal. Outside, a cool breeze made the leaves of the trees whisper. The laughter was gone but the branches above me moved frantically. Maybe there were monkeys.

I threw another glance towards Richard's tent. I could see no movement inside: he must have been sound asleep. How could he?

Peter and the car were not there. The car couldn't enter the forest, the path was too narrow, so we had left it some

15 minutes' walk away and Peter had stayed with it, in his tent on top of the car. We had cooked here, though, since it was just beside the water, and Richard had decided to put his tent up here. I did the same and pitched my tent close to his, although not too close. I so wished now I had put it closer!

Back in my tent, I decided once more that I had to get over these childish fears. I closed my eyes and stayed so for a while, my breath shallow, my senses all sharpened and on edge. Another crack, this time coming from the ground just to the right of my tent, and I froze again. It must have been a large animal. Or maybe a man?

I didn't even dare to unzip my tent this time. I stayed still inside and tried to breathe and reason, but I knew it was useless. I was trembling, and I noticed the small Swiss Army knife moving oddly in my other hand. I was having a panic attack. I felt too scared to move, to think, to dare to breathe. I soon started to wish someone would attack us; at least that would have liberated me from the overwhelming fear.

The laughter came back. It was as if the whole forest laughed at my fears. That was enough. I couldn't bear it any longer. I unzipped my tent, determined that this was to be my last time. I put on my boots and got out of the tent. I would go to Richard and ask him if I could sleep next to him, in his tent.

I was out now and had already walked half the distance to his tent, and I noticed I was feeling a bit better. It always feels better being outside. When one can see around, one tends to be less scared of strange noises. I stopped. I felt embarrassed. How could I possibly go to him and ask to sleep beside him? What if he thought I was trying to seduce him? What could I have told him? "Can I sleep with you? I'm just too terrified to be on my own in my tent!"

I walked back. This was ridiculous. And the worst of it was that there was no way out. I could not go to him. I could not go back. I just stayed out there for a while.

BOROMO

AFTER dinner it was toilet time. Peter was usually the first one to go, his head-torch nicely fitted on his forehead, a spade in one hand and a roll of toilet paper in the other. From his pocket, a bag of soft, moist toilet tissues hung. I had given up laughing about that a long time ago. In fact they were a brilliant invention, and when you couldn't wash your bottom for days in a row you would really start appreciating the importance of a moist toilet tissue.

"Have fun," Richard said. "I hope the kids behave tonight."

Giving details about the health of our bellies and all the consequent discharges took up a lot of the after-dinner talking time, and it usually happened between the last bite of pasta and the first sip of cocoa. "Dropping the kids off" was the name of the activity, and it was Richard who came up with this very visual description. The kids could be stubborn and refuse to get out of the car: they might not feel like going to school some days. Another day they might be quite willing and quite runny, and this was when the poor dropper knew he had a problem. The kids could sometimes be quiet, sometimes loud, and other times a bit lazy. One way or the other, dropping the kids off was a crucial part of the evening and giving details about their behaviour was another one.

We all preferred to pick a certain direction and called it our toilet range. We didn't really want to be walking in anybody else's footsteps, even though we usually tried to do our best to dig a small hole in the ground and bury everything in there. Back in our seats, we exchanged a few details and I found out that Richard's kids were quite well-behaved that evening and Peter's a bit stubborn. But we all dropped them successfully and this was quite an achievement.

The night was dark, there was no moon and it was quite tricky to spot the camp on the way back once the fire was dead and the torches switched off.

"It makes me remember a story from Mauritania," Richard said. "We were camping on the dunes in the desert outside Ouadane and there's this Corsican lad who feels like he needs to drop the kids off in the middle of the night."

This was before Peter and I met up with him, while he was backpacking on his own and had teamed up with a couple of other travellers for a camel trek in Mauritania.

"So he gets up, doesn't take his torch and thinks he'll just walk behind a dune and then walk back. Once he's there he thinks he should walk a bit further, since he doesn't want the others to hear – just in case the kids screamed. So he walks a bit further and drops his kids and it's all fine until he starts going back. He doesn't remember where the camp is.

He walks up a dune but there's no camp there. He wants to walk in the other direction but he's not at all sure where the camp is. So he decides not to walk any further 'cause if he was to walk in the wrong direction, he would just get himself deeper into the desert and the others would never find him the next morning."

"Why didn't he shout?" Peter had a practical answer for everything.

"Don't know. Maybe he thought he was too far away. Maybe he thought he would look too stupid, shouting for help coming back from dropping the kids off. Anyway, he waits there for a while, not knowing what to do, and then he starts freezing. The desert is cold at night, you know."

Poor lad, I thought. This was not as funny as it sounded.

"What happened? Did you find him the next morning?"

"The Canadian girl who was with us couldn't sleep and she turned on her torch to read. He saw the light and made it back to the camp. He was lucky. He would have been there for hours otherwise."

I made a mental note that dropping the kids off and carrying a torch went well together.

ON THE WAY TO BOBO-DIOULASSO

"*Je demande un cadeau.*"

The kid in front of me was looking deeply and seriously into my eyes.

"*Je demande un cadeau,*" he repeated.

He requested a present. It was a bit of a weird way to beg and I thought that maybe it made him feel better. One can't beg when one requests.

Why were they begging? Because they were poor. Because they knew we had things, many things, things they would have treasured immensely more than we did: a pen, a T-shirt, some money, some sweets. Whatever. Anything. He was a small, black kid looking into the eyes of a *toubab* who happened to be passing through his village and had stopped at this well, and he requested a present.

Maybe he had done this in the past, and some other *toubabs* in another 4x4 who might have passed through this village before had thrown things at him. He might have taken those home and his mum might have been happy. An empty plastic bottle, a handful of sweets. Whatever. "*Je demande un cadeau.*" It might have worked for him in the past. It might have worked for those tourists too. They might have felt less guilty to be so wealthy, so much wealthier and luckier in life than this small boy in a village at the end of the world, in Burkina Faso.

Today he would not receive anything though. We were filling up our water supply at the pump outside their village. The water was free, it was there for anyone to take, and they knew they couldn't demand payment for it. They just demanded a gift.

What could we give them? A bottle of water? Some sweets? Some pens? Why would we give them anything? Was a pen worth the loss of self-respect that boy probably felt as he begged?

I still didn't know if it was right or wrong, if it was fair or not. I didn't give him anything.

ON THE WAY TO WA

IT was Lariam night and we had all managed finally to come to the same day of the week, despite missed days and delays. We couldn't drink alcohol the night we took Lariam and it made sense for the three of us to try and stick to one night of the week. We took the pill after we had eaten, since taking it on an empty stomach would probably result in a large hole in the same stomach. It tasted really bad and we had developed a particular way of swallowing it: the pill was placed as deep in the throat as possible, on the back of the tongue somewhere where it was not easily tasted. Then the victim swallowed a large mouthful of water and hopefully the pill went down with it. Sometimes it went the other way towards the lungs, and we coughed so badly that we thought our lungs would come out. At other times it got stuck in the base of the throat, and this meant you needed to bring it back into the mouth somehow and try again, but by then the horrible taste had diffused everywhere and the unfortunate victim felt like throwing up for a long time after the pill was swallowed.

The good thing about a Lariam evening was that I was less afraid of the countless sounds in the night. This was because the small pill brought with it very powerful and deep dreams: another of its side-effects, just like the aggressiveness we all felt and that we usually blamed on

Lariam. Because of the dreams, the nights we took the pill became our cinema nights and we each went into our tents wishing each other a nice movie.

The dreams were weird and very vivid, and they usually had a story with a beginning and an end, just like a movie. I liked Lariam dreams. They made me sleep deeply and escape reality for a while, and I didn't even have to try and make sense out of them. Unlike this trip, which had a beginning and would eventually have an end, and which sometimes seemed like a long, weird Lariam dream. Except that I still struggled hard to understand this one.

CHAPTER 14 – A CAR WITH THREE WHEELS

(BURSA TO ACCRA, GHANA, MARCH 2003)

ELMINA CASTLE

THE voice of the guide slowed down and became almost a whisper.

"This is where they kept the slaves before they loaded them on to the ships. About one in four died before even boarding."

She opened a door and we could see a small, low-ceilinged dungeon. It was damp and the smell was heavy, even though it looked clean. I wondered how it must have looked back in 1750.

Elmina castle was the most famous slave trade castle on the Ghana coast. It was a pretty, fairytale-type fortress that lay on a rocky promontory at the end of a palm-fringed beach. Like all the other castles it was built by the Europeans, in this case the Portuguese, and it served one purpose only: as a trading post for the Atlantic slave trade. Today a professional guide will tell you in a pleasant voice that it was built in 1482 and it's the oldest European building in tropical Africa.

Then she went on to talk about the 6.5 million people who were shipped from West Africa to the New World over three centuries. More than a quarter died on the way. During the 18th century, at the peak of the slave trade, about 5,000 people were leaving the Gold Coast every year: crammed under the decks of ships, kept in appalling conditions, starved, beaten, raped and abused.

On the back of this flourishing trade, European powers grew richer and richer. Elmina Castle, like many others, changed hands several times. The Portuguese had to hand it over to the Dutch, who managed to defend it against the Swedes, the Danes and the Prussians.

The Dutch were Protestants and built their own new church in a corner of the courtyard, choosing to transform the old Catholic one built by the Portuguese into a slave market. Inside the church and outside in the courtyard, the trade went on.

At some point the castle became a British fort. It was not until 1807 that Britain declared the transportation, buying and selling of slaves illegal. Ownership continued to remain legal in Britain until 1834, however.

The voice of the guide was inflexible as she quoted all these figures.

"These were the dungeons for the women," she said, opening another door.

"Women and children were kept separately from men. Every evening the door of the dungeon would open and all the women would be taken outside into this courtyard."

She carried on through the door and we followed her.

"The governor of the castle would come out on that balcony and take a look at all the women. He would choose one or several of them for his pleasure for the night. The chosen ones would be escorted by the soldiers up those stairs."

She carried on walking up a wooden staircase at the end of the corridor. Her voice was as monotonous as when she quoted the figures earlier.

"At the end of the stairs she would be taken by the guards into the bedchamber of the governor. When he had done with her, he would leave her outside his door."

We had climbed the ladder and were now in the apartments of the governor. The story went on.

"But this was not the end of it. The guards would then take turns with her, and then they would pass her to the soldiers downstairs. By the time she was brought back to her cell, she would have been raped more times than she could remember. The next day the ritual would go on and another woman would be picked."

We were back in the small dungeons where more than 2,000 people were kept at a time, and she took us to a heavy wooden door in the basement. This was the Gate of No Return: this was where the prisoners were taken from the fort and boarded on to the ships that were waiting to take them to the New World.

It was the end of the tour and the guide told us we could walk round and take pictures if we wished. We did so, in silence. There was not much we could say: the only appropriate thing would have been to ask for forgiveness. Forgiveness for being Europeans, the descendants of those people who had become wealthy by trading in the lives of others.

Just as we left the castle, a plaque by the entrance read:

In everlasting memory
Of the anguish of our ancestors
May those who died rest in peace
May those who return find their roots.
May humanity never again perpetrate
Such injustice against humanity
We, the living, vow to uphold this.

I walked out of the door, feeling relieved to be outside. The smell of the dungeons was still with me, though, and I looked at the blue sea stretching in front of the palm-fringed beach and I tried to remember that I was supposed to be on holiday, after all. Some kids were playing in the water but it was far too hot to be outside, so I headed towards the shade of some street food stalls, thinking it must be time for lunch.

"Roxana!" I suddenly heard a voice calling my name.

I turned and saw Toby, the Swedish guy we had met first in Bamako and then again outside Timbuktu. It was a small world. We chatted for a while and I found out that they had been OK on the way back from Timbuktu on the Niger River, as we left them on to the boat that morning. They had eventually changed to the boat we recommended, but because they had already paid the whole fee in advance they ended up paying twice for the trip. Then they had various other adventures and eventually made it to Ghana.

"Where is Alice?" I asked.

"She went back to Sweden," he said, and I noticed that his voice sounded tired, really tired. "You know, the heat, the mosquitoes; she felt she had had enough. She wanted to go home."

I didn't say anything. When I had first met them, about four weeks ago, they said they had come to Africa for six months.

"I'm going back, too," he continued. "We've spent all our money. It turned out to be a lot more expensive than we thought, so... This is the last country I'll visit. I'll fly back from Accra."

I wished him good luck. There was nothing else I could say. He looked sad and defeated. I remembered the old, uncomfortable feeling I had in the courtyard of Bamako when we first met them. There had been nothing I could do for him then either. There was nothing anyone could do. It was simply about each of us learning the lessons we needed, and luckily or not, Africa had one for everyone.

THE ROAD TO ACCRA

IT was my turn to drive and Peter was reading the map on my right. On the back seat, Richard hadn't said anything for a while and I suspected he had probably fallen asleep. All those Nurofen pills he had taken that morning would have been enough to send an elephant to sleep. His foot was as big as a watermelon and it had all started with a swim on the beach at Busua, where he stepped on some sea urchins. The needles were still in his foot and it had become infected, although he had tried to prevent this by cutting the wound open with his knife. I always doubted cutting it open was such a good idea.

The road was not so bad: we were driving on tarmac, which was quite unusual. I was driving faster than normal but I barely noticed. It was hot, really hot, and really humid. My T-shirt was wet with sweat. Outside the windows, the scenery of a tropical paradise unfolded: on the right, the sea with golden beaches; on the left, the edge of the rainforest with huge tree trunks and lush vegetation. We passed through villages and towns but we didn't stop. We were going to the capital, to Accra.

We didn't talk a lot while we drove. The music was always on and since it was my turn to drive I got to choose, so it was Alanis Morissette today. I liked her. My travel mates didn't, and every time one of her songs was on I had to put up with comments like the one that came now from Peter.

"This whining cow again! Come on, let's switch to something else!"

I ignored him. I was quite stubborn sometimes, and Alanis stayed with us and went on about the love she lost and how depressed she felt about it. Out of the open window I saw a huge bug, maybe just a bee but the giant type, entering the car. To my horror, it decided to take a seat on my lap.

I hate bees. I get quite nervous and uncontrolled next to them. I had to stop the car urgently, otherwise we might have had an accident.

I pulled up on the right, as gently as I thought I could. The monster bee was still on my lap. The car came to a stop, gearstick neutral, handbrake on. I jumped out and the cry that had risen in my throat and was blocked there finally got out. I moved my arms in a strange dance, trying to get rid of the bee that now seemed like it wanted to find another spot on my T-shirt for its afternoon nap.

"Roxana, are you mad?" Peter's voice came from far away.

I was in the middle of the road now and I still fought my enemy.

"What on earth is this?" Richard's voice showed he was awake after all.

"Roxana's just gone mad." Peter communicated the situation. "She pulled up the car and jumped out dancing."

"It must be the heat." Richard gave his opinion. "She's gone mad with the heat."

I thought they must have been joking. I wasn't sure though. But my frantic dance had achieved its purpose and the bee was gone. I went back to the car.

"It was a bee," I said.

Two pairs of eyes looked at me and I saw more than laughter in them.

"A bee?"

"Yes, a horrible giant bee that came to sit on my lap! I needed to get rid of it. It's OK now."

I was catching my breath and tried out an indifferent smile.

"Next time it happens, please let me know so I can get my camera out!"

Peter wouldn't miss an opportunity to take an embarrassing picture of me.

"You looked like you'd gone mad!"

"I had to stop the car first, so I lived with that creature on my lap for a few minutes. How do you think that makes you feel?" I knew, though, that they couldn't understand such things; things such as why one would be horrified by bees. The same way they didn't understand why sometimes I felt paralysed with fear in my tent, listening to the forest laughing at me. They simply didn't get these things. Men were a different species sometimes.

We went back to driving. Alanis was back on and, having to put up with her "girly" songs, my travel mates were silent again. I felt revenged on them for their sarcasm.

At some point we stopped in a village. A woman with a large pot on her head came running towards the car. She was selling bananas.

"How much?"

"Three for 400 cedis. Only 400 cedis," she said, pushing through the open window a bunch of three small, ripe bananas.

"OK, I'll take five bananas."

"1,000 cedis."

"What do you mean? You said three for 400!"

"Yes, three for 400."

"And if I want five bananas, how much is that?"

"1,000."

I couldn't be bothered to tell her about economics and the laws of supply and demand. And about why price should decrease as quantity increases.

"OK, I'll take three."

"400 cedis."

I paid her.

"Do you have another three?"

"Yes. 400 cedis."

"OK, give me another three."

I bought six bananas for 800 cedis instead of five for 1,000. She was happy. I was happy. Who cared about economics anyway?

Some half an hour later I pulled up on the right again. This time it was not the bee: it was my hair that had escaped my ponytail and was getting into my eyes. Peter already had his camera out and the grin on his face told me he was expecting another show. I would disappoint him, and I felt good again about this small act of revenge.

"Another bee?" Richard's sleepy voice from the back showed some interest.

"No, this time it's her hair." Peter put the camera away.

I drove on, and although the car went well and the tarmac road made driving a lot easier than on previous days, I was feeling uneasy. And it was not a bee and not the hair this time. I felt like I was hearing some strange, metallic noises coming from the back of the car.

"Peter, do you hear that?"

"What?"

"That sound. Here it comes again..."

"I can't hear anything."

This, again, was about men being a different species. They also don't seem to hear the voice of the forest at night.

"There it is again. Did you hear?"

"No."

We stopped the car and went round it. Everything seemed to be all right. Peter must have thought I had gone insane. But I hadn't, and when all of a sudden the car pulled to one side and lifted its front right wheel off the ground I understood there was something terribly wrong. I could see fire or maybe just sparks coming from the back of the car, and it felt like we were about to roll.

"Don't brakeee! Keep on! Just keep oooon! Whatever you do, don't brake!"

This was Richard shouting from the back seat. Peter was trying to help me hold the wheel.

I did brake in the end. One always has to brake to come to a stop. We got out of the car, went round it and froze: one of the back wheels was gone. Completely; wheel and tyre and bolts were all gone, and the metal tube that normally went in it had left a long, deep cut in the tarmac.

We looked at each other and didn't say much. We didn't even try to remember that we had changed the tyre that morning and probably didn't tighten the bolts enough. We didn't even talk about the strange sound I had heard that must have been the bolts unscrewing. In silence, Peter went up to the roof and started unpacking one of the spare wheels, and Richard, dragging his swollen foot, went towards the edge of the road and waved to a couple of children who had come running towards us. They rolled a wide 4x4 Land Rover wheel between them.

After we changed the wheel, sent the kids off to find the

missing bolts and decided that the detached wheel was too damaged to be of any further use, we got back into the car, still in silence. This time even the music was off, but I didn't need it any more. I was feeling somewhat relieved and it had to do with two thoughts wandering through my mind. The first one was about gratitude: we hadn't rolled over and we weren't injured, after all. The second one brought a smile and it had to do with the three of us staring stunned at the tyre in the middle of the road, and then starting to unpack the roof rack in silence. Finally, it felt like we had become a team.

COCO BEACH RESORT

WE had arrived at this posh beach hotel just outside Accra by pure chance. We needed shelter for a couple of days while the car was getting all sorts of repairs done in a garage in Accra, and the city was too hot and too humid to survive. We thought we could persuade them to let us camp somewhere on the beach or nearby. We didn't want to pay the exorbitant prices they were quoting for a room. When you lived on £200 a month, which was about what I had spent in the last month, it was quite shocking to have to pay half of that for one night in a hotel room.

We spoke convincingly and the guy at the reception seemed pleasant and welcoming. He gave us a long speech about what a special place their hotel was, and we were afraid that our last offer of 20,000 cedis to pitch a tent for the night would have to be increased. And it was already a lot: about the equivalent of 150 bananas in this country.

The smile on the face of the receptionist got wider and he seemed to be about to reach the end of his speech. He had told us about the swimming pool we would have been able to use and the nice beach stretching in front of the hotel; about the pool bar and the air-conditioned restaurant available should we want to use it; about what an exclusive place this was and that they normally didn't allow people to pitch tents there. We were expecting to hear the last price increase, but no: 20,000 was all he wanted despite the impressive sales pitch.

We agreed. Within one hour we were in our swimsuits, resting on the pool chairs of the most luxurious hotel I had seen in a while. The car was badly damaged again and it was likely to need a few days' worth of thorough health checks, but we could hardly have found a better place to wait. Richard's foot was getting back to normal and he was also getting out of the *English Patient* mood he'd been in for the last week. Peter's jokes seemed to have become milder, too, and above all I was looking forward to sleeping within the walls of this hotel. Unlike wild camping, I thought that I would not get so worried about strange sounds here in this oasis of civilisation.

We ordered a pizza. This was a rare treat: something reserved for a great occasion, like when one reached a capital after spending days in a row in the bush. The pizza in question cost 40,000 cedis, double what we paid to pitch the tent, or the equivalent of 300 bananas. It didn't matter though. One needed a treat from time to time.

Then we put up the tent, and because we could put up only one it was to be Richard's, since it was the biggest. We thought we would just use it to store our things and we would sleep outside under the mosquito nets.

The night had fallen but it was still hot: too hot to breathe, too hot to sleep. Soon a steady stream of guests started arriving at the hotel. Most of them went to the pool bar and ordered copious meals. There were white expats and rich Ghanaians, with women wearing expensive dresses and glittering jewellery hanging on the arms of men with thick wallets. Their children were nicely dressed and were playing all around the swimming pool, coming occasionally to our tent to ask if there was anything we were selling in there.

I thought this evening entertainment would stop at some point so that we could get back to sleep. But it went on and on deep into the night, so I decided to ignore it all and slide under my mosquito net and try to get some sleep.

I couldn't. And it wasn't so much because of the music that was going on at the bar just three metres from our tent, nor so much because of the children running everywhere and the conversations and the sound of glass and plates that came by as people around us were wining and dining. It had more to do with the feeling of being utterly inappropriate, of feeling humiliated at sleeping there, on the bare ground of such posh surroundings. It was strange, but it didn't matter sleeping on the grass in the bush. But here, it was as if we had entered another dimension.

For the first time in my life I was seeing the world

through the eyes of a beggar, forced to sleep on the streets in front of a posh restaurant where others were having expensive dinners. And it didn't matter that I told myself that I could go to reception and get a room on my credit card if I wanted to, that I chose to be there, to live that experience, and there was nothing wrong with it. Nothing I told myself mattered. Only the disgusted expression in their eyes as they walked passed my net towards their cars mattered, and I know they must have wondered about these three strange, white people and what on earth they were doing there.

They left eventually; all walked past my net and I had to put up with more and more inquisitive looks, and I felt confined in a sort of a human zoo. Only that this time, I was the animal in the cage. I vaguely remembered the Fula village we visited near Djenné and how I took pictures of those people. How would I feel if some of them took out their cameras and took a picture of me, sleeping there in front of their eyes under my mosquito net? The thought was unbearable. What was even more unbearable, though, was that I knew I had done this to other human beings. I felt as if I was receiving my punishment.

They all left in the end, and then I thought it would get better and I would get some sleep. After all, Peter was sleeping under his net and he seemed a lot less bothered about what others might be thinking of us. Richard, on the other hand, was hidden in his tent, and in that moment I envied him deeply for being protected by the thin canvas of the tent from all those pitying looks.

People left but mosquitoes came. My net was small and I was touching it occasionally as I tossed and turned in search of a more comfortable position. Soon I realised they had entered the net. I was all bitten and started to scratch frantically. I felt I had had enough. I had to do something, otherwise I would explode.

The night in Banfora when I did not dare to ask Richard for shelter seemed such a long time ago. This time I got up and went directly to his tent.

"Hey Richard, are you asleep?"

"Sort of... I would be if I was allowed to be. What is it?" The grumpy voice inside sounded surprisingly awake though.

"Listen, I can't really survive out here. The mosquitoes have come through the net, I don't know how, but I'm all bitten. Can I come into your tent?"

"Sure."

No surprise; no joke; even less grumpiness than I imagined. I felt relieved.

He unzipped his tent and by the time I got in with my mattress and pillow, so had most of the mosquitoes as well.

I settled inside and realised that Richard's tent was hot, a lot worse than outside, and a bit smaller than I remembered it. There was a big pile of stuff lying around: clothes and shoes and bags. We unzipped the tent again and threw all that stuff out. Some more mosquitoes came in. Finally, after some moving around we were settled. Richard couldn't sleep diagonally any longer but had his legs crammed into a corner. I lay on top of my sleeping bag, on top of the mattress, in another corner. There was hardly any air to breathe and I felt the mosquito bites on my arms starting to get itchy again.

"Hey," said Richard.

"What?"

"I think you managed to bring all the mosquitoes with you."

This was true. I could hear them as well.

Richard turned on his torch, and for the next 10 minutes we tried to catch the mosquitoes that had made their way into the tent. I had no idea how many we killed, but we were dead too. The fight with the mosquitoes helped the temperature inside the tent rise by a few degrees. It was burning hot and I felt the sweat running down my forehead into my eyes. I thought it was about the same temperature and humidity as one would find in the steam room of a gym back home.

"Goodness me. It's worse than outside. How could you sleep in here?"

"I didn't. I was trying to."

I suspected the tent was a lot hotter now, with two sweaty bodies lying inside instead of only one, and I felt guilty for having brought the heat and the mosquitoes to Richard.

Silence. I wasn't asleep and he wasn't either. Every breath made the air inside the tent hotter and more humid. I was lying on my back, still, on top of a wet sleeping bag.

I felt Richard moving.

"Where are you going?"

"Out of here. I'll take a dip in the swimming pool. I need to cool down."

He got out, and during the process of zipping and unzipping the tent some more mosquitoes came in.

After a while he was back. There was no way one could survive outside. One would have been eaten alive by mosquitoes. The pool was the only place to escape them, but even then he had to keep his head out of the water and that was a feast for mosquitoes. He got back in and crawled on to his mat in the other corner of the tent. Because sweaty bodies generate more heat, we were trying to keep as far away from each other as possible.

I breathed in and out and concentrated on the movement of my lungs. I told myself that if I concentrated hard enough, the heat would disappear and the mosquitoes as well and I would enter another world. I desperately wanted to believe in self-hypnosis. Every breath I took brought a burning hot sensation into my lungs. Every breath I exhaled added another layer of sweat to my face.

Breathe in, breathe out. Concentrate. Breathe in, breathe out. Again. Breathe...

I was going to die if I didn't get out.

"Richard."

"What now?"

"I need to get out. I'll die of asphyxiation if I don't."

He didn't answer. He was probably concentrating on his own breathing.

I went out, unzipped the tent and zipped it back up. Some more mosquitoes must have gone in to Richard by now.

Outside it felt a lot better. For a few minutes, until I felt the attack of the mosquitoes. I went back under my net and tried to arrange it better this time. I soon started feeling itchy everywhere and I understood that it didn't really work. We were in the heart of the malaria region and being bitten by countless mosquitoes was not a joke. I'd better go back into the tent.

I didn't know how much time had passed since I got out. I didn't know if Richard was asleep by now or still struggling for a mouthful of air. I didn't know if he was alive, in fact.

"Richard."

"What?"

"Sorry, but I think I'd like to come back in. They've killed me out there again."

He unzipped the tent and I got in, trying to move as quickly as possible this time.

"No problem, young lady. Any time. Just let me know when you want to get out again!" He was sarcastic but surprisingly not grumpy. I was feeling stupid for my in-and-out movements all night, but it mattered less right now. All that mattered was to survive until the morning.

"Did you get any sleep in here?"

"You're joking? I'm still struggling to stay alive."

Back to the "breathe in, breathe out" technique. The night was dark and I didn't know what the time was. Morning seemed far away.

In the darkness of the tent I heard their sound and I knew there were still mosquitoes around, but this time we couldn't be bothered to try and kill them.

"Richard."

"Yes, young lady. I suspect you want to get out again."

His voice had an exasperated touch and I barely stopped a smile.

"No, but listen: let's keep the tent unzipped."

"Are you mad? They'll come in!"

"Yes, but at least we can breathe. Maybe we can spray some of the mosquito repellent around."

This was not a very good idea. All that would have happened would be that it would have got into our faces.

"Yeahhh."

Richard was not convinced.

I had another idea.

"We could use my mint patches: you remember? The ones I brought from Italy; we can stick them all around the tent opening and keep it unzipped. Maybe it will work."

"Or maybe it won't!" he said in a dry voice.

I knew he wasn't convinced, but there was no way we could breathe inside if we didn't unzip the tent. I put my torch on, looked for my small mint patches filled with natural mosquito repellent and stuck them all over Richard's tent. They smelled nice and we felt encouraged to unzip the flysheet.

For a while it felt better. Then, arms and legs started feeling itchy again and I knew my patches hadn't worked.

"I think you can throw your fancy Italian things away,"

Richard said.

"It would be a lot worse without them." I tried to defend my idea.

We'll never know if it could have been worse without them. We'll never know if it was even possible for things to get any worse, because we didn't bother to take them away and we didn't bother to zip the tent back up. We simply lay there in a semi-conscious state for the rest of the night, trying hard to stay alive: breathe in, breathe out. Another minute was gone. And minute after minute and breath after breath the night passed by, the way all hardships pass eventually.

And when I eventually saw the first ray of the morning sun, I knew we had survived.

Morning came and in the bright sun, all troubles seem less important. We had a whole day of lying by the pool ahead of us and the mosquitoes had left. Suddenly life was not bad at all. We went for a stroll, hoping to find some fat mamma with her pots serving breakfast. We walked past the shops that had started to open, even though it was still early. Nobody could sleep here after the sun had risen and they might as well have opened their shops at half past six in the morning. "In God We Trust Beauty Products" was open, and so was its neighbour, "Beloved and Rich Internet Café". Ghanaians were very creative people when it came to the names of their shops and businesses, and "Tears of Joy Ltd" was just another one of the many names I spotted on a sign. "Don't Mind Your Wife Chop Bar" was another wise name for a drinking establishment.

The stalls we were heading to that morning didn't have a name, though. It had just one small bench, and metal cups with Nescafé and condensed milk and lots of sugar. As I drank the brownish liquid, I noticed drops of sweat immediately forming on my forehead and dropping back into the cup. There was no need to drink anything here: it all got transformed immediately into sweat.

It was shortly after sunrise but one already needed the pool. Only there, surrounded by water, could one stop sweating.

I walked back and passed by another small shop that had opened its doors for business. I spotted its name: "People Don't Know: But Who Will Tell Them? Oh Father, Please Forgive Them". It was a meat shop and inside the barracks a bloke had already started chopping some cow legs. Maybe he, too, was vegetarian.

I used to think I'd like to have a hotel on the beach in the tropics one day. It used to be very close to my image of paradise on earth. I don't think so any more. It's simply too hot and too humid.

CHAPTER 15 – VOODOO AND BEDBUGS

(TOGO AND BENIN, MARCH 2003)

TOGO, ON THE ROAD

GRAEME was a handsome guy with strongly built shoulders. I have always been attracted by strongly built shoulders. He was blonde and had a clean-cut face with a strong jaw and shining, blue eyes. He was a fine young man, I thought. I also thought he looked like an available man. And I was in desperate need of one.

Graeme was travelling with Karl and another Dutch lad called Minded, and we had met the three of them by chance on the road. This time it was in Togo, in a small *auberge* just outside the capital, Lome. We stopped there for the night as well, and seeing Mavis parked in the courtyard we knew we would find some company.

We had a nice meal, one of those expensive ones we could only afford once in a while, and when all the others had gone to sleep I was left at the table talking to Graeme. He seemed a really nice guy and we talked about travelling and following one's dream, about how hard it was sometimes and about how some people felt as if they belonged to two different worlds.

Peter had already gone to sleep on the roof tent of the car. He would always choose to sleep on the car, even when we took a room somewhere in some decent *auberge*. He was too afraid someone would try to steal the car during the night and he wanted to keep an eye on it. As usual, Richard and I had taken a room together. It was expensive enough, and after having shared so many rooms and so many beds before, we were well past the *I cannot be bothered* stage. Most of the rooms had double beds and we would instantly go back to the routine we had developed in Guinea, in the small village of Sérédou. He left the room to me, I showered and changed clothes, I left the room to him, he showered and changed T-shirt, and when the night came we turned our backs towards each other and wished each other goodnight. And we were careful never to touch each other during the night.

To most of the locals we would pass as a married couple. Whenever I was asked if I was married I would say yes, pointing to Peter or Richard depending on who was around. Most of the other travellers we met assumed we were a couple too, although it must have been more difficult to figure out who exactly was in a relationship with whom.

The night was deep and I talked to Graeme, looking deep into his eyes. Richard had gone to sleep, telling me he'd appreciate it if I would be quiet when I came into the room. I knew that Graeme knew I was sharing a bed with Richard that night. I had no idea what Graeme thought about this. We talked some more and then it was time to go to sleep. Graeme didn't make a move on me. I didn't make a move on him. Did he think I was Richard's girlfriend? I'll never know. And he'll probably never know that I could have been easy prey that night.

I walked into the room as quietly as I could, and as I stretched my legs in bed and heard Richard's fast-asleep breathing I felt a mixture of relief and irritation. If I wasn't sharing a bed with him I would probably have shared one with Graeme tonight, and I wouldn't have slept much! I thought about Graeme's shoulders and about the deep look into my eyes and I felt a knot in my stomach.

Maybe it was better this way, I thought as I turned my back to Richard. To some degree it was amusing: it was as if Richard carried on looking after me even when he was in deep sleep. And this time it wasn't about protecting me from some aggressive local blokes on the streets of some town. It was about making sure I would be in the right bed that night, and he managed to do that simply by being there, deeply asleep.

ABOMEY, BENIN

IT was simply too hot, and in the burning sun of the late morning I felt like fainting. The man carried on talking but I stopped and lay down by a wall. I couldn't be bothered to listen any longer. I hadn't slept a minute the night before. And it was not because of fear of strange noises or because of mosquitoes. This time it was because of the bedbugs.

My whole body was itchy. Small, red lumps marked the places where I had been bitten. I had no idea where I got them from: maybe from one of the hotel rooms we had slept in previously. But last night, in my tent, it felt like those bedbugs had decided to have a party and they feasted on me until dawn. I had changed my clothes in the morning and I left all my bedding in the sun, sprayed with the most powerful bug repellent I could find. They say sunshine kills the bugs better than any repellent anyway.

We had come to see the local museum here in Abomey, the capital of voodoo culture in Africa, and we were curious to hear their stories. It was mainly about the cruel kings of Dahomey and the way they treated their prisoners of war. During the slave trade era, they would have at least one campaign per year with the sole purpose of capturing slaves from the neighbouring tribes. These were then exchanged for bottles of gin and sold to the Europeans. They would eventually gather all the slaves they procured and keep them in the coastal forts of the Gold Coast, nowadays Ghana, before shipping them off to the New World. Wherever we went in this part of Africa, we were followed by the ever-present history of slavery.

"The king had many wives. When the king died, all the wives would be killed as well. The tomb of the king would be here." The guide pointed to a corner of the courtyard. "The tomb of the wives was there, in the second courtyard. There was a tunnel built between the tomb of the king and the tomb of the wives so that they could continue to serve him whenever he demanded after death.

"We are here in the headquarters of the Amazons. They were an elite group of the army made up entirely of women. They would never marry and they would not have children. They would serve as guards for the king and would protect the king with their own lives."

The frescoes on the walls showed the women warriors

cutting heads off prisoners and drinking their blood. Apparently these warriors were fiercer than men. The order was created by King Agaja some time at the beginning of the 18th century. By the end of the 19th century, there were still some 4,000 of them. They were always the ones to lead the army's attacks, whether against other tribes or against the Europeans, who were the ones to name them the Amazons.

The guide went on about the temple of the warriors and about the ritual of getting drunk with gin supplied by the Europeans before a major attack.

I was lying down there, in the courtyard of the kings of Dahomey, desperate, mute and crumbling under the curse of bedbugs. I thought not even those wives buried alive, there under the very stones I was sitting on, could have felt more sorry for themselves.

Richard and Peter found me there, took me away and put me in the first room for rent that they could find in the village.

"Get into the bed and get some sleep! We're not leaving today. We'll get you disinfected before you bring the bedbugs into the car!"

"My clothes: there must be bedbugs everywhere."

"Don't worry, we won't burn them. Even though we should!"

I was desperate. After all the bug spray in the world, I still had new bites.

"I'll find someone to wash everything," said Richard, and he showed me two buckets of water. "Get rid of them."

I handed them the clothes I was wearing as they waited outside. Next, I poured the two buckets of water all over my body and I scrubbed and scrubbed until I was positive they must have all been dead. And as I slid naked into the not-co-clean bedsheets, the last thing I heard before falling into a semi-conscious state was a comment coming from outside about my mattress and pillow that would have to be thrown away.

And yet I fell asleep in peace. I knew they were there, outside, like guardian angels and that they would take care of me in moments like this when I felt I had reached the limit of my strength.

CHAPTER 16 – THE FIRST BAOBAB TREE

(LE PARC NATIONAL DU W, NIGER, MARCH 2003)

LEGEND says that the devil got angry with the baobab tree one day, pulled it out of the earth and stuck it back in upside down. That is why, to this day, its branches look like roots spread out in the air. It's not a tall tree; it grows on average up to 25 metres. But it's thick and solid, looking like it's stuck deep in the ground. It's leafless for nine months of the year and its bare branches reaching up into the air look as if they are desperately crying out for help. It looks dry: as dry as the earth it is stuck into. It seems frozen in the middle of a convulsion, and looking at such a tree one has the feeling its branches will start moving again, in some strange frenetic dance, reaching out to the sky and telling their story. It gives the impression of a magic tree, although it's not clear whether it shelters the good fairy or the bad spirit. But it transmits its magic to the people around, and above all, it does not go unnoticed.

For the locals it was a source of wealth: they made rope and clothes from the bark, medicines and condiments from the leaves and they ate its round fruits. To us, three foreigners lost in this strange land, it was a blessed sight. Since it grows in the savannah, the land where the air is hot but dry and the nights are cool, it meant that once we saw one we could be sure we would sleep at night. Humidity had gone and the Sahel climate, with its cool nights and hot dry days, had come back.

Although they can be found in various other parts of the

world – in India and Australia – baobabs and Africa are a perfect match. Above all they are a powerful sight, and the image of such a tree imprints the mind with the same force as the smell of the African dust, which is still in my nostrils today, and the taste of its mangoes, still on my tongue. *Mal d'Afrique*, say the French; Africa sickness, say the English. Both are right and this land, once touched, will stay with you forever, with its fire-like sunsets and the deep, red colour of its earth; with its mysterious, frightening sounds of the bush at night and the smiley faces of its people. And the baobab tree somehow contains all of these.

We were driving north, coming out of Benin and into Niger. The landscape slowly changed and the thick rainforest gave way to the savannah and the bush was thinner, and we knew that we were almost back to savannah and baobabs; we would be back in the land of the desert soon, back to the Tuaregs, although in a different country now.

It was another long day of driving. It was my turn again: I was blessed with extra-long driving days lately. Since it would have been too complicated to change seats every few hours, we had settled into the routine of one driver per day, no matter how long the day. Sometimes we only drove for two hours. At other times, like today, it was eight hours. I was tired, almost exhausted, and too proud to admit it. Having made such a big fuss about my right to drive and the need to find a fair system, I couldn't just admit I was too tired to do my part.

To my right, Peter had given up reading the maps. In the back, Richard had given up making his presence felt. It was a good seat, the one in the back; it was the seat of thoughtful meditation. It was like a reward for the one who had driven the day before. He got to do nothing on the back seat for the whole of the next day. There, one felt pretty cut away from what was happening in the front of the car, from the road and the maps, from where we were heading, from music and occasional conversations. But it felt good and we soon discovered that one could easily spend a whole day buried in thoughts, and we even started looking forward to our days of doing nothing on the back seat.

Peter had taken his sandals off. I didn't need to look down to know it. The smell of his feet told me all about it.

"Peter, could you please put your sandals on again? Your

feet smell."

"It's too hot, I need some air."

"I also need some air to breathe. Right now I can't!"

"There's nothing I can do, I know my feet smell but it's too hot."

"Come on Peter, I'm wearing boots and I'm not dying."

"That's your problem. I don't want to boil my feet."

I was getting angry. His feet really smelled, as if they had started a process of putrefaction.

"Peter, I can't take it: put your damn sandals back on!"

He wouldn't do it. He simply wouldn't do it. Strangely enough, we hadn't faced such a problem before. But there's always a first time for a new problem, and then a big struggle to find a solution. The second time it's usually easier: once a precedent has been set it will serve as the standard solution. This was what I was afraid of. I didn't really want to set a precedent of having to put up with Peter's smelly feet.

"Peter, you are selfish. You can't care only about your feet. I can't breathe in here."

"You're crazy. I can't smell anything. Richard, can you smell anything?"

As usual Richard avoided taking sides, and he did this quite skilfully considering the many arguments between Peter and me that took place every day.

"I don't know." That was the easy way out.

"What do you mean, you don't know? Do my feet smell to you?"

Peter tried to make him take a stand. Because we were three it was easy to vote. Whenever two of us agreed, the third had to follow. So now our dispute was up to Richard to decide.

"If you were here, would you have a problem with my feet?" Peter insisted.

"Fuck knows. I'm a guy and I'm less bothered. Maybe women are different."

Richard was trying hard to stay neutral. All very nice of him, but it left me and Peter with an unresolved problem. I went to plan B. I stopped the car in the middle of the road.

"What are you doing?"

"I won't drive until you put your sandals back on."

"Are you mad? I'm not putting my sandals on."

"Then we're staying here!"

"Then go away and let me drive."

"No, I'm not moving from this seat. We're staying here until you put your sandals back on!"

What could he do? Pull me away from the driver's seat by force? He would need Richard for this, and I felt Richard still wouldn't take sides.

"Roxana, move on!"

"Peter, I'm not moving anywhere. Put your damn sandals on!"

That was it. As ridiculous as it seemed, we were stuck over a pair of sandals. And in that very second, our whole trip south was stuck as well.

I turned the engine off. Peter looked puzzled.

"How long do you want to stay here?"

"As long as it takes. One hour. One day, one week. Until you put your sandals on."

I was feeling a bit ridiculous, and even more so when I heard Richard's voice from the back seat.

"Oh, great. Lovely. Absolutely wonderful. You two are like stupid little kids. Can you sort it out so that we can move?"

"Yes we can, if Peter puts his sandals on."

It went back and forth for a while, with Peter and I stuck in our positions and Richard swearing at the two of us from the back seat. Eventually it seemed that I won and Peter put his sandals back on. I drove on.

I was still tense and the victory I had just achieved didn't make me feel any better. The nasty smell disappeared, though, and we drove on for a while in silence. Then some 20 minutes later, I had a vague feeling that the smell was back. Peter had taken his sandals off again.

I stopped the car.

"Peter, do you think I'm an idiot?"

"Actually, yes. You're making a big fuss over nothing."

"You've taken your sandals off again. Do you think I can't smell it?"

"You've just driven on for the last 20 minutes while I had them off and it didn't seem to bother you!"

Now this was the wrong thing to say, and before we knew it we were back to shouting at each other with the car stopped in the middle of the road.

"Stopppp!" Richard shouted. "I'm fed up with the two of you!" He opened the door and jumped out of the car. At least outside he couldn't hear us.

Coping with the others around you is the most difficult thing while travelling, in fact. Why couldn't we just be perfectly nice to each other, polite and well-behaved, the way we would have been if we had met for dinner in a posh restaurant in the heart of London? Why couldn't we be more tolerant? Maybe because we were dirty and hungry and the heat had prevented us from sleeping well for more than two weeks. Maybe because we were living in a car, sharing it with two others, which meant we had a personal space of about 20 cm all round. Maybe because it was hard to be here: it was harder than we thought. And what was hardest was making allowances for the others, for their smelly feet and strange habits. Would we reach South Africa together? This question hung over us like a grey cloud and we didn't yet have an answer.

As for Peter's smelly feet and my sensitive nose, it took a while and some more yelling before we found the obvious solution. He took the plastic pot we used for washing dishes from the boot, poured some water from the jerrycans and washed his feet. The smell was gone and he could keep his sandals off. With over two hours wasted on this argument, there was only one question in the air as we drove on in silence: how come we didn't think of this solution earlier?

THE Parc National du W is set on the borders between Benin, Burkina Faso and Niger. Its name comes from the huge, W-like shape of the River Niger, which forms a huge bend on the park's Northern border. Apparently it's populated by a wide variety of species, from elephants to lions, and March is the best time to view them, since the animals are desperate for water at the end of the dry season and are easier to spot around the few remaining waterholes.

We had been driving in the park for about half a day and we hadn't seen a single animal. Wildlife in West Africa seemed to have evaporated, just like the waterholes in the bush. Animals were considerably fewer in this part of Africa, since the parks were relatively recent and many animals had been killed during the countless civil wars these countries had been through.

We were driving on a narrow dirt road, and the landscape around was the same as the one back home in Europe in the middle of the winter. There was no snow, but all trees, baobabs or not, were leafless and bare and seemed barely surviving, having sucked every little drop of water out of the cracked, dry land: they were now holding on with the last of their strength until the arrival of the rainy season. There was no breeze, no movement, and the still branches seemed frozen in the dry landscape rising high against the melting sky.

I drove with my eyes concentrated on the small dirt road instead of trying to spot animals in the bush. I was not losing much though. My travel mates and the compulsory guide we had had to load on the roof of the car had all been trying to spot a living soul for hours on end. There was nothing.

A small stone-like bundle, similar to many others, lay in the middle of the road. As I passed over it, I felt a small bump and I heard the cry of the guide on the roof of the car.

"Stop!"

"What is it? Did you see an animal?" There was hope in my voice.

"Yes, you just ran over it," the guide shouted back.

Had I just run over it?

He jumped down from the roof and Peter and Richard did so too.

"That was a tortoise. How could you not see it?"

The stone I had seen before...

On my seat I closed my eyes and tried hard not to think about it. Of all animals, it had to be a tortoise! We had a pet tortoise at home in my parents' back garden, and this animal has always been a symbol of home for me. I was feeling as if I had driven over my parents' home.

They got back in the car and the guide was angry and mumbled something about the animals of this park being protected. Richard asked me with an amused look on his face what on earth I was thinking as I drove over it, and Peter immediately produced one of his usual jokes.

"In the Parc National du W, there was only one animal left. It was a little tortoise, and it lived happily until Roxana decided to drive over it!"

"Maybe it's still alive," I said, trying to stop the tears in my voice. "They're very resilient."

"Or maybe not." Peter decided to put an end to my hopes.

I will never know if that little tortoise was still alive. We carried on driving, this time with my eyes piercing the road looking for other little, stone-like, brownish lumps. Tortoises are usually resilient creatures and I remember standing on top of ours in my parents' back garden as a little child. But that night, as we set up camp close to the borders of the Parc National du W, I couldn't think of anything else. My travel mates seemed not to be able to think of anything else either.

"Did you check under your tent? You might be able to find another one," Richard said as we set up the tents.

"No, she prefers to drive over them," Peter answered.

"I wonder if she did it on purpose, you know…"

"Stop! For God's sake, can't you two stop?"

They did, for a while. And then, as we were about to eat our mushroom soup made of powder from a sachet and cooked on the campfire, Richard added with an amused, evil-looking sparkle in his eyes:

"We should have collected it and added it to this soup; I wonder what tortoise soup tastes like."

Sometimes I hated them both!

NIAMEY was a busy, dusty and very hot city. It could have been any other city in West Africa. There were cars on the streets, goats wandering around and camels casually passing through. There were bicycles and motorbikes and countless black faces hurrying towards the central market. There were *toubabs* as well, embassies that we had to spend hours in waiting for visas for the next countries, nice little pizza places with exorbitant prices and countless souvenirs shops.

After coming out of the bush, this hassle was hard to bear. We were walking around, spending hours in Internet cafés trying to catch up with everybody else out there. We had a rest, washed our clothes, planned our road ahead and had a wander through the city, trying hard to keep our money away from the countless street vendors roaming around.

Escaping from souvenir sellers was a very tricky art, and one needed to practise hard until one became good at it. A simple "No" was usually not enough to prevent being dragged into such a shop, and multiple "Nos" didn't do the job either. The safest way was not to venture anywhere near a street with such small shops, but one was always curious.

The man looked at me with eyes wide open. I was about

to pay for the curiosity that made me enter his small shop.

"Please," he whispered. "Only 4,000 CFA."

That was quite a lot: about $8. One could survive many days with $8 here.

He grabbed my hand, and before I could say anything he dragged me to the back of his little room. On his fingers, he stretched out the glittering amethyst necklace with the big, heart-shaped stone in the middle that had grabbed my attention.

"Very, very nice," he said. "*Je vous en prie, c'est juste 4000 CFA. Je vous...*[19]"

I felt I had to go out. I didn't need to buy that piece of jewellery. I felt I should simply push him away, as he was blocking the exit, and get myself out of there.

But his hands were trembling. He was an old man with a face cut by countless wrinkles and huge, brownish eyes full of hope. He wasn't smiling: he seemed mute, desperate. His eyes, wide open, and his trembling hands said it all.

"*Je vous en prie...*"

Maybe I should have practised being tough. Maybe it was all about surviving and moving on. About sticking to the rules and not letting your emotions be played upon. But I failed. And as I walked out of his room with the necklace in my pocket and the exorbitant sum of $8 having changed hands, I felt that his trembling hands had taught me something important that hot afternoon on the streets of Niamey. Maybe one has to break the rules sometimes, simply to test their boundaries and maybe there's no one-size-fits-all answer for every situation.

---

[19] "Please, it's only 4000 CFA, please..." (in French)

CHAPTER 17 – FOUR CAMELS AND TEN GOATS

(TÉNÉRÉ DESERT AND THE AÏR MOUNTAINS, NIGER, APRIL 2003)

"I said no and it will be no. No way. I don't need you. You need me. So it's either my terms or, simply, no way!"

Richard seemed out of his mind. He was usually good at negotiating and we let him conduct the discussions, since he was the best one among us at getting a good price. But this time he was exaggerating.

We were in the building of the Office National du Tourisme in Agadez. A clerk looked at us with indifference. Next to him stood another man, the man that Richard was now shouting at. He was a Tuareg and a professional guide, and we were just discussing the price for which he would agree to take us into the heart of the desert for a week. The man seemed calm, but his round, black face was not easy to read. He could, in fact, be boiling with anger.

"Very well, *monsieur*. If you think these terms are unacceptable then I cannot be your guide. I hope you find someone else."

His voice seemed freezing cold. In the surrounding heat, which must have been over 40 degrees, it felt really odd.

Richard turned on his heel and told us, "OK, that's it. We're leaving!"

And then, just before exiting the room, he turned to the two men and added, "If you change your mind, you can find me at the Auberge Côtes D'Amour."

Despite the name of the *auberge*, there was not much love in his voice.

We all left in silence, and once out it was time to have a word with Richard.

"You're mad! You've just blown a deal. What's up with you? Why all this sudden anger?"

I had seen Richard's grumpiness before, but it was almost always a state he could command. He would be grumpy for a purpose, and that purpose achieved he would return to his usual smile. But today it was more than grumpiness. He had been aggressive, and this mood was not one to pass easily.

"OK, now are you happy? We're out of there with no deal, with no guide. I have no idea where we can find another one, and you know very well that we can't go to the Ténéré desert without a guide," I carried on.

"Didn't you see what a crazy price he was asking? This is pure rip-off. He'll come back," he added, and this time I sensed a note of doubt in his voice.

"He'll come back, you'll see. He wants this business, and he'll have it for a price which is more reasonable."

We were lodged at the Auberge Côtes D'Amour. To be more accurate, he and I were lodged there, as was most of the stuff from the car. The rooms were too small and too hot, but the roof was great and we had put two mattresses on top of the *auberge*. There was no courtyard, though, and Peter needed to find a suitable place for the car. As usual he would sleep in his roof tent, and tonight he was lucky. In exchange for a small tip to the guards, he was allowed to park the car and open his tent in one of the courtyards of the sultan's palace. It was probably the safest place in town.

The sultan of Aïr was around 40 years old and his ancestors had ruled over the Tuareg clans of the Aïr Mountains for about half a century. He was still the traditional ruler of the town today, even though his power was becoming more and more symbolic in nature. His palace was a low but highly spread-out structure of mud bricks. Several courtyards with gates in between one another. Lots of dogs, and I suspected Peter would have trouble getting a peaceful night's sleep in there. Some goats wandered aimlessly through the empty courtyards and out on to the dusty roads. The guards were half asleep in the shade, and the chief of the guards was enjoying his little, old black-and-white TV in his little barracks. He smiled, stretched out a hand for some money and suddenly Peter and the car were most welcome. He didn't turn down the volume of his little TV, though, and I wondered whether Peter would have more trouble putting up with the dogs or the TV through the night.

We were back in the land of the Tuaregs, and the ones here were so similar to the people in Timbuktu that we had trouble, sometimes, remembering that we were in another country. But for them this was not another country: it was still the Sahara, the only land they knew.

We were planning to go out into the desert and spend some days in the villages scattered around the Aïr Mountains. But for that we needed a guide. Someone who knew where the water wells were. Someone who could speak their language and who could somehow protect us from having our car hijacked, as so many other tourists had in the past years. Someone who was one of them. Someone just like the man with the round face and strong shoulders who we met at the Office National du Tourisme, and who had been recommended as one of the most trustworthy guides. His conditions were not easy to accept, however: the price was high, and above all he wouldn't venture into the desert with our car only. We absolutely had to have a second car, and this meant we needed to rent one, which in turn rocketed the price sky-high. We tried everything, and Richard put on his ultimate grumpiness show. But he let us walk out, and even though Richard seemed confident he would come back, I wasn't and I started doubting that our planned trip into the Tuareg lands of the Aïr Mountains would ever happen.

Richard didn't shave the next morning. He said he would keep his beard for when the guy "came back". He shaved very rarely, and only when we hit a town and had enough water around. Shaving took a few years off his face, and he usually feared this could hardly help the grumpy image he was trying to project for some hard bargaining.

We waited the whole morning in vain. Noon came and went and the heat of the sun increased, and we did what everybody else did in this town: found some refuge in the shade. And just before evening came, we saw the guide again. Richard said he would come back and he was right. But this time he had good news. He had found another car, a Mitsubishi 4x4 with two Spaniards on holiday and their driver from Côte d'Ivoire. They wanted to do a trip into the Aïr Mountains and hire a guide. And this meant we didn't need to rent another car and the guide's fees would be split in two.

I was not sure if this fitted within the boundaries of the "good things come to those who have given up expecting them" rule or if it was merely down to Richard's sense of bargaining. But one way or the other, we were leaving in the morning.

DAY 1

WITH the corner of my eye I could see his lips moving. His eyes were closed and his hands, turned palm up, were resting in his lap. I instinctively slowed down and tried to drive more carefully, as if I was afraid I might have disturbed his highly meditative state.

His name was Ibrahim, we had found out after the negotiations have been settled and we finally shook his hand on a deal. The price was right, the cars were there. The Spanish travellers were as eager as us to get going and Ibrahim seemed to think he had got himself some good business. It was April already and the start of the hot season here, and there weren't too many *toubabs* around interested in seeing the Sahara in the heat. The bulk of the tourists came here in winter and disappeared before the temperature hit the 50 line on the thermometer, just as it had at this very moment in the car. He must have been really happy to get some business before the season closed down.

We left the next morning after we had deposited most of our stuff in his house, another small, mud-brick building that he guided us to through the maze of the small streets of Agadez. He was obsessed primarily with two things. The first was forcing us to unload as many things from the car as possible. He kept on saying something about how we would thank him when we had to dig the cars out of sand; and we kept on arguing with him about those things we thought we couldn't leave behind, not even for a week. The second of his priorities was sugar for the tea. As part of the deal we had to buy all the food for the seven days, and he asked us several times that afternoon if we had bought enough sugar for his tea. Seeing a 1kg bag along with other provisions in the kitchen box, he almost had a fit. "This is what you call enough sugar?" Richard gave up trying to argue and just went and bought some more sugar.

The music was on and we had been driving for a while. I

didn't know if I should speak to him; if I should try to wake him up from his trance. I drove on in silence, trying to concentrate on the path ahead. Peter was on the back seat, too far away to speak to, Richard had gone in the other car that was following us, and Ibrahim on my right seemed to be lost in his own thoughts.

His palms came up slowly towards his face, and when he wiped them all around his forehead and cheeks I knew he had been praying and this was the end of it. He opened his eyes and seemed to have come back.

"Were you praying?" I asked him. I knew he was. And I also knew that a devout Muslim would pray before starting anything, like a trip into the desert for instance.

"Yes," he said.

"What were you praying for?" I went on.

"That we would come back. That the desert gives us back."

I suddenly didn't feel like asking anything else. I looked around. The landscape was more rocky than sandy, but there was sand in the air and sand on the horizon. It looked like we were about to lose ourselves in an ocean of sand.

"What is the biggest danger? That we lose our direction? That we can't find the way back?" I asked after a while, not managing to get my mind off his earlier comment.

"This, too, happens sometimes," he admitted. By now he was smiling, though, and I knew he was not too worried about this possibility.

"But you know the way. You said you've been here thousands of times."

"It is not the same. It is never the same. The desert moves. It changes. The dunes move, they change their shapes and their place. Everything changes."

We might have trouble finding the way, but I still didn't think this was the biggest problem we had. In the past month, 32 European tourists had disappeared from nearby Algeria. They still hadn't been found. We knew about it from the Internet news sites we used to check frantically every time we had the chance to go online. We also knew that the Tuaregs used to highjack cars from tourists not very long ago, and it happened even in the middle of the towns.

Agadez was also another hotspot on the Tuareg rebellion map in the mid-1990s. If in Mali the Tuaregs were demanding an independent state, here they only wanted an autonomous region in a federal country. They were as unsuccessful here as they were in Mali. And in both countries the central governments had sent troops against them and there were battles and blood. More than 100 people, Tuareg rebels, civilians and armed forces, died here following the beginning of the rebellion in 1990. At the height of the conflict, in 1992 Agadez became a closed city and the borders with Algeria were closed as well.

A peace treaty was finally signed in 1995, but it didn't make the region any safer. Banditry and sporadic violence were still reported, and some tourists had lost their cars around here. Some others had lost their lives, too, and right now all we were thinking about were the 32 people missing just over the border in Algeria, somewhere in the Sahara. This, I thought, was a bigger problem than the dunes that kept on moving.

"Do you think we'll have problems with the bandits?"

"Not really. Otherwise I wouldn't take you here, would I?" His eyes were sparkling with amusement. It was a dumb question. But if so, why was he praying?

"The desert takes us now and I prayed that the desert would give us back. May Allah's will be done," he concluded.

Then he told me a bit more about the Tuareg rebellion in Agadez a few years before.

"They were crazy people. They were driving around the town in their 4x4 cars armed with their rifles and they were talking of war. Madness. They scared all the tourists away. It was a very bad time for business."

"What did they want?"

"Autonomy and independence and all these kind of things. Stupid people. They should have known this would never happen. Not in this country," he said, with bitterness in his voice.

"But what do you think?" I insisted. "Do you think you should have an independent Tuareg state?"

"I don't know. I don't care. All I care about is my business and those people scared away my tourists," he said, as if he was avoiding answering.

"I think what they wanted was impossible. And you don't need all that shooting and killing to find out. You see, we're just too many tribes in this country; the Hausa, the Fula, us, the Tuaregs. Too many people; too different."

Maybe all conflicts were about one and the same thing in

the end.

"Anyway, I was happy when it was all over," he said after a while. "And we could go back to our business and take tourists around once more. It's reasonably safe now."

Reasonably safe. I had heard this before. This was what the websites said. This was what he told us as we struck the deal, when we asked him if it was safe to go there. This was what we told ourselves as we decided to go on and have a tour in the Ténéré, the desert of deserts, the most beautiful place in the Sahara; reasonably safe. What did this mean anyway?

DAY 2

IT was well into the afternoon when we stopped for a brief bite to eat. We had hit the sand already. The narrow, rocky piste that took us out of Agadez was a thing of the past. Now there was only sand. Sand ahead, building up in huge dunes that we could barely see because of the sun and the sand in our eyes. Sand all around, to the left and to the right, as if we had been swallowed up. Sand under our wheels, and this was the trickiest part since invariably cars got stuck. Sand in the cars, in our clothes, in our mouths and in our eyes. Worst of all, the wind had started blowing and I wasn't sure if this was called a sandstorm or simply a breeze in the desert. We could barely see a thing.

It was our second day in the Ténéré. Or maybe we were still in the Aïr Mountains: I had never really understood where one ended and the other started. But we were in the desert, judging from the sea of sand we had sunk into. The mountains were somewhere around us, too, and we could sometimes spot their sharp, metallic blue shapes reaching towards the sky. All around us lay the desert, the dunes, the silence. The Harmattan, the harsh wind of the desert that blew for half the year, was at its peak. The sun filtered through the many particles of sand carried by the wind and landed on the ground, creating the most amazing colour combinations. Today it was deep orange, and the harder the wind blew, the more the colour intensified. One couldn't see far away because of the wind, but one did not need to. We were in the middle of nowhere and the immensity around us was almost tangible.

"Bloody hell!" This was Peter. It was his turn driving and

I didn't need to ask what was up to know that we were slowing down. The clutch gave a loud roar and that was it. We were stuck again.

Out of the car. It was burning hot outside. Inside as well, but at least one didn't feel the wind inside. We were all covered, as covered as we could be, with long sleeves and long trousers and boots. I was wearing my Tuareg shawl called *tagelmust*, bought from Timbuktu, and it seemed perfectly appropriate here. The shawl covered half my face and my sunglasses covered the rest. I tried to expose as little skin as I could to the harsh wind blowing abrasive particles of sand. I had long ago come to understand why locals were so covered in the desert.

We got out of the car and started unscrewing the sand ladders. The metal was burning hot and we needed to be careful not to touch it bare-handed. My *tagelmust* came in handy for this.

Sand ladders came down and now we dug a hole large enough to fit them under the wheels, usually under the front wheels. Then Peter got back in the driver's seat and we pushed. Whoever was the driver for the day was a lucky person. Although responsible for having bogged down the car in sand, he was the one who could sit comfortably in the driver's seat while the other two pushed. The engine revved, the car moved a bit. We pushed harder and harder. The wheel spun again and we knew it hadn't worked. We knelt by the wheels and dug again, using our hands; it was just too complicated sometimes to get the shovel out. We dug another hole and put the sand ladders back in place. By now they had cooled down a bit so we could briefly touch them. We were back to pushing.

"You ready?" I heard.

"Yep."

"Now, let's go!"

I usually closed my eyes while pushing. It felt easier. My hands noticed that the metal of the car was starting to get heated as well. It was not burning hot though, like the sand ladders. Why was it, anyway, that the sand ladders got more heated than the body of the car?

"Again. Now. Push!"

On one hand, I so hoped that this time the car would move. On the other I so hoped it wouldn't, since I knew that what came next was harder than the digging and the pushing.

Somewhere far away I saw the other car, the one with the Spaniards. Ibrahim, the guide, was with them today. They drove around in a big circle. They couldn't stop. If they did, they would get stuck as well. They just drove around in this big circle somewhere far away, waiting to see if we could sort it out this time. We were doing the same when they were stuck. Only occasionally, when we saw they couldn't sort it out, did we look for a piece of hard sand where we could stop and then walked all the way to where they were and helped them push. They did the same for us and right now they were probably trying to understand if they should stop.

We pushed again and this time the car moved. Peter drove on. The sound of the revved engine got weaker and weaker. I knew there was nothing else he could do: if he stopped immediately after getting out of the hole, the car would be stuck again and we would have to go back to digging. The only way out was to drive on for as long as it took until he found some hard sand under the wheels or until reaching a small downward slope, usually on top of a dune.

He had finally stopped on the downward slope of a small dune. The car was now as small as a dot. Maybe it was because of the sandstorm that we couldn't see well, or maybe it was too far away. We picked up the sand ladders, I used a corner of my shawl to handle mine better and we started the long journey towards the car. We walked in silence, Richard somewhere ahead of me. He was always walking faster than me. It must have been because he wore sandals while I still wore my one and only pair of boots, which right now were sinking deep into the sand.

It happened so many times that I lost count. It happened to us and it happened to the Spaniards. We moved around and changed cars; Ibrahim jumped between us and the Spaniards, trying to give us more tips about sand driving. But it was all useless. We pushed and pushed and then collapsed on the seats for a short break when the car was finally moving. Then we dug and pushed some more. We let the tyre pressure down a bit more and by now they were half deflated. It didn't help much though. We didn't have sand tyres and we understood deeply what that meant: more digging.

At some point we lost sight of the other car. We were following their tracks in the sand and we suddenly realised the tracks were gone, or maybe just covered up by the sandstorm. We panicked for a while, stopped the car and climbed up on the roof, trying hard to see anything, anywhere around. Then we drove again and we found them again and we lost them once more. And then it all became of secondary importance as we got stuck again and had to dig some more.

By evening I felt knackered.

LATER THAT EVENING

I was lying awake in my tent and this time it was not Fear that kept me from sleeping. It was my belly. I felt sick immediately after I ate some of the couscous we had cooked that evening. I thought that everything would be fine once I threw it up, and I gave up eating anything else that evening. I crawled into my tent and hoped a good night's sleep would sort me out after that nerve-racking day. But it was not meant to be, despite the fact that it was cool enough and I even felt less afraid of darkness than usual. After all, we were a bigger group now, under the protection of a local guide, and this calmed down my ever-present paranoia about being attacked in the middle of the night.

But I was lying in a state between wakefulness and unconsciousness. I didn't know what it was but I was feeling sick, deeply sick, and throwing up the couscous didn't make it any better. Another violent pain stabbed my belly. Poison. All I could think was that I had been poisoned. I changed sides, tossed and turned. It didn't help. Nothing helped. My belly was on fire.

I felt another blow to my stomach and before I had time to understand what was going on I realised I was about to throw up again. Here, in the middle of my tent. Panic gave me strength and I jumped up, rushing to unzip my tent. The zip was blocked. As I struggled with it, some more of last night's couscous was also struggling to get out of my mouth. I couldn't get out of the tent no matter how much I fought with the zip so eventually I tore it, made a small opening for my head and threw up again, just there, in front of the tent.

The pain came back and I felt sick again. I was shaking. I was crying. I thought I was going to die.

I forced the opening of my torn zip and got out, trying to avoid stepping into my vomit. I tried to walk away but I fell down. I couldn't move any longer. In the light of the moon I could see the two cars parked some 50 metres away. The Spaniards' tent must have been somewhere on the other side of the cars: I couldn't see it. Peter was sleeping in his roof tent and Simeon, the Spaniards' Ivorian driver, was sleeping in the car. I had no idea where Ibrahim was. To my right, pretty far away, Richard had managed to find a thorny Acacia bush to hang his mosquito net on and I guessed he must be sleeping peacefully on his big pillow. All around us, the dunes were just as high and overwhelming as they appeared in daylight. Only now they were silent. The wind had stopped and there was no movement, no sound, no whispers. The desert was sleeping too.

My survival instinct took over my wracked body. I needed help. I didn't really know what type of help. I just felt I was about to die. I got up and staggered towards Richard's net.

"Hey."

No answer.

"Hey, Richard!"

No answer again. He was buried in his sleeping bag and I couldn't even see his face. I gave him a good shake.

"What?" Richard was as grumpy as someone just woken from a deep sleep could be.

"Richard, it's me. I think I'm going to die."

I sounded convincing.

"What?"

"I think I'm going to die."

He got up with slow movements. I didn't know if he had heard me or if he believed me.

He put the net away and I could finally see his face. His eyes were wide open.

"What are you talking about? What's this madness?"

"Don't know..." I was feeling too weak to explain anything, too weak to talk.

"What's up? What are you feeling?"

"Pain," I whispered.

"Where?"

"In my belly."

"Did you get bitten by anything?" I knew he was talking about scorpions.

"No... don't think so."

"What, then?"

"Don't know. I think I was poisoned. I think I'm going to die."

"Don't be silly!"

Just as I spoke, another violent spasm passed through my belly. I screamed and leaned down. I was lying in the sand by now and Richard was shaking my shoulder.

"Hey, get up! Come on, what's all this?"

I felt frozen. I suddenly felt like the temperature had dropped to freezing point and I was shaking. I couldn't speak.

"It's all fine! Don't worry, it's all fine!" Richard tried to calm me down. "Where's your tent?" He looked around and spotted it in the distance.

"I'll just carry it here. You're shaking. You need to get into your sleeping bag."

He got up and walked away, and I couldn't stop thinking of my tent with the broken zip surrounded by the traces of my sickness.

He came back shortly, dragging my tent along with him. There was someone else walking back with him. It was Ibrahim, our guide.

"What do you feel?" Ibrahim asked.

"Pain."

"Where?"

"Here." I put my hand on my belly.

"What kind of pain?" he asked again.

"Very sudden, very sharp."

"Did you throw up?"

"Twice."

"How about your head?'

"Sore... exploding. Ibrahim, am I going to die?"

"Don't think so."

This was not reassuring enough for me.

"I think I've been poisoned. The food... the couscous."

"It's not the food," he said convincingly. "It's the heat. You've got heatstroke."

I was about to protest but I hadn't any strength left. I just lay in the sand, feeling miserable. Nobody believed me when I said I had been poisoned and I was about to die.

Richard was listening to all this without a word. He had put my tent next to his mosquito net and seemed like he was not sure what to do next.

"She'll be fine," Ibrahim said. "It's just heatstroke. It happens. She'll be fine by tomorrow morning."

"Can I give her anything? Any pill?"

"No pill can help. Her body needs to cope with the heat."

I wanted to disagree. I wanted to tell them that it was not possible to have heatstroke after living in this temperature for four months now. I wanted to tell them that I felt frozen, in fact, and not at all hot. But I couldn't say a word. Another blow to my belly made me scream.

"Get her in the sleeping bag and get her to sleep. She'll be fine." Ibrahim seemed convinced of what he was saying. He then told Richard to wake him up if it got any worse and walked away.

Richard and I were looking at each other. I was still shaking. He put his mosquito net away and pulled his mat closer. He then pulled me up and got me seated on his mat. He sat next to me and stretched his arm around my shoulders. I was still trembling but his arm around my shoulders felt good and warm. I remembered the night when I had been crying in Burkina Faso and he told me that story about the old man and his soaps. He hadn't put his arm around my shoulders then.

"It's fine. You'll be fine. You heard him, it's just heatstroke."

"He's got no idea. This can't be heatstroke. I'll die of poisoning."

"Don't be silly."

I was more than silly. I was desperate. The pain came and went and I wondered if it was like one would feel in childbirth.

"You're shaking. You need to get into your sleeping bag. You need to get some sleep, it will make you feel better."

He got up and pulled my tent closer. He managed somehow to open my jammed zip and took out my sleeping bag. I noticed my tent looked clean. Was it that I was not sick on it as I thought, or had he managed to clean it somehow before dragging it over?

"Come on, get into the tent."

"I can't sleep... it hurts."

"You won't, then. We'll talk. But you need to get into this sleeping bag."

I felt like a two-year-old, incapable of saying no to her

mummy. I got into my sleeping bag. I felt warmer and a bit better.

"You know, I think Ibrahim is really funny. Sometimes he's like a child, with his sugar and all that." Richard still couldn't forget his many trips to buy sugar for our guide the day we left Agadez.

"Where has he gone now?" I asked. It felt better to be talking about something else.

"Fuck knows. Sleeping somewhere. Under the cars wrapped up in a blanket maybe, who knows? I don't think he's got a tent."

For a while we spoke about our weird guide and his multilingual habits: he spoke English to my two companions, Italian to me, Spanish to the Spaniards and French with Simeon, the driver from Côte d'Ivoire. At some point I felt my eyes grow heavy and I felt dizzy. I lay down inside my tent and Richard lay on his mattress, and we carried on talking through the thin flysheet. We talked about Ibrahim, about desert driving, about the dunes. Richard was doing most of the talking and I barely answered with some "uh-huhs" or "ohhs". Then, as I slowly drifted asleep and his voice remained somewhere far away, I felt a warmth flow into my belly and for the first time that night I thought that maybe I wouldn't die.

I don't know how much longer Richard talked to me that night after I'd fallen asleep. I don't know if he got any sleep at all. All I know is that as I drifted in and out of sleep and moved and tossed, I heard him on the other side of the flysheet every time, asking me if I was all right. And there was this force coming out of his voice, as if what he was trying to say was deeper than just asking me if I was fine. It was more a sort of "you'll be fine, you'll make it through the night and you'll even make it through this trip, and I'll be here for you in moments like this when you doubt that you'll survive". And his voice kept on going into the night and I fell asleep in the blissful certainty that he was there for me, and because of this, one way or the other, I was going to make it and I would be just fine...

DAY 3

THE next morning I was feeling better, the sun was bright and there was no sandstorm for a change. Ibrahim was not very pleased though.

"Tough driving today," he said laconically over breakfast as he sipped some more of his very sweet tea.

"Why? Will it be worse than yesterday?" I asked, thinking that the day before we had had to push the car out of sand more times than I could remember. Could it get any worse?

"A lot worse," he confirmed. "Not because of pushing. Because of the dunes. Very high dunes today. It will not be easy to get over them; not with these two cars. If you had listened to me and got my car it would have been a lot better. But with these two..." He moved his hand in despair. "Too heavy: your cars are too heavy. Too many things inside. That's why we need to push on and on."

I had no idea what else we could have taken out of our cars to satisfy him. Our entire luggage was left back in Agadez, but the cars were still too heavy for his taste. He had insisted we took his car but the price was a lot higher and it was one of the points on which Richard had lost his temper during the stormy conversation we had at the Office National du Tourisme. We won: he didn't take his car and we didn't have to pay for it. And as a result we might not now be able to get over those dunes.

"*Le Col de Temet. Il est dur... il est toujours dur*[20]." Ibrahim was lost in his thoughts.

"Everybody, listen. I need to tell you some things about dune driving today. It's very simple. But if you don't get it right, it can be very bad."

Silence. So far it made sense.

"So you need to get it right from the first trial. Otherwise, two things can happen. One: your car rolls, or two: you slide back to the base of the dune and get stuck there. We don't want any of those things to happen. Clear?"

Very clear.

"The dunes are very steep. What does this mean? It means the car needs to go up them straight. Bend the wheel to the right and you roll. Bend the wheel to the left and you roll again. What does this mean? If you don't want to roll, don't bend the wheel."

Clear again. It sounded easy.

---

[20] "The Col de Temet is tough... it's always tough." (in French)

"We need to go up as quickly as we can. Build up the speed at the base of the dune. Stay in a low gear. Let the engine push, keep it revved high in between three and four. Once you start going up, put the accelerator to the floor and pray. And keep the wheel straight."

His face was serious now and I thought that maybe it was a lot more complicated than it sounded.

"If your speed is right and if the weight of the car is not too much" – and here the look in his eyes seemed to add "this is not the case with yours" – "and if you're lucky. you'll make it," he carried on, deciding not to bother any more about the unsolvable problem of too much weight in the car. "If the car loses speed and stops, let it slide down to the base of the dune. But keep that wheel straight. Nothing bad will happen if you keep the wheel straight. If you don't, this is when you roll."

It made sense. It was almost like a Physics class about gravity and the result of applying force.

"If you need to slide down to the base of the dune, just drive away as far as you can. You need to have the space to build up your speed before attacking the dune again."

Silence. We were all listening and it seemed less funny.

"If you make it to the top, remember you must stop there. You must stop on the top but you must stop just as you reach the top. If you stop too soon, you'll slide back and have to let the car go back all the way. If you stop too late, you'll roll down the other side."

Again this bloody rolling.

"The dunes are not shaped symmetrically," he continued, and this time he drew the shape of a dune with his finger in the sand. "On one side they are less steep than they are on the other. This is usually the side we drive up. On the other they are a lot steeper. It's because the wind usually blows from one direction and shapes the dune on that side. On the other side, sometimes it's as steep as a precipice. That's why you need to stop on the top of the dune, before falling down the other side!"

All very clear. Suppose we manage to perform this masterpiece of equilibrium – then what do we do, hang on top of that dune forever?

"Before you go down, you need to understand how the dune is shaped. You need to be able to find the perfect, straightest angle and go down by it. If you turn to the right, you will roll. If you turn to the left, you will roll again. If you keep it straight you'll go very, very fast, almost like a free fall, but you will not roll. Clear?" We agreed in silence.

"Now, I'll drive the Mitsubishi," Ibrahim continued. "It is heavier than the other car and it will have more trouble passing over the dunes."

Simeon produced an instant smile of relief. He was the driver from Côte d'Ivoire and had probably never seen sand dunes in his life before.

"Who is driving the other car?"

Peter, Richard and I were looking at each other. We all knew that today was my driving turn.

"Oh, no!" Ibrahim cried when he found out the answer to his question. "Oh, no! Allah have mercy upon us! Allah have mercy upon us!" he repeated. "We're crossing the Col de Temet today and a woman is driving! Allah..." His voice became dimmer and dimmer as he walked away from us. It seemed that he had suddenly lost his appetite for tea. I suspect he went to pray for a miracle.

My travel mates didn't invoke God but they had also lost their appetites. I looked at them and they looked back at me. I knew there was trouble in the air.

"You're not driving today," Peter said, his voice as cold as ice.

"What do you mean?" I was already boiling.

"You heard him. You heard all about this dune driving. I don't think you can drive today. You've never driven on a dune before."

Ever since we had set the driving routine back in Burkina Faso, we had never, ever broken it. One of us drove every day, each day a different one, in the same order: Peter, Richard, and me. No matter how long the drive, how hard or how easy. Another day, another driver. And today it was my turn.

"Have you driven on the dunes before? Why do you think you can do a better job?" I was really furious now.

"Because this is my car. And if it rolls over a dune, I prefer to roll it myself." Peter was as inflexible as he could sometimes be.

Richard had been silent so far and I turned towards him with hope in my eyes. As always, when Peter and I disagreed it was up to him to strike the balance.

"Roxana, I don't think you should drive today," Richard

said, and his voice sounded frozen too. "Look, it's too dangerous; you've never done anything like this before. Peter is right, the car is his and he should take the responsibility..."

My eyes suddenly filled with tears and I tried hard not to let them out.

"Come on, don't you see? It's easy to understand!" he carried on convincingly.

It might have been easy and it might have been obvious. But all I could see was that I wasn't allowed to drive, just because I was a woman, and this made me mad. We went on quarrelling for a while and I tried all the arguments I could find. But it was in vain. As usual, when two of us took a decision, the third had to obey. And I obeyed with hatred in my eyes, and I felt even worse on seeing Ibrahim's wide smile when he spotted Peter in the driving seat. He must have thought Allah had listened to his prayers that morning.

I chose to get into the Mitsubishi that morning, next to Ibrahim. I couldn't stand being close to my two travel mates. Their unjust decision was too much for me to bear. If I thought hard, I knew somewhere deep down that it made sense and that Peter should be the one to take the risk of driving that day. It was his car, after all. But I would never have admitted it. All I could think about was that I was discriminated against for being a woman.

Ibrahim tried to make me feel better but a Tuareg was hardly the ideal partner to talk about the rights of women. We set off driving, and for a few hours those frightening dunes failed to materialise under our wheels. They were all around, tall and mighty in their soft, pink morning colours, but we drove around on a flat surface.

"We'll come to the pass soon." Ibrahim answered my impatient look.

"Does it really happen? Rolling the cars, I mean?" Ibrahim's frightening story of the morning seemed to be a bit surreal.

"I hope you won't see it. It happens. But it's not too bad. If everybody is wearing a seatbelt it shouldn't be too bad, as long as the car can be put back on the wheels."

"And if it can't?"

"We leave it here and we drive on in the other one to get some help."

This was one of the reasons one needed at least two cars

in the desert.

"Is this the worse that can happen?"

"A lot of things can happen. Cars roll, mines blow, people get attacked."

I knew he was referring to the gunpoint car hijackers that roamed these lands not very long ago.

"I was talking to a friend of mine the other day. He's a guide as well. He'd been out with a group of Italian tourists when they drove on to that mine in Chad, close to the Libyan border."

I had heard about this story. A landmine buried in sand, forgotten from who knows what war many years ago. A tourist jeep drove over it and blew up. Four people died.

"He was one of the guides of the group. The car exploded just in front of him."

"Were there more explosions?"

"Just one. The others were driving a safe distance behind."

One always leaves a large distance between cars when driving in the desert. I used to think it was so that one car did not get bogged down in sand when the car in front stopped as well. Now I thought there was at least one other explanation for the distance.

"There were four men in that car. All dead. One of them survived for a few hours but he was trapped under the remains of the car and the others could not get him out. He died there."

"Did they not go out for help?"

Ibrahim smiled grimly.

"They did. It took two days to find the closest army barracks and two more days to persuade the army to come and help. Not much they could do. They couldn't even lift the carcass of the car: they didn't have the tools, you see."

I could imagine that not much help would be available at the Chad–Libya border. How about here? We were still in the middle of the wilderness heading towards Timia, an oasis in the desert. There might have been some help there. There was surely help in Agadez, some two or three days' drive away. There was also the town of Arlit somewhere around, maybe another two or three days' drive, and which had one of the biggest uranium mines in the world. It still belonged to France, who fed all their atomic centrals with its production.

But in the immensity of the sand, all those things seemed

far away. Distance, much like time, was relative, and the help one could rely on was relative as well. I suddenly understood better why Ibrahim had been praying at the start of our journey.

"You know, everybody has a fate. You cannot escape your fate. If your fate is to die in a desert, you will die. If your fate is to survive, you will survive."

Like all Tuaregs, Ibrahim was deeply superstitious.

"Like with this car that blew up two months ago," he carried on. "A young girl had been travelling in it for the whole day. She was the daughter of one of the men who died. It was a big group, you know: several men, their wives and their children. Anyway, this girl travelled with her dad in the car in front for the whole day. Half an hour before they hit the mine, they had a break and her father told her to change places with a guy from another car. Her father wanted to talk to his friend. The girl did not want to go but the father insisted. That's why she is alive today while her father and his friend are not. You see, one cannot escape fate!"

His voice was mellow and I could sense his sadness. He probably knew many of these stories about people whom the desert had taken and decided not to give back. And yet he was here again, taking other tourists to other meetings with fate.

"Anyway, not all trips end badly," he said after a while, trying to cheer me up. "I had many groups who went back home happy: especially Italians. You know, I like Italians a lot. They are happy people; they talk a lot." He smiled.

"I need to talk, too, when I'm with them. I need to tell them something every second, otherwise they ask more and more questions. *Il sultano ha fatto, il sultano ha cagato…* you need to speak a lot for people who are paying €100 a day to be here."

We were paying a lot less than this and I concluded that Ibrahim therefore felt himself to be less an employed guide and more an occasional helper.

"So tell me, what's the story with you and these two men you travel with in your yellow car?" he asked, changing the subject abruptly.

"No story. We're just travelling together."

"Are they your relatives?"

"No."

"Are they your boyfriends?" Did he mean either of them, or both of them at the same time? I didn't ask him to clarify.

"No."

"Neither of them," I added.

He paused. I guess that, in spite of his perfect command of the Italian language and years of exposure to *toubab* tourist mentality and culture, he struggled to understand.

"What on earth are you doing with them, then?"

"Going south. We're crossing Africa."

"Why?"

This was a tougher question than he probably imagined.

"Because we felt like it."

I didn't really have a better answer.

"Because we always wanted to do this and we found an opportunity now."

"And then?"

"Then what?"

"When you have gone all the way south and the road has stopped at the ocean?"

He probably meant when we reached Cape Town, the agreed terminus point of our trip.

"Don't know."

I really didn't know, and this was one of the questions that started haunting me day and night.

"Go home, I guess. Carry on with our lives."

I knew it didn't make sense to him. It almost didn't make sense to me either. But it was simply the way it was. I was thinking a lot about what I was going to do at the end of the trip. I had written several emails to Chris, my Namibian guide of last year, along the way and I'd asked him if he had a job for me. He said he could use me as an assistant safari guide for a few months at the end of my trip and I accepted immediately. I thought it was the perfect solution: it would give me some more time in Africa and it would give me some more money too. But the question remained in my head...

I didn't have an answer yet. But that morning, in the immensity of the ocean of sand, this question seemed too far away – much like the unlikely help we would expect to get if things didn't work out well with all that dune driving.

We did do some dune driving in the end. And we did slide back to the base of the dunes many times, just like Ibrahim had said we would. And then we flew over dunes at full speed, praying with all our hearts that we would find the right place to stop on the crest just before falling down the other side. We drove up and we drove down again and we drove up again, until the whole world seemed reduced to these mighty piles of deep, pink sand. Peter drove first and then, with one of the sudden attacks of generosity that he experienced sometimes, he turned to me and asked if I wanted to try my hand. It was an armistice offer – after all, I hadn't spoken to either of them for the whole morning – and I accepted it immediately.

With my heart pounding, I pressed the accelerator to the ground far, far away from the next dune so that the car could build up speed. The engine was over-revved, the needle of the indicator was oscillating ready to break the glass, the dune came closer and closer and off we went up it, and I tried hard to remember to keep the wheel straight, not bend it to the right because we would roll, not bend it to the left...

We went up, straight up the dune, and it all seemed so surreal. And I felt the adrenaline pumping as the speed of the car gradually came down, the accelerator still pressed deeply and desperately into the floor, as if I wanted to push it through the carcass of the car. And I prayed with my eyes wide open and my jaws tightly closed that God would help us get over that dune, just as Ibrahim had prayed to Allah that the desert would have mercy upon us, and I felt my veins pulsating with blood as I witnessed the miracle happening and the car become as light as a bird, and it came docilely to a stop just on the crest of the dune before falling down the other side. I was breathing heavily; and I still couldn't believe we hadn't rolled, not even when I pulled the wheel to one side in a last-minute panic attack over whether we would hit the other car that Ibrahim had managed to bring to a stop in front of us, on the crest of the same dune.

It was too much for words and I couldn't say much. I got out of the car with my eyes still wide open and my hands still trembling, and the mixture of fear and excitement that was pumping blood heavily into my temples started to slow down, and I knew that even if the car was to roll on the next dune and my fate was to die here in this desert today, it would be without regrets: I'd die having experienced the miracle of flying over a dune.

Peter, Richard and I shared the driving for the rest of the

day. It felt as if we had once again found the middle ground in a dispute. And we all got to know the adrenaline pump and we all got to experience our own victories and failures. Occasionally the car slid back. At other times, dunes were conquered only on the fourth attempt, but one way or the other the miracle kept on happening and at the end of the day, when we set up camp at the base of another tall, deeply pink-coloured dune, all three of us felt racked but happy. And the memory of our flight over the dunes stayed with us long into the night and for many more days and nights to come.

DAY 4

IBRAHIM was talking in a whisper and it started as soon as night had fallen.

"No fire tonight, we will not cook. We'll eat some of the couscous left from lunch."

This did not sound too encouraging. What he said next sounded even less encouraging.

"Listen to me," he said as all of us gathered around the leftovers of the couscous. "This is not a very nice place. We are very close to the Algerian border here. A lot of things may happen close to the borders. When there is wind and sandstorm it's better, but tonight is too clear and we can easily be found. We should be prepared. I think it's best that everybody gives me their passports for the night. I will keep them for you and will give them back to you tomorrow morning."

Our passports, what was he talking about? What could he possibly do with our passports in the middle of nowhere?

"If they come and take everything, at least you'll be left with the passports."

"Who are they?"

"The smugglers. The bandits. Bad people. They sometimes come to attack in the night, and we are close to them here."

This either sounded like a horror movie or Ibrahim was even more paranoid than I was, which was quite a difficult thing to achieve.

"Listen to me," he whispered. "If they come, do not oppose them. Give them everything they want. Your money, your clothes, the cars, everything. If you do, they will not kill you. They usually don't kill tourists; they let them walk back after they have taken everything. I will hide the passports and some water. If we need to, this will help us make it to the next oasis."

"Ibrahim, you're joking, right?"

"No, I'm not. But don't be afraid. The main thing is that they will not kill. They usually avoid killing if they are not opposed. They only take the things, rape the women and then go."

Rape the women. He said "rape the women" and he said it in such an indifferent voice that it sounded even less important than taking the cars away.

"So please: no light, no torch. Even if you go to the toilet, do not use a torch. Be as quiet as you can: no noise, no voice. Sound travels fast in the desert."

We were looking at him in disbelief. It sounded more like a story made up for tourists.

"If they can hear us, we can hear them too. We can hear them if they come." Peter had a logical answer for everything. "We can hear their engines and we can jump into the cars, leave everything else here, the tents and all that, but at least we can jump into the cars and drive away."

Ibrahim threw him a wry look from under his shawl. His eyes were uncovered for once, free from the ever-present sunglasses, and I could read pity in them.

"Yeah, if they come by car. But if they come by camel, you won't hear anything until it's too late."

I didn't feel like eating couscous or asking any more questions. I put up my tent in silence, and I knew even before I got into my sleeping bag that I would not sleep that night. Ibrahim's phrase kept lingering in my mind – "they only rape the women". It was worse than rape, it was potential death. I remembered the statistics that said one African man in four was HIV-positive. And I doubted they would use condoms.

The night was long and silent and I listened to the darkness around me in terror. This time it was not about laughing monkeys or the sound of a rusty bicycle with a broken tyre. It was about "will I get raped tonight?", and this threat seemed a lot more credible than any of my imaginary ones.

Just before crawling into my tent, I heard Ibrahim whispering with Peter and I saw them handling some machetes. Then he went towards Richard's tent. Maybe he had changed his non-resistance approach and was organising our defence. He didn't come to my tent to give me a machete. It must have been because he thought women were as useless with machetes as they were with cars. With no other weapon around, I just clung on to my small Swiss Army knife and my almost useless self-defence spray. And for the rest of the night I tried hard to build up the hope that being raped tonight was not part of my fate.

DAY 5

"RICHARD, can you pass me the foot pump please?"

We were having a cup of tea. It was early morning and the campfire was burning. Food containers lay open everywhere: bread, jam, margarine, open tins, tea – lots of tea. Richard put down his mug and looked around.

"Richard, the foot pump please!"

This was Peter and he was insistent.

"What does he want?" I asked.

"Fuck knows." Richard looked around, trying to locate Peter or the foot pump.

Peter's voice came from somewhere under the car, and there was no way of understanding what on earth he was doing there so early in the morning.

A fourth request and Richard went on and found the foot pump, and a small argument followed over Richard's request to be left alone to finish his tea and Peter's concern over a flat tyre.

So far, nothing unusual: a morning like many others. I decided to enjoy my own tea and let the two of them sort out theirs or the flat tyre, whatever came first.

Ibrahim lay on the eating and all-purpose carpet next to me. He was smiling a lot this morning. Maybe it was because the fears of the previous night were gone. He was having one of his usual cups of tea half filled with sugar. We were seriously running out of sugar.

"Today we arrive in Ifreuane, please tell Richard to buy more sugar!" Ibrahim pointed to the remains of the bag. For one reason or another, he had decided that Richard was the one in charge of his sugar supplies.

I nodded. He would get his sugar today when we found the oasis. And I would finally get a night without terror, since we would sleep in that village.

My travel mates were still arguing, but their voices were low and somehow controlled. A British quarrel, as understated as everything else they do. My Latin temperament would have got overheated already.

Ibrahim was watching them, then he looked at me: a long, silent stare.

"You see, you see how much trouble you cause?"

"What do you mean?"

"You see, all this tension, they are quarrelling. You, the three of you, you are always quarrelling!"

Tension was in the air in our small group day after day, and no wonder Ibrahim could feel it. Yesterday it was me against the two of them over who got to drive; a few days ago it was Richard and I against Peter, defending our right to have our bedding packed up in his tent, away from dust and sand. And today it was Richard and Peter against each other over a flat tyre and the right to have breakfast first. There was always something.

"It's just a tyre. They'll sort it out."

He looked at me again: the same deep, long look.

"No, it's not the tyre – it's you!"

"What do you mean, it's me? Do you think they are quarrelling about me?"

"Not about you but because of you. It's you who are the cause of all this – the cause of all this tension. You shouldn't be here with them. They are fighting like two cocks for a hen."

I was getting frustrated now. This was more than unfair. This was even worse than saying I shouldn't drive.

"Ibrahim, I think you're seeing things that are not there!"

He gave me a hopeless look.

"It's you who is not seeing things that are there. One woman and two men. The woman does not belong to any of the men. What do you think they are quarrelling about?"

I had serious doubts that Peter and Richard were having an argument over who was to "own" me as this guy suggested. But Ibrahim's opinions could be very strong sometimes.

"Look, my friend." I tried to make him understand. "In our world, it's not all about men and women and their relationships. People have other issues too."

"Everywhere it's about men and women... everywhere.

It's the essence of life. You'll see when you meet someone."

Now this was dangerous territory and I didn't want to go into any details with Ibrahim over when and if I would meet someone. I decided to change the subject.

"Yeah, sure, why don't you ask around to see if any of your countrymen are looking for a wife? I was offered the price of four camels and ten goats by the Tuaregs in Timbuktu." He looked at me in silence and I felt weighed by his looks, as if I were a goat on sale.

"How old are you?

"Twenty-eight."

"Are you joking? Four camels and ten goats for a 28-year-old woman? I paid half that for my wife and she was 15 at the time!"

He was laughing but I was not sure this was a joke.

So I was not in high demand here. I made a mental note that I'd better hurry up and find a husband, otherwise my value would deteriorate to one goat only.

"Did you really pay in goats and camels for your wife?"

"Of course. She was very expensive. Women are always very expensive. Before they marry they want things, after they marry they want more things. Always expensive."

"Like camels, for instance?"

"More expensive than camels. And they cause a lot more trouble. A lot of effort to a get and keep a woman. I had to court my wife for many months. She belonged to another tribe and she was living with her family far away from Agadez. I sometimes rode a camel for a whole night just to see her for a couple of hours before sunrise!"

Tuaregs had very independent love lives. Unlike young men and women in other traditional societies, they were free to marry whom they chose and their courtship involved many rituals.

Ibrahim seemed to be lost in his memories and our bargaining for goats and camels stopped there. Richard returned to his cup of tea after the short, stormy episode with Peter. Peter still hung out under the car, doing something only he understood. I drank some more tea and thought about getting up and getting ready; my tent needed to be put down, the cars loaded. I thought about driving and I felt relieved that it was not my turn to drive. I thought about the oasis we were to reach that afternoon, about my hand that I had cut the other day and the wound that did not seem to heal well. And beyond all this, there was another thought in the back of my mind and it was linked to what Ibrahim had told me: were my travel mates really quarrelling because of me?

SHE was the only one who did not smile. The bones of her face were long and thin, her chin pointy and perfectly designed. Her nose was small and a bit round, the shape of a strawberry. She wore round earrings and a necklace of red beads that seemed to match the long, dark blue dress with a pattern of red roses. This was not a traditional dress: it looked rather European. Maybe a French girl had worn it at some point, when it was all bright and new. Now it was dusty and the colour had faded. But the shape was still there: a good cut is always easy to spot. After the little French girl the dress must have stayed with some NGO for a while, and then it must have been shipped as aid to Africa. It somehow arrived here, in this hot oasis of the Aïr Mountains, and it found a new owner: the little Tuareg girl who was now standing in front of me.

She was pushed in front by the other children. There were many of them, talking, shouting, begging: "*donnez-moi un cadeau*[21]". The old phrase was again on their lips and, as always, it seemed to indicate a place where tourists had been before. Like the barbarian tribes of the Middle Ages, who used to leave behind ruin and pillage, we modern barbarians of our age move around in a constant search for new territories that we call holiday destinations, leaving behind beggars: *donnez-moi un cadeau*.

The girl with the red beads was quiet. She did not ask for anything, she did not smile; she did not hang on to my clothes. She stepped aside, leaving the other children in front, and she looked at me with her eyes wide open. She looked at me intensely, as if trying to imprint my image into her mind. What did she see, I wondered. A tourist woman wearing dirty trousers and an even dirtier top with long sleeves, and a Tuareg indigo shawl wrapped around her head.

"*Madame, donnez-moi un cadeau!*" The voices sounded far away now. I looked at the little girl and she looked back at me, probably not realising that under my sunglasses my eyes were as wide open as hers. The voices around me faded even

---

[21] "Give me a present." (in French)

more. Children must still have been hanging on to my trousers but I didn't feel anything. Under her clearly contoured eyebrows, the deep, brownish colour of her eyes spoke of the desert. I could see the dunes in her eyes: huge, silent, immobile. I could hear the wind blowing over her face, the same harsh, hot wind of the desert that blew on to our faces and into our food for days on end. I felt that somehow, impossibly true but inexplicably sure, I had met her before. I felt I knew her, and my staring at her must have told her I recognised her in the same way her staring at me told me she knew me. And this knowing came from somewhere beyond time and space, beyond me being a *toubab* tourist and her being a six-year-old Tuareg girl.

Thoughts flashed through my mind. I wanted to know more about this girl. I wanted to help her somehow. I wanted to know who her parents were and what I could do for her. Maybe give her a pen, some more clothes, give her parents some money. The harsh reality of the situation was that all I could possibly have done for her was transform her into a beggar, help her become just like the other kids who were still hanging on to my clothes in the desperate hope they would receive something. Anything. Her eyes still stared at me, soft and silent, and they told me she didn't want anything. She just wanted to fill her eyes with my unexpected presence in her small world in the same way I wanted to fill my eyes with hers.

Meanwhile, the jerrycans had been filled with water and packed back on the roof. Everybody was in. The engine was revving. That was it, I needed to go.

I still had my eyes sunk in hers as I felt the tourist in me taking over. I waved her to come over to me. I pointed to my camera in a silent attempt to ask if I could take a picture of her. She nodded. I took my picture and hoped this small piece of coloured paper would manage to preserve the magic of this encounter. Like all tourists before me and like all those who would come after, I took my picture and left.

And like all the tourists around me, I gave up and succumbed to the voice of guilt in my heart. I took her hand, my eyes still deeply sunk in hers, and I hid a small sweet in her palm. She didn't look to see what I had given her; she still looked into my eyes. I closed her small fist around the sweet and I turned around and got into my car with broken movements. We were leaving, and I still felt her eyes following me, us, the car...

The children ran around and banged on the windows and I looked above their heads, trying to see her one more time as the car built up speed. There she was, hidden behind the walls of the well; she had finally opened her fist. She must have been pleased with the sweet because suddenly she threw her head back and her arms in the air and waved at me, and I waved back at her and I saw a timid smile growing on her lips.

In a fantasy world in which I was a grown-up woman with a settled life, such an encounter would probably make me think of adoption. But the reality was that our car was driving away from that small oasis, and this told me that I would never ever see her again. Maybe it was better that way: maybe if I was to see her again she would be like all the others, hanging on to the clothes of another tourist in the hope of getting something because once upon a time another *toubab* tourist gave her a sweet.

I felt guilty.

RICHARD was not himself that day. It wasn't because he was grumpy: that was as natural to him as brushing his teeth with the dusty, worn-out brush he kept in the glove compartment of the car. Grumpiness was his natural state, but it would usually go away and be replaced by a sudden excess of joy, and when that happened he would scream with pleasure as he hit the accelerator and drove full speed over some dune. And it wasn't because he was going through one of his solitary phases. "I need to be on my own," he would say, just before he went away for a wander with his camera round his neck. He went for wanders almost every morning, just after the sunrise and before breakfast, and he went for more solitary wanders in the evenings: as we set up camp, he would go climb some dune and "listen to its music", so he said.

The dunes were singing, and at the beginning we thought this was a metaphor that Ibrahim had come up with because he thought it was the kind of thing tourists wanted to hear. But we soon realised that it was true, that the dunes really did sing a kind of soft, pale melody which blended perfectly with the soft, peach colour of the sand. The dunes sang best in the early morning as the sun rose and in the early evening just before the sun went down, and it almost seemed they were singing for the sun. The wind was carrying particles of sand all around, and sometimes the surface of the dunes would be covered by a thick crust built up with countless intricate models, like a masterpiece of embroidery crafted with skill and patience. The wind would change this pattern over and over again and the dust would change its form and other shapes would come to life: small, wave-like patterns or others that looked like flowers. It was almost as if we were at the bottom of the sea and the wind was doing the job of the waves: shaping and sculpting, changing and modelling...

It might have been the desert and the immensity around us, or the song of the dunes he climbed every evening, but one thing or another had managed to push Richard into a state of mind I did not see him in often. He was sad.

Sadness is difficult to fight against. It's a cunning state of mind and it comes along when you least expect it. At least Fear was straightforward. She would usually come by at night and she would go away in the morning. She had her rules and she would stick to them, even though she was a stubborn thing at times. There were ways to deal with Fear and I had slowly learned that simple things like putting the tent up closer to the car made her back off a bit, and sleeping in a village instead of in the middle of nowhere almost reduced her to silence. But above all, she would run away from light like a vampire of the night, afraid of being destroyed by the first ray of sun.

But Sadness was different. She chose to come whenever she pleased: by night, as she had come to me that evening when I cried and listened to Richard's story, or by day, as she had come to him today.

Richard was not himself today, and no matter how beautiful the dunes and how bright the purple of the sunrise, nothing seemed to bring a smile to his face. Not even the sight of his sandals with the sole almost completely detached, which would usually get several comments per day. Not even Coldplay songs. Actually, Coldplay made it more difficult, especially lines like "nobody said it was easy". Not even my timid questions attempting to check if he was fine, which were left unanswered, and not even the ever-present worries of Ibrahim that we didn't have enough sugar, managed to bring a smile to his face.

"Shut the fuck up about your sugar. I'll get six kilos for you next time. Then you'll be happy!" he finally burst out as we arrived in Ifreuane, and Ibrahim pointed towards a small hut that was likely to sell sugar.

He got out of the car and slammed the door. Ibrahim was speechless.

"Is he crazy?" He turned towards me.

"He's just not himself today." I tried to defend Richard. "He'll be back to his usual self."

"Heatstroke?" Ibrahim followed a one-size-fits-all strategy.

"Don't think it's the heat. I think he's just not feeling well," I said.

It was probably a mixture of everything. Not only the heat but the dust and the sand and the couscous we had been eating for a whole week. They all melted together and created an illness that was not easy to deal with. It was called being homesick. I didn't tell this to Ibrahim. He would probably have asked why on earth we were away from home if we were homesick. And for this I didn't have an answer.

"I'll talk to him," I told Ibrahim.

I meant to talk to him, but I didn't quite manage it. Maybe I simply couldn't find a way. I looked for Richard, who had gone on one of his usual wanders around the village, and I found him. I asked him if everything was OK.

"I'll be fine," he said "It's just one of those days, you know – when nothing works. When you think about all you've left behind. When you wonder if it was all worth it...'

And then, in a sudden moment of openness:

"It's M, I guess. I can't stop thinking about her today."

I didn't ask more and he didn't say more. M was the girl he had left behind in London. He had told me briefly about her before and I knew she was a friend he had known for a long time. And just before he left, he discovered in her a woman to love. But he still wanted to go on this trip. What was meant to be would be and what was not meant to be wouldn't happen. This was his philosophy, and it was much like the Tuareg belief in fate. He left for this trip and she stayed back in London to carry on with her life as usual for the many months he would be away. They parted friends, leaving the future open. But I knew that despite his belief in fate, there were days and nights he would think of her. And he would probably ask himself at times, like today for instance, if this trip was worth being away from her.

"It'll be fine," I told him. "You'll see."

"Yeah..."

I felt awkward. He had been there for me in one way or the other whenever I needed him. Now he was the one in need and I felt incapable of telling him anything else but the empty phrase, "It will all be fine, you'll see." I wished I knew a story as absurd as his, about the old man and his collection of soaps, but I didn't know one. I wished I could give him a hug but it felt improper. It was not part of the British way of expressing emotions and I wasn't sure he knew enough about the Latin ways to be able to handle them. I wished I could find something to tell him that would make a difference, even though nothing could bring him back to London and he would just have to carry on with his life in that little, dusty, sandy oasis village in the heart of the Aïr Mountains.

"It'll be fine, you'll see," I repeated, feeling useless as I sometimes could.

I let him carry on with his wander and returned to the camp. The music in the car was still turned on and the song we had listened to for the whole day was playing again. It was Coldplay.

Nobody said it was easy
It's such a shame for us to part
Nobody said it was easy
No one ever said it would be this hard...

No wonder Richard felt depressed after listening to this for a whole morning.

"Hey, what's up with him?" Ibrahim shot at me as soon as I came back.

"He's just sad. You know it happens to everyone; we're all sad sometimes."

"Why is he sad now? We had a nice trip and we have reached the village! What's the problem?"

"I think he misses his girlfriend," I said.

"Where is she?"

"Back in London, I guess."

Ibrahim looked at me with puzzled eyes.

"If she's in London and he misses her, why has he left her there?"

I guess he really found us hard to understand sometimes.

"I need to talk to him," Ibrahim decided. "He cannot go on like this. He cannot shout at me like this just because he's sad and because of a woman in London…"

"Ibrahim, please, don't. If you speak to him it will just make things worse!" I begged him with a sudden attack of panic. "Please just let him cool down: I'll buy you sugar!"

The sugar bribe worked and he agreed to forget about Richard's loss of temper. And as I came back from the shop, I saw my travel mate was back and reading his book in a chair in the courtyard of the house where we would be camping for the night. He looked like he still needed some time on his own.

I wanted to tell him something, anything, that would make him smile and feel better: something that would get him back to his usual "whatever happens, I'll be fine" state when he purred like a big, happy cat and he smiled at the world on his own. I wished I could somehow bring the sparkle back to his eyes and summon back the contagious happiness he spread around. The world seemed strange without them and I suddenly realised, now that he was sad and quiet, how much ease and enthusiasm he brought to our small group. I wished I could have told him that he would be fine.

But I couldn't find the words. Maybe because Richard is a very private person and I feared he would have preferred to be left on his own, or maybe because I am inclined to talk too much to myself and too little to others.

I went back to the shop and bought a big bag of sweets. I came back to the house. Richard was still there, reading his book under the tree.

"I have something for you," I said, handing him the black plastic bag.

They always wrapped things in several plastic bags here. He unfolded them in silence, one by one, his eyes wide with curiosity.

"Thank you!" His eyes looked deep into mine and they felt warm. He had finally arrived at the sweets inside the many plastic bags.

A smile started to form on his face, although his eyes were still sad. I felt my attempt was only half successful.

"Thank you," he repeated. "These will really give me a boost."

I wished I could have said something. But I couldn't. I just let him sit there under the tree, with his book and his big bag of sweets. He sat there for the rest of the afternoon, turning the pages and unwrapping the sweets one by one in silence, his thoughts probably wandering between Africa and Europe, maybe silently asking his own questions and trying to find his own answers. And I sat under the shade of another tree for the rest of the afternoon, wondering why it was so difficult sometimes to tell someone you really care.

THEY say hell is other people. After weeks and weeks of silent tensions, sudden bursts of argument, frustrations over smelly feet, overcooked pasta or one of the other small things our lives consisted of, we came to a crossroads. And it happened just as we returned to Agadez and went straight back to Ibrahim's mud-brick house to recover all our possessions, which had been stored there in an attempt to reduce the weight of the car.

And as we loaded all those small things into the car, it almost felt like we were loading our own worries as well and the car became heavier under the weight and we became heavier as well under all those thoughts that can bring one to desperation.

I had a problem with Peter; Richard had one with Peter and another with me. Peter had a problem with both of us. It looked as though we would simply have to admit that not all conflicts can be talked through and not all issues can be solved. To a greater or lesser degree, all three of us were thinking that the time had come to split up.

We had several beers that night on the terrace of one of the hotels in Agadez, and we quarrelled hard and we yelled at each other, and we felt we had reached the limits of our tolerance levels. As usual, it was Richard who managed to bring the three of us together. Then we tried to talk, maybe for the first time in all those long and tense weeks, and tell each other what it was that we felt went wrong, what we were happy with and what we were unhappy with.

In fact, it didn't matter what we talked about that night – whether it was about Peter shouting orders to the two of us as if he was still in the army; or about Richard and me not taking enough interest in looking after the car; whether it was right or wrong if one were to jump in the car and take it away to a safe distance, then leave the other two to the mercy of bandits should we be attacked in the middle of the night, which Peter found an absolutely valid principle and I found a scandalous one; whether it was about me being inflexible and unwilling to compromise and Richard being fed up of acting continuously as a peacemaker between Peter and me; it didn't even matter whether it all came about because of the dust, the sand or the heat, or that we did not find a solution to all our problems that night. What really mattered was that, for the first time since the three of us had started to travel together back in Timbuktu, we had managed to talk about what we didn't like about each other.

And once we started, we went on and talked deep into the night until the waiters came and told us that they had to close the terrace: the only terrace in town where we could find both a seat and a beer. It felt like once the words had found their way out we had to carry on talking and talking until dawn, taking out all our frustrations and clarifying all misunderstandings, talking some more about all those things we had kept inside for such a long time. We had to leave the terrace eventually, and we went to sleep still feeling we could talk some more.

We left Agadez early the next morning, the three of us and the car, still together. We hadn't found the answers to our problems that night, we didn't set new rules as I had hoped we would, we didn't even manage to listen well enough to each other. But in the light of the morning, any problem somehow seemed less of a problem, and as we drove away and the city of the desert and its dunes and its nomads remained far behind us, I remembered the silhouette of a mighty, peach-coloured dune and its song in the early morning and I understood, once again, that peace was not to be found inside our small group. It was there, in the song of that dune and in the harsh Harmattan wind of the desert. It was on the face of that little girl with the strawberry-like nose and a necklace of red beads, who carried the immensity of the desert in her eyes. It was in the joy of driving over a dune and in the relief of waking up alive in the morning. There was peace all around us, in fact, and the dusty road south that stretched out in front of the car that morning seemed to smile wryly at us and say that our time together had not come to an end just yet and there would be many more wonders to come.

CHAPTER 18 – THE ROAD TO NOWHERE

(LAKE CHAD – APRIL 2003)

THE night had fallen and it seemed that finally all those animals in the courtyard had gone to their rest. The goats and the sheep had gathered in one corner, towards the mud-brick wall that separated the open-air toilet from the rest of the courtyard. They were silent, immobile, tightly pushed one on to another, and I wondered if this was how they would sleep for the rest of the night. The chickens and ducks seemed to have cleared out of the way too. I had no idea where they went, since I could see no cages or shelter for them. I suspect they simply went into the house, into the only dark little room, and they must have entered through the small door that was always open. The dog stopped barking, as if it had come to terms with the short chain bound around its neck that limited its movements. The cow in another corner of the courtyard was chewing slowly, as silent as it had been throughout the afternoon.

I had put my tent up between the dog and the cow, thinking that would be a pretty quiet spot if the dog kept up its current silence for the night. Above all I wanted to avoid the chickens, and even though I had no idea where they had gone, I hoped they would not come anywhere too close to the dog.

The car was parked outside; the opening of the courtyard was too small for it to pass through. Peter, who was to sleep in his roof tent as usual, would be the one to have the quietest night, I thought. I didn't know where Richard would put his tent up or whether he was thinking of putting it up at all, or if he would just go for a simple net as he did most of the time. As for the family, it looked like they would sleep on the two mattresses they had laid in the middle of the dusty courtyard, close to the entrance of the house, under no net or tent whatsoever. I suspect they always slept outside. It was a lot cooler and therefore more bearable than inside the small room.

The family we were staying with had already made the fire for the evening meal, and we decided it would be polite if we were to use some of the couscous we still had from our desert provisions to feed all of them. There were not too many: the man, his wife and their three children, the smallest of which was still a baby strapped on to his mother's back. One kilo of couscous would feed us all.

They seemed pleased with our offer and we used their fire to cook. We sat down on a piece of cloth laid out in the middle of the courtyard and we placed the big bowl with the couscous in the middle. Each of us had one spoon, and the custom in these places was that we would all eat from the same bowl. The man, his wife and the two oldest kids kneeled down in front of the food. We thought we should start. And as I brought my first spoonful of couscous to my mouth, I froze as I heard the voice of the older of the two kids.

"Our Father who art in heaven..."

His voice was shy but clear, and after the first line in French he went on – in his Hausa mother tongue, probably – and I recognised the cadences of the most well-known Christian prayer. His name was Abdullah, meaning the Slave of Allah. He was Christian though, like his father: the man who had given us shelter in this small border village. And he was praying with his eyes down, his voice clear in the night, his parents and his brother kneeling next to him, the large couscous bowl in front of him, while we, three puzzled foreigners, were looking at each other unsure how to react.

We decided to keep our heads bowed as they did theirs, my mouth still filled with the couscous I did not dare swallow, and we didn't move until the boy finished and raised up his eyes with the last word: "Amen".

The sound travelled out to the courtyard, to the sleeping goats and sheep, to the chewing cow and the dog lying in the dust at the end of his chain, and out into the dark night beyond the mud-brick walls of the compound. It felt like everyone was listening.

"We always pray here before our meal," said the man, and took his first spoonful of couscous.

I started chewing again. This time the meal had finally started.

WE were lodged with the only Christian family in the village of N'guigmi, on the border of Niger and Chad. In fact, this was where Niger ended. Nobody knew where Chad started and the sandy stretch of land opening up after the last border point was a No Man's Land. Chad was to be found somewhere in that direction, following the small row of thorny acacia trees under the constant, dusty wind. It was as if the country itself had decided to run away and hide, and maybe escape from being found by three *toubabs* and their car that clearly didn't belong there. No tourists travelled those roads.

We were really lucky to have found them. The unspoken rule in those parts was that one camped either deeply hidden in the bush, where one was as sure as possible that the camp would pass unnoticed through the night, or in someone's courtyard. Being allowed to camp on someone's property, near their house or in their courtyard meant we would be under the protection of that person and very likely not to be attacked by anybody. Camping next to a village but under nobody's protection was the worst choice one could make, since then the camp was in plain view of everybody but nothing stood between the poor campers and possible intruders. And when we came to a border, things were usually tougher: there was always less of law and order next to a border. We had needed a safe place to camp for the night, and this man had given us a night of peaceful sleep in his courtyard.

"I will pray for you," the man said next morning as we loaded the car and gave him some money for his hospitality. "I will pray for you," he repeated. "The road you take is difficult and dangerous. Not many people pass by here on this route. I will pray that God protects you and delivers you safely."

For a second, I remembered Ibrahim's lips moving as we left Agadez.

"*Insha'Allah*," we responded. "May God's will be done."

PETER'S DRIVE – FIRST DAY

COLDPLAY was on again and the sound was turned up to maximum. I was on the back seat. Peter was driving and Richard had given up making any sense of the map. There was no need for a map here. Outside the sandstorm had started again: not a particularly heavy one – we had seen much worse in the Aïr Mountains, after all – but hazy enough to prevent us from seeing more than a few metres around us. There was no road, not even a piste, only countless tracks in the sand that crossed each other in all directions. Some thorny bushes appeared out of the foggy wind every now and then. The air was dry and hot, judging from the thermometer still stuck at its upper limit (somewhere just above 52°C). The sand carried around by the wind outside sucked out every drop of moisture from everywhere: from the bushes, the thorns, the ground, our lips.

"We live in a beautiful world" – the words of the song seemed to mock us; mock this whole surreal landscape, the reality of the sandstorm outside and us being totally, utterly and hopelessly lost. We had been driving the whole morning, hoping in vain to get to the Chadian side of the border. There was no border, no road, and we had started doubting that a country called Chad ever existed. In fact it didn't. It just existed on a nicely coloured map displayed in a bookshop back home. There you could see a line dividing Niger and Chad: one country finished, the other one started. But here, under this sandstorm, Niger finished as we drove past a wooden hut with two soldiers who stamped our passports and wished us "*bon voyage*". But Chad did not start. It was the same rough, sandy land scattered with thorny bushes, but without a border post, a flag; any sign whatsoever. It seemed a place that had escaped our modern maps. And so we drove on into nothingness – desert, bushes, sand, more sand.

Sometimes, silhouettes all wrapped up in countless layers of robes and shawls came out of the wind for a brief moment. We tried to stop and shout after them. Sometimes they would simply run away. A car with three strangers would probably not be a pleasant sight somewhere in this No Man's Land between Niger and Chad. At other times they would come closer and we would try to ask for directions.

"Chad? Where is Chad?"

They always pointed straight ahead.

"*Tout droit.*"

Straight ahead, it was always straight ahead. It didn't matter that you were going the wrong way; you had to keep on straight ahead. It didn't matter that they had no idea what we were asking, as if the country we asked about simply didn't exist here, or was maybe known by a different name and our stumbling French pronunciation couldn't give them any idea of what we were looking for.

But we followed their directions and we drove straight ahead, ahead into the storm, ahead into the bushes, ahead into nowhere.

By noon we realised we had gone in a big circle. The compass mounted on the dashboard of the car seemed to have gone mad. We were following the sand tracks we could see in front of us and they seemed to be heading north one minute, then west, then back south, then east again. It was all useless: totally, utterly useless. It was as if we had finally escaped the boundaries of our civilised world and ventured somewhere beyond: somewhere that did not exist on any map or in the mind of anybody; somewhere even a compass would be overwhelmed and give up. We were not in Niger, not in Chad, not in any country named on any map. No Man's Land. Hardly a more appropriate name for it.

The road was supposed to take us around the lake, and we desperately hoped we would see the water of the lake amidst the dry wind that was constantly blowing. If we had seen the lake it would all have been nice and easy: we only had to drive east around it, taking care not to come too close. But there was no lake, no water whatsoever, no border post and no villages. Only countless tracks in the sand, each going in a different direction as if Fate was smiling at us, trying to see which pair of tracks we would bet on.

We thought we could outsmart this labyrinth when Peter decided to take out his GPS equipment and try to figure out scientifically where we were. Richard and I were more inclined to rely on our gut feelings. But Peter did not listen: he measured and he calculated and measured again, and then the map on the bonnet was about to be blown away by the wind, but he measured again and again and again. Eventually he got back into the car.

"According to the GPS coordinates, we're in the middle of the lake," he said, with a blank expression in his eyes.

The map he held had one small cross made with a red pen. It was where the GPS coordinates he took met and it was in the middle of the bigger blue spot: the Lake Chad.

I was trying hard not to burst out laughing. We were hardly in the middle of a lake. We were actually in the middle of a sandy track. In the middle of nowhere, to be more precise, and GPS equipment was even less useful than biased intuition. We found out later that the lake which was shown on all the maps in the world was never in the place it was shown. It was, in fact, a constantly moving lake, shrinking with the dry season and growing in size with the rainy season, moving around and reshaping like the sand it was surrounded by. Like the borders of the countries shown on the map, this lake seemed to be as surreal and non-existent as the country whose name it bore. And we three Europeans with our sophisticated equipment and detailed maps were as powerless before this as the nomads on their camels whose silhouettes we had seen earlier that day emerging from the storm for brief moments. Only that I guessed their gut feeling was considerably more accurate than ours.

In Africa, they say that every journey ends by sunset. One way or the other it always happens: one always has to stop and camp by sunset since one would not even dream of driving into the night. And as Peter stopped the car that late afternoon, the wind was still blowing and the particles of sand still piercing mercilessly every little inch of exposed skin. But in the blur in front of us we could somehow, miraculously, spot the silhouette of a wooden hut and a small flag with unclear colours nearby, and we figured out that one way or another we had made it and this was the Chadian border point. Had we driven in a large circle for a whole day? Or were the borders a day's drive apart? We would never know and it didn't matter. One way or another, a journey always ends by sunset and that day it ended well.

We parked in front of the hut. The wind was blowing and countless black plastic bags flying around marked the people's intrusion into the desert. These bags seemed to be a part of the Sahara, from Morocco and on to Mauritania and Senegal, in Mali and Niger and now in Chad. Black plastic bags were flying with the wind in the desert and were settling on the thorny bushes, looking like huge, black flowers: the black flowers of the desert. But this time it was a pleasant sight. It meant there was a village around: people, border officials, hopefully a road, even a lake, and who knew? Maybe this country called Chad existed after all.

It meant we had arrived somehow, and in the process we had discovered rule number one of surviving in Chad: just drive *tout droit* and you will get somewhere.

RICHARD'S DRIVE – SECOND DAY

RICHARD yelled from the bottom of his lungs and for a fraction of a second I had the impression he had gone completely insane. But we must have seemed a good pair of mad people as I yelled too and this time it was with excitement when I saw we had made the right decision regarding which pair of tracks to follow. Peter was sitting on the back seat that day and he had given up trying to make sense of all that yelling.

Today the visibility was better, which meant we could see about 20 metres ahead and this counted for a lot when you were trying to decide which pair of tracks you should follow to get up the sandy hill in front of you.

We were still driving on sand and today the sand was worse. This simply meant more digging and pushing whenever the pair of tracks we had decided to follow ended up not being the best bet. We left the border post in the morning and were delighted to find that we had finally entered Chad. We were less delighted, however, when we realised there was no hope of any clearer indications. Once again, *tout droit* was to be our way. And so we kept *tout droit* for the whole morning, trying to stay out of sand as much as possible.

Staying out of sand usually resulted in driving like maniacs. The desert driving skills that we had acquired in the Aïr Mountains under Ibrahim's careful mentoring came back into use now on the sandy piste around the Lake Chad. We still hadn't seen any part of the lake but we were less concerned about that. We were told that it was there, somewhere on the right, and it was all fine that we couldn't see it. Apparently the last thing in the world we wanted was to see it, since that would mean we had come too close and would be in danger of getting bogged down in its moving sands.

Richard pressed the accelerator down to the floor and we drove at full speed in low gear, the engine revving as if it was about to explode, the car flying over the sand following some tracks, then abruptly changing to other tracks that seemed more suitable.

"There, go left! Leeeft!" I screamed, spotting another pair of tracks that appeared out of nowhere, and Richard swung the wheel, trying to catch the new tracks. He had his eyes fixed in front of the car, trying hard not to roll, while I had mine far into the horizon, trying to follow the labyrinth of tracks ahead and decide which ones were the best bets. The speed was up, there was no time to think: if we stopped or slowed down we would sink into the sand.

"Change, go to the right, now! Not this one, further to the right!"

Another sudden swing and the car shook and leant dangerously to one side. This was close to rolling. Richard kept up the speed, though, and we fell nicely into the new tracks.

Each pair of tracks would leave two deep cuts in the sand. You wanted to be inside, since it made driving easier, but only as long as the axis of the car did not touch the sand. The moment this happened, we would get stuck. And since most of the tracks had been made by trucks with much deeper wheels than our car, it was essential to understand when the tracks would start becoming too deep for us and then change to others before we lost speed.

"Which ones?" Richard shouted. We were coming at full speed towards a steep hill.

I had about two seconds to make a decision. At least ten pair of tracks went up this one.

"Which *ones?*" Richard shouted again.

A flash of inspiration.

"Left, go left!"

The wheel swung, the car slid and up we went. This time it was the wrong decision. Halfway up we got stuck. The tracks were too deep.

We got out of the car and unscrewed the sand ladders. We needed to push the car out, but backwards this time, let it slide down to the base of the hill and then start again.

"Left, hey? You liked the tracks on the left, hey? Did they look like the right ones to get stuck or what?"

Richard's voice came from the other side of the car, digging under the front wheel.

"Maybe you should try and pick them up yourself: let's see what happens then," I muttered while I kept on digging under my wheel.

Back into the car, and after drinking about one litre of water each, hardly equivalent to what we had lost while digging and pushing, we tried again.

"Which one? Hey! Which one do I take?" Richard's shout was barely covered by the over-revved engine and I instantly forgot my decision to hold back from offering him any more suggestions.

"Go right!" I shouted back, and this time as the car flew over the top of the hill and built up speed going down the other side, it looked like it was a more fortunate choice.

Later on we realised we had lost the way completely. The tracks became fewer and fewer and my job of choosing between them less complex. But it also meant we were going away from the main road – if the high concentration of different tracks could be called a road.

The shape of a house appeared from out of the dusty wind. We thought that we could stop and ask for directions. We drove towards it and we could spot a few people in the courtyard. They'd obviously seen us. One of them ran into the house, and minutes later he came out holding what appeared to be a very large gun – pointed towards us.

We stopped. We looked at each other. We were about 20 metres away from them. He still held the gun pointed towards us and I thought it looked like a bazooka. I got out of the car. They would feel less threatened by a woman.

"*Bonjour, excusez-moi, est-ce que c'est la direction pour Liwa*[22]?" I spoke loudly, hoping that he could hear me. I walked slowly towards him, showing my bare hands.

He shouted back: I didn't understand but I thought he was angry. The gun was still pointed at us. I gave up any hope of getting directions. I stopped and then walked backwards towards the car, slowly. He stood there, still. I got back into my seat.

"Turn around, turn the bloody car around!" said Peter from the backseat.

---

[22] "Good afternoon. Excuse me, which is the direction for Liwa?" (in French)

I didn't say a word. I was shaking. Coldplay was back again and it somehow seemed stuck to the same melody today – "We live in a beautiful world" – and on the small screen of the MP3 player I could read the title of the song. It was called "Don't Panic".

They didn't fire and we turned the car slowly, as slowly as we could, and we drove back on our own tracks this time. To this day I still don't know if they were regular soldiers, or smugglers, or some sort of rebels, or simply friendly citizens of Chad defending their home from intruders. We drove on, back into the maze of tracks, and we eventually found other tracks, and then others, and one way or another we made it to the small village of Liwa where we hoped to fill up with water and camp for the evening.

We stopped by the well in the centre of the village. The well was always at the centre of any village. We said *bonjour* and we asked if we could fill up with water. We didn't get any answer, although it looked like the entire population of the village had gathered in the little square in an instant. Women, all wearing coloured robes; men, all with their heads wrapped in countless coloured shawls; kids, barefoot and dirty.

We filled our jerrycans with water and as we did so we sensed the hostility around us. They were not smiling, they were not begging, they were not even talking to us. Only the occasional shout from some kid, and it didn't at all resemble the usual *donnez-moi un cadeau* that we had heard so far.

The crowd surrounded us. Their eyes were full of hatred. Was it because the war in Iraq had just started and Chad was one of the most fundamentalist countries in Africa? Did they see us as invaders of their country? Did they even know about Iraq? It was hard to say, but one way or the other we were clearly not welcome there.

The first stone was thrown at us. It hit the back window of the car. It didn't break it but I wondered how many stones that window could take before it was broken. The kids shouted again, and this time the teenagers joined in. The adults didn't say a word. Not yet, and for as long as they were quiet we knew we wouldn't be attacked by the kids.

Peter pumped water into the jerrycans I held for him, my back turned away from the crowd. I didn't need to look back to sense that they were coming closer. Slowly, slowly, like a giant snake that was tightening up around us, the crowd was advancing. I was thinking that this was how one must feel before one got mobbed.

"You there, keep away. Get your hands off the car!" Richard shouted at one of the teenagers. Then he picked the oldest man he could see around and he talked to him in French, hoping to get him on our side. If we managed to bring the elders on side we knew we wouldn't be attacked.

"You there, yes, you! You should be controlling him! You see? He's thrown a stone at us. We are guests of this village. You should be ashamed of this, you should be telling him off!"

This strategy seemed to work, and although the old man did not answer back or even look at Richard, he said something and the kid moved away. But they didn't leave and the hatred in their eyes didn't go away. They were still there, slowly advancing. I had no idea what they wanted, what they would do next. I believed they didn't know either. One thing was clear, though: we were not welcome there and the longer we stayed, the more we tested their patience.

A kid tried to open one of the car doors on the other side, where Richard couldn't see him.

"Go to the left side," Peter shouted at me. "We must stop them from getting into the car!"

I let him handle the jerrycans and I went to the left. Richard was on the other side. I pushed the cheeky kid away and yelled at him. Another stone hit the car, somewhere next to my head. I wondered if it had been meant to hit me instead.

On the other side of the car, I could hear Richard shouting.

"Move away! Move the fuck away from the car!"

"Peter! This looks like trouble! Are you done?" I shouted.

"What's going on? Are they entering the car?" I heard back.

"Not yet on my side!"

Bang! Another stone hit the car.

"Back off!" I shouted at them, this time in English, and I pushed another kid. By now I realised that it didn't matter if we spoke French or English. All that seemed to work was if we matched their aggressive looks. I didn't know why, but I had the feeling that they would only attack if they sensed we were afraid; if they sensed we were about to run away. For as long as we could face them and shout at them and show we were confident, they would stay where they were.

Peter had given up filling the jerrycans. He threw them into the open boot just as two other kids clung on to my arm.

"Let's get the hell out of here!" Peter shouted. "Drive, drive on!"

Richard jumped into the driver's seat. I managed to push away the kids who held on to my arm and got into the car.

"Drive away!" I shouted to Richard in terror. "Just drive away!"

"Peter! He's still out!"

I managed to lock my door and I could see countless angry fists banging against the window. There was no way I would dare get out now. The crowd had already sensed we were afraid.

"Drive on!" we heard Peter from outside. He had climbed up the ladder on the back door of the car, halfway to the roof. Richard hit the accelerator and the wheels swung away. There was a wall of human bodies blocking our way out and they looked even more threatening now, seeing that we were rushing away.

"Drive, just drive through them!" I cried out in panic. I was convinced by now that if we didn't get away from here they would just kill us.

Richard hesitated for a second, and then he hit the accelerator once again and somehow drove out of the circle without hitting anybody. They just jumped away, seeing the car coming at full speed towards them.

We drove like crazy on the streets of that small town, trying to get out of there before we got bogged down in sand and had to stop. Stopping here now would have been equal to suicide. Men shouted angrily and showed us their fists, kids threw more stones, and I couldn't stop thinking about Peter who was still out clinging on to the ladder. We drove out into the wind once again, and once we were a safe distance away Richard stopped and we collected Peter, all covered in dust from the back of the car. By a miracle he hadn't been hit by any of the stones that were thrown at us.

We were safe and the car managed to miraculously survive without any windows being broken. And we were wiser after having learned rule number two of surviving in Chad: don't ever dream of stopping to fill up with water in any little village on the way!

MY DRIVE – THIRD DAY

WE woke up in the governor's palace that morning. We were still camping and I still slept in my dirty, dusty tent, but it didn't matter. The main thing that mattered, the only thing actually, was that we could put up the tents in the courtyard of the so-called "palace" and fall asleep knowing that several armed guards were patrolling around the walls and that we were safe: possibly as safe as we could be in this country.

We had arrived in the small town of Bol late the previous night, almost by nightfall, which was often a very bad time. Usually by nightfall, we would have been lying down in our tents after having already figured out a safe place to sleep. We drove around for a bit and found the town pretty calm: no angry, threatening mobs here, but none-too-friendly faces either, and we soon realised we still needed protection. And this time the house of an average villager would not be enough. We needed to be in the courtyard of someone powerful, where we could be sure we wouldn't be disturbed.

We asked around to find out who the most important person in the town was. We were told that the governor of the whole province of Bol had his headquarters here and we were showed in the direction of his "palace". We didn't know the man and neither did we know anybody who knew him. But we went on and knocked at his gates with a mixture of self-confidence and naivety that seemed totally out of place to us but very acceptable to the guards. We said we wanted to the see the big man. Did we know him? No, we didn't. Did he know us? No. What did we want from him? Protection. We wanted to be his guests for the night.

A miracle happened. The chief of the guards returned with a man wearing a long robe. He was still chewing and he seemed to have been disturbed in the middle of his dinner.

He asked us who we were. We said we were travellers. He then asked us what we wanted. We said we had just arrived in town and we didn't know where to camp, and that we needed protection.

We were still standing in front of the gates and he didn't make any attempt to invite us in. He was probably trying to figure out what he should do with us. He seemed surprised to find a woman among these three strange, dirty foreigners. I explained to him where we came from and where we were going and then, in an attempt to be as charming as I could, I pointed to the Chadian flag tied on to the front of his building and I told him that the country I came from had the exact same colours: blue, yellow and red.

"It's not possible," he said, smiling at me. "You must have stolen the colours from us, then."

I thought that it was more likely to be the other way around, but it didn't seem the right thing to say.

"Probably," I said. "But we put them in another order: still vertical stripes but red, yellow and blue."

"What a coincidence!" he laughed. And then to all of us, "You can camp here tonight if you want. You'll be considered as my guests. Since Madame has the same colours as us..."

It was a very powerful argument, apparently. We thanked him. He wished us goodnight and vanished back into the house. I thought back to our "civilised" countries in Europe and tried to imagine three hungry, dirty travellers knocking at the gates of some MP and asking to camp in his courtyard for the night. I doubted the same laws of hospitality would apply and once again I realised that what we called "civilisation" was something very relative.

The soldiers opened the gates, and as we drove the car in we knew we had reached heaven. We knew that no one in this town would ever dream of harming a single hair on our heads for as long as we were guests of the most powerful man in the province. Sometimes when one needs protection, the best thing one can do is ask for it.

After a night spent behind safe walls, I started my day of driving full of joy. We even had a glimpse of the lake: the Lake Chad was to be seen from the central square in the town of Bol and we had a long look at it. We didn't dare to take pictures though. In this country they could apparently arrest you for a lot less than taking what could appear to be suspicious spy pictures.

We drove on, and I was pleased to discover that the sandy tracks of the previous two days were gradually melting into a dirt road. My joy was diminished, however, when I realised that this whole road was covered in a very fine, grey powder like dust, called *feche*, that entered every single corner of the car. We soon started to see other vehicles on this road, and judging from their increased frequency we thought we must be approaching the capital. Huge trucks overloaded with people completely wrapped up, their faces covered by colourful shawls, passed by. Armed guards were invariably sitting on the boots of each of those trucks and I wondered whether they were soldiers or bandits or simply armed citizens. They didn't have any uniform whatsoever and I doubted that the largest part of the Chadian army would have any type of uniform.

When we hit the tarmac at the end of a heavy drive along the *feche* road, we knew we were very close to the capital. A soldier, again judging by his gun, waved at the car to stop. I slowed down.

"What are you doing?" Peter looked at me.

"I'm stopping. He waved me to stop."

"So what? He just wants a bribe. Just drive on."

We were coming closer to the guy now. I was in doubt, but the memory of the other guy who stopped us just as we got out of Boll was still fresh. Maybe Peter was right.

"Do you think I should just drive on?"

"Yeah."

This was coming from both of them and I felt they were right. I hit the accelerator. From the corner of my eye, I could see the surprised look of the soldier as we drove past and then I could see the rest in my back mirror: he suddenly swung around, pulled his gun off his shoulder and pointed it at us. I hit the brakes that very second. The whole car shook, and then eventually came to a stop in a few metres.

He was quite angry judging from the amount of yelling that came from the lower part of his face, hidden somewhere under the huge shawl that wrapped his head. He was yelling at us – surprisingly – in French, and demanded to see our documents. We gave him everything: passports, driving licences, insurance, the carnet[23]... everything.

"What were you doing? Why did you not stop? I know you saw me, I saw you looking at me!" he shouted at me.

What could I tell him? That I didn't stop because I knew he would ask for a bribe?

---

[23] The Carnet de Passages en Douane is a customs document that identifies a driver's motor vehicle. It is required in order to take a vehicle into a significant number of countries in Africa.

"I wanted to stop," I told him in the most docile voice I could find. "Only that…"

"Only that what?" he yelled back.

"Only that I hit the accelerator instead of the brake. I don't know how it happened, I'm sorry. I did not mean to cause offence."

I tried hard not to smile. To my right, Peter must have thought I had gone insane.

But I knew that this was a winning tactic. Playing the fragile woman who admits her incapacity always works in front of a macho type. The soldier seemed to swallow my explanation.

He was now busy going through our passports, and my travel mates got a sermon about why the UK should not have helped Bush invade Iraq. He then moved on to clarifying the next issue on his mind.

"Why are you driving?"

I knew what he meant but I couldn't be bothered to think of an explanation.

He then asked my travel mates:

"You two in there, and a woman is driving? How did you let this happen?"

To him, this was as an insult to the manliness of my travel mates. Peter decided to serve him the full explanation.

"Because we're on a very long journey, we all drive. We rotate. One of us drives every day. Today it is her turn to drive."

It was beyond his understanding and obviously he did not get it. Peter gave up.

"Look at you, two men in this car, letting a woman drive. Who can understand…"

He went on for a while, but he didn't get any more explanations so he turned to another subject, his main subject in fact, and the one that he had left until the end:

"You need to pay me 5000 CFA."

It was useless to ask why. It was a bribe, just because he happened to be there, or just because he had a gun, or just because he held all our documents.

"No."

This was in fact three "nos" combined into one. He asked again. We refused again. Then some mumbo jumbo started and Peter told him about our friend the Governor and our other friend the ambassador and somehow he believed us. Or maybe just didn't know what to do with three white tourists who refused to pay a bribe.

As we drove on, I checked my back mirror again. His gun was pointing down this time. I couldn't see his face, all wrapped up in his many layers, but I bet he had a doubtful expression. He might have learned two new things today: it was possible not to receive a bribe when you asked for one, and yes, women could drive. I wasn't sure which one he found more puzzling.

As for us, we had just learned rule number three of surviving in Chad: when a man with a gun waves at you, you stop. Immediately.

WE arrived in the capital, N'Djamena, and we left it as soon as we could. We were lucky enough to find a plush Novotel hotel to camp around. At €150 a night, the rooms were far too expensive for us: after all, we could survive two weeks with this money. We negotiated a much lower amount and they allowed us to camp in their grounds. Once again, this was safe territory and that was all that mattered.

N'Djamena was the last place where we could make a decision regarding the route to follow for the rest of the trip: we could either try to get a Sudanese visa and drive east through Sudan into Ethiopia and Kenya, or south through Cameroon and Congo into Angola. The time to take a decision had arrived, and when we took it, it was one of those rare instances when the three of us agreed totally. We were not here to see the touristy Africa, and the route from Nairobi to Cape Town was more or less the route all tourists, backpackers and overland trucks took. We had come here to see the real thing, the authentic Africa as I liked to call it, and there was so little left of it already and so much taken up by mass tourism that we felt it was a pity to try and avoid it. We had heard the way south through Angola was now open – we had been emailing with several travellers who seemed to have made it safe and sound through the country – and we looked on the maps and found a road going south through Cameroon and Congo. And we decided to take it.

N'Djamena was right on the border with Cameroon, and as soon as we had our visas in our pockets we couldn't wait to get out of there. Chad was definitely not among my favourite countries, and it was not so much because of the harsh wind that kept on blowing day and night or the potholes in the *feche* road that was in no better condition than the sandy piste with its countless tracks of the previous two days. It had more to do with the attitude of the officials, who, with the notable exception of the Governor of Bol, were all in a constant search for a bribe. It had to do with the scary power a man with a gun had in this country. It had to do with the hatred I had seen in the eyes of the people in the village where we had stopped to fill up with water. In a way I could understand them: maybe they had given up hope of a normal life. After all, Chad was a country where some 10 years ago, a warlord marched into the capital with his private army of 2000 soldiers and took over the presidency. He was still the president today, after some "democratic" elections. Maybe all those people were tired of it all: of the army and the ruler in the capital, of the harsh wind of the desert and the abuses; tired of the continuous conflicts the country had been experiencing for the last 30 years – there were still fights going on in the northern Tibesti area. Or maybe they just didn't like foreigners and had not yet started to figure out a way to use them to their advantage as their neighbours from the much more tourist-friendly West Africa had.

One more encounter with the officials, the last one in Chad: the border point. Sure enough, they took our passports and then demanded 5000 CFA. For what? For returning the documents with the exit stamp.

We knew better than that. We said no, thank you. They kept us waiting on a small, wooden bench. It was a time game and we knew it. We took our books out and started reading patiently. After a couple of hours we got our passports back with the precious exit stamp and no charge.

As we crossed the river that separated Chad from Cameroon, we learned that we needed to pay for a return ticket over the bridge. No, it didn't matter that we would never be crossing that bridge back into Chad; it didn't matter that we would never again come back to this country. They only sold return tickets over that bridge.

We bought the ticket. We got out of Chad. We threw away the return. And we felt that in fact, it was quite a good deal.

CHAPTER 19 – DO NOT BOTHER THE OFFICIALS

(CAMEROON, APRIL 2003)

WE were in Northern Cameroon, in the small town of Buea, and for the first time on this trip I was totally alone. Richard and Peter had gone to climb Mount Cameroon, some 4000 metres high – the highest peak in West Africa. I had no desire to push my already weakened limits with this endeavour so I remained in a Protestant mission. I was to be alone for a couple of days but I had a clean bed to sleep in. That was all that mattered for the moment.

It was evening and I went out alone for a bite of street food. After five months in Africa, I was finally not afraid of walking by myself on a small, dark street of an African village at night. There were petrol lamps on small tables and the mammas with the big pots were out, like everywhere in Africa.

A tall teenage boy was following me for a while and I was very well aware of his walking behind me. I was in the midst of other people, though, and I knew that nothing would happen as long as I was among the others. But the way back to the mission was dark, along a lonely path, and I wouldn't have been too happy knowing that this lad was still following me.

I decided to turn around and speak to him.

"Hey you, what do you want from me?"

I looked directly into his eyes and I came close to him. I had spoken loud enough to be heard by some of the people around us. I knew that if it came to trouble, the people around were the only ones I could rely on for help. My travel mates must have been well away up Mount Cameroon by now.

"Excuse me, Miss; I just wanted to ask you a small question..."

His voice was weak and he almost whispered. He spoke English. They all spoke English in Northern Cameroon; it was the only country in Africa where they spoke both English and French as their official languages.

"What do you want?" I still looked him straight in the eye, but by now I felt pretty reassured that he had no violent intentions.

"Miss... you know... I was wondering..." he stopped.

"What?"

"I was wondering if there is any way I could enter your life?"

I was puzzled.

"As a lover boy, I mean."

He was serious: his eyes, wide open, and his trembling lips revealed the effort he had gone through in order to pronounce the words.

Was he trying to make a move on me? Or, more likely, was he trying to sell his body to me just like a young teenage girl would probably try to sell her body to a white male tourist?

I didn't feel afraid any longer. I didn't even feel embarrassed; just amused and sad at the same time.

"I don't think so, my friend, I really don't think so."

He did not insist. I turned around to carry on my search for a fat mamma with a big pot of fried yams. He didn't move, standing right there where he had stopped, his eyes following me and his thick lips still trembling. I couldn't tell if the expression on his face meant he was feeling rejected or relieved.

SEVERAL days later, the three of us were back together and we were also back to our driving routine. We took the road south, straight through the rainforest towards the Congo border. Our initial plan had been to head down on the western route, through Gabon and then Congo, but after speaking with a French expat we had met in a garage in Douala we had been persuaded to give up this plan. Apparently the roads were really bad and the ferry crossing a nightmare. He told us of another way, a way we had not thought about: going east, deep into the rainforest, we would eventually come up to Moloundou, the last human settlement we could see on the map. From there, we would be able to cross the border into Congo, where we would hit a reasonably good road that our Michelin map showed to be a full tarmac one. It all made sense and we decided to take his advice. From what we could see on the map, it looked like we would safely emerge on the other side in Namibia in a couple of weeks or so. We had no idea that once again, planning would turn out to be totally useless in those lands.

Everything seemed to be breaking apart in the car. The driver's door had not worked for a few days now, and whoever was the unfortunate driver for the day had to jump on and off through the other door. The back window couldn't be opened but this was something we had put up with for some time now. Apparently, electrical windows were a lot more fragile than good old mechanical ones like the two in front. The compass on the dashboard had gone insane. Either that or we kept on moving in circles: it swung from north to south, east and west in a matter of seconds. The suspension was broken (so said Peter and I had to believe him, since I didn't understand much about suspension anyway). All I could feel was a weird sensation of having no springs left every time we landed, after having jumped over yet another pothole.

The road looked like a red wound through the lush, green forest. It was my driving day again. I seemed to get the worst drives lately. This one, although not nearly as tough as the *feche* road of Chad that was still fresh in my memory, was still a harsh one. The road would wind through the rainforest, and despite its holes and sudden bends it was all fine and manageable. The problem was when you met a huge truck coming from the other direction. The road was barely wide enough for two cars to pass side by side. The trucks were driving at a mad speed. I didn't think they would have been able to stop, not even if they had wanted to. I usually tried to squeeze as close as I could to the trees marking the edge of the forest. The truck came down, shaking on all its wheels, not even dreaming of slowing down, and then the miracle happened and it somehow got by.

All of these trucks were carrying huge tree trunks, sometimes one trunk only, sometimes two, very occasionally three. The tree trunks were long, much longer than any driving regulations would allow, and very thick, so thick that sometimes their trunk was as wide as the front cabin of the truck. Slowly, slowly, one after the other, they were all carried away, first by trucks, then by ships, then they would eventually be cut into expensive furniture and sold, living out their lives holding the expensive clothes of some rich European family. In other words, the rainforest was being harvested just as the logging companies said, although they "harvested" something they hadn't planted in the first place.

"Keep both hands on the wheel!"

Peter was trying to teach me – once again – how to drive. He would occasionally enter such teaching moods, and when he was stuck in one of them he could carry on for a whole day: "get your thumbs outside the wheel", "keep your hands at an even distance around the wheel", "don't turn it with a sudden movement", and so on; he had a lot of valuable advice and my only regret was that when we set the driving turns, mine came after Richard's, which meant that I always had to put up with Peter as my map reader while Richard had his day of rest on the back seat.

I ignored him. I always tried to ignore him when he got into the "I'll teach you how to" mood. But I couldn't always manage to, and when this happened, we got bogged down in one of our endless arguments and it was much more unpleasant than when the car used to get bogged down in sand.

Another pothole in the road materialised in front of my eyes. I was driving fast, over 40 km/h, which on those roads was simply too fast. But driving at this speed allowed us to fly over the small corrugations in the road, which meant that everybody had a more bearable day. Otherwise our muscles would have had to take in every little shake, and this would have been far too much for our backs, as well as whatever was left working from the car parts.

Driving fast meant that I couldn't always avoid such potholes. Like now, for instance, when I saw it coming: I panicked a bit, squeezed the wheel and off we went. A big shake. We were back on the road.

"If you see it coming, why do you close your eyes instead of just moving away from it?"

I didn't see Peter's expression, but I guessed he must have

had that sarcastic look in his eyes again.

"What do you mean, I close my eyes? I don't! It's not true!"

Another hole in the horizon. Instead of figuring out how to avoid it, I was now busy trying to see if I really closed my eyes. We went straight into it and then we were back on the road. We had a short flight and the landing was not one of the nicest.

"Bloody hell!" Peter was shaken. "Will we be flying next?"

"Come on, Peter, you saw how deep it was. Of course we got a bit shaken."

"Yeah, right. It was pretty deep; seems like a good idea not to go in it if it's so deep!"

I didn't have the time to build up an argument. Another hole speeded towards me. And this time it was really big.

"Attention!" Peter shouted. "This time we'll fly!"

I don't know if we flew. What I knew was that it hurt as we touched the ground again.

"Do you think all four wheels were in the air this time?" Richard, from the back seat, took a sudden interest in my driving.

"Yeah, that was a real take off," Peter agreed. "At least keep your hands on the wheel when we come back to the ground, otherwise we'll really roll next time," he added.

Another hole, another jump. I was thinking that I should slow down and I did so, until the car started shaking badly. We had reached the speed where the corrugations started to make themselves felt.

"Oh no!" Richard shouted again from the back seat. "Better the jumps than this."

"Come on, speed up. We'll go crazy with these shakes," Peter agreed.

I wished I could have listened to Alanis Morissette playing. I could have turned up the volume to the max and not have heard the two of them. But the MP3 was dead, like many other parts of the car, so I had to put up with listening to Peter instead.

I speeded up. Then we jumped again. Then I came dangerously close to some chicken in the road in front of someone's hut, and I had to put up with Peter's remarks about how close we were to having a decent soup tonight. Then I saw a heavy lorry speeding towards us on the narrow dirt road, and I panicked and this time almost closed my eyes. It went on like this for a few hours and I was concentrating so hard and feeling so exhausted that I didn't even hear Peter's helpful driving tips any more. I noticed that it had started to rain.

Our strategy of taking our time on our way south had finally turned against us and we had caught up with the rainy season. We should have crossed the equator by now and thus be on the safe side once again. The rainy season was travelling north, and south of the equator the dry season was just starting. We were still on the wrong side.

And in Africa everything was pushed to the extreme. When it was hot, it was hot, when it was humid it was humid and when it rained it really poured down every day.

The rain was never far away here. It came back every day, sometimes in the afternoon, sometimes in the evening, sometimes all day long. The water made the clay of the road even more slippery. In fact it turned it into a sort of ice surface. We were skidding deeply now, and the car moved from right to left with almost no response from the wheel.

"Bloody hell!" yelled Peter next to me, having probably seen the huge truck coming down at a mad speed in the middle of the road.

"Pull up, to the right! Pull up!"

There was nowhere to pull up. There were trees on both sides of the road and that maniac driver seemed ready to drive right over us. I could spot a huge tree trunk on the back of that truck. If the truck and the trunk decided to pass over our car, there would be nothing left of the three of us.

But it seemed we had a good angel on our side. I slowed down and almost stopped as he passed by, miraculously without even touching us even though there must have been only a few centimetres separating the two vehicles. I gave a sigh of relief and I tried to move again. It was impossible. The wheels were sliding and spinning on their own axis. We were stuck.

We got out of the car. The road surface was transformed into a deep mud field. Our boots sank into this sticky mixture up to our ankles. We got ready to push the car. I let Peter drive and I placed my hands on the boot next to Richard's, under the rain, wondering how much mud we would get in our faces as the wheels started spinning. But no, there was no need for this, there was no need for pushing. With one hand only, Richard moved the car. And it was not a new form of magic. The heavy, overloaded Land Rover was sliding on mud, just as it would on ice. It felt weightless.

It poured down with heavy rain, we were up to our ankles in deep mud and we were laughing hysterically in the middle of the road as Richard pushed the car with one hand only, then four fingers, two fingers...

Back in the car, we realised the problem now was not ending up in the ditch. The road was somehow curved, and since it felt more or less like ice the car tended to slide away towards the sides. And when this happened, one of us got out into the rain again and pushed it back into the middle of the road with one hand.

I remembered the sand and the heat and the heavy pushing in the desert. Was that better than the rain and the mud and the ice-like surface of the road now? Hard to say.

I was back in the driver's seat. Peter was back to telling me how to keep my hands on the wheel. I didn't listen; I couldn't be bothered to.

"You know, back in my country you wouldn't pass your driving test."

But we were not in his country. We were in Southern Cameroon in the heart of the rainforest, driving south towards a hypothetical border with Congo under a heavy downpour. And my driving felt just fine here.

MOLOUNDOU was a small sleepy village in the middle of the rainforest. In the middle of nowhere, to be more precise. I somehow had the feeling that we were close to the border, although the whole concept of a border was as foreign to this never-ending rainforest as the concept of countries. We had arrived here the night before, at the end of the muddy ice-like piste along which we had left our suspension. As soon as we arrived, we learned that we must leave again since there was no border crossing here. We were told to go further east, deeper and deeper into the forest. There we would find the mysterious town of Sokodou, which did not feature on any map. There would be a crossing there, they said.

We found an *auberge* and I shared yet another dirty, small and smelly room with Richard. We woke up next morning. We loaded everything into the car. We went to look for a bite to eat before we left. A man came by and asked Peter for his documents. A lot of them did: everybody was up for hassling some foreigners in this town, as in all the others; we had learned this by now. The man did not give up. Peter, instead of ignoring him, which was usually the best strategy, started an endless debate.

"And why do you think I should show you my documents?"

"Because I ask you to," the fat little man said.

"And why should I listen to you?" Peter seemed to be having fun.

The wrong type of fun, I thought.

"Because I am the chief of police."

"If you are the chief of police, where is your uniform?"

"At home: I don't wear it every day. But you must come with me now. And you must give me all your documents."

You're not the first one to try, my friend, I was about to jump in. A lot of lads were interested in making a living from "confiscating" the passports of travellers and then returning them for a fee. I had no doubt our friend here was in this game too.

"Peter, just ignore him," I said.

Peter was having fun, though.

"So if you don't have your uniform, then maybe you can show me your ID to prove that you're the chief of police."

The man had no ID. All he had was an angry face. He was threatening us by now. Peter was laughing.

"I am the chief of police and you have to report to me!"

"Yeah right, and I am the Queen of Great Britain," said Peter with a grin.

I thought it had gone too far. I stepped in and told Peter that this was the most stupid form of morning fun that he could find. That he should shut up and ignore the hassler.

The man suddenly turned to me.

"You too, I need to see your documents."

I was not as polite as Peter. I was not as patient either. I was fed up and I was eager to leave this border town and I didn't have time to play the game with an idle hustler who claimed he was the chief of police.

"You're not gonna get any documents, clear? Now get the fuck away from me, go to hell or wherever you want."

It turned out that he was indeed the chief of police.

Three hours later we knew we were in deep trouble. The little man's veins had become so thick that I thought he was about to have a heart attack. Strangely enough, he didn't mind Peter's mockery so much: what he couldn't put up with was my insult. He went home and he came back, dressed in his uniform and with three other soldiers. We had to give them all our documents, passports, carnet, driving licences and all that, and we had to do so in a matter of seconds. Richard, who had just come back from one of his wanders, was looking at the two of us in total astonishment, not understanding what on earth we had got ourselves into.

We were then taken to the police station and waited for the small fat man to be kind enough to open the door of his office and let us in, and maybe even give us our documents back. And we waited... and waited. We were still waiting, and by now we realised that we were going to see the full extent of a small African border town police chief's revenge for his wounded pride.

"What on earth could you do to him that he's so pissed off?" Richard was still struggling to understand. "I leave the two of you for a minute and when I'm back we're almost arrested; what have you done?"

"Nothing," said Peter. "I just explained to him that I needed to see his ID if he wanted to see my passport."

"Yeah, Peter, right." I was simmering with anger still. "If you weren't in one of your funny moods, telling him you're the Queen of England, we wouldn't be here. It's because you mocked him that we're here. You should have ignored him."

"I rather think we're here because you sent him to hell. That was a lot worse than my mockery."

It turned out that he was right. The chief of police in Moloundou was offended, as deeply offended as one could ever be, and it was not so much because of Peter's jokes but because of my remark. A woman, incredible but true, had shouted at him. A woman had dared to send him to hell in full sight and earshot of his fellow villagers. He felt overcome with shame.

And he would be avenged. We sat on the wooden benches for the whole morning. Then he came out of his office – yet another small wooden hut – and went home to eat. He didn't even look at us. Then, a couple of hours later, he came back and passed us by again. Then we waited for the whole afternoon. Then, just before evening, he called us in.

He gave us a sermon and we had to apologise. Then he told us about the rules of polite behaviour with the representatives of the authority in Cameroon and we apologised again. Then he came towards me and he gave me an even bigger speech about how I should never, ever dare to raise my voice to a man again. I smiled and I apologised, despite the anger I felt in my stomach. There was nothing we could do. He had our passports and for as long as he kept them we were going to be waiting on his small, wooden bench in front of the office.

Then he told us that he forgave us, just because he had a big heart. But he warned us to seriously reconsider our behaviour, because on the other side, in Congo, the policemen were not as nice as he was. We apologised once more.

And then he produced our passports and just before he handed them out to us and just as I thought we would have to apologise one more time, he stopped in front of me and spoke to me.

"Madame, next time, control your temper. It is a very good skill to have; to control one's temper. You seem to have some work to do here." His head was a few inches away from mine and I could see the hatred in his eyes.

Maybe he was just a corrupt official in need of showing off his huge ego. But in one thing he was right. Maybe I did need to do a better job of controlling my temper.

We got our passports back eventually, and wasting a full day on the wooden benches of his highness the police chief meant that we set off out of the town as the sun was close to setting. This was a big no-no on the roads of Africa. But staying in this town for another night and risking another encounter with our friend over next morning's breakfast seemed a hell of a bigger no-no.

CHAPTER 20 – MR FRANK THE FAN

(POKOLA, CONGO, MAY 2003)

WE had managed to cross the river Sangha into Congo, just outside a town that didn't exist on any map. A mysterious ferry arrived and took us to the other side, where a grumpy official stamped our passports and unsuccessfully tried to get some money from us. He seemed to have accepted that he had to let us go but he followed us outside his hut and just before we left he asked us with a glimmer of amusement in his eyes: "So, where are you going?"

"To Brazzaville; to your capital."

"And how are you getting there?"

"We will follow this road, cross the forest and get to the capital."

He looked at us, puzzled, or maybe simply amused.

Peter unfolded the Michelin map and showed him the road, the solid, red-coloured road. Red stands for tarmac on Michelin maps.

"There is no road."

"What do you mean, there's no road? It's here, look at it!" Peter pointed it out on the map.

"No road," he repeated stubbornly. "It was a road, but not any more."

He must be joking, we thought.

"This road will carry on for some 40 km to Ouésso. Then it will stop. There is no road from Ouésso on."

The chilling feeling that he might not be joking started to take shape in my mind.

How did people travel to the capital then? By plane from Ouésso, he said. Obviously the plane was too small to get the car on board. How did all the trucks we saw around move in and out? Using the route through Cameroon and Gabon and then re-entering Congo just near Brazzaville: in other words, using the route we had discarded in favour of this non-existent one. What were we to do? He shrugged his shoulders. It wasn't his business. We remained there, outside his hut, standing still around the useless map. If he was right and there was no road further on, we were in trouble. We only had one entrance visa and 10 minutes ago we had been stamped out of Cameroon and into Congo. We could not go back. The road they took, through Cameroon and Gabon, was forbidden to us. We did not have another visa.

It turned out that we might get some help in the mysterious town of Pokola, another place not included on any map but which apparently was "just around the corner", some 20 km further down the road. "There are white people working there." I remembered the lad on the streets of Guinea who told us he would take us to "white people". Was another miracle about to happen? We had nothing to lose, so we decided to go on and have a look.

POKOLA was a little village with a busy central square. We soon spotted the main place in town: it was a huge compound with tall wire fences and lots of guards by the gates. On the building we could read the name of the company: CIB – Congo International du Bois. We were in front of the headquarters of a major logging company, the end of the jungle road and the starting point of all those trucks with huge trees we had seen on the way. It was French-owned and apparently there were a lot of *toubabs* working there. Maybe they could help us understand where we were and where to go next. Maybe they would tell us that the policeman had simply been joking with us.

But before we could try to make our way through the 20 guards by the gates, we needed to stop somewhere else and we were reminded as soon as we pulled up in the car that in this country there was one authority only and that was the local police.

"You need to report to the police. Immediately," the first black face we saw told us.

Determined to get things right this time, we immediately set off for the police station. It was easy to spot; it was the only wooden hut in the square with a Congolese flag on top of it.

Madame Adjutant was not there, we were told by a half-asleep soldier, but we must leave our passports and return in a couple of hours. We did as we were told. Was there a road onwards to Brazzaville? He didn't know. Only Madame Adjutant knew.

Next we headed towards the headquarters of CIB, back in the main square. We didn't talk to each other: we didn't say a word about this story of a non-existent road. We were too shocked and too afraid that it might be true. But we needed to have someone we could trust confirm this, and we hoped to find that someone inside the well-guarded compound. The only problem was that the guards wouldn't dream of letting us in.

"Who are you looking for?"

"For the manager of this factory."

"What's his name?"

We didn't know.

"What is your business here?"

We didn't have an answer.

We were trying to persuade them to let us in but they wouldn't listen. We were soon surrounded by people passing through the square: the chief of the guards was shouting, we were shouting back. I hoped that somehow all this noise in front of their gates would attract the attention of one of the managers inside, but it seemed in vain.

I felt somebody tapping my shoulder. I turned and he smiled. A wide, white-teeth smile on a dark brown face.

"*Din ce tara veniti dumneavostra domana?*"[24]

He was speaking Romanian. For a second I didn't react. Hearing my mother tongue spoken in the middle of the jungle in Congo somehow seemed to be the most natural thing in the world. In his hands I could see the cover of my passport. He must have got it from the police station.

"*Voiam sa va uram bine ati venit in tara nostra!*"[25] he carried on, and his smile widened.

I was still speechless. I was afraid that if I opened my mouth and spoke, the illusion would disappear.

He carried on in Romanian and told me that he had been among the 200 students that their Government had sent

---

[24] "Which country do you come from, Miss?" (in Romanian)
[25] "We just wanted to say, welcome to our country!" (in Romanian)

away to university in Romania some 20 years ago as part of an aid programme between the communist government of Romania and that of Congo. He had spent four years in my country, learned the language and come back with a diploma in "Management of Forests and Waters". And he could still remember the language he had learnt 20 years ago. It turned out that he was the husband of the mysterious Madame Adjutant. Madame was the chief of police in this small village and he, being her husband, had no problem entering her office and having a look at the passports of the three foreigners in town. And, seeing my Romanian passport, he thought he would give me a warm welcome to his country.

I was still speechless, but somewhere in the background I could hear Peter and Richard shouting at the chief of the guards. I suddenly remembered why we were there and decided to use my new friend to good purpose.

"Do you know the French people who work here?"

"Sure. Everybody knows them."

"How many are there?"

"A lot: they have a whole village only for themselves. They are here with their families, some with their children too. About 20 or 30 of them in total."

I thought he was exaggerating but it didn't matter. We only needed to talk to one of them.

"Do you know the name of one of them? Someone who may be in there today?"

"Sure," he said with his ready-to-help smile. "Try Pierre Dupont."

I didn't have time to thank him. I rushed to the gates and I looked straight into the eyes of an angry chief of the guards.

"We're here to see Mr Pierre Dupont. We have an appointment with him," I said with as much confidence as I could muster. The miracle happened. The gates opened instantly. Now that we knew a name we were suddenly worthy of some respect. And as we walked in and headed towards the first building that we saw, my travel mates looked so puzzled about the unexpected namedropping that I decided to give them clarification.

"A little bird whispered his name to me," I said. "In Romanian!"

We were soon talking to the man with a name. He was a middle-aged French expat who worked as a manager here, in the middle of this never-ending rainforest. He was smiling and he seemed really pleased to have us there. His office had air con, a large desk and a real office chair. There were maps all over the walls, books and a bookshelf. He called his secretary and offered us a glass of water. For a moment, we felt we were suddenly out of the rainforest and back in the office of a European company.

The first thing we asked was about the road.

"They were right to tell you the road stops. There is no road. It is impossible to reach Brazzaville by road from here."

"But the road on the map, look..."

"I know there's a road shown on the maps," he smiled. "But it's no longer a road. During their last civil war, about five years ago, they blew up the bridge on this river here." He showed us a small spot on the map. "Since they could no longer cross the river, the trucks stopped using the road and the trees have grown through it. There was no tarmac, you see, it was just a dirt road. The forest has taken it back."

"But then how do your trucks reach the capital?"

"They don't. They cross over the border to Cameroon, the same way you came, and load the timber on to the ships in Douala."

Douala was the biggest port in Cameroon and its de facto capital. So this was why we had seen all those trucks loaded with huge tree trunks on the narrow jungle roads in Cameroon. They were all coming from here.

"And if we need to drive to Brazzaville we do it through Cameroon and Gabon. There is no other way. But we don't drive too often. When we need to go there, we take our small plane. We could take you by plane to Brazzaville, if you wanted to."

"And the car?"

"Sorry, no space for the car. If you want to drive you may want to go back into Cameroon, drive all the way back to Yaoundé and then take the other road into Gabon. There is also a small dirt track into Gabon from here if you wanted to take it, but I really don't recommend it. There's been a recent outburst of the Ebola virus in this region." He pointed out the border of Gabon and Congo on the map. "Besides," he continued, "you need a visa to enter Gabon and the only place you can get that is in a capital. And that means back to Yaoundé."

We remained silent, looking at each other. What he didn't know but we did was that there was no way we could go back to Cameroon now. Our passports had been stamped out of the country and into Congo. Our visas for Cameroon were valid for one entrance only and we had used that already. There was no way they would have let us in without a new visa and we couldn't get one in the small village of Pokola or anywhere nearby. We were stuck. Really, deeply stuck.

"You know what? I think you should come to dinner at my house tonight. We can talk more about it!" Like every respectable French citizen, Pierre thought there was no problem a good dinner couldn't resolve.

And then, opening the door, he showed us how things were done the easy way in Pokola.

"Victor, please make sure these guests are lodged at the *auberge*," he told his assistant. "Please accompany them there and tell Marcel to give them rooms. Please also tell the guards that they can come into the factory whenever they choose. After that, please go and get their passports sorted out with Madame Adjutant. Tell her they are my guests and they are not to be disturbed by anybody!"

And then, turning towards us: "I'll come and pick you up by 7 tonight. And don't worry. We'll figure out a solution."

He seemed the man to make everything happen in the small village of Pokola. The only thing he couldn't do was build a road for us. But he could do all the rest, and dinner, *auberge* and no trouble with the police looked like a good enough piece of miracle for the day.

WE had no road and slowly, slowly we had come to terms with this reality and with the fact that we had to spend some more time in Pokola. But we had a lot of other things which made our life more bearable for the next week or so.

The *auberge*, for instance, was an unexpected small miracle. Built mainly to accommodate guests of the big company, it was surprisingly clean and well-kept. A few small rooms with clean bedsheets were aligned along one side, and even if they all seemed to be full, two of them became suddenly available when Pierre's name was pronounced. We got the rooms. As usual, I shared one with Richard. After all those months, this had by then become an automatic decision, plus the rooms were expensive for our budget and we were not yet sure how long we needed to stay there. Peter decided to take the other one.

Richard and Peter would never, ever take a room together, and you had sooner kill them than ask them to share the same bed. Neither of them had any problem sharing beds with me, even though they had never given me any sign that they were interested in the woman they travelled with.

I had got used to how things were. I felt much more at ease with Richard, though, and appreciated his quiet, gentlemanly manners. He would always make sure I was comfortable, that I got the best part of the bed or the first access to the shower, and he did that usually very matter-of-factly and with no jokes. I was grateful for the way he always managed to make me feel at ease but I never said anything.

The room was reasonably clean, with a small bed and a mosquito net. We even had a fan and, wonder of wonders, electricity. The *auberge* had a small generator. Peter was delighted and the first thing he did was to plug in his laptop and turn to computer games for days and nights together.

The loo was outside, the hole-in-the-ground type but clean enough. There was also one small room where you could take a bucket shower and that looked clean enough too. A small restaurant with a few tables and a smiley manager completed the picture. It was almost too good to be true.

The next good thing in Pokola was the French, with all their wonders: Pierre, Christian, Mandy and all the others, their bars and their drinks, their spotless air-conditioned houses, and we felt we were sliding again into another world as evening came and Pierre came by in a huge, clean 4x4 and took us to his house, hidden in the middle of another well-guarded compound that started where the locals' village ended. It was, in fact, another village, the one of the white expats, with beautiful wooden houses built of the most expensive mahogany. Pierre had luxury furniture, air con and a fully equipped kitchen. He had a real table with real chairs, and the table was laid out by a maid dressed in a uniform. We were told that inside their small compound they had their own swimming pool, tennis court, bar, hospital and pharmacy. There was a small supermarket stocked with imported goods from France and two nuns were running a school for the few kids who were staying with their parents in this small community. They had their own power generator and their small plane, which was ready to take them on a short flight to Yaoundé or Douala in case of any emergency. They went back to France every three months and they had one month off. They seemed to be enjoying their life, making a lot of money and not spending a penny on living. Everything – the house, the food, the maid, the hospital and the school – were provided by the company in a desperate attempt to convince employees to live in the middle of the jungle.

It felt we were reliving the miracle that happened in Guinea, where Richard and I were the unexpected guests of the guys from Rio Tinto. The same openness, the same readiness to help another European in need, the same feeling of sliding in and out of a parallel world: the world that reminded us of home, of good food and clean beds, of everything we had left behind.

The solution to our dilemma, they told us, was to wait. Waiting was the miraculous solution to all problems in Africa. The most obvious way to Brazzaville for us was by water, they said. The river Sangha, the same one that divided Cameroon from Congo and that we had crossed on the ferry, was flowing through the village. This would ultimately flow into the River Congo, which would pass through the capital, Brazzaville. If we managed to find a boat big enough to load the car on to and that would go down to Brazzaville, we would be sorted. The problem was that no such boats were going down the river. We were at the end of the dry season and the water level was low, so low that the big boats would not leave for fear they would get stuck in some sandbank on the way. As soon as the water level rose enough there would be a boat, they said: the boat of the captain Kikuli, which would go down to Brazzaville as it did every year. And this boat was big enough to fit the car on.

So wait, they said. How long? Who knows? Maybe a couple of days, maybe a couple of weeks. It could even take longer than a month. Wait for the rain.

So we waited, day after day, in our small *auberge* room. We got to know the village inside out and we set our routines, and we soon felt like we had been living there forever and we would live there for the rest of our lives. Pokola was not shown on any map, and when Peter took the GPS coordinates, 01°24' north and 16°19' east, and we plotted this on the maps, we found out that we were in the middle of the rainforest, just north of the equator. To the rest of the world, Pokola simply did not exist. To us, it was our new universe.

There were good things we got used to, like the occasional dinners and drinks with the French expats. There were also less pleasant things we had to get used to, but this was simply the way life carried on in this small village and one had to face both the nice and the not so nice, like Madame Monique for instance.

Monique was the mysterious chief of police, Madame Adjutant as she was also called, and we finally met her the third time we came by her office in the small wooden hut in a vain attempt to recover our passports. She was a middle-aged beauty, fat as all respectable mammas were and boasting an impressive amount of facial hair. I suspect she had to shave every day, just like a man. I never quite understood how important the grade of adjutant was, but she was displaying her uniform and carrying her decorations on her huge breasts with such dignity that it seemed she was second-in-command only after the president in Brazzaville.

Her original hair was black, very curly and short. On top of that she had attached long extensions of soft, blonde hair in the form of a ponytail. We instantly decided to name her Monique, the Dragon Woman.

"So what do you want from me?" she said, after having asked all possible questions about where we came from and where we were going.

We told her that we didn't really want anything from her except to get our passports back. But this was not so easy. Our visas were not to her liking, our passports were not to her liking either, and she told us we were in trouble. Unless, of course, we agreed to pay her 25,000 CFA each, which was a lot of money: about five times the usual figure for a bribe that we had been quoted all around Chad, Cameroon and at the border post in Congo. She would then stamp another visa in our passports and do us the honour of signing on top of this new stamp. Just because we were the guests of Monsieur Pierre, she added, and also because her husband had studied in my country, she could be persuaded to offer us this very good deal.

We were tempted to refuse this bribe as we had refused all the others on the way. To tell her that no, we were not paying and our visas were perfectly acceptable, and to tell her that we had all the time in the world to wait for our passports to be returned. After all, there was nowhere we could have gone anyway. But we were too tired and maybe a bit wiser, and by now we had come to understand how things worked in this country. And maybe we had a glimmer of intuition which told us that this price was well worth it to avoid all the trouble that would otherwise come, and the long, soft, blonde ponytail of Madame Adjutant seemed to tell us we shouldn't mess around with her, and even Pierre suggested we do as we were told. So we paid what she wanted and got the precious stamp on our passports. Later on, it proved to be our lifejacket.

A DAY LIKE MANY OTHERS IN POKOLA

The morning:
I lay in bed, awake ever since the sun came out. There was no way one could sleep. It was too hot and the sticky bedsheets were already wet with sweat. To my right, Richard read his book. He was out of the dirty, greenish mosquito net which by now hung over my half of the bed only. In his corner, the fan kept on turning its blades with the same slow rhythm I remembered from last night, yesterday, the day before. It could hardly make a difference, but psychologically one feels better next to a fan. I wondered how long it could carry on before it broke down. It had been turned on non-stop for a few days now.

"What's up outside?"

"Not much. Sun. Hot."

"Any clouds?"

This was the big question, the question we would go to sleep with and the question we would wake up with. We were still waiting for the rain.

"Nope."

Having clarified the main issue of the day, I slowly got into my morning routine. I climbed out of bed, trying not to step on Richard's long legs as I got out. It must have been early morning still, but it was burning hot. Like yesterday. Like the day before. Like all the days in this town.

As I got out, heading towards the toilets, I noticed a couple of locals whispering outside Peter's window. One of them carried a small bundle covered with several cloths under his arm.

Peter had a deep interest in stripping the African villages of their artefacts. He had bought a turn-of-the-century hunting gun from the Dogon country and a bow and arrows from a Nigerian hunter he had met on the border in Northern Cameroon. I had no idea what he was up to now but I hoped it would be something less risky. I had almost scratched my back on his arrows, thrown somewhere on the back seat of the car, when he told me to beware: they had poisonous tips!

I got back into bed. I took my book. I started reading. Later we would venture out to find some food, but this usually happened only after Peter decided to take a break from his endless computer games.

Having found electricity in the small *auberge* with a noisy generator, Peter was in heaven. This meant not only could he recharge his many gadgets, among which were his electric toothbrush and his PDA, but he could also plug his laptop in and play computer games, and he did this for the whole day, disappearing into his darkened room with the windows covered in a vain attempt to keep the heat out. His favourite game had something to do with the World War II, a sort of a nostalgic attempt to slide back into his former military life. He played on the side of the Allies and therefore he killed Germans. On good days he killed as many as 25 or 30, on bad days only a couple. Today, the sparkle in his eyes as he came by to take us out in search for food seemed to indicate a lot of killings. But no, it wasn't his war: it was his new acquisition.

It was a small wooden statue about half a metre tall. Instead of a head it bore a monkey's skull. Around its waist it had all sorts of magic herbs tucked away in a small purse. It had weapons, something looking like a spear, and some hair stuck to the skull. It looked disgusting.

"He's my guardian spirit," Peter said.

"He's hideous."

"What do you mean? He's very authentic. I paid a lot for him. He's a fetish, a real one. The blokes who came with it were a bit afraid they would be seen selling something like this. It's something very hard to find. Apparently he's got magic powers."

Peter was all excited and I decided to make no further comments on the beauty, or lack of it, of his new best friend.

Richard was less impressed though. "If he can do magic, try asking him for the rain," he suggested.

We went for breakfast. The hot spot in town was a wooden hut kept by a runaway Chadian man with a large, white smile and a very ugly wound on his left hand. I suspected he had troubles back home and the wound was only a pale reminder of his past. He had found a new life in the quiet village of Pokola, in the heart of the tropical forest. Unlike his fellow countrymen, who would be forever remembered for their rather harsh welcome at the wells of their villages, he was a very peaceful and friendly guy. He served the best haricot in the world, and beans and bread was our main diet for days on end.

After breakfast it was time for another wander through the village, and we went towards the market this time. I looked for a couple of bananas and I found them on a straw mat in front of a small man with a square and much-wrinkled face. He looked like a ten-year-old child, prematurely grown old. I got my bananas and I gave him a few coins. He smiled and I froze. His teeth were sharp and pointy, like those of a vampire. He had probably spent many hours filing them.

He was a pygmy, one of many who came to market in Pokola to sell their fish and game, and sometimes fruit or honey they gathered from the forest. They were the people of the forest, the original inhabitants of the Congo basin who were then pushed deep into the forest by the settling Bantu populations. Apparently there were only about 150,000 of them left in the forests of Central Africa. They were short and delicate people, the colour of their skin lighter than that of the Bantu majority. They lived deep in the forest in their own huts, surviving on hunting and gathering, much as they had lived for thousands of years, and they were almost untouched by civilisation. For some odd reason their flesh was believed to have magical properties, and there had been acts of cannibalism reported against the pygmies of the neighbouring country, DRC (Democratic Republic of Congo, formerly known as Zaire), which was currently being torn apart by civil war. In the deep forest, pygmies were hunted much like animals and their flesh eaten by warriors on both sides of the conflict, who considered the gentle little people as some sort of sub-human species, like monkeys for instance. One survivor told a journalist how he had seen his whole family cut up into pieces and roasted over a campfire by rebel soldiers fighting a war with no end in DRC[26]. But their Government did everything to keep such rumours under control, and the world was too busy thinking about interest rates and the budget deficit and many more important things. Who cared about the pygmies in the jungle anyway?

The evenings were more animated than the rest of the day. After a full day of doing nothing, at least we had something to do: bedtime routine. We changed into our night T-shirts, we spread the net all over the bed and we tucked it in carefully under the mattress. Then, lying in bed, we would start a long conversation with Frank, as we had decided to call our fan. He was our newest and best friend and we needed him badly, especially during the night when the hot, still air in the room felt even hotter.

Frank was working hard but with little effect. I was wet with sweat and the bedsheets were wet as well.

"I think Frank isn't doing a proper job tonight!"

"It's the net, I think. He's blowing, poor guy, but we can't feel it through the net."

"Then let's get him inside the net."

"Get Frank into the bed? Could be one idea." Richard was receptive. And then he turned towards the fan.

"Frank, do you want to sleep with us tonight?" We pulled out a corner of the mosquito net from under the mattress and wrapped it around the fan. It wasn't much better though.

"You're blowing but your lungs are getting weaker." Richard's voice got sweeter.

"I think he'll die soon. He'll somehow reach the end of his working life and just collapse. I can't believe he's gone non-stop for a week now."

"If he dies, he'll be fondly remembered. He was a good lad."

We talked more nonsense for a while, then we slept. Then we woke up in the morning and we waited for the evening: another day of doing nothing.

The days were long and empty. Life in the small village went on. We woke up and read, went to the market, came

------

26

http://www7.nationalgeographic.com/ngm/0509/feature5/

back and read. Frank was still alive. Peter too, it seemed, although he spent more and more time in his dark room with his computer turned on under the protection of his new best friend, the guardian spirit. Marcel, the manager of the *auberge*, offered us beer and more beer. We were counting lizards. We were hoping for a dinner invite into the *toubab* village. Sometimes it happened and then we ate incredibly well. At other times it didn't, and we were back at the market for some haricots and putrefying monkey meat (for the non-vegetarians). We postponed going for a wander into the forest to see the gorillas for another day.

The rain did not come. Not only that, but we were told soon that the level of the water in the river was decreasing instead of increasing. How much longer? We knew already that this was a pointless question there. Like everywhere else in Africa, time did not exist and any questions starting with "how long?" were totally, utterly pointless. The rain would come when it came, and the boat would set off when the right time came. And right now it was the right time to be doing nothing, until one morning when it all came to an unexpected end.

Good things come to those who have given up expecting them. Just as we allowed our rhythm to slow down and melt into the quiet rhythms of the village of Pokola, just as we had given up counting the days or asking about the level of the water in the morning, just as we started to manage the art of doing nothing, change kicked in. And the piece of paper stuck to the walls of a street food hut, where we read that there was a boat leaving for Brazzaville the next day, seemed as surreal to us as our whole new existence in the village of Pokola. The boat was a *baleniere*, a small cargo boat not big enough to fit the car on. It was the first boat that ventured down the river, being small enough to fear less trouble from sandbanks. The big Kikuli cargo boat was to follow soon, they said.

We were to split again: Richard and I to go down to Brazzaville with this small boat, try to arrange visas and get our bearings in this new city. Peter was to follow on the big Kikuli boat. And if the big boat didn't come down soon, he was to try and bribe his way back into Cameroon without a visa and drive around via Gabon. We were to meet again in Brazzaville at some point.

We said goodbye to Frank the next morning and I felt

sad leaving him there. Richard disappeared for a while and came back just as the boat was about to leave, carrying some bulky parcel that turned out to be a big, spongy pillow.

"Roxana, please meet Mr Pillow. Mr Pillow, please meet Roxana."

We moved. On the bank, Peter waved.

"Have a good trip. And see you in Brazzaville."

"*Insha'Allah.*"

It was the only appropriate thing to say. May God's will be done. If we were meant to meet Peter again in Brazzaville, then we would meet him. When the time was right, as Africans said.

People were shouting and the boat was moving and we could see the village of Pokola slowly disappearing, with Peter on its shores still waving at us.

I was sad: sad to be leaving behind this strange town in the middle of the tropical forest, where a fan had a name. I felt I was being pulled away from it just as I was finally discovering the pleasure of doing nothing

I was also sad to leave Peter there. Strangely, slowly but surely, things had become different between us in the last weeks and even his ever-present jokes were less of a nuisance. Somewhere in this rainforest, a new, friendlier Peter had started to take shape in my mind and I became aware of that only as we left him there with no certainty that we would ever see him again.

And then, I was also sad because we didn't see the gorillas. "We'll go out in the forest tomorrow," we used to say. "Today it's simply too hot." It all came to an abrupt end, and as the boat slowly left Pokola behind and we still hadn't attempted to see the gorillas, all I could think about was that there are only so many tomorrows.

CHAPTER 21 – "BETHLEHEM VOYAGES"

(SANGHA RIVER, CONGO, MAY 2003)

"OH Lord, may thy name be praised. Oh Lord, turn thy face on to us poor mortals who invoke thy protection and thy grace."

In the darkness of the night, his voice sounded clear and powerful and his words filled the space and ruled over the river and the forest on the shores, over the silent boat and over the two of us tucked under a mosquito net on the roof.

"Oh Lord, to thee I pray and thy protection I seek. Bestow thy mercy upon us, Lord, and take us all in safety to Mossaka. Because I have not built a fetish to pray to, Lord, like so many others, but I pray to you, since you are the creator of the earth and the universe and you are my Lord, and you will help me better than the fetishes will help the others..."

Next I heard a chant with no words. Only occasional "hallelujahs" broke the rhythm. I knew it was the captain. It was the second night we had spent on his boat, and we had grown accustomed to his early morning prayer habits.

The boat flowed slowly downriver the whole day. When night fell, the boat anchored and we spread our mats on the roof, crawled under our mosquito nets and tried to get some sleep. To avoid mosquito attacks, we got under the net as soon as the sun had dipped below the horizon. Everybody went to sleep early. Everybody woke up early. The first to wake up was our kind captain, who introduced himself as Dieu (meaning God). His boat, the "Bethlehem Voyages", reflected the very Christian views of the captain. His day started early, around 4 am, with a long prayer, and by sunrise he had completed the prayer and the hymns and we had given up trying to get any sleep, since his powerful voice resonated less than a metre away from our ears.

"Oh Lord, listen to my prayer. I pray for the success of my business. Please, Lord, make it happen so that we reach Mossaka with all the fufu and cassava sacks undamaged. Please, Lord, remember that I have 55 sacks of cassava on board. Please make it happen so that I reach Mossaka with all of them and that I sell them at a good profit. Please, Lord, make it happen so that I sell them for more than 4500 CFA a sack; please, Lord, make it happen so that I earn this money."

I heard some other numbers being mentioned, and I believed Dieu was in the process of telling God how much he paid for the cassava and how much the market price was, and how much he could go down with the price if the Lord could really not help him sell for 4500 CFA as he wished. This took place in a lower voice, more like a whisper, and I took the opportunity to drift back into sleep.

"Oh Lord, praise be to thee!" His voice came back in all its force and my sleep came to an end.

"Please look after my family, Lord: please look after my wife and my children. The older one, Lord, cannot walk well: please look into this 'cause you are the Lord of all. Please, Lord, grant us good understanding and peace in my house, and please, Lord, make the women obey their husbands and do as their men tell them. Send away, Lord, the quarrel and the uneasiness from their hearts and let them be guided by our judgement. Not like in my brother's house, where my sister-in-law does not obey my brother and she argues all the time... no, no, Lord, this is not how things should be! Please, Lord, bestow thy attention on this matter and make women obey..."

He then carried on giving the Lord some more details about the specific situation. When he thought the issue was well covered, he moved on to the next point of interest:

"Oh Lord, praise be to thee! Lord, please fight the Evil in the heart of the policemen, of the police of Pikunda and of Mossaka and of all the villages we will pass on the river. Please, Lord, make them have mercy on me and my boat, and please, Lord, help me and my boat to survive!" This did not sound as funny as the first part. This sounded a bit worrying. I didn't really know what he had to hide and why he seemed to be on the run from the police.

"And, Lord, please guide and help us all. I pray to thee for all the people on this boat, for my crew, for Bartholomew my assistant and for his family, for his unborn child: may you, Lord, ensure that he comes well into the world."

This must have been the other man and his pregnant wife. There were three men, two women and two small kids on this boat. Dieu remembered them all and each of them got a special mention in his prayer.

"And I pray to thee, Lord, for the souls of these two travellers that we are taking to Mossaka."

I stuck an elbow into Richard's ribs. I didn't care if he was asleep or not, this was too important to be missed. This was Dieu's special intervention to God on our behalf.

"Because only thee, Lord, know their sorrows and their joys, where they come from and where they go, what they do with their life and what they are looking for here. May thee, Lord, guide them and bring them to their aim, and make them find what they are looking for..."

"Amen," I felt like adding.

"I think this was for us," said Richard. Just like me, he had been wide awake for some time, listening to the prayers of the captain.

Dieu was back to some more hallelujah hymns and then he prayed for several of his friends and then for his enemies, mostly competing fufu and cassava traders. At the end we heard a very long song, which he shouted from the depths of his lungs into the thinning darkness. The sun was about to rise and our captain was about to end his morning prayer. The engine started and the boat was moving. We were set for another day on the River Sangha.

We were still under the net. We didn't dare to get out until the sun was up, driving the mosquitoes away. There was usually one last attack just before sunrise.

There was not much space inside the net, and with Richard tossing and turning the whole night the space seemed even less. We were lying on top of our sleeping bags – it was too hot to be inside – and we were very careful not to touch any part of the net. The night before, Richard had woken up with a swollen elbow. He must have touched the net during the night and the mosquitoes rushed to feed on the little piece of meat exposed. He had bites on top of other bites, now all swollen into a big red sore.

The boat had left the bank where it had been anchored during the night and was slowly heading towards the middle of the mighty river. On the shores I could see the forest: huge trees growing directly from the water, the same trees as the day before. The trees of the rainforest, as silent and immobile as always, stretching on for days and days without end. I had never seen so many trees before!

The air was misty and it smelled of rotten leaves and mud. It smelled of forest and wilderness. It was still cool: the sun hadn't yet risen. It was the only moment in the day when one could feel a cool breeze. It seemed like everything was still: still in their silence, like the trees, or still in their movement like the boat and the river. I breathed in this stillness.

"Hey, did you get some sleep?" Richard broke the silence.

"Yeah, not too bad. How's your head?"

Richard had complained of a horrendous headache last night.

"It's better. I fell asleep when the Nurofen kicked in. But then I woke up again and I needed a pee."

I remembered. I had woken up in the middle of the night with the strange sensation that Richard was outside the net. He must have been mad; the mosquitoes must have devoured him.

"I was peeing and spraying mosquito repellent at the same time! They killed me, I tell you, they killed me."

I knew it was not supposed to be funny. Being bitten by mosquitoes in the most sensitive spot one can imagine isn't funny! But I couldn't stop and I burst into laughter, and my laughter travelled far into the stillness of the morning, reaching across the water and the trees, just like the captain's prayer had reached them all a few moments before.

"Shall we put the net away?" Richard had had enough of my laughter and moved to more practical things.

On the horizon, the sky had already turned purple and by now was pink. The sun was coming out.

"Not yet. I think they will come one more time."

They came. In a huge swarm they came; I could hear the buzzing and when they met the net they banged into it, shaking it as if it was being hit by a huge, invisible force. The mosquitoes were back in a desperate attempt to get one more drop of blood, like vampires of the night, being forced into the shade by the rays of the morning sun.

In a couple of hours, the captain came to check on and greet us. He seemed to treat Richard with considerably more respect, since he always called him "mister". As for me, he had already baptised me with a name – Tarkana – that sounded easier to pronounce.

"Monsieur Richard! Tarkana! How are you today? I hope you slept well."

Yes, we had.

"I hope you were not disturbed by my praying."

No, we weren't.

"We will arrive in Mossaka today."

This I doubted. Every single day so far, he had said we would arrive in Mossaka that day.

The days on the boat were long and, for an outsider, boring. For us they were not boring though. Nothing was boring once you had managed to "break inside". "Breaking inside" doing nothing meant stopping the obsession with doing anything. Like the nomad Tuaregs and their days that went by as they slowly poured tea from one cup to the other to mix with the sugar, here time passed as the trees on the shores went by and were replaced with similar trees on similar shores. Sometimes we read. But we only had one book about African history, and that was really boring. At times we talked, but this did not happen much. It was far too hot and we had spent far too many days and nights together to find new topics to talk about. Most of the time we just stared at the bank, sometimes seeing a small *pirogue* (canoe-like boat) carved from a tree trunk emerging from underneath the branches on the bank. They were full of pygmies. The men rowed with oars longer than their tiny bodies. They were dressed in shirts and trousers too big for them, as if they were kids who had stolen their parents' clothes. They came close to our boat and they always had something to sell.

The women of the crew were fascinated by this trade, and often bought items such as bundles of smoked fish held together by ropes made of tree bark. At other times we could spot a hut or two on the banks or in a small clearing. But most of the time, nothing would happen. Time would just go by as the boat would slowly float downriver: the sun as hot and immobile as always, the trees on the shores as mighty and never-ending as always. The forest was immense, impenetrable and mysterious. As we floated on this river, I remembered what I had been told by the French guys in Pokola. Apparently a team of Japanese researchers were organising an expedition to the heart of the forest on the shores of Lake Tele, looking for live dinosaurs. They had reason to believe that the rainforest of Congo would be the last place on the planet where dinosaurs still lived.

The boat was about 20 metres long and split into two parts: the lower deck – the real deck – was filled with countless sacks of cassava, a tropical root crop also known as manioc. It played a very important part in the local diet, much like bread did for us. They sometimes called it fufu, but I soon understood that fufu was more like a cooked meal, the equivalent of our mashed potatoes, and that it could be eaten with everything from rice to cassava. One way or the other, the sacks of fufu or cassava or manioc seemed to attract swarms of bees every time we got close to the bank. On top of these sacks, life would go on as usual: the kids would cry, the women would cook and the men would lie in the shade. Dieu and all his crew retired for the night to a small cabin at the stern of the boat. They would lay out their bright pink mosquito net, which was so full of holes that I doubted it offered any protection. They had a little gas lamp and would gather to eat before taking the mattresses out and finding a comfy spot for the night. They usually invited us to join them, but I was afraid that their mosquito net had too many holes in it and we preferred to spend the evenings tucked away under ours. The cabin was also the place where all navigation took place: much of it based on intuition or experience, I believed, since apart from a wheel they did not have compasses or maps or anything. The river was flowing south and all they needed to do was stay in the middle of it.

Richard and I, with all our belongings, spent our days and nights on the roof of the boat. That gave us a lot of space and it also kept us away from the bees attracted by the cassava. But it didn't give us any shade and we spent day after day under the hot equator sun. We would sit on our mats and quarrel ferociously over who got the privilege of leaning on Mr Pillow. Although it was Richard who bought him, I attempted time and time again to steal him from his rightful master. Leaning against him made life much easier.

Sometimes we would go down and have a chat with Dieu or Bartholomew. At other times they would come up and offer us a plate of manioc and smoked fish, which I would politely decline and Richard would gladly accept. Richard could eat anything. At other times we would set off for a trip to the toilet. Even though it was more like a hole on top of the water at the end of the deck, I was deeply grateful that this boat had a toilet. At least it had wooden walls all around and one could get a moment of privacy when one really needed one. Occasionally we would go down and collect drinking water, sinking our bottles deep into the river. So that at least some of the germs got killed, we would throw a pill or two into the bottle and leave it in the sun for a couple of hours before drinking. We only took drinking water from the front of the boat though. Water at the end of the boat was reserved for our toilet needs.

We ate little, and as the days passed we ate even less. A combination of heat and humidity turned all the food we had bought in Pokola bad. We had hoped that it would keep us going for several days. A couple of hours after we left, we noticed that the small plastic bags with haricots bought from our Chadian friend had started to swell, and by noon they were as big as a football and in an advanced state of putrefaction. Everything turned bad. My "Vache Qui Rit", as incredible as it sounded, had melted and it was the first time that I thought that maybe it was not all plastic! The bread was colonised by a layer of green fungus, which grew at an alarming rate, and by the time we decided to throw it into the river it was already rotten. Richard's meat sandwich also went into the river, and we soon realised that we were in trouble. We had nothing else to eat. Dieu and his crew ate manioc and smoked fish, and Richard embraced this life-saving alternative without too much fuss. I initially refused to eat the manioc, but as hunger set in I had to try it. It was a white substance, like an uncooked bread paste or polenta, all wrapped up in leaves. It tasted sour and fermented and I didn't really like it. We had hoped that we would finally find food in the village of Pikunda, which the captain said we would reach any moment now. We were not really sure when this would happen. All we could get from him was "*maintenant*". Like everywhere in Africa, time did not exist.

WHEN we arrived in the small village on the banks and we looked for food, I realised that there was no "La Vache Qui Rit" but there was some bread and I was happy enough with this. Richard got some tins of sardines and then we negotiated at length for bananas. We ended up buying a whole branch with about 50 green bananas on it. The woman who sold them said they would ripen soon, and we trusted her.

And just as we got ready to leave this nice little village in the middle of the forest, we were asked by our smiley Captain Dieu, this time with a wrinkled and serious look on his face, if we had registered with the police.

"No, should we?"

"You have to. We cannot leave before you register with them."

We said we would do so, got off the boat again and went to speak to a soldier casually leaning against the anchored boat.

We soon discovered that not only was he waiting for us, but his boss was as well. The boss was fat and did not smile. He sat on a chair in front of his wooden hut, which was apparently the police station. He said *"bonjour"*, but it sounded more like a threat than a greeting. He showed us inside.

As the door banged behind us and my eyes adapted to the semi-darkness of the room, I saw the chief of police taking a comfortable seat at his desk. He pointed to a wooden bench in front of his desk for us to sit on. Two other soldiers stood at the door. There was someone else in the room. In a corner I spotted a man squatting on the floor, his arms around his legs and his head in between his knees. I could not see him well, since the desk of the chief was blocking my view. Was the man bound? Was he under arrest? Had he been tortured? I didn't know and I was too much of a coward to ask.

"Your passports, *s'il vous plait.*"

We gave them our passports.

"What are you doing here?"

"We're visiting your country."

"Who gave you permission to visit my country?"

"Your ambassador did."

We opened our passports and we pointed out the visas. The first visa was from the embassy in Cameroon, and the other was the residence permit that Monique the Dragon Woman had stamped in exchange for an exorbitant amount of money.

"This is not valid here." The chief seemed convinced of the truth of what he said, and he smiled.

This village was only some 20 or 30 km away from Pokola but it was a small kingdom in itself, and the chief of police was the feudal lord. We had a feeling that this was not going to be easy.

"Yes, it is valid. Madame Adjutant, Monique, signed our passports in Pokola. Do you know Madame Adjutant?"

He didn't.

"Madame is a very important person. She has a lot of connections in Brazzaville. She said that if anyone questions her signature on our passports, we have to tell her straight away and she'll take care of it."

Now we were in dangerous territory, threatening a local chief of police while he was sitting at his own desk, in his own wooden hut in the middle of the village he ruled over with the absolute powers of a king. On top of that he had got two armed soldiers guarding the door and a man with his head hidden in between his knees, squatting in the corner of the room. I was getting nervous.

I felt Richard's elbow touching my arm. It will be fine, his elbow said, let's just play with them a little.

The chief looked a bit puzzled. But he still did not smile.

"Madame is a very powerful person." I echoed Richard's approach. "Maybe you can give her a call and talk to her, and I'm sure she can explain that we're here by special permission."

There were no phones here and that was why I felt so bold. If this chief were to call Madame Adjutant, all he would probably hear was the amount of the bribe we paid her and he would then feel encouraged to ask for the same amount. But we knew that this time we would not pay.

"I need to register you," the chief said after a moment of silence, and we knew that we were close to winning. Our threat might just have worked.

He looked at me and then at my passport, and then at me again.

"Your name?"

"Roxana."

"Roxana and what?"

It's in my passport, you idiot, I was about to shout. But I just told him my name instead.

He had started writing down my answers in a large

notebook.

"Born where?"

"In Bucharest, Romania."

"Where?"

I spelt my hometown. He wrote it down.

"Profession?"

Sometimes I was a businesswoman; some other times I was a teacher. Today I decided to revert to my BA degree and become a journalist. I also hoped this vague reference would send a subtle message about good manners to him.

He was not impressed. Maybe he did not know what a journalist was.

"You father's name."

I told him.

"Your father's surname."

"Valea."

That shouldn't have been hard to guess: it's just like mine, after all.

"Your father's date of birth."

I told him, and he wrote my father's date of birth in his small, dusty notebook.

"You father's birthplace."

Then he asked about my grandfather. I couldn't remember my grandfather's birthday and I made it up.

"Your mother's surname."

"Valea."

He stopped writing and looked at me.

"Your mother's surname, I said."

"Yes. Valea."

He was not writing. Something was wrong, I could tell. He did not like my mother's surname.

"Impossible. It cannot be the same."

"It is," I insisted. "Her surname is Valea, just like mine."

"But this is the surname of your father."

"Yes, we all have the same surname."

He paused. He looked at me again, and this time his eyes were telling me he thought I was an idiot.

"It is not possible," he repeated. "It means your father has married his own sister!"

For the next ten minutes I explained to him in detail how most women changed their surname upon marriage and why my mother and my father have the same surname without being brother and sister.

He looked at me with an expression of doubt, but eventually all my mother's data was entered into his dusty notebook and he started the same procedure with Richard.

"Your father's surname."

"Leon."

"Your mother's surname."

"Leon."

He paused.

"This is impossible!"

We didn't laugh. We didn't look at each other in amusement. We even didn't tell him that this was the same discussion we had 10 minutes ago. We were too hot and too hungry, and the image of the man squatting in a corner with his head between his knees was not encouraging at all. He hadn't moved since we entered the room. In a low, patient tone, Richard explained to the chief that in England women usually take their husband's surname upon marriage.

It took another half-hour before we left the wooden hut. But we were lucky. There was no other explanation for how we emerged from the hut with our passports in our hands and our money in our pockets. And as we walked towards the boat, I could see a smile of relief on the face of our captain.

"Welcome back. We were worried for you. Now we can go again."

I remembered the words of his prayer in the morning. "Lord, please fight the evil in the hearts of the policemen everywhere, of the policemen in Pikunda..." His prayer must have done wonders.

The boat moved and the village of Pikunda, with its empty shops and fat chief of police, slowly drifted away from us.

Bartholomew came to sit with us on the roof.

"How much did you pay?"

"We didn't."

He shook his head in doubt.

"This is not possible. You must have paid something. Everybody does."

We told him the story of our passports and the visas we had, and we told him that there was no need to pay just because someone demands money.

He shook his head with doubt again. I could tell he was wavering between belief and disbelief. I could also tell that he and the other members of the crew had been paying as they always did, and as they always would. For them the question was not whether to pay or not, but rather how much to pay.

"And they did not get violent with you?" he asked.

"No, they didn't."

"Then you are very lucky people," he concluded.

Yes we were, unlike the poor man squatting in the corner of the chief's room. Most likely he was among those who did not pay either. Only that he was black and we were white, and this meant the difference between violence and non-violence in Pikunda.

Later that afternoon we forgot about the whole incident. With the branch of bananas next to me, I felt nothing bad could happen. At least we had got food.

We started dinner as soon as the sun was low on the horizon. Richard opened a tin of sardines and we politely refused the smoked fish that one of the women placed in front of us. We didn't refuse the manioc. I ate bread and bananas. Richard ate manioc and sardines, with an occasional bite of the smoked fish that lay on the plate in front of us.

"Oh come on then, I know you want it."

"What?" I was trying to figure out what was going on.

"I know you can't stop salivating for it, so go on, take it."

"Richard, are you nuts?"

"The fish head, I mean. I know it's your favourite!"

Its mouth was open and its teeth were sharp and as black as the rest of the body. The fish head danced for a while in front of my eyes until I told Richard I would end up throwing it at him if he didn't give me a break.

But Richard was in a good mood and nothing could stop him.

"Yum yum, I love my food. Don't you think it's lovely?"

After starving for two days I could somehow understand his enthusiasm. But no, I didn't think it was lovely.

"Yum, yum, yum, this is the best food in the world: manioc with sardines. Better even: manioc with smoked fish and smoked fish head. What a delicacy! I couldn't have a better dinner tonight. How about you?"

"I'm having strawberry ice cream," I said as I took another bite from a not-yet-ripe banana. "With little strawberries on top," I added.

"How about the cream?"

"Cream as well. It just tastes delicious."

For the remainder of the dinner, we set free our wildest fantasies. For me it was mostly about sweets: chocolate cakes and tarts, ice cream and various fruits I hadn't seen in what seemed like years. I wanted an apple so badly! For Richard it was about ham and eggs in the morning, roast beef and lemonade.

After dinner I was about to get under the net, while Richard stripped to his boxer shorts, preparing for his evening swim in the river. The boat had already anchored for the night and if he hurried, he could be back under the net before the mosquito attack.

"Come on, come for a swim," he said. "The water's great!"

"Yeah."

I was not convinced that swimming was a good idea. I was terrified just thinking of all the creatures hidden in the water.

"Don't worry, they'll swim away from you. Remember that you're the biggest animal in there."

This was not really reassuring.

"Plus, you haven't taken a shower in a century. Soon you'll be banished to the other corner of the roof!"

"Do I smell that badly?"

"You will do if you don't come for a swim! Come on, you'll feel so much better afterwards!"

Maybe. But I had one more problem. I didn't have a swimsuit.

"Neither do I," he said. "We'll find a quiet spot for you and another one for me. We'll swim naked. That's what I've been doing every night!"

I got my towel and soap. I told Richard that he must promise to stay close, close enough to hear my shout if something went wrong. We got off the boat and realised that we had stopped on a sandy half-island. This was just perfect. I found a sandbank in between some bushes and Richard disappeared into the water on the other side of the bushes. The sun was down and the night was approaching quickly. I needed to get into the water before the mosquitoes started to feed on me, and the horror of this thought made me overcome my hesitation. I stripped naked and stepped into the muddy water. The bank collapsed and I found myself suddenly waist deep in the river. There was no current and I felt safe enough to venture a couple of metres from the bank when I felt a sudden movement in the water, very close to my leg.

"Richard?"

"What?" I could hear his answer not too far away.

"Richard, there's something moving in the water next to me!"

"Don't worry. Some fish probably. They'll swim away. Remember you're the biggest animal in the water and they are more afraid of you than you are of them."

Feeling encouraged by his advice, I started swimming towards the middle of the river. I could hear his voice far away. He was done now and wanted to go back to the boat. Now that I wasn't afraid any longer, I didn't feel like getting out. I was floating peacefully in the middle of the dark water and feeling like I was slowly melting, and I became one with the water, the sky and the silence...

"Hey! Hey, you!"

Two silhouettes were approaching. Although it was already dark, they could probably see my head in the water.

"Hey, you! We want to ask you a question!"

I was naked in the water. On the bank, two men were standing right next to my clothes. Richard must have been back on the boat already. I started to shake.

"Go away!" I shouted in French. "Just go away!"

"Just want to ask a question. Are you with this boat?"

"Yes."

"Is this Kikuli's boat?"

Kikuli was the boat Peter was waiting for in Pokola. It was a much bigger boat, transporting lots of people and goods and stopping at each village. These guys on the bank must have been waiting for this boat.

"No it's not, it's the 'Bethlehem Voyages'. Now go away. Just go away!"

They went. I got out and into my clothes. No matter how quickly I dressed and how desperately I ran towards the boat, I still got bitten by mosquitoes. Back on the roof, the net was up and Richard was already under it. I pulled a corner of the net out and desperately threw myself on my mat. I was still wet.

"How was it?" he smiled.

"Shit, I'm all bitten!"

"Well I told you to run once you're out, didn't I? Why did you feel like taking a stroll instead?"

I gave up trying to explain why a woman needed more time to dress than a man.

"Turn away, I need to change out of my wet T-shirt. Shit, I got so scared by the two blokes. But it was good: I must say, the swim was good."

"I told you, it's a great place to swim. And guess what? You smell a lot better."

I hoped this was a joke, even though I was not really in the mood for jokes.

He went swimming every night, and I ventured out a couple of times again. For some odd reason for which I'll never have an explanation, we never really registered the potential presence of crocodiles. We simply did not make the link between images of pygmies rowing in their *pirogues*, coming to sell their catch from the river and amongst which were big fat crocodiles, and our peaceful evening swim in the same river. We simply failed to make the connection.

THE rain came down unexpectedly and powerfully in the middle of the night. The rain that we had been waiting for in Pokola had arrived. Possibly Peter, the car and the Kikuli boat would now be able to set off down river. For the two of us, tucked under our mosquito net on the roof, it all was most unpleasant. We forgot about the mosquitoes, got up under the downpour, pitched the small tent and eventually settled down to sleep again. It was stifling so we slept with the flap open, hoping that the heavy rain outside would keep the mosquitoes away.

It didn't, and I woke up feeling depressed. It wasn't raining any longer but heavy clouds were covering the sky and it looked like it could start again at any minute. My body was aching and I realised I had been bitten all over by mosquitoes. Richard had gone down on to the deck below and found a cassava sack on top of which he could stretch his legs.

I woke up with the fresh memory of a powerful dream. I had dreamed of my ex-boyfriend, who I still thought about sometimes, although this trip had managed to pull me more and more into the present tense. It was a goodbye dream: I was telling him at last that I had loved him and that he had broken my heart into so many little pieces that I was afraid it could never be mended again. That I was now ready to let him go and it was not easy; that I needed more than five months of this trip to stop thinking about him, but that I was ready to let him go for good now because I understood that one needed to let a part of oneself die in order to be able to move on and maybe live again, and that here and now I would let that part die in me, and I was ready to be reborn again as if the trees of this immense forest and the river and the silence around had been telling me that it was time for a new beginning...

Richard climbed back on to the roof and came to check if I had opened my eyes. It was not raining any longer and he picked a wet banana from the branch sitting in a corner of the roof next to the tent and peeled it.

"Guess what?" he said, with a twinkle in his eye.

"What?"

"We've crossed the equator!"

"When?"

"Dunno. At some point. Last night. They say we've crossed but they're not sure when."

We didn't have any fancy navigation tools. The GPS stayed with Peter and the car. We didn't even have a compass.

"They say such storms as the one last night are frequent around the equator at this time of year. It's the rainy season passing from south of the equator to the north.

"Hey, welcome to the southern hemisphere. Do you want a banana? Or do you prefer strawberry ice cream?"

I was in no mood for jokes. But I took a banana, and as I peeled it I couldn't stop thinking that maybe this whole equator story was an omen. Maybe I had finally managed to cross my own internal equator.

I smiled. "The equator, hey? Who would have thought?"

Then we had an argument over Mr Pillow, who ended up in my possession for the morning under the agreement that he was to be returned to his rightful master for the afternoon. On the banks of the river, the trees stood as huge and silent as the ones from the day before. Only these ones belonged to the southern hemisphere: they just didn't know it. We ate and we sat and we watched the world go by. My dream melted away, maybe sunk into the water or absorbed by the trees, or maybe just hidden under the cassava sacks on the deck. The women under the roof sang. The babies cried.

We were silent. Life went on and we were moving on. I was moving on...

MOSSAKA

WE arrived in Mossaka the next day, even though we had given up hope that the concept of "*maintenant*" would have any link with reality.

Dieu and his crew were overwhelmed with joy. They had all put on their new, bright orange lifejackets and were yelling at all the passers-by as we entered the port area.

"Pokola to Mossaka. We have arrived. We're 'Bethlehem Voyages' and we have done a great trip. Just two days from Pokola to Mossaka!"

Two days were more like five, but who cared? Time was a volatile concept.

Mossaka was a small town with no roads leading in and out of it, no electricity, no cars and no telephone or mail. It was, however, the only town set at the point where the Sangha flowed into the Congo River and this was a very strategic site for a town. On the other side of the river, the forest belonged to the neighbouring country called Congo, or RDC (République démocratique du Congo) if you're French, or DRC (Democratic Republic of Congo) if you're English, or simply Congo-Kinshasa after the name of the capital and to differentiate it from Congo-Brazzaville if you were just one of the many people living or travelling on the banks of the river. All very confusing!

We all got off, Dieu and his crew still proudly wearing their fancy, bright orange lifejackets and Richard and I in our dirty clothes, in total disbelief that we had arrived at last. Dieu shook our hands and pointed out yet another wooden hut that he said was the headquarters of the local police. We should hurry to register, he said, and thanked us for having been his guests for the trip. We were to part here. He would be trying to sell his cassava at the price he had told the Lord about and then attempt to go back to Pokola, maybe with something else he could trade. As for us, assuming we would survive another encounter with the police, we were to find another means of transport to Brazzaville.

The chief of police was not there. We left our passports for "his highness" to check upon his return and we went off to search for some food. After five days of rotten bread, bananas and manioc, we needed to eat. I was weak with hunger.

We ate, we found a decent *auberge* to stay in, we asked about boats to continue our trip to Brazzaville and we found out that "*Oui, il n'y a pas*[27]". We decided to leave it until the next day to worry about it. For now we had one major task left: go to the police to meet yet another chief.

"His highness" had returned and was carefully studying our passports. He didn't smile and didn't say *bonjour*. He pointed us to the classic wooden bench. There were three armed soldiers in the room.

"When did you arrive?"

"This afternoon."

"And why did you not come straight here? What have you been doing for the whole afternoon? Do you know that foreigners are supposed to register with the police first thing when they arrive in a town?"

His voice was deep and serious. He was barking his questions with a sort of strange, neutral tone, as if he was doing it out of duty with no feelings involved, either good or bad ones.

"We came here as soon as the boat docked. We were told to leave the passports and return to see you."

We carefully avoided mentioning that he wasn't there: most likely having a siesta.

"What is your business in Mossaka?" he barked again, changing the subject.

"We're tourists. We have arrived from Pokola on a boat and we're looking for another boat to go down to Brazzaville."

"Who allowed you to go to Pokola in the first place?"

This chief here seemed to forget that his country was not a country at war any longer but one that was supposed to encourage and welcome tourism and foreign investment.

"Madame Adjutant," I said. "Madame Monique. She is the one who signed our passports and allowed us to be here. And we also have the signature of the chief of police from Pikunda. See? Here."

I pointed to the open pages of my passport. Also counting the original entrance visa we had got in Cameroon, the various signatures and permits for this country stamped

---

[27] "Yes, there are none!" (in French)

into my passport already took up three pages.

The chief took a long look, and then leant back in his chair with a serene expression on his face. He had figured out the way to deal with us. If other chiefs had signed our passports, it meant they had probably taken their share of our money. After all, this was how things worked here. So he wanted his cut too.

"10,000 CFA each for registration. This is what you need to pay."

He forgot to say please. Somehow this disturbed me more than the absurd amount of money he demanded. If he did not say "please", it meant he felt too much in control.

"No," Richard and I said at once, our voices united.

"What do you mean, 'no'?"

This came from another guy, one of the soldiers standing next to the chief. He was about two metres tall and one metre wide. He had a gun. He was not yet pointing it at us.

"What do you mean, 'no'?" he shouted again. "Have you heard what *monsieur le chef* has said? We're doing you a great favour by registering you here. You need to pay!"

"No we don't," said Richard. "We don't need to pay. We've already paid for our visas and we're not paying anything else. We have the legal right to be here in your country."

I suspected that the concept of a visa was to them something like a bribe we might have paid to someone else. Police chiefs were much like the medieval lords back in Europe, who'd figured out they could make a living by demanding some "tax" from each passer-by.

"You are going to pay. Do you hear me? You are going to pay if you want to step out of this room!" This was the giant soldier with the gun. I suspected that he was not an ordinary soldier but it was impossible to figure that out by looking at his uniform. The chief didn't say a word. It was probably beneath his dignity to quarrel with us.

"But Madame Adjutant...." I tried to say.

"To hell with Madame Adjutant. Do I know her? Who is she? Why should I care about Madame so and so? You need to pay. All foreigners pay!"

He was gesticulating and the gun was waving about all over the place. I wondered about the safety lock and whether it was on.

"There was a recent congress meeting in Ouésso,"

Richard seemed struck by inspiration. "We have come from there. The congress decided that once a foreigner had a visa stamped into his passport he did not need to pay anything to anyone else. Look, we have a visa. That's it."

"You have nothing, this is what you have. Do you understand?" the soldier with the face of a paid killer yelled. He then threw our passports at us.

"You have nothing!" he yelled again. "We are the law here and we are telling you what you need to do. And now you need to pay 10,000 each!"

I didn't know how much longer we could hold out. I got closer to Richard. He put a hand on my arm and I felt better. I thought of the river that flowed just outside the hut. If they decided to shoot us and throw us into the river, nobody would ever know. Nobody would ever know what happened to us and where we had disappeared. In this town they were the law, and this place was too far away and too remote from any form of civilisation to expect that anybody could intervene on our behalf. It was just them and us.

Richard's hand was still on my arm and I felt he thought we could push it a bit further.

"Look, *monsieur chef.*" He now talked directly to the chief, ignoring the yelling soldier. "You represent law and order in this town. You are a man with authority and you have the respect of everyone. I know you understand our situation. We're travelling to Brazzaville and when we arrive there we'll certainly mention your help and your cooperation. You know your Government is trying to encourage tourists in this country and your efforts will be much appreciated."

The chief did not say a word. But it was clear he was the decision-maker and all that the broad-shouldered guy with a gun could do was yell. And if the chief gave the order, I had no doubt that he would shoot us in a blink of an eye. He now looked at us with ferocious eyes and the yelling melted into a whisper.

"You bastards! You don't know what could happen to you. You really don't know!"

The chief sat quietly. We were all waiting for him to speak, and I felt that my life depended upon what he would say next.

Silence again. I felt that I couldn't take the pressure any longer. After all, it was just 10,000 CFA, a lot of money here but only £10 back home. My life was worth more than £10.

But the deal was a lot bigger for us. We knew that once we gave in to fear and paid a bribe, we would do it again. We would lose the self-confidence we had, which allowed us to get out untouched from such unpleasant encounters, and we would become easy prey for them. We were fighting hard and it was not for that 10 quid. It was for what would happen if we gave in. If we let them frighten us, we would end up like Toby and Alice, who had to go back after three weeks because they had spent their money. The future of our trip was at stake.

"You will leave your passports here and you will go to your *auberge*. We will discuss your situation. You will come back in the morning and we will decide then."

"His highness" had spoken. It was final. If something was going to happen to us tomorrow, at least we were granted another night.

We nodded. The soldiers silently stepped away, leaving the door open. We were free to leave.

We stood up. I realised that my hand had been grabbing Richard's knee and I had squeezed it with all my might. His hand, in turn, had been squeezing my arm. Richard remembered to say "*merci*" just before we stepped out.

Out in the night, I took a deep breath – it felt so good to be free again! Free but without passports, with no transport coming or going through this town, and with hundreds of square kilometres of rainforest all around us, there was hardly anywhere to go. We had to come back there in the morning.

I woke up from a nightmare that night. I was dreaming that I was running on the streets of Bucharest, trying to hide away from the Securitate, the former secret police in communist Romania. I was being followed closely and I knew that if they got to me, I would be dead. I grew up in a communist totalitarian regime that had no respect for human life and even less for human rights. I had always known that police could kill, and the soldier yelling at us that day with his machine gun pointing in all directions had triggered all those memories. They could have fired at us that evening and they could fire at us tomorrow. They were just like the Securitate on the streets of Bucharest.

I woke up sweating and panting. I got up and sat on the edge of the bed, outside the net. There must have been mosquitoes, but I didn't care. I needed to breathe.

"What's up?" It was still dark outside but Richard seemed to be awake. He sat up next to me.

"Hey, what's up?" Richard asked again.

I couldn't answer. I was still shaking, trying to catch my breath.

"It's fine. Don't worry. It will all be fine."

He put his arm around my shoulder. This was very un-Richard-like behaviour. He did not "do" hugs. The last time it happened was in the Aïr Mountains back in Niger, the night I thought I would die from poisoning.

"It's them, isn't it? You're thinking of them. But it'll be fine, you'll see. We'll get our passports in the morning and we'll carry on, and we'll somehow reach Brazzaville and we'll forget about all this."

"The dream," I said. "I dreamt... I mean... I was followed on the streets... police."

I couldn't say more and what I dreamt about didn't matter anyway. The only thing that mattered was that we needed to go back to face the police chief and his machine-gun-waving soldiers.

"It'll all be fine, you'll see. It'll all be fine." Richard's arm was still around my shoulders.

I went back to bed. There was nothing we could do until the morning anyway. Richard stretched his legs out in the bed beside me. We turned our backs to each other and as I tried to fall asleep, I thought that maybe Richard was becoming more and more Latin in his behaviour. It was not only the hug: I realised that it had been a while since he stopped apologising every time his elbow touched me during the night. I still felt the terror of the dream, but the thought of Richard's British coolness slowly melting away to be replaced by Latin warmth brought a smile to my face.

"It'll be fine, you'll see," he said that night, and the following morning his prophecy came true. We went back to see the chief. The gorilla with the face of a paid killer wasn't there. The chief smiled and gave us back our passports, just like that, with no more threats and no more demands. He had probably figured out that two white tourists going missing in his town would bring him trouble, and he chose the safest way out.

We then went to the port, where we found out that there was a boat and one boat only, the Kikuli boat, that was expected down the river at some point. This was the same boat that Peter was probably still waiting for in Pokola and that could take days or weeks to arrive. We searched more. And sure enough, we found something else. There was no boat but there were small *pirogues* – the same type of *pirogues* the pygmies moved in, small boats made of the carved trunk of a tall tree – loading up with people and merchandise, about to sail to Brazzaville.

I took a close look at the *pirogues* and they didn't look too good. They were small and uncomfortable. There were no benches, chairs or anything: people would squat on the floor on top of sacks with all sorts of goods and there was no roof and no space to put up a tent. There were no toilets on board and the bottom of the boat was wet, so there was no way you could lie down without getting wet. And under those conditions, the trip was to take two days and a night.

I wished there was another way, I desperately hoped we could find something better. Compared to the reality of the small *pirogues* loaded up with passengers and goods, our trip with "Bethlehem Voyages" seemed like a first-class cruise. But right now there was nothing else and I knew, looking at Richard, that we had to take it. One way or another, we had to reach Brazzaville.

We left Mossaka early the next day. Or rather, we went to our *pirogue* and we loaded our bags and waited. We were leaving "*maintenant*", we were told, and sure enough by 2 pm we were still there, anchored to the dirty, crowded bank waiting for more passengers. After all, a *pirogue* was still a form of bush taxi and the "leave when full" rule applied here as well.

When we finally did leave, I soon wished we never had. The two *pirogues*, attached together and pulled by one small, inefficient outboard motor, moved very slowly. We chose to sit in front of the *pirogue*. Most of the people chose to cram into the stern or on top of the many sacks of dried fish stored in the centre of the small *pirogue*. We soon learned why the front of the boat was still free. As soon as we left, the waves of the river managed to pour over the bow and in a matter of minutes our clothes were wet, as well as the mattress, placed on top of some plastic sheeting. We had thought we could sleep on it to keep away from the dampness in the bottom of the *pirogue*. Our bags were wet, as were all our clothes inside. The faster the *pirogue* went, the wetter we got. We were squatting in a tight space already filled with our bags and the useless, wet mattress. Richard was grabbing Mr Pillow and I suspected Mr Pillow was the only one who hadn't got wet, since he was all wrapped up in a big plastic sheet. I looked at Richard in despair: how were we to survive like this for two days and a night? But he didn't have an answer and as I looked back and saw the bank of Mossaka slowly disappearing into the mist, I knew there was no way back.

To make matters worse, I noticed that the big stones I thought the other *pirogue* was loaded with were in fact huge turtles turned upside down. They were still alive. They were moving their flippers desperately in the air in a vain attempt to turn over. A guy sitting on top of them was kicking them every time they moved. I could hear the shell of the poor turtle cracking under the blow of his boots.

"No!" I shouted. "Stop! Stop it!"

But my voice was swallowed by the noise of the engine and the waves, and he didn't hear or didn't bother. He didn't stop and I couldn't stop my tears. I started to cry hysterically, and it wasn't clear if I was crying for the plight of the turtles or for self-pity, for being a prisoner on this horrible little boat.

Richard shook my shoulders.

"What's up? Have you gone mad?"

"The turtles!" I sobbed. "The turtles... he can't do this to them. The turtles... we have a turtle at home, we always had a turtle at home. My parents... the turtles..."

I knew I was not coherent. There was no point in explaining anything. I was wet and my legs already ached from squatting. The bloke in the other boat kept on kicking the poor creatures and I just wanted to be away from all this, away from this trip which had become a nightmare. I just desperately wanted to be at home with my parents.

"Hey, it's OK." Richard was still shaking me. "It's just the way things are over here. Come on, it's not the first time we've see this."

I didn't listen. I cried and cried, and by now all the people in the boat were looking at us wondering what on earth was happening.

Richard grabbed the ropes of the other boat and pulled it closer.

"Hey, you!" he shouted to the man. "You there!"

I don't know what else he said or what he did. I'd stuck my head between my knees and was crying and crying until I felt his arm around me, just like the previous evening.

"It's fine," he said. "It's all fine now". His voice was warm.

"We'll make it. We'll make it to Brazzaville and we'll make it after that too. Don't worry, you'll make it!"

I lifted my head from in between my knees. The first thing I noticed was that the turtles were gone. For a second I had the silly idea that maybe the bloke had released them back into the water. But that would have been a miracle.

"I asked him to move them to the back of the *pirogue*. So you won't see them any more."

That was also a miracle. A smaller one, but I didn't know how Richard had done it – whether he had to threaten them or pay for it – but he had done it. I stopped crying. He opened his book and started reading. In the mist of the river, the boat was moving and the sound of the small, dingy engine covered everything else there was to say.

SOME hours later it started to rain. By then we had almost dried our clothes off in the wind. The waves had thankfully calmed down and the *pirogue* seemed to take a shortcut along an arm of the river where large weeds made it seem more like a marsh. But we were still on the Congo, going down towards the sea, floating in the middle of No Man's Land: on one side, one Congo; on the other side, the other Congo!

We had feared rain and we knew it wouldn't be easy to find a solution when it came. But when one is desperate one becomes very inventive. We immediately pulled up the flysheet of the tent and tucked ourselves under it. The flysheet now covered the bags, the mat, Mr Pillow and us and hung out over the edge of the boat. We thought this was a pretty good deal, especially since the mat was now dry enough that we could attempt to lie down and stretch out.

The only slight problem was that there was not too much space under the flysheet. The boat was narrow, so narrow that Richard and I could barely lie alongside each other. Since we were at the front of the boat, it got narrower and narrower and we had put the backpack at the pointy corner to serve as a pillow. Mr Pillow, on the other hand, made a second pillow, a more comfy one. Richard, suffering a sudden attack of generosity, pushed Mr Pillow into my arms.

We were moving and tossing under the flysheet in darkness. Richard managed to crawl backwards and rested his head on the backpack. The boat was as narrow as his shoulders at one end but then got a bit wider, wide enough for both of us, and I stuck Mr Pillow somewhere about the height of his hips and attempted to lie down as well. We tossed and turned for some time until we found a position that we could survive in. I was thirsty but I didn't have anything to drink. I was terrified that I'd need to pee and then I'd be in trouble on this small *pirogue* with no toilet. Men peed freely into the water from the back of the boat and Richard had no problem doing the same. Women, on the other hand, had to pee into a bowl. They would stick it under their skirts as they squatted. The bowl would come out and be emptied into the water. Nobody seemed to have a problem with this method. Except for me. I was not wearing a skirt and I was terrified I might need a pee. I decided not to drink anything whilst on the *pirogue*.

Then the maggots came. At some point, in the deep darkness under the flysheet, I felt something crawling slowly on my skin: a hairy, wormy crawling feeling. I had seen Richard tossing and turning before and sticking his hand out of the flysheet as he threw something into the water. I had no idea what he was doing, but when I told him what I was feeling he said in a calm voice, "There are some things crawling on us. I've no idea where they've come from. Don't worry, they don't bite: just pick them up and throw them into the water."

I thought it wasn't a big deal. But when I first felt the hairy touch of a small living creature on my neck, I shook with horror and shouted out and grabbed it desperately, trying hard not to let it go again despite the sick feeling I had as it was still moving in my fist. I threw it into the water.

"What on earth are they?"

We switched on the torch and I realised that this was the wrong thing to do. There were many other huge, long, hairy maggots on my trousers, on my T-shirt and on my pillow. They were all around us, but in the darkness we hadn't seen them.

I shivered. Richard grabbed my shoulder and kept me still. He yelled, "Whatever you do, don't jump into the water. You can shout if you want but don't move. I don't want to be fishing you out of this river in the night."

I calmed down. Actually I froze there, in the narrow space between Richard's legs and the edge of the boat. By the light of the torch I saw Richard picking them up one by one and throwing them into the water. When the last one was gone, I breathed again.

LATER, the rain had stopped and we pulled the flysheet away. Outside the stars were bright, and the boat floated slowly across the swampy landscape. Our travelling companions were asleep, squatting or lying across the sacks. In front of us, an old woman was squatting just where our feet ended. She held a metal bowl in her hands and when we shone the torch on her face she smiled. In the metal bowl, the same one she used for peeing, we could see she had been gathering the maggots. They were all around her as she picked them up one by one and placed them into the bowl, and when the bowl was full she threw them into the water. She pointed to the white sacks loaded with smoked fish next to her.

"*Poisson*[28]," she said. "They come from the *poisson*."

This meant there were many more. I was terrified. Richard was terrified as well, but for a different reason. He couldn't stop thinking about how many of those smoked fish he had eaten over the last few days.

It started to rain again and we had to go back under the flysheet. We had to switch the torch off and lay awake in the darkness, waiting for the next hairy invasion. We knew we could only feel them once they touched our skin, and then we picked them up and threw them out. I tried hard not to imagine hundreds of big, hairy maggots all over my clothes, slowly advancing towards my face. I felt their soft, hairy touch, and it took all the self-control I could muster not to jump up and possibly end up in the water. I continued to pick them up and throw them as far away as I could into the black waters. Sometimes I got them as they reached my hands. At other times I only got them as they came on to my neck. Some of them fell inside my T-shirt and I picked one out from inside my bra.

The boat was moving and the raindrops were hitting the flysheet again. My back was aching and I asked Richard to

---

[28] "Fish" (in French)

change position. The old trick we had discovered on the green truck in Guinea seemed to work here as well, and one always felt better after one changed position. I picked up more maggots. I tried hard not to fall asleep for fear that I would wake up with one of them in my mouth.

By morning I was so tired, so indifferent to the maggots and so achy in my back that when the boat pulled on to the bank and we were told we needed to go register with the police, I felt there was no power in the world that could make me move. Richard was up and he looked for his passport.

"Come on. We need to go."

"Tell them that Madame cannot be bothered. They can arrest me, they can do whatever they want to do. Tell them that I really cannot be bothered."

No comment. He took my passport and disappeared to the bank. As for me, I instantly conquered all the space he had left available, embraced Mr Pillow, forgot about the maggots and for the first time that night I fell into a long, deep sleep with no dreams.

I don't know how long we stayed there, but when I woke up we were moving again and Richard was squatting next to the mamma with the bowl of maggots and reading his book. I felt guilty for having taken up all this space and I drew my legs closer together.

"How did it go with the police?"

"The same story. They wanted money."

"And?"

"I told them we couldn't be bothered. How was your sleep?"

"Good. I don't know how long I slept for."

"A while. Next village it's your turn to deal with the authorities and I can stay here and stretch my legs and get some sleep, how about that?" He was sarcastic as he hinted at the inequitable distribution of space in my favour.

Fair enough, I was about to say, but as I looked around I forgot to say anything. For one reason or another, the maggots had disappeared. Maybe they were like mosquitoes and they stayed away during the day. A naughty thought came into my mind and I tried to hide it for a while, but then I couldn't resist and let it go with a wide smile of my face.

"If you're hungry there's some smoked fish on the boat! Garnished with maggots on the side!"

Richard lifted his eyes from his book and threw me a disgusted look.

"Thank you, I'll keep that in mind!"

We squatted for the rest of the day with no more maggots but no food either. We were told we were about to stop at a larger village where we could get something to eat. Richard had probably stopped thinking about the smoked fish with maggots and he was now in a more cheerful mood, occasionally shouting from the depth of his lungs, "Brazzaville, we're coming! We'll make it. Do you hear me, someone up there?" I believe he was invoking God. "Whatever you throw at us, we'll make it. Smoked fish or corrupt officials, the maggots or the waves. We will make it!"

WE reached Tchikibaba. By now we knew well that we had to go to the police first.

This time the chief was politer and had another soldier who would carefully repeat each of his questions. All questions came twice: first from the chief, then from the soldier. "Where are you from?" "Where are you from?" the echo repeated. We only answered once. "What are you doing here?" "What are you doing here?"

I felt as if I had drunk too much and I was hearing double.

"And what's the purpose of your tourism?"

"What's the purpose of your tourism?" the echo man repeated.

"No purpose. We're just visiting. We're going from village to village and we're hoping to reach the capital, then we'll cross over into Congo-Kinshasa and we'll go on to visit that country as well."

It seemed the chief didn't like to hear Congo-Kinshasa mentioned. The relationship between the two countries had never been too cordial.

"I want to see your *ordre de mission*."

"Your *ordre de mission*," the echo repeated.

We had no order of any mission. I suspected that this was something related to the bureaucracy of the army. All we had were our passports.

"Passports are not enough," the chief argued. "I need to see something else: if not an *ordre de mission* then a *fiche d'hébergement.*"

"*Fiche d'hébergement,*" the echo jumped in again.

We didn't have a lodging document, which was an approximate translation for what these guys were asking for.

"Then you must surely have a *laissez-passer?*"

"A *laissez-passer,* no?" came the echo.

No, none of those things. I pointed to the passport in his hands and I asked him if I could show him where my visa had been stamped. He agreed. I opened it up and pointed my finger to it.

"Here. This is the only document we have. This is what gives us permission to be in your country. Your ambassador signed it. Madame Monique, the Madame Adjutant of Pokola, signed it too, and all the other chiefs of police have signed it too. You can sign too if you want. If you don't want to, that's fine with us."

He now carefully studied my passport again.

"*Ambassade de la République du Congo dans la République du Cameroon.*[29]"

"*Dans la République du Cameroon,*" the echo only caught the last bit of the phrase.

"*Le titulaire de ce visa*[30]..."

One by one, all the words stamped in my passport were slowly and carefully pronounced by the chief and echoed by the echo man. At least I was convinced now that he could read.

"Very well," he decided. "I will register you." And he took out a school notebook, the same type of notebook I had seen before at all the police stations we had passed.

It all started again. Your father's name... your mother's name... it's not possible... the birthplace of your grandfather... and so on. Then the conclusion that we already expected.

"Now please pay me 5000 CFA each."

This was half the price we were asked for in Mossaka. The registration bribe seemed to fluctuate a lot in this country. They would do a better job if they could collectively agree on a set figure.

"No."

---

[29] "The Embassy of the Republic of Congo in the Republic of Cameroon" (in French)

[30] "The recipient of this visa..." (in French)

We had to go on for a while, the same story again and again: the congress in Ouésso that established foreigners no longer needed to pay registration fees if they had a visa stamped into their passports, the same story about talking to our ambassador who was waiting for us in Brazzaville, the same story of Madame Adjutant, and all the possible stories we could remember that we had successfully used before.

It took two hours. The *pirogue* waited, heavily laden with its maggots and smoked fish, sacks and many people. They all waited for us to be released from the chief's hut, and when we finally emerged I was sure that they had all heard every single word of what was going on inside.

The first thing we noticed as we walked towards the boat, with our passports back where they belonged in the back pockets of our trousers, was the captain running towards us.

"*Excusez-moi* – well, I just wanted to ask you something."

"Sure."

"Will you pay me?"

"What do you mean?"

"Will you pay for the transport? What we have agreed back in Mossaka, will you pay for your tickets?"

Of course we would. But we never paid anyone in advance and we were waiting to arrive in Brazzaville before we paid him. But the captain looked really unsure of us and we suddenly understood what was going on in his mind. He thought that if we managed not to pay the police and get away with it, there was no way he could hope we would pay his fees.

We paid him there and then. He felt better. Then, just as we got back on to the *pirogue*, a young boy ran towards us.

"Monsieur, Madame, *le commissaire* wants to speak to you!"

The *commissaire* was another grade of the bureaucracy in a small Congolese village. I suspected he was representing the Government while the chief of police was representing the army, and the army and the Government were never too friendly to one another. Usually the army overthrew governments, and every government was both in fear of, yet courted, the army. We wondered if there was another show about to start and another bribe request, but this time things were a lot easier.

"*Am auzit ca sunteti din Romania si voiam doar sa va salut*[31]." The

------

[31] "I heard you come from Romania and I just wanted to say

round, well-fed face of the *commissaire* spoke to us in the purest of Romanian accents.

He was another student sent to Romania 20 years ago for training. He was another one who did not forget the language. And because he had heard from the chief of police that a Romanian was in the village, he reckoned he could do something for us.

"Oyo is only 20 km away from here. From there you can take a quick minibus to Brazzaville: the road is good."

Apparently this was the only good road in the country, and it connected the capital to the birthplace of the president.

"Don't get back into the *pirogue*. It will take too long: another day, probably, to Oyo, and then a lot more to Brazzaville. I can arrange a car for you from here. Some of my colleagues are leaving soon and I'm sure they won't mind giving you a lift to Oyo."

He smiled again and added in Romanian, "*Doar un mic serviciu in amintirea vremurilor bune in tara dumneavoastra*[32]..."

The man in the dark blue suit from Pokola, the husband of Monique the Dragon Woman, had said there were 200 of them scattered all around the country: former students in Romania who would still be able to speak the language. And it so happened that the *commissaire* of the small village of Tchikibaba was one of them.

We got into the car provided by the *commissaire* and we said farewell to the captain and the *pirogue*. We drove on an incredibly potholed road through the jungle, stopping at every village on the way to Oyo. We soon understood that the "colleagues" of the *commissaire* were political activists, representatives of the ruling party, and their mission was to drive from village to village to "wake up" the population and the opinion leaders like teachers and chiefs. In short, they were preparing for the next election.

In one such village, the teacher came running out of his house as he heard the car stop. He was wearing a pair of very colourful trousers featuring the face of the current president on both legs. Two women, each dressed in a skirt made of the same material, hurried out. We noticed one small problem: one of the women had cut the skirt straight

---

hello." (in Romanian)

[32] "This is just a small favour, in memory of the good old days spent in your country..."

through the president's face so we could only see one eye, one ear, half a mouth and half a nose. She seemed to be happy with the strange portrait. They got out of the car and started yelling at the teacher.

"What have you done? How many people have you recruited? How many faithful supporters can we say that we have here?"

Richard and I were sitting on the back of the pick-up truck and tried hard not to listen to this. For some strange reason, they spoke French and not one of the local languages. It probably made the whole scene seem more official.

The teacher tried to defend himself: he didn't have enough time, but yes, he would gather the people, and yes, he would spread the word.

"When? My question is when? We came here two weeks ago and you said the exactly same thing. I want to know, when will this happen?"

The one who was yelling was a good-looking young woman. She wore blue overalls, which reminded me of the communist regime in my own country and the communist party people dressed as the "working class". She had nicely manicured hands and I doubted whether she was doing anything more than dressing up to appear as part of the "working class".

The whole show went on and on while we sat and listened. We had no idea how long they would spend here and if they would arrest this poor teacher, or just decide to give him more time. They all ignored us and we tried hard to ignore them. The *commissaire* had managed to get us a place on this pick-up truck but he didn't tell us how long the journey would last and he didn't warn us we were to travel with a band of political maniacs terrorising the population in every village we passed through.

They eventually finished their business and the teacher was left alone. We reached Oyo just as the sun was ready to set. We were not surprised when we were dropped off in front of the police station. Everybody knew that the first thing one needed to do when one arrived in a town was to register with the police.

We knocked at the small window. The sleepy face of yet another policeman appeared. We gave him the passports.

He studied them for a while. I now expected the classical question about my mother's maiden name.

"Do you have a camera?"

Of course we had. But this was the birthplace of the president and therefore a very strategic place in the middle of the jungle.

"No," said Richard, with enough confidence to blow an elephant away.

"Do I need to search your bags?" the policeman enquired.

"No, you don't. We don't have a camera."

Apparently he believed us.

"Are you two married?" he asked.

To everybody else except the police, we said we were married. It made life easier in *auberges* and Catholic missions whenever we asked for a room. But lying to the police was different.

"No, we're not married."

"What are you doing together?'

"We're travelling together."

"And what do you do at night?"

"We sleep."

"Where do you sleep?"

"Usually in an *auberge*."

"And what if you cannot find an *auberge*?"

"We have a tent."

"And what do you do there, the two of you alone in a tent?" The policeman was by now really interested.

"We sleep." I could read the irritation in Richard's voice.

"Oh no, no, no, I don't think you sleep. With Madame next to you... and moreover, you are not even married. What a shame. Where did you meet?"

"Listen, are you registering our passports or what? We cannot stay here for the whole night. We need to go to Brazzaville."

The driver who brought us there had told us that we could get transport to Brazzaville that evening. Since the road to the capital was paved, bush taxis travelled throughout the night. All we had to do was get registered with this imbecile and get to the Gare Routière.

"Ah, Brazzaville, yes. Don't worry. Every minibus that passes on this road goes to Brazzaville: you'll find something," the policeman said, not realising what a precious piece of information he had given us.

"So as I was saying, where did you meet?" Back to his topic of interest.

There was not much we could do about it and we had to tell him that we met in the UK, that we started our trip in Morocco and were heading towards South Africa. The policeman had all the time in the world and he was holding our passports, and he was fascinated with interpersonal relationships or what was going on in our tent at night.

Salvation arrived in the form of an overcrowded minibus. We waved it to stop. It did. We asked where it was going. To Brazzaville. We asked if they had two spaces for us. They did. And then we knew that our next move would take us away from the nasty, smiley policeman and his fantasies. We broke from our rulebook and paid the driver the full fare for two seats to Brazzaville. In advance. Then, we turned towards our friend and I heard triumph in Richard's voice when he asked, "Now can we have our passports back?"

He had lost and he knew it. We knew it too. Once you paid for your seats, a minibus would wait for you, no matter how long it took for you to strap your luggage on top or finish your argument with some policeman. They didn't run on a schedule and they didn't mind waiting for customers. The thing was that all the people in the minibus, about 20 or 25 in this case, would be waiting as well. And with all this audience looking over our shoulder, we were quite confident that our smiley policeman would not feel like taking any more time to play with us.

He didn't. He stamped our passports and gave them back to us. We jumped into the minibus and felt that we had been given a passport to paradise. As always, the principle of "get a local by your side" had worked. We were one night's drive from Brazzaville and for the first time in the last two weeks I started to believe that we would actually get there.

The night, however, was not to be as trouble-free as we hoped. And it wasn't so much because our seats were crowded, dirty and half broken, and it wasn't because the minibus was so full of people and their belongings that one could hardly breathe; it was once again because of road stops and more policemen.

By midnight we had already passed through four roadblocks. It worked like this: there was a barrier. The driver stopped. A torch in the face. A handful of banknotes, the agreed bribe. Then the faceless owner of the torch – and there was more than one, judging from the noise they made

– moved the torch to check on the passengers inside the minibus. They invariably picked on Richard and me, the only two white faces there. They asked us to get out. They pointed their guns at us and escorted us to a wooden hut. Chiefs always sat at a desk in a wooden hut. The chief asked to see our passports. Then we went into the mother's-maiden-name type of questioning and he wrote everything down in a notebook. Then he wanted money. We said no. Then he threatened us. We threatened back, always careful to be subtle enough, mentioning ambassadors, *commissaires*, Madame Adjutant and the minister of foreign affairs for Congo, who coincidentally was our best friend.

Some haggling and then we were eventually released without paying. We went back into the waiting minibus, where everybody was asleep. We drove on. Another roadblock came and the whole story started again.

By 2 am I wanted to cry. I hadn't slept the night before because of the maggots. I wasn't expecting to sleep that night because we were travelling in a crowded bush taxi on a potholed road. But I felt I was getting dangerously close to the end of my patience, and the sight of yet another gun pointed at us in the darkness of the night made me tremble, and yet another question about my mother's maiden name made me pause and choose my words with utmost care. The only answer I could think of was a "go fuck yourself" type of yell, which would mean I would spend the rest of my life in a Congolese prison.

We were dirty, hungry and we hadn't slept for ages. Richard had an overgrown beard and deep-sunken eyes. He was answering the questions in a patient, monotonous voice and swearing at them in a whisper. I didn't swear, but his whisper cooled me off. We had entered an autopilot mode where their barks, our answers and their guns all looked and sounded both far away and surreal, as if they were happening somewhere in another world or in a movie. Time and again, we got picked up by the torch, dragged out of the minibus and interrogated. The old questions came back, again and again, and it all started melting away in my mind. The torch was in my eyes:

"*Laissez passers*, passports, why are you here, where are you going, what are your birthdates, where is your *ordre de mission*, give me money, 5000 CFA, give me money, money."

The closer we got to the capital the more the controls

intensified. At what was going to be the final stop, the discussion with the driver took a while. We heard some "oohs" and "aahs", and eventually the driver turned and said to us all, "1000 each, please. We need to pay 1000 each."

Loud protestations. Everybody was now awake. Everybody was unhappy. It appeared that the price of the ticket had included all the customary bribes and people were not expecting to pay more. But this was an extra bribe. Some police chief had decided that he needed to have 2000 CFA as a tax for each of the big white sacks of merchandise strapped on top of the minibus. The problem was that the sack owner wasn't travelling inside, he had merely strapped the sacks on the roof and paid for their transport to the capital. Now the driver didn't want to leave the sacks there: after all, he had been paid to take them to the capital. The people didn't want to pay for someone else's sacks and so we had a little riot. The policeman waited, patiently. He knew he had all the time in the world. He also knew people would pay.

We did. Eventually, each of us put 1000 CFA into the driver's hand. The driver eventually paid the policeman and we were ready to go. But no, the torch shone again and I instinctively got closer to Richard.

"Oh no, not again..."

He asked to see our passports. This was how it usually happened: they took our passports through the window and then we had to get out of the minibus to get them back and we would be escorted into another wooden hut at gunpoint. But no, this time the torch returned on the owner's face: a smiley black one with a small radio strapped to his ear with a piece of cloth. It was turned on and it sounded like he was listening to a football game.

"*Aveti pasaporte frumoase doamna,*[33]" he said, and the miracle happened again. He spoke Romanian.

"*Merci. Trebuie sa coborim?*[34]" I asked nervously.

"*Oh nu, nu. E sufficient ca v-am vazut pasaportul. Calatorie placuta si bine ati venit in Congo. Stiti, Romania e tara noastra sora. Am studiat pe vremuri acolo. Ehei, bune vremuri. La Academia Stefan Gheorghiu.*[35]"

---

[33] "You have nice passports, lady." (in Romanian)
[34] "Thank you, do we need to get off?" (in Romanian)
[35] "Oh, no, no. It's enough that we have seen your passport. Have a pleasant trip and welcome to Congo. You know,

The school he mentioned no longer existed. It used to train the communist elite. But my friend here didn't know that. And I would not be the one to tell him about the regime change in my country.

I thanked him and burst out laughing as Richard looked at me in disbelief. I would never have thought the day would come when I'd bless the communist regime in my country and their policy of exporting communism to countries in Africa through training their youth. But here in Congo, nothing surprised me any longer.

This was the last stop before the capital but we had another problem. Despite the delays and the potholes, despite the long discussions we had with officials in each and every one of those wooden police huts, morning was still far away. By 4 am, the driver decided to stop the minibus just outside Brazzaville and have a rest. He didn't want to arrive too early in the city. Nobody wanted to arrive too early in the city. It was not safe and the passengers would have stayed in the minibus anyway. Only sunlight made the city safe, and apparently this was what we were waiting for. We were to enter Brazzaville by sunrise.

We got out and stretched our legs. We were in the middle of the road, in the middle of some fields. We decided to put the tent up. We fell inside in a sort of semi-consciousness. We lay there for a while, but there was no way we could sleep. We soon felt the tent being shaken and heard the voice of the driver yelling, "Monsieur, Madame. We're leaving!"

We arrived in Brazzaville as the purple light of the dawn was breaking through the horizon. The minibus stopped in the Gare Routière of what appeared to be a big, busy, dusty city. We got out. We asked about the best *pâtisserie* in town. We were told that we could find one on the main boulevard, but it was too early and it would open only at 9 am. We went there, nevertheless. It was too early and we waited for a couple of hours, sitting on the stairs in front of the closed door. Too exhausted to speak, too dirty to try and clean the dust from our faces and too desperately hungry to want anything other than the best croissants and coffee in town,

---

Romania is our sister country. I was studying there a long time ago. Hey, hey: good old days. I went to the Stefan Gheorghiu Academy." (in Romanian)

no matter the cost.

Eventually the door opened. In any other country we would not have been allowed in. But under our dust and dirt we still had white faces, and in Africa this was a source of both sorrow and joy. We had experienced the sorrow last night and the days before, and it was usually connected with hassle from the police and authorities. We were now to see the joy. Nobody dared to stop a white face from entering a posh place in Africa, no matter how dirty the white face was. We sat down. Then we washed our hands. They had real toilets and running water in the bathroom. We ordered coffee and croissants and we paid 4000 CFA, four times more than what we had been spending during the whole of the last week. They were the best coffees and croissants I ever had.

Next, we went to an Internet café and checked our emails. After all, we were back in civilisation. As expected, no news from Peter: he must still be somewhere in Pokola, or maybe on the Kikuli boat if it had finally left. We had an email from Karl, the biker:

"I'm waiting for you at the Mission Catholique. Not feeling like crossing Angola on my own. How about a convoy?"

We headed towards the Mission Catholique. Since the email had been sent three weeks before, we had little hope of finding him there. As we climbed the hill we noticed a guy of East Asian appearance coming out of a gate, next to the imposing Catholic church. He stopped and looked at us.

"I know you! Karl talks about you all the time. I think you must be the ones he's waiting for!"

We didn't have time to ask him any question. There, through the open gate that the guy had come from, I spotted an old acquaintance: Mavis. Karl was never far away from his bike and sure enough we found him on a balcony, overlooking his bike and reading a book.

"Oh dear me! Very luverly to see you both. Kinda given up hope! Me 'n' Mave have been stuck here for over a month now. Not mucho fun, Brazza on your own. Not mucho fun at all…"

This was not an illusion. It was Karl's voice. And then and there, I suddenly realised that we had arrived. Maggots and smoked fish, chiefs of police and *pirogues*, the rainforest and "Bethlehem Voyages": somehow, all those things that had shaped our world for the last three weeks suddenly became a thing of the past. As we opened bottles of beer and chatted with Karl and checked into a room with a shower, I became more and more aware of the fading image of the rainforest and its inhabitants. Maybe it disappeared with the dust as I washed it off my face or maybe it was drowned in the beer, or the taste of its bananas was covered by the pizza we had that night. We slept in a real bed and washed our clothes, shared our stories with Karl, who shared his about his own wilderness that he still carried in his heart and that he discovered alone on his bike on the mud jungle roads of Gabon.

And we laughed about it and slept for days on end and ate well and wrote emails to friends back home and started planning the next leg of our trip, crossing Angola. But as we started looking ahead to what was to come, a part of me was still looking back and I knew that, even though the last three weeks had been the most difficult of this trip so far, there was one thing that would never go from my being, no matter how many showers I took or how much pizza I ate. A part of me was still there, lying on the roof of that boat, gazing at the banks of a wide river with tall trees growing straight from the point where the water ended, and the river was flowing swiftly and silently. And I knew that part of me would stay there forever, since it was there that I had come as close as I would ever be to the concept of eternity.

CHAPTER 22 – BECAUSE I AM WHITE

(BRAZZAVILLE TO KINSHASA, CONGO AND CONGO, MAY 2003)

THE day we crossed the Congo River into Kinshasa started very early in the morning. A knock on the door and the black head of Madame Nicole, our very kind and very talkative neighbour appeared through the door.

"Monsieur Richard!"

No answer. We were trying hard to pretend we hadn't heard her.

"Monsieur Richard, *il faut prendre de l'eau.*"

"What the hell does she want?" Richard was too sleepy and too grumpy to bother with understanding French so early in the morning.

"She says you need to take water."

"Monsieur Richard, *il est six heures déjà*[36]. The water is here. If you don't fill your bucket, you will not have water for the whole day," she insisted. She was already half inside the room where we were sleeping.

She came into the room, waking us up with the same story she told every morning. The door could not be locked. We had to fill the bucket with water every morning at six o'clock sharp. After this the water would be cut off, most likely for the whole day, and we would not be able to wash. These were the rules at the Catholic Mission of Brazzaville, and after spending a week in the city we were well aware of them.

What she didn't know, though, was that we didn't need

---

[36] "Mister Richard, it's six o'clock already!" (in French)

water today. We were leaving; we had got a ferryboat to Kinshasa to catch at some point that morning.

We were crossing over with Karl, who finally met up with the two other bikers he was waiting for. Minded was the same Dutch guy we met in Togo and Ed was another English biker who Karl had previously met up with in Cameroon. Ed was a medical doctor and was on his way to a job in a private clinic at Johannesburg. And he had got his bike out to get there. To my deep disappointment, Graeme, the handsome blonde biker I had talked to at length that night in Togo, wasn't there. Apparently he had had enough of the mud and the potholed roads of the rainforest and had decided to fly back home from Cameroon. All three of them had come down via Gabon, taking the same road we thought we would cunningly avoid by our shortcut through Congo.

Peter arrived too, about a week after us on the large Kikuli boat that proved to be more like a floating village than a boat. He couldn't get the car off the boat, though, and he got stuck in the port, lost in endless negotiations for several days in a row. It wasn't clear why there was a problem but it was most probably down to the "because I am white" concept that Richard had elevated to a rule which explained it all. Both good and bad things happened to us because we were white. "Because I am white, I am not being beaten up by the police in the same manner they would do to a local." "Because I am white, I am allowed inside the most expensive pâtisserie in town even though I am carrying more dirt and dust on my trousers than the whole of the road outside." "Because I am white, I am getting dragged into yet another wooden police hut for yet another set of questions and a passport registration show." And "because I am white, I am usually expected to pay more for everything." In this particular case of Peter and the car stuck in the port, the "because I am white" concept meant the authorities requested a sum of money equal to the whole cost of the journey from Pokola to allow the car to be taken off the boat.

He managed to get the car off the boat eventually, having agreed to pay the same exorbitant amount he was initially asked for, but this time he was late in submitting his passport to the Angolan Embassy for the visa. On top of everything, the car needed yet more work on it: the same suspension problem left as the legacy of the roads in Cameroon hadn't been fixed yet and Peter was already talking about finding another garage.

More days passed. The bikers decided to go. Richard was impatient. He could be very impatient sometimes, and this time it was all about the Glastonbury music festival he couldn't afford to miss. We were approaching the end of May and he wanted to be back in the UK by mid-June, just in time for his concert. And for the sake of a music festival he was now ready to rush through what was left of our trip. Maybe it wasn't Glastonbury after all. Maybe it was just a disguise for the homesickness we all felt, but one way or another he decided to get going. He was to cross the river into Kinshasa the same morning as the bikers. And they were going today.

Once more I had to make a decision. Peter and the comfort of the car were on one side, but so was the frustration of a much slower pace and the big doubt that I'd be able to survive with Peter without the constant mediation work usually done by Richard. More attractive was the thought of going ahead one more time, crossing into the unknown and getting ready for another adventure with Richard on public transport through the former Zaire and Angola, two of the most no-go countries in Africa. We had crossed Guinea together and more recently the rainforest of Congo, and both experiences were among the hardest and most memorable parts of my trip. Now I was being offered the chance to go for a third and final adventure. I decided to go with him.

We said goodbye to Mr Pillow that morning. Sadly, he was to be left behind. He had served us well, on "Bethlehem Voyages" and on the small *pirogue*, in the minibus and here in the Mission Catholique. Richard stripped him of his T-shirt. Mr Pillow used to wear one of Richard's T-shirts as a substitute for a pillow case.

Then we said goodbye to Peter. We told him we were to meet in Luanda, the capital of Angola, if he was quick. If not, I was to meet him in Namibia and Richard was to meet him at some indefinite point in the future, "when the time is right", as the Africans said. Richard was to go on from Namibia into Mozambique and finish his trip with a few days on the beach.

I felt the end was in the air that morning as we left Peter

and Mr Pillow behind and ventured down to the port to see if we could get on the ferry. We didn't expect to spend more than a week crossing DRC, which I always called Zaire, and then Angola. Then, once we reached Namibia, it would be practically over. Richard would go on his way. I would stay and try to find Chris, see if his promise of employment was still holding. And Peter was to continue on his own to Cape Town. It was to be over soon and I felt sad. But then I remembered I had the same feeling of the end being close in Cameroon and, before that, in Agadez, and yet there were so many more things that happened – roads lost and then found again and days that unfolded with their unique mix of normal and extraordinary events – that I told myself I shouldn't try to anticipate what might happen. Anticipation is a bad habit: I had learned that in Africa.

ALTHOUGH I had given up hope, we did get a place on the ferry. We spent the whole morning trying to resist any further attempts by the officials to extract more money from us before we boarded the ferry. When we finally got on board, we were pushed and tossed and I almost lost hold of Richard's bag, which I was holding on to much like a puppy holds on to the trousers of his master. Madame Nicole had warned us about the major chaos we were to meet on this ferry, but it was way beyond what we had imagined.

"Keep your eyes on your bag, and keep your bag in your arms!" Richard yelled as the crowd pushed us with the force of an unleashed hurricane. I worried more about holding on to him than I did about my backpack. I clutched his bag with all my strength, but the force of the crowd prevailed and soon my hands gave up and the straps of his big blue backpack slid away.

"Over here!" I heard his shout. "Towards the cabins!"

I fought my way through countless black faces pushing me in all directions. More people were boarding the ferry and pushing the ones already in towards the edges. I felt I was being pushed further away from my travel mate. With my remaining strength, I held on to the small, black day pack that contained all my belongings.

"Richard!"

I couldn't see anything. Someone's elbow had hit me in the eye.

"I'm here. Towards the cabins. Keep your bag in your

arms. Whatever happens, don't let it go!"

His voice faded away somewhere to my right and I realised I was being pushed in the opposite direction.

I fought. I struggled. I pushed. I turned. I hit with my elbows. I managed to get to the other part. I grabbed Richard's arm fast, with a strong determination not to let it get away again. The last thing I wanted was to find myself on my own on this ferry, crossing the Congo River between Kinshasa and Brazzaville. We put the bags in front of us and grabbed hold of a steel pillar. We had found a place. We were somewhere on the upper deck and every single inch around us got filled up with bodies and sacks of goods. I tried to look around and see if I could spot the three bikers who boarded that morning with us, but I couldn't see anything. There were too many people all around, too many sacks; too much chaos.

At some point the turmoil started to settle down and I understood it meant everybody had boarded. I heard a whistle and the ferry started moving. We were in No Man's Land – or more precisely, in No Man's Water.

The actual crossing did not take long. Brazzaville and Kinshasa are the two capitals in closest proximity to each other in the world, with only the River Congo separating them. Having already learned how things worked in Congo-Brazzaville and with fresh memories of the countless bribe requests and the many chiefs of police I had met along the way, I was already nervous thinking about the other Congo. DRC was a country torn apart by civil war. The capital and the west part of the country were fine, but in the eastern provinces about 300,000 people had reportedly been killed in the previous weeks. How were they going to behave? If we had all those troubles with the police in Congo, which was not a country at war, how would it be on the other side?

In no more than 20 minutes we anchored on the other bank of the river. We were now officially in the other Congo, the Congo-Kinshasa or DRC or RDC or whatever the official name of the country was. The same chaos started again, with hundreds or maybe thousands of people pushing into the gates, breaking through the rows of soldiers on the other side. Everybody wanted to get out, as soon as possible. It didn't matter who they stepped over, it didn't matter that the soldiers tried to keep the crowd under control and whipped the people with long leather lashes. We tried to keep hold of the pillar and not let the crowd push us away. When the hysteria of the crowd started to dissipate, we noticed the three bikers on the lower deck getting off as well and we decided that it was time to move.

We grabbed our bags. I noticed one of the zips of my small day pack was open and I wondered what I had lost. We got pushed. We got separated again. We fought our way on to the bank. As soon as we disembarked we found other people, more people, selling things, shouting, pushing. There were faces that whistled at us, others that called us "*ey vous, les blancs*", others who told us to follow them or stuck some fruit, cigarettes or who knows what else in our eyes. I tried to keep going on through this madness, but I lost hold of Richard again and the crowd pushed me away. I felt a hand grabbing my arm.

"Madame. Give me your passport!" He was a guy like so many others, dressed in a coloured shirt like so many others.

"Madame, your passport!"

The noise was deafening. I couldn't see Richard around. I was afraid. I was hysterical.

"Let me go!" I shook my arm from his grasp.

"Madame, you need to give me your passport."

He didn't let go of my arm. I was getting panicky.

"I won't! You can go to hell, you hear me? I won't give you anything! You idiot, do you think that I'm going to give you my passport so that you can extort some money from me next?"

"Madame, I'm the police!"

I looked at him. His short-sleeved, brightly coloured shirt with only a few buttons left did not look like a uniform.

"No, you're not. You're just another son of a bitch like all these other ones who try to steal something from me!"

"Madame..."

"Fuck off!"

"Shut up!" This was Richard's voice. He had arrived next to me, by some miracle.

"Shut up and give him the damn passport. He is the police!"

I shut up instantly. If he was the police then I was in serious trouble.

The image of the chief of police of Moloundou danced in front of my eyes for a moment. I couldn't believe I had been stupid enough to repeat exactly the same scene.

I gave him my passport. He took it and nodded to us to follow him. I had no doubt he would take us directly to a prison. I also had no doubt that he had understood every single one of my insults. I had made a point of barking them in French. The only thing that I doubted was whether I'd ever leave that country again. This was not Cameroon, which still saw white tourists. This was Zaire, a country in the middle of a full-blown civil war. Why could I not learn from my own mistakes?

"How did you know he was a policeman?" I asked Richard. "He was wearing just a shirt, like all the others!"

"I've seen him checking documents. People were showing him their ID or passports or who knows what. Where on earth were you looking? Didn't you see?"

"No, I didn't," I said. Maybe because of the crowd or the push or all the scary things we had heard about Kinshasa.

"I thought he was just another one of the street sellers around, and I panicked. I just wanted him to leave me alone."

"So you thought telling him to fuck off would make things better, did you?" Richard said sarcastically. "What else did you tell him before I arrived?"

"You don't want to know. Trust me, you don't want to know..."

The air in the small corridor was hot and heavy. I closed my eyes. This may be the end of it, I thought. This may be the end of this crazy adventure. I may never leave this country, except for maybe at the end of a diplomatic dispute between two governments while we rot in prison. After so many struggles, to have made it up to here, after all we've been through and all we've managed to get ourselves out of, this is where it will all end.

But, once again, good things come to those who have given up demanding them. Despite my worst fears and Richard's predictions as he found out eventually more details about the conversation I had had with the plain-clothes policeman, we were not imprisoned that afternoon. We were received in a small room with a huge desk and our passports were stamped, and another official, this time dressed in a complete uniform, smiled at us and wished us *bon séjour* in his country. The guy I had called an "idiot" was standing next to the door.

"Have a good time in Kinshasa," he said in a friendly

manner. "You are most welcome here. You see, our president, he wants to encourage tourism and foreign investment in DRC. So we're very happy to have you here."

No bribe. No vengeance. No registration in a small, dusty notebook. No mother's maiden name. Just welcome to DRC. Compared to Congo-Brazzaville, it felt like heaven.

LATER that night we met the bikers again. We were all staying at Hotel Jumbo on a busy, dirty road, with countless more-or-less wrecked cars parked on both sides of the road. We got some rooms but because they were too hot, too smelly and too full of mosquitoes, we all ended up asking the hotel owner for permission to put up our tents on the roof.

Kinshasa was a much bigger city than Brazzaville and a lot dustier. The streets were wide and there were many such wide avenues. I suspected it was a legacy from their communist past, which probably aimed to build Kinshasa as a faithful replica of Moscow. Brazzaville, on the other hand, had a much more colonial flavour and despite the half-destroyed buildings and the marks of bullets on the walls, which all spoke of their last civil war that ended only five years before, it was a reasonably safe city. The people were friendly and helpful and I realised once again that in Africa there was a very strong inverse correlation between the attitude of the police and that of the people. The nastier the chiefs, the nicer the locals, be they some boat captain or the people we travelled with in the bus, or even Madame Nicole.

Kinshasa, on the other hand, looked rather scary. Maybe the people were just as friendly here, but we had heard so many stories and the sight we had upon arrival of policemen beating up the crowd was so scary that we decided to move away from this town as soon as possible. We were to leave the next day and were looking for a form of transport that could take us up to Matadi, one of the border towns with Angola.

Night fell and we got hungry. The guys grabbed some meat from a mamma with cooking pots just in front of the hotel, but I decided to look for something vegetarian and I ventured out on my own. I got two hassling guys following me within the next ten metres. Some others joined in later; mostly kids, some teenagers as well. There were a lot of people on the street so I still felt safe. But then I got pushed. I got whistled at. I got called again and again, "*Madame, viens ici,*

Madame!" I hurried on. They hurried on. I panicked and wanted to run away. They ran after me. I pushed them away, they pushed me away. I fell down and it happened to be just by the side of the ditch at the side of the road. It was full of mud, garbage, excrement and urine. For a brief moment I thought I was going to roll into it. But I didn't. I was just lying next to it, and the smell that came from it was so disgusting that I felt I was about to throw up. I got up. The kids were still around and by now they were all laughing. "*Madame, Madame!*" I had had enough. I hurried back to the hotel, forgetting about food.

Back on the roof of the hotel, I realised my travel mates were still somewhere down on the road enjoying their meat. There was no way I would venture out on my own now so I decided to wait for them there. I noticed I had cut my palm as I fell down in the street. It was a deep cut, full of dust and dirt, and it already looked swollen. I didn't know what to do about it so I didn't do anything. I just sat there, my head on my knees, and I started feeling sorry for myself.

Self-pity is another powerful enemy, just like Fear and Sadness. Self-pity makes you think you are the most unfortunate creature in the world. And now I was thinking I was to be pitied indeed, because I was hungry, alone on that roof, and I had a deep, ugly cut on my palm. The night had fallen and I could hear the mosquitoes. I ignored them. I already had so many old and new bites on my body, on my arms and my face, through my T-shirt and my trousers, that I found it useless to fight against them any longer.

Eventually Richard found me on the roof, looking at the stars.

"So here you are, young lady, I've been looking for you everywhere. Even thought that you fancied a stroll on your own in this lovely city!"

He was smiling, like always. I was tempted to blame him for my wound and my empty stomach, as if it was his duty to constantly make sure I was safe. I knew it was not fair but I hardly resisted throwing him a hint.

"Yes, I went for a stroll. Until I was followed by a crowd half the size of this town and I almost fell into a ditch running away from them."

"You did what?" His expression was halfway between disgust and amusement. "Don't tell me you fell into one of those stinky holes?"

"No, I didn't," I admitted. "I managed to hold on to the edge. But I got a wound on my palm. Here." I opened my fist, and to my surprise the wound already looked a lot worse than the last time I saw it. It was now purple, bloated and it looked really infected.

"Let me see. It doesn't look too good. Did you put something on it?"

"No," I said feeling stupid.

"Well, don't put anything on then. Let the infection grow until we need to chop off your arm. A very good idea. Very, very clever." Richard wasn't amused any longer; he was pissed off. My wound didn't look too good and dealing with an infection in Zaire or Angola was not the easiest thing in the world.

"Let's go to the room. We need to get this dirt out."

We went into the room and we looked for all the disinfectants that we had. The light was dim; it came from the only bulb, hanging lonely from the ceiling in a piece of metal that was once a lampshade. There was no door to the bathroom and no running water either. The tiles were broken in the bathroom and the greenish linoleum that covered the floor of the room had big holes that revealed the concrete underneath. The huge bed in the middle looked like it had seen better days. One of the legs was gone and the bed leant dangerously to one side. We wouldn't use it though. We would be sleeping on the roof in the tent.

We could see that there was no point pouring any disinfectant over my wound, since the edges had now closed around all the dirt inside.

"We need to open it up and clean the dirt away," Richard decided, and he started to play jungle doctor. He took out a needle and heated it in the flame of his lighter until the needle turned first black, then a bit red.

"Are you ready?" he asked.

I wasn't but I never would be. He grabbed my palm. I turned my head in the other direction and waited for the biggest pain in the world to follow.

"Aaaayyy!"

"What? I didn't even touch you!"

"Yes you did. I felt the needle inside."

He tried again. I screamed again and he stopped. Despite the ferocious look on his face, Richard seemed more afraid than me of cutting my wound open.

"Are you doing it or what?" I was still looking away but I could tell my wound was intact.

"If you stop pulling your arm away I'm going to do it!"

I felt the needle attempting to enter my palm again.

"Ayyy! It hurts!"

Every time the needle came close to the wound, I screamed. It was simply beyond my control. We gave up eventually. My wound was still closed and still purple around all the dirt inside. But I didn't want to be tortured with a flame-heated needle and Richard had no intention of putting up with my screams any longer.

"You know what? Let's ask Ed. He must know, he's a doctor after all."

It seemed like a good enough solution to me and we went back on the roof, waiting for the bikers to return.

WE spent the entire next day in a bus station, a sort of a Gare Routière, where we waited for a real bus just as we were told. It would take us to Matadi and it would leave *maintenant*. It was afternoon already. I suspected it would be leaving in the evening. Unlike West Africa, where no bush taxi would venture out after dusk, here they preferred the night rides. It must have been a legacy from the countless civil wars, where moving by night was probably less visible and therefore safer.

The bikers had gone their own separate ways. Ed said I wasn't to worry about my wound until I started to feel pain going up my arm. Then I should worry. He failed to tell me what I was to do then. So I poured all the antiseptic powders I could find on it and I decided to let it find its own treatment.

A girl of about 17 or 18 sat next to me in the over-crowded waiting room. She was waiting for the same bus, like us; like all the others. She didn't have any luggage, just a small bundle covered up with a piece of cloth.

A fat policeman came and sat next to her. I don't know why, but most of the policemen were fat in this country. Maybe it was because they ate well. He attempted to talk. She answered hesitantly, throwing terrified looks around her. They spoke one of the local languages and I didn't understand. He probably asked her to show him what she carried in her small bundle, and she opened it reluctantly.

One of the rules of safe travelling in such countries is to

get involved in as few problems as possible. One should just mind one's own business. But this girl seated next to me seemed so desperate that I decided to break our rule.

"What's your name?" I asked her in French.

"Nadine." She looked up at me, surprised that someone other than the policeman had spoken to her.

I tried to find out more about her. She was 18. She was working in the city. She was going back to her village now because her mother was ill and she needed to bring her medicines.

"What does he want from you?" I asked her, pointing to the policeman.

"Nothing," she said.

"Oh yes, there is something. He keeps on coming back."

"He wants money. He says I need to pay a tax for the medicines I carry for my mother. I have shown him the receipt. I have bought this from the pharmacy, not from the black market as he says; still, he says I need to pay him a tax." She looked down again. "They always want more money, you know," she whispered.

"Do you want me to talk to him?" I asked her. This was a stupid question and I knew it. The only thing I could achieve by talking to him was to get me and Richard into trouble as well.

"Oh no, no," she answered quickly. "There's no need. He'll probably leave me alone anyway, if the bus comes soon."

This country might have been led by a more open-minded guy who wanted to encourage foreign investment into DRC. But he still had a long way to go in taming his police force, the same way the neighbouring Congo still had a long way to go in changing the mindset of their chiefs of police. Being a policeman in these parts was a ticket to free income for the rest of your life. Protected by a uniform and a gun, each of them could demand whatever "tax" they could think of from anybody they wanted to pick on. In the Nadine's case, it was a tax on medicines.

The bus arrived eventually, just before nightfall. We had been sitting in the Gare Routière waiting for the whole day. The policeman came back one more time, but I started talking to Nadine again and he went away, sat on another chair and kept on following her with his eyes. I suspect he wanted something more than just tax money from her. We got into the bus. I held Nadine's arm as we passed in front of him and he let us go.

With a sound of rusty iron, the bus got ready to go. Richard and I shared two seats and, a true miracle, we actually had two full seats all to ourselves. It was not at all bad. I was getting ready to spend a quite comfy night, when an unexpected voice pounded over our heads, "*Merci Dieu!*[37]"

The shout came from the front of the bus. A young guy with a very powerful voice stood up and turned towards the audience. The bus was shaking and puffing, but it was slowly moving along the wide, dusty roads of the city.

"Let's pray to the Lord for everything the Lord has given us! Let's thank the Lord for our life and for all the gifts he had bestowed upon us!"

"*Merci Dieu!*" the crowd answered.

"Let's pray to the Lord that this trip ends well and we all arrive safely in Matadi. Praise be to the Lord!"

"Praise be to the Lord!" the crowd repeated.

The guy now walked up and down through the middle corridor. He changed from French into a local language and I couldn't follow what he said next. But since the crowd answered with "*Merci Dieu*" every time he stopped speaking, I suspected it was still about praying.

"Thank you, Lord, for the life you've given me!"

"Thank you, Lord, for the life you've given me!" the crowd repeated.

"*Merci Dieu* for all your blessings."

"*Merci Dieu,*" the crowd answered.

They all prayed for a while and I wondered if this was going to go on for the whole night, until we reached Matadi at dawn. But as he sang a "hallelujah" hymn, I understood that the end of the prayer was near.

He then moved on to payment. He collected cash from each and every passenger and each and every passenger gave him a couple of banknotes. The reward from this business was remarkably good. He then came to us.

"*Merci Dieu,*" he said, with his hand outstretched.

We smiled. We didn't intend to pay him.

"*Merci Dieu,*" he repeated and then, with a sudden look of inspiration on his face, he switched to English.

"Jesus, you are my life. Thank you, Jesus! Please deliver

---

[37] "Thank you, Lord!" (in French)

us safe to Matadi!"

He still waited with his hand outstretched. I remembered a word that we had learned up north, where other people also prayed at the beginning of their journey and they all prayed to the same God, only they named Him differently.

"*Insha'Allah*," I whispered.

We still didn't pay and he gave up on us and went to others. When he thought he had collected enough, he jumped off the bus. We were driving by the outskirts of Kinshasa by now. People smiled and felt happy. They felt blessed and they felt nothing bad could happen to them now. As for the preacher, he was probably counting his cash and working out what share of it would go to the driver for letting him do his speech to the captive audience. A very profitable business.

"You know what? I think we should have taken Mr Pillow with us," I said, contemplating the broken window on my side and the bare iron back of the chair in front of me. There was nowhere to put my head down for the night.

"I guess you'll have to make do with my shoulder instead," said Richard.

"May I?" I said, pointing to his shoulder.

"You may indeed," he said.

A proper British dialogue, one would say. I went on and tried to get some sleep with my head on his bony shoulder. It was a lot less comfy than Mr Pillow. He stayed awake. There was nowhere he could put his own head. Then, giving up on the sleep that didn't come, we switched and he rested his head on my shoulder. I guess he must have fallen asleep because his head felt heavy. Maybe my shoulder was less bony than his. The bus drove away into the night, shaking and puffing from all its rotten joints. People had stopped speaking. Some of them were sleeping in convulsed positions, others just staring into the night with their eyes wide open, immobile. I, too, stared into the night with my eyes wide open. *Merci Dieu* – the words of the preacher were still in my ears. This was a country in the midst of a civil war. Most of the people on this bus had been born after this civil war had started and would probably die without knowing any moment of peace. And still they thanked God for the life He had given them. They didn't pray for more success or money or a new house or this or that. They simply thanked God for their lives. This, to the ears of a spoiled European, sounded rather incomprehensible.

We got off in Matadi the next morning. The prayer of the preacher worked and we had no major incidents through the night except for the occasional breakdown of the engine or the tyres or who knows what. We were told to keep our bags with us at all times and pointed towards the border point.

The exit formalities were a lot easier than expected. They stamped us out of the country and wished us a safe journey. On the Angolan side it took a bit longer, but they, too, managed to stamp us in after waiting more than half a day for a soldier they had sent back across the border into the DRC's town of Matadi to make a copy of our passports. Apparently the technological revolution had kicked in and Angola was no longer dealing with dusty little notebooks where all sorts of details about passers-by would be inscribed: they would prefer a photocopier, no matter that the closest one would be in another country. They had their copies eventually and we had our passports back. We walked away from the border point, with Angolan soil under our boots for the first time, and we felt pretty good. It was easier than expected and above all, no bribe requests.

We walked into the village of Noqui, which stretched away from just outside the border post. We asked for an *auberge* for the night. There wasn't one. Then we asked for transport to the capital. There wasn't any, they said. We thought they didn't understand the question and we asked again. Then we became suddenly too afraid to ask anything else, but the man squatting in the dust outside his front door smiled and casually answered the question we did not dare to ask.

"There is no road to Luanda," he said. "No road going out from here. There was one, once upon the time, but it has been destroyed by the war."

This was worse than a Lariam nightmare. This was a real one.

CHAPTER 23 – THE GOVERNOR'S PALACE

(NOQUI, ANGOLA, MAY 2003)

HE had entered through the open window. He flew around the room, banging into the walls. He kept on looking at me with his big, dark, devouring eyes and a sly smile on his muzzle. He was the incarnation of evil and he had come for me.

"No!" I shouted out, and covered my head with my arms. "No! Go away, go away!"

"Roxana!"

"Go away, go away!"

"Roxana, wake up! Wake up! It's me, Richard. Wake up!"

I felt his grasp on my arm. It was very dark, too dark to see anything around me, but I knew the intruder with the face of evil would still be somewhere in the room.

"What's up? Another nightmare?"

"Big bug! Big bug!" I couldn't articulate anything else.

"Where?"

"Up there!" I pointed somewhere above the bed, where I remembered having seen the sly smile of evil.

"What did it look like?"

"Batman."

"What?"

"It was Batman... a bat. I mean... don't know."

Richard paused.

"Then I shouldn't put the light on, should I? You may see your Batman again."

"He was evil. He was really evil. He smiled at me... he came for me."

Richard lay back on the bed with a sigh.

"Lariam," he said.

"What?"

"It's no bat or Batman or whatever else. It's Lariam. You had another nightmare."

I remembered that last night was the Lariam night. For a month or so I had started having nightmares every time I took Lariam. After six months, the secondary effects of the strong medicine had finally kicked in. I closed my eyes again and tried to erase the sly smile of the creature from my mind.

WE were still in Noqui, the small village just across the DRC Angolan border with no road connecting it to the rest of the country. The situation was scarily similar to the one we had in Pokola. We were stamped out of DRC and we only had one entrance visa. We couldn't go back. We somehow needed to make our way towards Luanda, the capital of Angola, only there was no road. There was a river though, the same mighty Congo River that upstream was dividing Congo from DRC, and now, just before floating into the sea, was marking the border between Angola and DRC. We asked if there were boats going down to Luanda. There weren't but we might be able to get one going to Soyo, a small town on the ocean, just where the river flowed into the sea. The owner of the boat wasn't there, though, and we were told that he would come to talk to us at some point soon, "when the time was right".

We waited. We took a room in a half-built house that we were told was an *auberge*, or used to be an *auberge*. Except for the family looking after the place there was only one other client, a tall, well-dressed guy who could speak a few words of English. He told us he was from the capital, Luanda, and that he was employed by some company to look after the rebuilding of their operations on the Congo River in Northern Angola. Something about transport on the river, I believe.

The little village was so much a ghost town that it was really difficult to imagine anyone willing to invest in any type of business here. Half the houses were a ruin and unlike in other parts of Africa, where you could see villages slowly developing into towns, Noqui seemed to have been quite a flourishing town once upon a time, now turned into a destroyed village. There were no fat mammas with big pots of cooked food coming out on the streets in the evenings. There was no market or people going about in the streets. There were no kids running around shouting *toubab*, *toubab*. Here and there we would spot the locals, hidden in their wood and corrugated iron huts or in their half-destroyed brick houses. On a plot of land just in front of our *auberge* lay a big pile of bricks which once used to be a house. A woman with one leg stumbled around trying to clean the bricks away. She was rebuilding her house. She was cleaning the bricks one by one, jumping around on the only leg she had left. I couldn't see anybody helping her. I doubted she had any family left.

Angola had just woken up after a 30-year-long civil war. Most of the people there had lived in continuous war for as long as they could remember. At the border post, a chatty soldier told us he had been in the army for over ten years now. He looked like a teenager and I asked him how old he was. Eighteen, he said. A former child soldier. Many people had died and many others had lost their limbs to the landmines still scattered around. Children became orphans. Houses and roads were destroyed. More armed clashes took place. More people died. For the last 30 years, while the rest of the world sent the first man to the moon, listened to pop music, watched communism falling in Eastern Europe and discovered the Internet and mobile phones, these people continued to fight and die in this country, in the most forgotten corner of Africa.

Two days had passed and we still hadn't spoken to the mysterious boat owner. With not much to do except wait, we went for a stroll around. We spotted a beautiful building at the edge of the town, something that looked like an old colonial building. We climbed up the hill that led to it and went inside. A few workers were lying in the shade and having a casual chat. They told us they were rebuilding the house and did not mind us having a look around.

Half an hour and about ten pictures later, we came out of the house only to realise that there was a smiley soldier with wide shoulders waiting for us. He pointed first to us, then to himself, then he said a few words in Portuguese. It looked like we had to go with him and I wondered if it meant we were under arrest.

He escorted us to a wooden hut down the road which served as the military's headquarters. I started feeling more and more uncomfortable. The fresh memories from Congo and the police chiefs were playing on my mind. These ones were not the police though. They were the army. I suspected there was not yet a police force in this country.

To our relief, we found out that their commander spoke French. He sat at a table, smiled and chatted loudly to other soldiers scattered around. There were many soldiers around, too many to feel comfortable with, and we still didn't know why we had been brought here.

"Do you have a camera?" the commander asked, and we held our breath.

Of course we did, and Richard had just been taking countless pictures of the ruined colonial house. He decided it was too risky to try to bluff his way out. All they needed to do was to search the small, thin bag he was carrying on his shoulder to find his camera.

"Yes, we do."

"Did you use it?"

"No, we didn't."

The camera was now out of the bag and the officer was studying it. If we were lucky, this whole thing could end up with the film being torn out of the camera. If we were less lucky they would confiscate the camera. If we were truly unlucky we would stay under arrest for a longer period.

"You cannot take pictures here. This is a highly strategic point. This is the border. And that is a palace," he said, pointing to the ruin. "That is the Governor's palace and it is being rebuilt."

He had stopped smiling and seemed chillingly serious by now. The soldiers had stopped laughing. They had stopped chatting as well and they were all staring at us. My feeling of being uncomfortable grew stronger.

"If you have taken pictures with this camera, then I have to confiscate the camera," the chief continued.

I didn't want to look at Richard's face right now. His camera was his most treasured possession.

"Look, my friend, we did not take pictures. We were just looking at it. The workers said we could take a look at it. We didn't mean to disturb anyone," said Richard, probably trying desperately to find a good enough explanation that could save his camera.

And then, with a flash of inspiration, he added, "We're guests of Gomez. Do you know Gomez?"

Gomez was the strange businessman with a clean, well-cut suit who was staying at the same *auberge* as us. A guy like that would probably not have passed unnoticed in this town. And it was also reasonably safe to assume that in order to go ahead with his business, he must have already greased the palms of all the officials in the area.

"We're his friends. He told us we could go to take a look at this ruin." And then he corrected himself immediately. "At this palace. At the Governor's palace."

This was a stroke of genius. The officer was now silent, but this time it was a different silence.

He looked at us, a long, distant look, then at the camera and then back at us.

"*Bem, bem,*" he said.

I don't speak Portuguese but this sounded like an agreement to me.

"*Bem,*" he said again. "You can go this time. But remember, you cannot take pictures of highly strategic places in this country."

We thanked him and we went, quickly, before he had time to change his mind. If this ruin was a strategic place then we had better keep our cameras hidden throughout this country.

WE eventually left the next day, on another boat going down the Congo River. The owner of the boat was waiting for us at the *auberge*, and he immediately asked us for the exorbitant sum of $600USD each for the five-hour boat ride to Soyo. After a couple of hours the price came down to $50, which I still found exorbitant for the service. But he wouldn't go down further and he was in a somewhat privileged position: he was the only man with a boat capable of making the trip to Soyo and we were in a village with no roads. We took him up on his offer.

We arrived in Soyo just after sunset, which meant we couldn't find transport to Luanda until the next morning, so we went into the automatic default mode for arrival in a new town: find a place to sleep, leave bags, find a bite to eat and make sure you walk back to the *auberge* while there are still people on the streets. We were taken around town by a teenager who had lost both his parents in the war. When we asked him why such a big crowd was gathering around us every time we showed up on the roads, he told us that they had never seen a white person before.

We spent the entire next day in a minibus on a very potholed road connecting Soyo to Luanda, paying $25 for the privilege. This country was amazingly expensive. I realised that we had spent more money in three days in Angola than in three weeks in Congo and was starting to get worried that my cash reserves were rapidly approaching their limits. But I had a credit card and travellers' cheques and I guessed it wouldn't be a problem to get some more cash in the capital. So far, all through Africa, this had never been a problem. But Angola was to be a different experience, as we were soon to find out.

The minibus was shaking. Although it was in much better shape than the ones we had become accustomed to, the road it travelled on was in a much worse condition. The result was that we were driving at a pace slower than walking. The road had been tarmacked once upon a time, but since then many tanks and heavy military vehicles must have passed over it, tearing the asphalt to pieces. Then some bombs and explosions probably accounted for the large potholes, and the rest was down to vegetation that was trying hard to reconquer the land. So we were driving on a dirt track on the side of the road, following the road sometimes on the left, sometimes on the right. We could tell immediately when this dirt track disappeared and we were back on the road. It was usually then that the car stumbled and shook and leaned dangerously to one side as it tried to emerge from a pothole double the length of the vehicle.

The night was falling and Richard's hard-acquired travel wisdom told him we should not arrive in the capital after dusk. We would be easy prey for thieves and Luanda enjoyed quite a reputation for crime. Therefore we asked the driver to drop us off at a hotel in Caxito, a town which was just outside Luanda and from where we could easily find transport into the capital the next day.

At the outskirts of town there was a police roadblock. There always was. This time, as with the soldiers in Noqui, I was not sure if they were police or army or both, or if police and army were one and the same thing here. The commander looked at us in disbelief, two white faces in the middle of the minibus, and for a fraction of a second I had the feeling I was back in Congo and the whole bribe request story was about to kick in again. But no, it didn't. He scratched his head, looked at us, talked to the driver and then looked at us again. They all spoke Portuguese here and it came as a surprise. They didn't have any local language left. We didn't speak Portuguese and they usually didn't speak anything else. Noqui was an exception: they spoke French there because they were just across the border from Matadi, the DRC town, and their lives all revolved around that town. But here we were a long way away from the borders, in the heart of Angola. We used gestures extensively and at the end of a dialogue in French, English, Italian and with bits of Spanish thrown in, we managed to explain that we wanted to stay there for the night. This seemed to be a problem and after some more talking, the policeman decided to follow us into town. The minibus was now driving into the darkness, with a military car by its side.

We stopped at a hotel. At least they said it was a hotel, although it sounded more like a nightclub or a disco to us, judging from the pounding music inside. We got off the minibus. Everybody else got off the minibus as well and we entered the hotel, with about 20 people following us and the policeman leading the way. Inside there was no reception, no lounge: only a huge room with fluorescent lighting and a few tables dotted around. The music was loud. The room was rather empty, but despite the darkness and the thick cigarette smoke we could see several groups drinking around some small tables. We were in the middle of what looked like a local disco.

Someone came to talk to us. The driver of the minibus and the policeman started a long conversation, pointing at us. We all went outside because the noise made hearing impossible, and eventually we found out that they had a couple of rooms on top of the disco that they could rent out for the exorbitant price of $37 a night.

We simply didn't have the money. We had paid for the boat and the minibus and the last three nights in *auberges*, and everybody wanted US dollars. We had reached the end of our cash supply and the small amount we still had we preferred to keep for emergencies.

We told them that we couldn't pay so much. They talked a bit more. The owner of the disco didn't want to lower the price. By now everybody had gathered around us in a large circle, taking part in the negotiations, offering their advice or who knows what. Everything went on in Portuguese, and we were trying desperately to concentrate so that we could understand something. Anything.

Eventually the policeman pointed back to the minibus, we got back in, everybody else got back in too and we left. Maybe they were taking us to another hotel.

But no, that had been the only alternative. Now we had to go all the way to Luanda, like everybody else. We said goodbye to the kind officer at the entrance of the town and we carried on.

We made the driver promise to deliver us to a hotel in Luanda and he did so, some one hour and many more potholes later. This time we decided not to be difficult. We were already in Luanda and that was all that mattered. We decided to take the room, no matter how noisy, dirty or expensive it would turn out to be.

We got our bags out. We walked into the hotel, this time with only the driver on our side. The rest of the passengers were asleep – or maybe they had just given up on us. We woke up a sleepy guy by the reception and asked how much for a room.

"Do you want a room by the hour or by the night?" he asked, and for a moment I believed my Portuguese comprehension had disappeared.

"By the hour or by the night?" the bloke repeated, and this time he pointed out the price list printed on a piece of A4 paper and stuck on the wall next to reception.

I looked at it but didn't notice the figures. I looked at the words. There were two categories of prices here and the words said per hour and per night. We were in a very authentic and straightforward brothel.

I looked at Richard and he looked back. Somewhere under the deep crust of dust that layered his face, I could see the beginnings of a smile.

"Hey, what do you think? Shall we go for a night this time?" he asked.

"Yep, I think a night would be just perfect," I laughed.

We got the key and just before we walked away from the reception, Richard had another of his great ideas.

"Do you think he would mind if I took a picture of that price list?" he asked.

"I wouldn't dare ask if I were you. It's probably a very strategic place here," I answered.

The night was dark. The room was dirty. It didn't

matter because we were dirty too: too dirty to mind laying our sleeping bags open over the sweaty, stained bedsheets that probably hadn't been changed since the start of the civil war. *Não faz nada*[38]. We were in Luanda and we were still going south. *Não faz nada*...

---

[38] "Does not matter." (in Portuguese)

CHAPTER 24 – NÃO FALO PORTUGUÊS

(LUANDA, ANGOLA, MAY 2003)

THE woman waved at us desperately but we didn't move. We were not quite sure what she wanted and her shouts in Portuguese didn't help our understanding much.

"Get in!" she suddenly switched to English. "Get in, quick!"

She had stopped the car just outside the circle of people who surrounded us. She was gesticulating feverishly and pointing to the car she had just got out of.

We came closer; she grabbed our bags and attempted to pull us inside.

"Hang on," Richard said. "Where are you taking us and how much is it?"

We were somehow reluctant to believe that we had finally found the taxi we had given up hope of.

"No money," she said. "Just get in. Quick!"

We got in. She had an old car but it still had doors and windows, which meant it was quite comfortable. A young guy was driving. She, a woman of about 40 years old with a bright, educated look on her face, sat in front near the driver.

The car moved but had trouble finding its way through the huge mass of people outside. People banged on the windows, on the windscreen. The driver sounded the horn. They didn't care. We pushed, almost driving over some of them, and at some point emerged in the streets.

We still didn't understand where this unexpected taxi had come from and Richard made another attempt to ask where we were going and how much it was.

"*Nada. Nada.*" She shook her head. "You just don't understand what danger you were in!"

"Danger?"

"Yes, in the middle of that crowd. What were you doing there? What were you thinking of?" She shook her head in disbelief. "You must be crazy!"

What were we doing there? We were trying to get into the centre of the city. We woke up in the brothel that morning and found a bit of comfort when we noticed that their business wasn't really booming and the place was rather empty. We spent the night terrorised by the bedbugs, which had managed to make their way from the filthy sheets through my sleeping bag, and now a whole new set of bites appeared on top of my old mosquito ones and I had started the day scratching like a maniac.

In the light of the morning, the city seemed somehow less threatening and we had packed our bags, left the brothel behind and tried to figure out how to get to the centre of the city. The plan was to try and find the Romanian embassy, leave the bags there, then go and get a Namibian visa, change some money and get out of this crowded city in the first bush taxi we could find. Piece of cake, we thought. After all, we had survived so many other African towns and cities so far that Luanda did not seem such a threat.

Out on the streets, we soon discovered there were no taxis in this city. There were very few minibuses either, and there was no way to get into one since they were already packed with people, or understand where they were going since all the shouting went on in Portuguese. We had stood there in the middle of the street, trying to figure out where to go, and we hadn't noticed that people had started to gather around us. This was when the women arrived and she pulled us out of there into her car.

"Where do you want to go?" she asked.

"To the Romanian embassy. Here, this is the address." I showed her a small piece of paper where I had printed the details of all Romanian embassies in all the countries in Africa. I'll never know when I might need one, I thought as I did that before we left, and I was right.

She only spoke a few words of English and the conversation was limited. The only thing she managed to transmit was that we were in danger and we should never do this again. Do what? Go out on the streets? She seemed to be exaggerating, I thought.

We drove through long roads with high communist-style

blocks of flats which looked half empty, and we figured out we were a long way away from the centre. Then we drove through an overcrowded market with people selling all sorts of things, but above all cans of Coke and Fanta. It looked like the soft drinks industry had just entered Angola and everybody was selling those cans in every corner, on every road. At the market she pointed towards the huge crowd and said that this was where she wanted to go, and then something about her having a little shop on the outskirts of the city and coming here to buy stuff for her shop. We then thought this was our destination and we expected to be left on our own. But no, we passed the market and she and the driver engaged in a long dialogue about the address I had given them.

Eventually we arrived. It was a small street with nice little houses and the car stopped in front of a green fence.

"Romanian embassy," she said, smiling.

Then she held my hand and looked deep into my eyes.

"You must take care here. Very dangerous. Luanda, very dangerous city. Don't go out."

As we took our bags and asked her how much we should pay, she smiled again and said

"*Nada. Nada.* You were in danger, that's why I stopped; but no money. Once in my life, maybe, I too will be lost on the streets of a strange town and I too would like someone to stop and help me out."

We thanked her and we went. I hoped someone one day would return to her the kindness she had shown to us. I couldn't stop thinking, though, that in Europe nobody would have done it. Once again, Africa was teaching us a lesson.

We rang the bell at the gates of the embassy and they spoke Portuguese, and when I answered in Romanian there was a long silence before I heard:

"Do not move away from the gate. Someone will be with you shortly."

And sure enough, a couple of minutes later someone unlocked the heavy gates. And it took a few minutes before the guy fully comprehended that he could speak Romanian to me.

"Whatever you are doing here, you should not be out on those streets. Come in! Quickly! You should never be out on those streets again," he said as we passed through the gates.

There must be something wrong with those streets, I thought. People here seemed to be obsessed with staying away from them.

We left the bags and found out several important things: the first was a repetition of the warning to stay away from the streets, plus the added comment that Luanda was a dangerous town and we should hurry to get out of it as soon as possible. The second was that we could not sleep there as we had hoped. We had to find a hotel and this was not going to be an easy business.

Despite their warnings we were back on the streets, and this time, before changing money or getting a Namibian visa, we decided that our priority was finding a place to spend the night. We walked around trying to find the centre, following the vague indications we were given. We entered a couple of places with a big signpost saying "hotel" above their entrances. A bunch of girls were counting money on the stairs. Another bunch of them were waiting in the lobby. After several further tries, we gave up. I couldn't bear the thought of another night like the last one. The bites of the bedbugs were still fresh and itchy. We decided it was an emergency and we moved on to Plan B, which we kept for real emergencies only: moments like this one when we felt we truly could not carry on. We went straight to a luxury hotel, a real hotel that probably cost a fortune. So far, in seven months in Africa, we had never done it, except for Christmas Day when Peter got that wonderful room in Dakhla. We felt it would be a sort of betrayal; we had come here to see the real Africa, not to look at it from the other side of an air-conditioned room. But this time we had no choice. It was either that or another brothel.

As soon as we stepped through the door, we felt the temperature change and the air-conditioned breeze struck our unaccustomed faces. The lobby was luxurious and there were white people around. It smelled clean. It felt unreal.

We went directly to the reception.

"How much are your rooms for the night?"

"$250USD for a double, $174 for a single," we were told.

That was my budget for a month. It was worth asking for a discount. It always is. I spent the next ten minutes trying to persuade the receptionist to give me a single room and allow Richard and me to share it. He didn't agree. He said this was not the procedure. I somehow distantly remembered that this was really not the procedure in a 4-star hotel back in Europe, but this was Luanda and I was still impregnated with the dust of the streets and I felt that somehow it should be possible here; everything should be possible here. And on top of that, the difference was quite substantial.

We argued for a while. He called his boss; the boss said this was impossible. I pushed a bit more, and the old feeling of arguing with the police in Congo came back. But this was not the police. This was a civilised, 4-star hotel and they looked at us as if we were mad.

I almost felt like giving in. The bites were aching. I knew outside it must have been hot and dusty and there were no taxis or minibuses in this town; plus everybody kept on saying we should stay away from the streets.

"Fine, we'll take a double room then."

"Perfect. For when?" the receptionist asked.

"For tonight."

"We regret, madam, but for tonight we have no availability left."

I thought I must have heard him wrong.

"What did you say?"

"We don't have a double room free for tonight, I'm afraid."

"How about a single one?"

He threw a quick glance into a big registry.

"No, madam, I'm afraid we don't have a single room either. I'm afraid we're fully booked."

This sounded like a bad joke to us. But no, it was true. They were fully booked. They knew they were fully booked all the time: when we argued about the discounts and when he called his boss to his rescue. They were fully booked and so were the other few luxury hotels in town. I don't know what conference was on; I don't know what subject was being discussed in Luanda in those days.

"Thank you," Richard said to the professionally smiling receptionist. "Thank you so much for having wasted our time."

There was nothing much to say. We went through the polished glass door once again, but this time it was the hot, dusty air that greeted us as we exited the hotel. We carried on walking and soon it felt like our brief encounter with luxury never even happened. We were back to the real Luanda.

We spent the whole afternoon trying to find a hotel. The evening was approaching quickly, and although we didn't have any further incidents while walking around the city that day, we knew we had to be off the streets by nightfall. But good things come to those who have given up expecting them. And there, on the streets of Luanda, this principle kicked in again and when the miracle happened and we spotted the little, tucked-away "Hotel Paris" and we decided to give it one more try and see how bad this brothel would be, we were greeted by a nice man dressed in a clean shirt and shown up to a room, and there were no girls waiting in the lobby and no girls sharing money on the stairs and the bedsheets smelled, incredibly, clean, and it cost only $30 for a double, which we had learned was cheap by Angolan standards.

"We'll take the room," we said at once.

Outside, night was falling fast and after all we had heard about that town we didn't dare go out on the streets after dark. The luggage had to stay at the embassy and we were to stay at the hotel overnight with nothing else except the clothes we were wearing.

THE next day I reached the limits of my language skills.

"*Não falo português.*[39] Do you speak English?" I shouted, trying to make my voice heard above the heads of people who kept on pushing in front of me.

But he either didn't speak English or hadn't heard me at all. He kept on talking to me, in this strange language that I couldn't understand despite its Latin roots.

"English. *Français. Espanol!*" I shouted again. Whatever. Whatever else you can think of, but please not Portuguese, I was about to add.

"*Não. Não,*" he said, and I knew that this meant "no". It also meant he would not change my travellers' cheques at this bank, just as the other three or maybe four places we had tried would not change them.

He said something about the central branch. He wrote down the name of it on a piece of paper and pointed his hand behind his back, to the wall. I guessed this was the

---

[39] "I don't speak Portuguese." (in Portuguese)

direction we should walk once we got out of the building. Apparently they would be able to help us at the central branch and we might finally change the travellers' cheques we were desperately trying to convert into cash.

We went out on the streets again. It was mid-afternoon and we hadn't eaten anything since the morning, ever since this mad rush for cash had started. We had woken up in that small and miraculously clean hotel and gone to get my visa at the Namibian Embassy. I managed to get it without much hassle and I had the piece of paper stuck in my passport in exchange for $30USD, the last cash in my pocket. We then thought we would get some money out or we would change some Amex cheques, and we would be out of this town by sunset.

But there was no place in this town where we could take money out or change the cheques and we were slowly sliding towards panic after the fifth unsuccessful attempt. The central branch was to be our last hope. It was Friday afternoon already and we needed to find cash somewhere, before all those institutions closed for the weekend. We simply didn't have enough money to survive here over the weekend.

We waved at a minibus to stop. After a day and a half in this town, we had figured out that there were minibuses going towards the seafront centre. We got on and took the last two seats.

In front of us, a group of four guys were speaking loudly. The minibus stopped again. A teenage girl got on. She was dressed in a denim jacket and clean trousers. She took money from the pocket of her jacket and paid the driver. Then she took the only available seat on the minibus, in front of us, next to the guys. Then a series of events occurred. I saw the hand of one of the guys hanging over the back of their chairs, just in front of my eyes. He got a handful of banknotes. He must have taken them from the girl's pocket. His mate's hand leaned back too, and he gave the cash to the other one. The other one then gave it to a third. Then, some more movement on the seats in front of us and the girl gave a brief shout. She started crying and her sobs filled the minibus. The guys were laughing. She had just been robbed and the notes I saw dangling in front of my eyes, being passed from one hand to the other, were the same banknotes she had put into her pocket after she had paid the driver.

On the back seats Richard and I were frozen. I felt the revolt building up in my throat and the sobs of the girl, the laughter of the guys, all that, pushed my blood into my head and I felt ready to jump up.

But I couldn't. Richard's hand held my arm tightly.

"Don't even think of saying something," he whispered. "Don't even think of it. There's nothing we can do. You know very well. There's absolutely nothing we can do, is that clear?"

It was. Crystal clear. They might have had guns. Even if they didn't, they were four and we were two and we were on the streets of Luanda, in Angola, and all this meant we stood no chance. But the girl kept on crying and the guys still laughed and teased her, and when the minibus stopped and we got out I was very careful not to look in her direction. I was feeling like a coward and I didn't say anything for a while. But then I told myself that we were alive and the girl was too, and maybe that was more important than feeling like a coward.

At the central branch of the biggest bank in Angola, after waiting in a queue for an hour we met the same avalanche of Portuguese words.

"*Não falo português. Não falo...*" I tried desperately to make them understand.

The guy stopped talking and went away. Then he came back with another guy, his boss probably. This one could speak a few words of English.

"Cannot change cheques here. No Amex cheques. Not possible process. No possible in all Luanda, in all Angola."

So this was one of the two possibilities crossed out.

"How about cash on a Visa card? Do you have a cash machine?" I asked, with all the hope I could muster gathered in my eyes.

"Yes," he said, and he smiled and for a moment I could see the gates of paradise opening.

"Yes. Possible. But next year. We sign contract now with Visa. Next year cash machine!"

Next year and right now: somehow these two notions were interchangeable to this man. Once again, time did not exist there.

I felt like fainting. I had absolutely no cash left in my pocket, in whatever currency, and Richard had got only enough to pay for a single ticket on a bus to the border. I was feeling desperate.

One idea crossed my mind. With a sudden regained hope, I asked one more question.

"Do you have Western Union here?" I was thinking that if I could somehow communicate with my parents and get them to send me money, then we could still get out of this nightmare.

"No. No Western Union here."

And then, as I tried to explain our desperate situation, he gave us one more suggestion.

"Try the hotels. They take credit cards. They may give you cash on a credit card."

We got out of the bank and for a moment I felt like just sitting down on the pavement in the dust. Richard looked at me very seriously and his ever-present smile was gone from his face:

"Listen. We're in trouble. I only have enough money to get myself to the border. I don't have enough money for your ticket. And if I stay here another night I won't have enough money for my ticket either. We need to find a solution. We need to sort this out now. I need to leave tonight."

This was chilling. For the first time in eight months in Africa, I was contemplating alternatives to being left all alone in the most dangerous city we had passed through.

"Let's try the hotels," I said. Somewhere deep down, I hoped with all my heart that this last alternative would work.

It turned out that it didn't. We walked from one hotel to the other and we soon realised we had asked the same question to all of the few luxury places in town who would take a credit card. None of them was willing to give us a cash advance, maybe because of the exorbitant commission, maybe because fraud was rife and they didn't trust our cards. One way or another, there was no way to get cash out.

"But what shall we do?" I asked desperately at the reception of the last place we tried. "Who else takes a credit card in this country?"

"Try the airlines," we were told, and for a moment I held my breath. This was something that we hadn't thought about, but it was the worst possible solution for me. A lot worse than anything I could have imagined could happen to me on the streets of Luanda. If the only place I could use my card was an airline, it meant my trip would suddenly finish, then and there, since I would just have to jump on to a plane and go back to Europe.

We went out on the streets once again and Richard was determined to find the first airline office before it closed down for the weekend. This meant we had about two hours left.

"This is it. This is the solution. You'll need to use your card to buy a flight ticket and that's how you'll get out of here," Richard said.

"But... I don't... but you don't understand... the trip... I can't take a flight... not yet!" I was feeling sad, desperately sad, sadder and more desperate than I'd feel if I were told I should stay here for one more year until their Visa card agreement would kick in and the cash machines would become available.

"You need to do this. There's no other way out... do you understand?" Richard was yelling at me by now.

"I don't want my trip to be over yet! Can't you understand that?" I was yelling back at him.

"Don't you dare shout at me! Not after everything I've done for you in the last few days. I'm here because you need a Namibian visa and because you don't have enough cash! I wouldn't even have stopped in this town if I was on my own. So don't you dare shout at me!"

I shut up. He carried on, "Do you understand that I need to go on and I can't pay for your bus ticket to the border? Do you understand that if I stay here another night, I won't be able to pay for mine either? Do you understand that I need to go and leave you here?"

He was still yelling. This was so unlike Richard. He'd never yelled at me before. Even when we had disagreements, even when we were at the end of our strength and our patience, he had never yelled at me before the way he was yelling at me now.

I started crying instantly. I felt suddenly that my life had transformed into a series of horrors, much like the nightmares that kept on coming back to me in the night. Richard yelling at me and telling me he would leave me alone in Luanda. The only solution was to take a flight away from Africa...

We walked on the dusty streets aimlessly, Richard silent

now but with his veins pulsating in his neck and me, stumbling and crying at the same time. I didn't know where we were going and I didn't care. I was to take a plane and go away and end my trip abruptly, and I didn't care about anything else.

"We can try Air Namibia," Richard said after a while. "We can check if there's a flight between here and Namibia so you take this one and then carry on from Namibia."

This was a better alternative than flying back to Europe, but it still felt wrong, deeply wrong. I somehow stupidly felt that if I took a flight I would betray my old dream of crossing Africa over land, with all the hardships and joys that came with it.

But Air Namibia could indeed be a solution and I knew he was right. I swept my tears away and we carried on walking, asking for directions and not understanding a word, getting into minibuses and out of minibuses, getting lost in a big, dusty town with no taxis.

At some point we stopped in front of the polished glass doors of an office. There was a sign outside and it said "Travel Agent". The building looked new and incredibly modern. We stepped in. There was aircon and it was clean and I felt like I had just stepped back into the lobby of one of those hotels.

"*Eu… nada… Namibia, plane… ici?*" I managed, trying a combination of Spanish, Italian and French, hoping that I could somehow make myself understood.

A young, white man with a well-cut suit, clean shirt and tie walked towards us:

"First of all," he said in English, "which language are you speaking?"

I couldn't believe he spoke English. I was still in shock and my standard phrase, the only one I had learned in Portuguese, came out:

"*Não falo português.*"

"It's OK, we can speak something else then. Is English good enough?" he laughed.

It was.

"Do you want to sit down?" he said, pointing to two leather-covered chairs by the side of a nice, brown, solid wood desk.

"Do you want something to drink?"

We did. We drank some Coke and then we were silent

for a while. We had arrived in paradise.

It turned out that Miguel, our new acquaintance, was Portuguese and had just come to this country to open up a business: more precisely, a travel agency. He had high hopes: the country was just out of a civil war and the infrastructure was almost non-existent. Everything needed rebuilding and there was money to be spent everywhere. On top of this, the prospects were encouraging. Angola was the richest country in Africa, with oil and diamonds in its soil among other things, and he guessed there would be soon a solid business clientele that he could serve.

We told him our story. He told us we must be mad. Not so much because we were left without cash in this country, but because we were walking the streets.

"You must be mad to be walking around this city. You must be totally insane. You probably have no idea how many times you've risked your lives today."

Miguel was giving us the same warning as everyone else. Something bad must have happened out there, but except for the robbed girl, we seemed to have been spared any bad experiences.

"I tell you, this country is wild. You must get out of it as soon as possible. This is not a place to come for tourism."

Then it should be no place to come for business either, we said, and he agreed. But he was an adventurer, and chose to come here just because it was so unusual, just like we had chosen to cross through this country because it was off the beaten track.

"The other month, at the airport, when I came back from Portugal, one of the officials told me I couldn't enter. Why? He didn't like my face. It didn't matter that I had bought an expensive ticket to get here, that I had a regular visa in my passport and a lot of cash in my pocket. It didn't matter that I was a business traveller and that I had come to invest in his country. He just didn't like my face.

"And what happened?"

"I didn't enter. I had to take a flight back to Portugal, the same plane I came in actually. I couldn't get out from the airport. I then came back two days later, having paid for another ticket, and this time another official who checked my passport let me in. He must have liked my face."

He smiled.

"Hey, hey, there are many stories in this country. Many,

many. It's interesting, in a way, being here and dealing with all these things. It's so unlike anywhere else."

We could somehow understand this: it was the same for us, and even though we were going through a nightmare right now, about the cash and the airlines and all that, we knew that there was always a price to pay for the privilege of being off the beaten track. And in this case, for both Miguel and I the price seemed to be an extra flight ticket.

The office was cool and Miguel was really pleased to have us there and we chatted some more, oblivious to the clock that was ticking and the office of the Namibian Airlines that was about to close. We heard some more stories, about the ruling family who practically controlled all the administration and who managed the country like feudal lords would manage their private lands. We heard of oil and diamonds being sold and whole islands being bought abroad, most notably on the shores of the Portuguese-speaking Brazil to serve as a refuge when the family was eventually overthrown. A government was always destined to be overthrown here, it seemed. We heard about Alcatel, who wanted to make an offer for the telephony company in Angola only to find out that the business they wanted to buy was plagued by enormous amounts of bad debts – notably, the Government and their extended families had been using the phones free for the last 20 years. We found out that oil was being extracted in this country with no way of measuring the output, and this because nobody really wanted to be held responsible for the tons of barrels that went missing. Angola seemed the last wild frontier of Africa, and above all, Miguel told us that the worst thing we could do was to venture out on to the streets.

"Carlos," he said when we told him we needed to leave. "Please drive my friends to the Air Namibia offices." He handed a bunch of keys to the driver. "And make sure you leave them just in front of the door," he added.

We couldn't buy a ticket from him, since his agency wasn't yet registered to issue plane tickets, but he had called Air Namibia and made sure they would be waiting for us and now he was lending us his driver and his car.

"Take care. And stay off the streets. Get the hell out of here as soon as possible. You must be mad."

"No, you must be mad!" Richard said. "You're the mad one, to be doing business in this country!"

"Well, one also has to have some fun in life," he said as he waved us away.

A part of me could understand him. The other part, the one that had briefly stopped crying but was about to start again, was saying that this was by no means funny.

We arrived at Air Namibia. They had a flight leaving in two days. It landed in Windhoek, the capital of Namibia. It cost a fortune. I looked at Richard in desperation, as if he could do anything: a miracle, as he had done at various other moments throughout the many weeks and months that we had been travelling together. He looked back at me. There would be no miracle this time.

"You have to do it. There is no other way."

I gave the woman my credit card. She swiped it and processed the $500USD ticket, and I started crying again and I cried and cried from the bottom of my heart. My trip was ending right here, right now, under my eyes full of tears.

It didn't take long and we were back on the hot, dusty streets. My flight was to leave in two days. Richard said we should go back to the embassy and make sure they would give me shelter for those two days, while he was to leave that very night, getting into the first minibus he could find.

I still cried hysterically, standing in the middle of the dusty street, in the middle of the heat that started to dissipate under the breeze of the early evening.

"Come on! Stop it! Stop it!" Richard shook my shoulders again. "There was no other way... you know very well!"

"There was!" I shouted out. "There was another way that we just haven't thought about, and now it's too late!"

The sudden flash went through my mind like an explosion, and in its light I could see that yes, there might have been another way: if only I had thought about it earlier!

"What do you mean?" Richard looked at me as if I had suddenly become insane.

"The ambassador!" I shouted. "The ambassador!"

"What do you think? That he would have given you money? You know that's impossible. You know no embassy would give you money because there is no way they could be sure you would repay it."

"Yes, there could be a way. My parents in Romania could give the money to some of his relatives. Maybe he's got some relative in Bucharest; it could have been done! We could have tried it, at least we could have tried it. But now it's too late," I sobbed.

I could feel the weight of the $500 flight ticket in my pocket.

"Let's go to the embassy," Richard said after a brief pause and started walking briskly.

I didn't know if my late solution sounded feasible or if he just wanted to make sure I was behind a safe fence before he left. But it somehow didn't matter. It was too late anyway.

We went to the embassy. I was still crying. I asked to see the ambassador. I fell down on the sofa in his office, crying hysterically, and I tried to explain to him that we were out of cash, that so many things had happened since the previous day when we had left our bags there, that I had bought a plane ticket and that I was broken-hearted at having to end my trip there and then. I told him about my idea.

It turned out that he had a daughter in Bucharest who could receive $200USD cash from my parents. He asked me for my parents' phone number in Bucharest. He then made the phone call.

"Hello, is this Mrs Valea? This is the Romanian ambassador in Angola. Please call me back on this number; I'll let you speak to your daughter."

My mother called back. I think that she must have been terrified to get such a phone call: after all, the last time I spoke to her on the phone was more than two months ago and since then I had just sent some emails saying I was fine but not giving too many details about the route we had taken. I didn't want to scare them.

But that afternoon, in the office of the Romanian ambassador in Luanda, when the phone rang I picked it up and said, without much consideration about scaring or not scaring her, "Hi, Mum. It's me. I'm fine. Listen, I can't talk much, I can't explain anything to you but please do me a favour. Please go at once to this address and give the lady $200 dollars in cash. It has to be done now: it has to be done tonight. And please tell the lady to call her father when she receives the money!"

Then I dictated the address of the ambassador's daughter and I hung up.

"I will explain it to you, Mum. One day, I will explain," were my last words to her.

The ambassador's daughter called her father in the next

30 minutes while we were all still waiting around the desk in silence. She had got the money. My mum must have been working miracles back home.

Next, the ambassador counted out the equivalent of $200USD in local currency into my palm. I felt I was floating. This meant we could pay for accommodation that night. It also meant I could take a bus with Richard in the morning. It also meant my trip would carry on. It wasn't over yet. It wasn't meant to be over yet.

I took the non-refundable $500 ticket, now useless, out of my pocket and I knew I would never use it. A huge price to pay for not having thought of this alternative earlier.

"Give me the ticket," Richard said suddenly.

"What?"

"Give me the ticket! I'll try to give it back."

I looked at the big clock hanging on the ambassador's wall. It was half past five. Namibia Air offices closed at six.

"Give me the ticket," Richard repeated.

I didn't say anything. I gave it to him and he ran out of the door.

WE went back to Hotel Paris that evening, and this time we had the bags with us and I could finally change out of the dusty T-shirt I had survived in for the last two days. As incredible as it sounds, Richard had managed to get to the airline office before it closed. He had stopped one of the jeeps being driven around and asked for directions and the man, another expat, looked at him in astonishment and told him, "Get in. Get in at once. You must not be walking these streets. Tell me where you want to go, I'll drive you there!"

He then managed to persuade the woman who sold me my ticket to tear it apart and cancel it. Because they didn't have a direct phone connection, my Visa card transaction had not yet been processed. He tore the voucher into pieces and she tore the paper ticket into pieces. It was as if the transaction never took place. He then managed to make his way back to the embassy, under the constant terror of the approaching night when the streets of Luanda would become even more unsafe.

He smiled at me when I saw him back at the gates of the embassy, the same old smile that reminded me of the Richard I knew, the smile that had been wiped off his face for the whole day.

"It's fine. It's all good. The ticket is cancelled and we're leaving tomorrow morning. Together."

I was still shocked and I couldn't react too much, not even when Richard came back with this good news and not even when the ambassador himself took out his car and, together with his wife, drove us to our small Hotel Paris. They gave us a big bag with all sorts of food nicely packed for our bus ride the next day and wished us good luck.

"And stay off the streets," they said as they left. "Don't leave your hotel until tomorrow morning! Just stay off the streets."

There must be something happening on those streets, I thought again. And I even felt tempted to step outside, just to check if the street would melt away during the night and swallow up everybody on it, which would be the only explanation for the horror in everybody's voice as they told us to stay off those streets.

But we didn't go out. We got straight into bed and I was feeling happy, as happy as someone could be when waking up from a nightmare. And Richard was bursting with joy too, and for the first time in the many, many nights that we had shared the same bed, we didn't go to sleep with our backs politely turned to each other, wishing each other a good night's sleep. Instead we laughed and fought each other for what we believed was our rightful half of the bed and kicked and hit, and then we started fighting with the pillows. And the laughter in the room went deep into the night, and the pillows kept on flying around the room. And then we calmed down a bit, exhausted but still thrilled with the idea that we had cash in our pockets, and we fell asleep eventually like two little kids tired from too much pillow fighting. We knew that our trip was to carry on and it was the only thing that mattered. What we didn't know, though, was that we were still close to the end, maybe a lot closer than we thought, and the night that we spent in Hotel Paris in Luanda was to be the last night we shared a bed together.

The following morning we left Luanda on a bus heading towards the border, and I promised myself never to return again. We went to the Gare Routière and asked for a minibus to Lubango, a city towards the Namibian border, and we found one straight away. In fact, we were practically lifted by an army of unwanted helpers and carried over to one bus, then carried over to another one among shouts and fights and our useless attempts to recover our bags left on the ground.

But once again, "it will all be fine" seemed a miraculous formula that worked. After three days and two nights we were leaving this city, and as we sat down in our seats in the middle of an overloaded minibus, Richard stuck his elbow into my ribs and said, "Hey, you see: I told you it would all be fine and it is."

And then, in a more serious voice, "I'm really happy you're here. It was haunting me, the thought of going out of this city on my own; and yesterday I just lost hope that this would work out and we could continue together." I smiled. Our yelling of yesterday and the chilling distance that it brought between the two of us seemed a long way away now, and I suspected the pillow fight of last night had something to do with the significant improvement in our relations. I felt good. The minibus was shaking, then it started to move slowly and when I saw the road stretching out in front of us as we went out of town, I knew that we were back on track and that road, that long, red road south, was still there and my trip hadn't ended yet.

The minibus was pretty modern: it had a radio and I saw the driver push a tape inside. Surprisingly, it was English music and the words said:

> *Sometimes living up your dreams*
> *Is not as easy as it seems.*

There could hardly have been a better way to put it.

CHAPTER 25 – THE OTHER SIDE OF THE MOON

(ANGOLA TO NAMIBIA, JUNE 2003)

RICHARD'S hair had grown into long curls the colour of honey. It would soon be as long as mine, I thought. Having tried once to cut his hair in Senegal and having emerged from the barber shop almost bald, he decided to keep whatever was left of his hair for the remainder of his time in Africa. "They don't know how to cut 'white' hair here," he used to say.

A sudden shake of the minibus woke me from my thoughts. We were stopping again. We had been stopping every hour ever since the morning, when we had left Luanda in this minibus.

Everybody got out. Everybody always got out at every stop, and this process took about 15 minutes. Then everybody started to pee, right there in the middle of the road. Men usually walked some two or three metres in front of the minibus, turned their backs to the rest of the crowd and peed standing up. They were so close that I could hear their urine hitting the dust of the road. Women, on the other hand, didn't bother walking so far. They just squatted down in no specific order, right there around the minibus, and pulled up their many layers of skirts. They usually left the last layer hanging out so as to cover their bare bottoms. They didn't use any paper. Once they were finished, they shook their squatting bodies for a bit and then they stood up and let the many layers of skirts fall down. They were done.

Angolans pee a lot, I thought. Every time the minibus stopped it seemed that everybody needed a toilet break, and every time we left again the minibus had to drive through the many wet spots left in the dust of the road.

Richard usually joined the men for a pee, only he made the effort to walk a bit further before he turned his back to the minibus and faced the empty dusty road ahead. I suppose men were used to peeing together; after all, they do it in every public toilet back in Europe. But I had never peed in a group and I felt so inhibited that I was sure nothing would come out, even if I tried.

I decided to go and look for a quieter spot. I walked away from the minibus, following the road in the opposite direction from where the men were, which meant that I was heading backwards. After a while I realised that I was far enough away, but still in plain view of the others. The road stretched outwards in an open space, with very few bushes on the sides of the road. Here and there, some baobab tree sent its convulsing, empty branches to the sky. The rainforest was far behind us by now and we were back to the savannah climate, back to baobab trees, and spotting this old acquaintance from West Africa brought about a feeling of wellbeing.

There were no bushes by the road so I decided to start walking over the land to the baobab tree I could see some hundred metres away in the fields. I figured out I could hide behind its thick trunk.

As I finally squatted and did my business behind the trunk, I heard voices, some shouts in Portuguese. Maybe the minibus was getting ready to leave. As I walked back to the road, casually stepping over the fields overgrown with weeds, I realised they were all gesticulating and shouting at me.

"Look where you step!" shouted Richard, and I suddenly made sense of all the yelling.

I was walking through a potential minefield. That was why they were all peeing in the middle of the road, avoiding taking even a step aside. That was why the fields were not cultivated. That was why we had never seen cows or other animals in the fields. That was why they were now shouting at me.

I tried to look down at where I stepped, but the earth looked as red and dusty as always. "What did a landmine look like?" I wondered.

"Very clever, very, very clever," Richard said as I came back. He was not joking. He was rather pissed off. "What did you think you were doing?"

"I went to find some shelter for a pee. Do you think I can pee in the middle of the road like everybody else?"

"So you went searching for a landmine instead? Very, very clever!"

"Come on, there can't be mines everywhere. They must be exaggerating."

"I guess it's better not to find out!"

Maybe he was right. Maybe I shouldn't drink water any more.

WE arrived in Benguela by sunset and we found that there were minibuses going towards the border: more precisely, to the city of Lubango halfway to the border. We took the decision instantly. We were to continue through the night and get into the other minibus straight away. It must have been the fresh memories of the cash crisis in Luanda, or those of peeing in a minefield, but I felt I wanted to get away from this country as soon as possible. It was expensive. It was dangerous. And, even though surprisingly we didn't have any problems with the officials, the population seemed rather hostile. There were three categories of people, and it made me think of the social system in my country back in the communist era. There were the nice ones, like the lady who picked us up from the streets of Luanda, or Gomez, the strange businessman from Noqui who would go across the border in Matadi to buy food for us since we couldn't cross on our passports. There were the indifferent ones: people that would talk about us, would comment when I walked into a minefield, but would be mostly neutral. And then there were the nasty ones, the loud ones, who were drinking in minibuses and shouting, the ones who would yell questions at me in their incomprehensible language and then laugh loudly; the ones who had run after us that night when we arrived in Luanda and we had had to take shelter in the brothel in the suburbs. This society was severely shaken and I guessed the aggressive guys must have been recently released soldiers who had grown accustomed to terrorising the population. Moreover, we were told by Miguel back in Luanda that ever since the UNITA, the opposition force supported by South Africa, had lost the war there was a very strong anti-white feeling in the country which came across in slogans like "let's throw the whites away and rape their women". I didn't really like the sound of it and thought that maybe rushing to get out of this country wasn't such a bad idea. Richard, on the other hand, was obsessed with a bet he'd got on with the bikers, arranged with Karl, Ed and Minded back in Kinshasa before we all went in different directions, and it was something about whoever got out of Angola first would have to buy a certain quantity of beer for the others somewhere, at some point when we would meet again. With the three of them on their bikes and us on public transport, the odds seemed heavily against us but he held on to his hopes.

WE travelled for the whole night and then we travelled for the whole of the next day. My mind went blank: I didn't know if there would be an end to this minibus story, I didn't know if there was a point of arrival. The road was in a total state of destruction and the large holes in it spoke of war again. I remembered the camels we had in the desert. It was a lot more comfortable to be travelling on their backs.

The car stopped, people peed. I still went into the bushes, but tried to reach for the ones close by. We bought bread and fruit at some ghost towns. There were no lively villages in this country with fat mammas cooking by huge pots. There were only ghost towns fallen into ruins and shops with broken windows selling imported cans of Coke. Everything around spoke of war.

We got off minibuses and into cars, out of cars and into jeeps. The sun was rising and setting, day followed night, then it was day again. We didn't notice anything any longer: we had entered a sort of zombie state where all that mattered was reaching the border of Namibia, to make sure that we would never again be trapped in this country.

Three days and two nights later we arrived, just before sunrise. The car stopped and as we got out with unsteady steps and shaky legs, we understood we were witnessing a miracle: in front of us the tall wire fence marked the place where Angola ended and Namibia began. We had arrived at the border.

We put up the tent one more time, the last time, and fell into a dreamless sleep. They said they would open the border at 9 am and we had got almost a whole night's sleep ahead of us.

THE next morning we remembered instantly why we hated any encounter with the police in general and the ones at border points in particular. We were waiting in a queue. They had taken away our passports. They said they needed to register them on a "computer". We deeply doubted that the wooden hut with no windows contained such equipment. There was a huge crowd around, all of them pushing, all of them waving their passports or IDs or whatever piece of paper they could produce. The crowd yelled. The policemen yelled. Our passports had been gone now for more than two hours and we started to feel restless.

"Give me my passport back! Do you hear me? I want my passport!" Richard shouted at one of the officials.

"*Não há pressa... Não há pressa.*[40]"

"Yes *pressa*, damn *pressa*: I'm in a hurry and I want my passport now. Right now!" Richard yelled like he was out of his mind.

Maybe they would arrest us. Maybe they would simply stop us from leaving this country right here, as we gazed at the civilised world across the border. We were so close!

But Richard had a sixth sense that told him when he could yell and when he should keep his mouth shut. And this time his yelling worked. Our passports appeared miraculously in the hands of the policeman.

"Just stamp me. Put your bloody damn stamp here. Right here!" Richard pulled his passport from the hands of the policeman, opened it and pointed to a blank corner.

"Just stamp me out of this country!"

His yell had managed to cover all the noise and the other yells and his furious face did the trick. The policeman seemed convinced, opened a big register and copied the data from our passports. Then he stamped them. Then he pointed us towards the gate. We crossed it, and as I set foot on Namibian soil I felt a sudden and instinctive need to cry.

But there was no time for crying. Smiling, polite officials dressed in clean uniforms welcomed us. They stamped our passports and it all happened in a matter of minutes. They searched our bags. They searched all the bags of everybody coming across the border in detail, as if afraid of smuggling from their neighbouring country. Then we were free to go and I heard one of them comment. They spoke English.

---

[40] "There's no hurry, there's no hurry." (in Portuguese)

English was the official language of Namibia.

"Look at them; poor them. Look how dirty they are. They must have come from far away."

"Yes my friend, from further away than you can possibly imagine," I felt like adding.

In front of us, just outside the Namibian police post on the other side of the fence, a new road began. It was tarmac and it was grey, and it suddenly replaced the red dirt road we had been travelling on so far.

The air was dusty, it was hot and I felt hungry. I could see a few shops lined up further along the tarmac road and I could even spot a sign above one of them which said "Supermarket". We walked towards it. It had a shiny new ATM machine next to its glass doors. I felt like crying again and I wanted to go and touch it, so as to believe it was real.

"No. No," Richard said. "You can't enter the supermarket. At least not for the next 30 minutes. Otherwise you'll have a heart attack!"

We stayed outside. We were just standing in the middle of the road. Shaking, looking at each other, we were too exhausted to say anything and I felt a mixture of joy and sadness building up in my throat and pushing to come out in tears. We had made it.

We wanted to take a picture once we stepped out of Angola, and we'd talked about it time and time again during the last three days in the various minibuses. We wanted to take it just beside the fence, with our passports open and our fingers pointing to the fresh exit stamp from Angola. But now that we were here we forgot all about it, and maybe taking a picture right next to a border point would have got us arrested anyway. We just rushed into the first shop we saw and ordered a big sandwich, and to my delight it was filled with cheese: with real cheese, not the ever-present "La Vache Qui Rit". And then we took cash out at the ATM and we entered the supermarket, and it was a real supermarket with shelves filled with all sorts of products, and we wandered through it looking at everything with eyes wide open as if we were in a museum.

Then we found a nice new minibus with comfy seats and expensive tickets to take us all the way to Windhoek. It would take us there in six hours, they said; the road was tarmacked and pretty good, and we realised that in fact it was the same distance that we had covered in the last three days and two nights, from Luanda to the border.

We felt we were living in a dream world. The sandwich and the people smelling of clean clothes and perfume and the supermarket and the cash machine: it was all unreal and we joked about it for a while, and Richard came up with the brilliant idea that they should put a signpost just before crossing the fence from Angola to Namibia saying, "Attention! You will experience a culture shock!" as a warning that one was about to enter another world.

But as we sat down in the minibus and started the easy and painless drive to Windhoek, I felt a deep, inexplicable pain stabbing my stomach and I knew that I was sad, as sad as I felt in Luanda buying that plane ticket. For it was the same thing, and this plush minibus was now coming to give me the same message the flight had done a few days earlier: my trip was ending and the real Africa was left behind, somewhere on the other side of the big wire fence we had crossed that morning...

TODAY I was to say goodbye to Richard. I woke up with this certainty and I carried it around throughout the day in the hectic rush from one place to the other. We were in Windhoek and the level of facilities around us, as well as the prices, reminded us of a world where one needed a job to pay the bills. It also meant things could be done a lot more quickly, there was no need to walk halfway across a town to find an embassy, one could make a quick phone call from the reception and they had all the visa information printed out anyway. Richard had quickly and easily found a bus ticket to South Africa and would go from there to Mozambique. The trip was to last some 20 hours and cover a distance as wide as the one we had covered in the last month. I, on the other hand, decided to take another bus in the opposite direction and go to Swakopmund, the second largest city in Namibia, where I was to meet Chris, my guide of last year who had promised me employment as an assistant safari guide. We were to leave today, both of us, in two opposite directions: I by noon and Richard in the evening. I was glad my bus left first: it would make me feel less abandoned, I thought.

My head was full of thoughts. We had arrived in Namibia and in the middle of its civilised capital, time started to rush and we had to rush away with it. And our trip seemed totally out of place here, where one could jump on to a luxurious bus to cover huge distances in just 20 hours. It was over. It was all over, and even though we were looking for ways to add some more to it, we knew deep down that it was over.

I thought about doing a tour on my own in Zimbabwe and maybe Madagascar. I still had money in my pocket and felt too sad to be going home just yet. I felt like I had a once in a lifetime opportunity to think about what I wanted to do with my life next, and I still didn't have an answer despite the eight months I had spent thinking about it. This was scary. Even scarier than this was the thought of being left on my own, for the first time since the start of this trip. Peter was still up north, crossing Angola probably, but we had no news from him. I knew that at some point he would turn up in Windhoek and this gave me some comfort. If my employment didn't start immediately, I could continue my trip with him to Cape Town. Richard, on the other hand, was in a hurry to get back: again, the Glastonbury Festival playing a big part in this, and he wanted to spend a couple of weeks on the beaches of Mozambique before returning to England. As for me, I was being pulled in all these opposite and contradictory directions with an overwhelmingly sad feeling ruling over everything else: even if I was to wait for Peter and go to Cape Town, even if I was to catch another bus and find Richard on the beaches of Mozambique, even if I was to go on my own to Zimbabwe, one way or the other this trip was over: it would never, ever be just the three of us and the car again.

I had half an hour to catch my minibus. This one was leaving on a fixed schedule and they had never heard of the "leave when full" rule. I rushed back to the hostel and looked for Richard, with my heart beating fast and the tears building up in my eyes. I was about to say goodbye.

I found him in the lobby. He was back from a stroll on his own in the town and he had also been looking for me.

"Hey, here you are! I was... I... I need to leave," I said, my voice choking.

He stood up. He looked at me. Around us people were laughing, talking, and somewhere far away a phone was ringing. I heard everything dimly and far away. I stared into Richard's greenish-blue eyes and I remembered the first time I saw them, on a rainy, cold evening in London, and I remembered how I stared into them the same way then. Only that now they were filled with so many memories.

"I was looking for you as well. I thought you'd left already. I thought I'd come back too late and I really... I really wanted to be here to say goodbye," he said.

We shook hands. This was the British part. Then I leaned over and gave him a brief kiss on both cheeks. This was the Latin one. I was still concentrating on my tears and I forgot to say anything else, as if there was something else to say, something that could contain it all... the joy of driving over the dunes together or the pain of sharing yet another bush taxi in Guinea... the hours spent being interrogated by police in Congo and the days of lying on the roof of the "Bethlehem Voyages". As if there could ever be a sentence that could contain everything we had shared together and the immense sadness that all those things had come to an end. Monsieur and Madame were to travel on different roads from now on.

"See you later," he said with his hand on my shoulder and his eyes still staring deeply into mine.

I smiled. Richard always said "see you later", even to people who he knew he would never see again.

"Yes, later. Somewhere, sometime. See you at some point again," I said, and then I added silently in my mind, "*Insha'Allah.*"

No, we wouldn't see each other later. But we might meet again at some point, when the time was right as the Africans say, and when we'd probably talk about all this and the warmth I felt then would still, hopefully, be there.

That was it. I left and tried hard not to glance back. I also tried hard not to cry, and for a while I managed. I got into my minibus and tried to think of something else for the remainder of the day.

I arrived in Swakopmund. I got in touch with Chris: I even met him briefly, and he told me the job he'd had for me was no longer there due to a drop in demand from Italian tourists. Disoriented and depressed, I walked on my own through the streets of the quiet town. I thought about everything again and again. One moment I felt like I should go home: I felt like I missed that world, where people went on with their life, celebrated birthdays, got married and had babies, a world where people were settled. The next moment

I felt I should email Richard and tell him I wanted to come to Mozambique to spend two more weeks together. But it was useless and I knew that even if I ran after him, it wouldn't be the same: nothing would ever be the same again because it was over and the sadness that was eating my heart away right now was the price I was paying for the privilege of having lived such an extraordinary experience.

I tried to contact more embassies. There was a riot in Zimbabwe and the buses had stopped crossing the borders. On top of everything I couldn't get a South African visa: they were not used to processing Romanian passports here and getting a visa would have taken a lot longer than my current Namibian visa allowed me to stay in the country. I didn't know what to do. Then I received an email from Peter saying he had crossed the border and he would be waiting for me by the northern border if I wanted to join him for a tour of the Etosha National Park.

More walking on the streets, more thinking. What was I waiting for? Something: an omen that would make me accept that this trip was indeed over. I had met Chris but he seemed distant and busy preparing for his next safari; too distant and too busy to be giving me any advice about what I had to do next. I was feeling lost, deeply lost, and, worst of all, alone.

I hadn't cried when I said goodbye to Richard that day and I hadn't cried during the following two days in Swakopmund. My mind was busy, caught up in all the different alternatives I was considering. But I carried the pain with me, and for the first time after six months of spending each and every day next to Richard I felt I was alone in the world. He had been more than a friend to me: he had been my whole universe and my main point of reference in all the madness we had gone through. I always felt that nothing wrong could ever happen to me as long as I was around him, and his way of saying "It will all be fine, you'll see" had some kind of magic in it and it was all fine, time and time again. But now that I was alone, I doubted that the magic formula would work for me any longer.

But the sadness in me was building up, and I eventually found a way out one early morning as I woke up in the eight-bed dorm of a hostel in Swakopmund.

I was still between sleeping and waking and I gazed

around with half-open eyes. I wondered which of the many beds around was Richard's and where was it that he had gone so early in the morning. I looked around. I saw the faces of people asleep, unknown faces: none of them was Richard's. I thought hard, really hard, as if I somehow knew there was something that I should have remembered but I couldn't. And then, the thought came like an explosion and I realised that none of those beds around would be Richard's, simply because he was not there.

After two days of resistance I gave up the battle: my tears came out and I cried, with my head under the pillow; I cried desperately and without end, and I somehow remembered crying last year in the middle of the plain at Twyfelfontein, and I knew that now, like then, it was the sadness of being alone and going back without my answers that made me cry.

When I had no more tears left I got up, washed my face and thought that maybe going up north to meet up with Peter and have a tour of the Etosha Park was not such a bad idea after all.

I checked out of the hostel and jumped into another minibus headed for Tsumeb, the city from which Peter had emailed me. As we hit the road out of town I realised not only that I didn't feel like crying any longer, but that a timid smile had taken shape on my face. Life was going on and we had to go on with it. And I remembered Richard's energy and his constant enthusiasm for the next leg of our journey, and his planning and smiling in front of an open map, the sparkle in his eyes and the enthusiasm in his voice. And I realised that even if he had gone now and I didn't know if I would ever see him again, there was something he had left behind, like a hidden gift that I had just unwrapped, and I knew this was something that would stay with me forever: the joy of moving on.

CHAPTER 26 – EPUPA FALLS

(NORTHERN NAMIBIA, JUNE 2003)

THE woman smiled and told me her name. I couldn't understand it. I really wanted to know her name so I asked her again. I don't know why, maybe because she seemed friendly and she let me take a picture of her without asking for money in exchange as all the others did; maybe because she had offered me some of the strange seeds she was eating; or maybe because the small toddler she carried on her back in a sort of a little, handmade leather backpack had a smiley, round face and kept on trying to reach his little hands out to me.

I wanted to know her name because I had spent the last hour trying unsuccessfully to talk to her and I no longer felt that taking a picture could preserve any of the magic of such encounters.

She smiled again. Then she took a small stone with a pointed end and started drawing carefully in the dust of the road on the side of which we were sitting. I followed her shy letters: first N, then A, and then I could suddenly make sense of it.

"Naukukui," I said.

She smiled and touched her bare breasts. "It's me," her gesture said, and I realised I had got it right this time.

She could understand a bit of English and I was surprised to see that she could write. I then asked her how old she was, and she wrote the answer in the dust: 25. How many kids did she have? Four. I did not ask if this meant four in total or four of them alive. She belonged to the Himba tribe, one of the last authentic pastoral tribes left in Africa. The women of this tribe took a long time every morning painting their naked bodies with a red mixture made of clay and butter fat, and this gave them an intense red colour which was regarded as very attractive, in addition to being a protection from all sorts of insects. They wore heavy metal and leather jewellery and had intricate hair fashions, with their long braids usually covered up by the same red mud. The married ones would wear a pair of little horns on their head, which made them look like little gazelles, while the unmarried girls would have their hair pulled up into thick braids coming over their faces.

I had met her on the outskirts of this small town in the heart of Kaokoland, a northern province of Namibia. She looked at me and waved and I came to sit with her, and I instantly felt close to her despite the lack of words or understanding. Like other people I had met throughout this trip, she was a proud, free inhabitant of this land, oblivious to the "civilisation" of the 21st century. She wore her heavy, copper ornaments around her neck, hanging down between her full, bare breasts, and her many layers of metal beads around her ankles and wrists. The only piece of clothing she had on was a little leather miniskirt strapped tightly to her waist by a richly embroidered leather belt. Her bare feet melted into the red dust of the road and it was hard to say where was it that Naukukui ended and the red African earth started.

I sat down with her for a while, staring at her copper-red body, the colour of the road that brought me south. The smell of the clay mixture she had spread all over her body was so powerful and the colour so intense that I suddenly felt like I was back in the Africa I loved and that I still felt I had left behind the fence at the border between Namibia and Angola.

Peter called me. It was time to go. I waved to her and she smiled again, and, like the tourist that I was, I took another picture of her and then, once back at the car, I opened my notebook and wrote down her name: Naukukui. And I knew that it would be her name and not the picture that would keep her alive in my memory.

I was back with Peter in the Land Rover. I met him and the Camel in a petrol station on the road, just as the minibus I travelled in had filled up with petrol and was hitting the road again. I shouted out. The driver stopped. I got out and told him not to wait for me. He probably thought I was crazy. But I was not crazy, just happy, really happy, and I ran over to the car, opened the door and threw my bag on the back seat and then turned to an astonished Peter and said, "Hello, hello! Here I am. I thought you had had enough of being on your own!"

There was warmth between us. It felt almost like all the endless disputes we had gone through had been left behind, on the other side of the wire fence separating Angola from Namibia. We were at the end of our trip and we knew it and now, with Richard gone, I felt time was flowing backwards and we were back to the roads of Morocco, the two of us and the Camel, and we were somehow back to the same endless conversations where he mumbled something and I asked him to repeat it again and again; where he made a joke and I failed to laugh at it. This trip was ending the same way it had started.

Peter had had no troubles crossing Angola, apparently, and he wisely avoided the capital, which meant he stayed out of trouble. He even spent very little money, since petrol was cheap and he always slept in his roof tent. He said he thought people were friendly and it was altogether a very pleasant experience – a very different point of view from mine.

Kinshasa and the former Zaire, on the other hand, although a trouble-free stopover for Richard and me, had been a nightmare for him. The next day after we left on our bus to Matadi, he had been kidnapped from the main boulevard of Kinshasa by two guys who claimed to be plain-clothes policemen. Stuck on the back seat of their car between two others, he realised he was heading towards trouble and decided to fight his way out of there at all costs. Apparently the fact that they were caught in slow-moving traffic and the presence of another policeman, a real one this time, by a junction helped him escape alive from the car.

We talked about what next. He was following his way south to Cape Town and I was seriously considering flying back to Europe from Windhoek due to the messy visa situation I was in.

But there was something else that I needed to do before leaving Africa: have a chat, a real one, with Chris.

When I met him in Swakopmund, Chris seemed to be somewhat pleased to see me but caught up in a thousand other things he had to do. He was leaving on a safari the next day and he briefly told me about his itinerary, then added, "If you meet your other travel mate and the car, then come and find me in one of those camping places; we'll chat some more."

I felt I needed this chat, even though it was not really clear what it was to be about. I felt that somehow this trip had started back there at Twyfelfontein, last year when he had told me all those things about the path which lies dormant in each of us and about the courage to get up and follow your dreams. I felt that I had listened to him and this whole trip was the proof that I had got up and followed my dreams. And now, at the end of it, I felt empty. I had always carried with me the hope that I would find what I was looking for, whatever that was: the answers to my questions, my direction in life, what I wanted to do next. But I didn't, and now that I was about to leave I was about to panic, just like the last night of my safari experience last year when I had had to return to my grey life. One way or the other I wanted my answers, and I somehow hoped that another chat with Chris would send me in the right direction.

He said he would be taking a group up north to see the Himba tribes close to the northern border of the country, and then to camp for a few days at Epupa Falls on the Kunene River. Peter was fine with the idea and we started driving towards the Falls at once.

I had asked Peter to let me drive that day, which he reluctantly accepted. I hadn't driven since before Pokola, since the potholed, muddy road in the heart of the rainforest in Cameroon. Now it all seemed to have taken place in another life.

The road was bad, full of stones, and I managed to destroy one of the tyres completely. Peter was complaining. I was trying to concentrate and stare into the road, trying to see and avoid each and every stone, each and every hole. I didn't manage too well, and feeling discouraged, I lifted my eyes for a bit and there I saw a beautiful, magnificent baobab tree just beside the road. Its trunk was thick and solid, its branches spasmodically dancing in the air, reaching up towards the sky. It was almost like a human presence but I didn't have too much time to contemplate it. I turned my eyes back on the road, as I felt I had just hit another rock.

The drive was long and dry. We knew we would have to

hit the river, but the landscape seemed so dry and desert-like that I doubted there would be any river close by. And yet, despite the dust and the dryness, it was there and it appeared in front of our eyes unexpectedly after a sharp turn. It was a strong river with whitewater whirls and I could see the vegetation completely changing on both banks. There were palm trees and green bushes, even some baobabs in the distance, and the narrow stretch of land on the side of the river looked like a hidden garden emerging from the dust of the dry lands we had been driving through. There was white foam rising from the middle of the river, from the place where its waters tumbled down into a narrow gorge and then into a series of small cascades. We took another long look at it and we knew we had arrived. We were at Epupa Falls.

FROM the other side of the fire his eyes stared at me and I could read warmth in them, the same warmth that came out of the small, yellow flames of the fire dancing on the remaining logs. He stared at me, a long, silent stare, and then my words died one by one and all that I wanted to say was lost somewhere in the darkness around us and my voice died into silence as well.

"You're such a fool," Chris said, and there was warmth in his voice.

I didn't understand, but I tried hard not to misunderstand either.

I was happy to meet Chris here at Epupa Falls, in the exact place he had told me he would camp. I had started telling him about our adventures and I spoke about the desert drives and the rainforest, about surviving the police in Congo, about bush taxis and the endless road we had travelled for the last eight months. And I didn't understand why he interrupted me to tell me that I was a fool.

But the warmth in his eyes was still there and I couldn't get angry.

"You're such a fool," he repeated. "But it's OK, you know, we all are; we are all fools at some point or another. But one day the fools will become wise and the wise will become fools. Whatever you do, try not to pretend you're wise. It's a lot better to remain a fool!"

He took another sip from his can and then reached out for the bottle of brandy on the table and poured himself some more.

"It's the disease of the *I*," he carried on, with his eyes turned towards the river that flowed silently under the white light of the moon. It was a full moon night tonight, another full moon, just like this time last year. And just like then, it was late in the night, and the others were in their tents: his three tourists tucked away in theirs and Peter lying asleep in his on the roof of the car. We had remained outside, the two of us, and I had a very small hope that the depth I had reached when talking to Chris last year would be reached again.

"The disease of the *I*," he repeated. "This is the disease of the century. I did this, I did that, look at me and applaud me: I, I and I again. You're such a fool."

"What do you mean? I talk too much about myself? But all those things really happened, and I feel I want to write about them. I feel I've been really privileged to have those experiences and I want to write about them so that others can live them too!"

"Yeah, write then," he said, and the warmth in his eyes had turned into sarcasm. "Write your book and it will be another explosion of the disease of the *I*. Your ego will be satisfied. And you will have achieved nothing. Nothing."

I kept quiet. I felt he was unjust; after all, I wanted to write a book about searching, daring and finding that would inspire others.

"Will inspire others to what?" he interrupted me. "What makes you think you have a message to pass on? What makes you think you can write about Africa, what makes you think you have seen the 'real' Africa? Do you think the real Africa is about poor people and corrupt officials? This is the essence of this continent, do you think?" He was now heavily sarcastic.

"But Chris, I've spent eight months on this continent. I've seen the good parts, I've seen the bad parts. I've lived and survived through all of those things and maybe, yes, poor people and corrupt officials are part of it."

"You have seen nothing. Or maybe you've simply passed by the meaning of what you've seen. If you want to write about Africa, write about the herds of elephants, write about the huge spaces where animals roam free and where Bushmen or Himba tribes hunt them in the same way they hunted them thousands of years ago. Write about the forest of baobab trees you have passed by on the way here."

"Which forest of baobab trees?" This was strange. I didn't remember having seen it, and moreover baobabs don't really grow together in a forest, they are more like lonely trees on a plain.

"There was a forest of baobab trees on the road: the road passes right through it. It's very rare and amazingly beautiful... you must have passed right through it when you came here, there's only one road anyway."

Silence. I remembered the one and only baobab tree at the sight of which I had marvelled as I lifted my eyes for a brief moment away from the road.

I felt ashamed. He was right. Maybe I had been passing by the true meaning of the many things I had seen on this trip, too busy to control each and every small detail, too busy to look for the small stones in the road.

"Listen to me," he continued, and he leaned forward above the fire. "Listen to me. You have started well, but you're a long way away from the end. What you have experienced is the Africa of people. All your stories, the Tuaregs and the camels and the pygmies and the police, all this is the Africa of people and this can be pretty wild. Pretty scary wild," he added.

"But the thing missing is the dimension of nature." He pointed to his T-shirt, with a big logo that read "Nature Adventure".

"You have missed the dimension of nature and you need to get in touch with it, because only the day that you will be able to transmit and put into writing the overwhelming feeling of meeting with a herd of wild elephants on the top of a hill, only then will you have woken up both of these dimensions within you and then you can write, and then I will read your book."

"But how do I find this dimension of nature that you say I'm missing?"

"You look for it," came the answer, and for a brief moment I felt I had gone back in time and it was the Chris of last year talking to me again.

"You go out and spend days or maybe weeks in the wilderness. I can set up something like this for you if you want. I'll take you somewhere far away, in the middle of the savannah, and leave you there with a tent and some food and water and come to find you after a week, let's say. There, in complete solitude, you will understand what nature means."

I wasn't too tempted to follow his advice. I wouldn't have survived, not even one night. I would have been too afraid. I did not ask him anything else but I felt discouraged.

The river was flowing silently, and once again I marvelled that such a mighty river could be flowing through what was practically bare desert. The Kunene River marked the border of the two countries: on one side, Angola, on the other, Namibia. My best and worst experiences in Africa were separated by its course. I thought again about going back home...

"Chris, I'm afraid. I'm afraid to go back," I carried on. "I left for this trip with high hopes that I would find my answers, that I would understand what I want to do with my life. That..." I stopped. I didn't know, in fact what exactly it was that I expected from this trip and what was still missing, but it was something important that I had to take home with me, something I had not found yet. Something that I was so scared I might not have any time left to find...

"Then why are you going back?" Chris asked.

Because I had no money left, I wanted to answer. But no, it wasn't only that. I was going back because on the other side I felt ready to go back, to face again the world that I had run away from and to which I belonged, after all. And there was something else. Independent of my own will, this trip was ending, as if it had a life of its own and decided for itself when it was to start and when it was to be over. And it was over right now, in these last days, and it had decided to end right here in Namibia, in exactly the same place where it had started a year ago. It was ending with Chris by the fire, as it had started last year, with Peter at the wheel, as it had started in Morocco. It was ending and I couldn't do anything but accept that a part of me was ending with it as well.

I had another sip from the tin and I realised the drink was finished. We looked for some more brandy but it was all gone. Then I had a brilliant idea: Peter's single malt whisky, a bottle that he had been carrying all the way from Spain and from which he would occasionally enjoy a small sip. I knew it was one of his most treasured belongings, but at times like this one turns selfish in a matter of seconds. We had just started talking and we needed a drink to keep us going. After all, I had been travelling for eight months for the privilege of this chat. I felt that only another bottle could keep Chris talking, and I had a desperate need to clarify my thoughts.

I got the bottle out of the car, taking care not to slam the doors so as not to wake Peter, who was sleeping in his roof tent. The whisky tasted worse than the cognac and in my opinion it could have been improved with some syrup from one of the peach tins we had opened for dinner.

"You told me to believe in dreams. Last year at Twyfelfontein, this is what you said. You told me to get up and go follow my dreams and here I am. I've done the trip of my life; and now, at the end of it, I find myself without any other dream to hang on to."

"Good. Congratulations. It means you're waking up." He smiled wryly and I felt I was about to start crying. All that he talked about seemed so contradictory.

"Once you get up and go live your dream, then you align your life to that dream and it becomes less of a fantasy and more of the real thing. Then you see it as a loss, because you don't have anything else left there, in the fantasy land, to hang on to. It's OK even if it's hard as well."

The lines of the song I heard in Angola came back to me: "Sometimes living up your dreams / Is not as easy as it seems". And what if the song and Chris were trying to tell me the same thing? And what if the sensation of emptiness and sadness I felt now was in fact coming to tell me that I was waking up, that I had left the fantasy land and descended into real dreams?

"You see, we never arrive, in fact. We always rush and hurry, hoping that there will be a place, a moment, when we can reach somewhere that we can get our answers. And you know what? This is another illusion, because in fact we will never arrive."

"What do you mean?" I asked, feeling frustrated. "Look at you. You are someone who has it all in life. You have a beautiful wife and two kids who seem to be two little angels. You have just moved into a new house. You're earning good money doing the job you really want to be doing, living out your passion. How can you say we never arrive, when you, you have arrived!"

"You fool!" he said. "You don't understand. You don't understand that even when we have it all, a family and kids, and when we have found a partner and we get married and even when we have a new house, you don't understand that the questions will never go away."

I could take a lot of frustration from Chris but this last statement seemed like a bad joke to me. I had left my job and my life because I was looking for the answers to those questions. And now, the very person who encouraged me to do so and who managed to transmit the sparkle of enthusiasm that lit the fire of all these amazing experiences for me, the same man was telling me now that the answers were not to be found.

"What do you mean?" I asked in a quiet voice, with all the disappointment built up on my face like a child who has suddenly realised she is never going to receive the gift for which she has waited for one full year.

"You will never arrive," he repeated, "because there is nowhere to reach; because it's only the road we travel on that matters, and there's only death waiting at the other end of this road. So we had better take the time to look around instead of hurrying to arrive as soon as possible. It's an illusion, it's all an illusion..." he said, and his voice wandered away and melted into the fire.

"The only thing we can do is to try to get a bit closer to those answers," he continued "Where do I want to live? What type of work do I want to do? Who will I marry? How will my kids be? There is no clear answer to all those things. There is trial and error; there's the will to find out that brings you a bit closer to the answers. But the real answers will never reveal themselves. It's a mystery, one of life's mysteries."

"How about passion, then?" I asked, still not convinced. "How about my deep desire to be here, in Africa, to have done this trip and to think that one day I will be back? Is this also an illusion?"

"No, passion is real. Passion is the fuel, you see. You cannot do too much without passion. But you must learn to control it. Passion is a dangerous weapon sometimes." He paused and took another sip. His eyes were now reflecting the flames and I could see in them the reflection of his own deep flames.

"I am struggling with this myself," he carried on. "With taking control over passion, I mean. Sometimes I control it and this is when it takes me in the good direction; at other times it controls me and this is when trouble comes. You see, I'm an extremist and sometimes this passion that I have chosen to let live in my own life, this passion opens up and I can see the dark precipice beneath and I'm pulled down, deep down where I can see the scary face of the other me."

Chris looked back into the fire and I noticed the wrinkles on his forehead getting deeper. For the first time I had the impression that he must have been dealing with his own questions, and even if he sometimes managed to give me the right answers, maybe he had still not totally found his own. The scary face of the other me, what did he mean? How could it be that this man, who gave so much to those around him, who gave so much to me, could still be vulnerable when facing his own demons?

"Then what is the solution? What can someone do to stay alive and balanced in the middle of all this turmoil, in the middle of all those questions without answers?" I asked, and I hoped that at least this question would receive an answer.

"You turn to the memories you carry in your heart; you remember the images you have seen and which have touched you. You'll understand more when you discover the Africa of nature," he said with a brief smile. "There are small things like the memory of a sunrise or the elephants in the dawn or the immensity of the fields. These things are there even if the answers have not come, and they give you the strength to carry on. You see, after all we struggle for, the only thing we take back with us when we die are memories."

Memories. I may not have had my answers, but memories I had a lot of. As I stared at the fire I saw them all coming and going, dancing with the flames. All the memories of these eight months were coming back. And I understood that I might not have seen the Africa of nature, as Chris called it, but I had lived the Africa of people and there was beauty in there, a beauty that I was to carry with me forever.

There was an afternoon spent in the tent of the nomads in the desert, their chants and their women with henna-painted fingers drumming into the night. There was Ibrahim speaking Italian from under a Tuareg shawl, and Dieu, the captain of the "Bethlehem Voyages", praying for us in the stillness of the rainforest morning. There was Richard and his mad run on the streets of Luanda to return my flight ticket. There was a car and the three of us flying over a dune.

Yes, I was carrying all those things with me and they

would stay there and live in me in the same way that the miraculous meadow of my childhood lived in me for many years. And then, still watching the dying flames of the campfire on the shores of the Kunene River, I understood that I had found, in fact, my little meadow, the one I had started looking for last year, and I was now ready to go back home carrying all those little treasures that I had found with it.

With the fire dead and the bottle empty, there was not much that could keep us going. I thought of last year's night, with the joint and two bed rolls side by side in the middle of the fairy circle. It was all gone. There would be no joint and no fairy circle tonight. But I didn't need them any more. I didn't need to sleep outside either; I had been spending too many nights sleeping outside during this trip.

It was time to say goodbye.

"We won't meet again," Chris said. "Not on this tour, at least. I know we said that we would meet again at this other camp, but the reality of the situation is that it's hard to arrange such meetings with two cars driving on different routes and we will just miss these meeting points. So I just wanted to say goodbye to you here and now. Tomorrow morning everything will be hectic."

It was too dark to see his eyes, but I could feel the depth of his words. I couldn't stop feeling that "on this tour" meant, in fact, "in this life". I felt I was never going to see him again, as if his mission in my life ended right there and then.

"One day we may meet again," he said, probably reading again my silent thoughts.

I didn't answer. But in my mind the old praying word came back again: "*Insha'Allah!*"

I went back into my tent and felt my limbs trembling because there was no fire and nights were very cool in Namibia at that time of the year. I was still feeling sad, but there was more than sadness in there. It was a deep, underlying feeling that things were as they were meant to be and things would work out. It was a feeling which said that beyond anything good or bad that happened, I would be fine. For a moment I remembered Richard's words from that night when I cried under a tree and he came to tell me the story of an old man and his collection of soaps. He spoke about feeling sad and feeling fine at the same time and I didn't understand it then. Now I did.

CHRIS was right and we did not meet again for the remainder of the days we spent in the north. We headed towards Etosha Park and then we had a puncture in one wheel, then another one, and with the reserve being by now trashed during my drive in Kaokoland we felt we needed to head towards a proper garage urgently. We thought we could still stop on the way for a drive through the Etosha Park: after all, it was to be the first proper park with animals that we had found on this trip so far.

We entered the park and we stopped to pay the entrance fee, and just as we got ready for our drive we heard a bang on the windows and someone yelling and waving desperately in the middle of the street: it was Karl.

This time he was without Mavis. They didn't allow bikes in the park and he told us he was looking for a ride to see the animals. A perfect match, since we were on our way to the same destination.

With Karl in the car the afternoon went by quickly: the "Africa on telly" expedition, as Karl called it, watching the animals from the safety of our car. I couldn't stop thinking that this was another omen, though. I had met Karl in Morocco, on my second day in Africa as I was travelling with Peter in the car; now I was meeting him again, a couple of days before leaving Africa, as I was travelling with Peter in the car. Once again, my trip was round.

But right now we were in a park, taking pictures of springboks and gazelles, and I was happy – too happy to be thinking about leaving. Even Peter, who had been deeply shocked on discovering the missing whisky bottle, had by now come to terms with it. What he could still not forgive was the fact that I had drunk the remainder of his treasured single malt in a mixture with the peach syrup. This, he said, was betrayal. He also said I was lucky that the powers of his magic guardian spirit had not worked, since I might have been transformed into a frog. I had a good laugh about it and he laughed too, and for the remainder of the day I felt I had rediscovered the warmth under his apparently distant behaviour, the same sensation I had in the Atlas Mountains in Morocco. Once again, time seemed to be winding back.

IT was almost dusk and I went to sit on the benches far

above the waterhole and watch the animals coming to drink. I was there among other tourists, with their clean and perfumed clothes. They were people who had come here on holiday, tourists that I had never seen before in all of Central Africa, in Congo and Zaire or Angola. We had left the land of adventure and had landed in full-blown tourism. I was sad and I didn't understand what I still had to see there, in the middle of that perfumed crowd. Was there anything I could share with those people that could touch me as deeply as the people of the desert had touched me? The Africa of nature and the Africa of people, said Chris. And now, seated on that wooden bench like a tourist lost in the middle of the other tourists, I was looking at nature waiting for something to happen. Nothing happened though. The waterhole was still under the last rays of the setting sun.

I remembered the days of doing nothing in Pokola, the days on the boat and the afternoons in the tents of the Tuaregs and slowly I managed to move away from the feeling that I was waiting for something to happen. And as I did this, the waterhole, although still with no animals around it, seemed to have suddenly changed and its colours were a lot more intense now, and the sky reflected in the water was a lot more blue.

The sun was close to setting and it sent out a myriad of bright red and orange tones which slowly turned into pink and lilac. The colours changed quickly and there was an entire silent symphony taking place far away on the horizon. Of all that I had seen in Africa, the sunrises and sunsets of Namibia were still the most spectacular of all. The surface of the water shivered, touched by a brief breeze, and its colour changed, reflecting part of the colour explosion in the sky above. The night was falling and the immense African savannah seemed as frozen or as alive as one chose to see it.

The elephants came first. Maybe because they were the tall, mighty owners of the plains and nobody could have contested their supremacy. A whole herd of them came and they bathed in the pond and the water didn't reflect the sky any longer but became muddy and whirly. They drank it and they played with it, the young bulls in the middle of the pond, the mothers and calves drinking on the sides. They took water up through their long noses and they splashed it on to each other, and although the light was getting dimmer and dimmer the artificial lights had been switched on, and they were dim enough not to disturb the animals but strong enough so that I could see the smiles and joy in the eyes of the elephants. They had the eyes of humans, I suddenly thought with a shiver. They had eyes that reflected as much intelligence as ours but much more joy, enthusiasm and passion.

They played for a while and then they went away: as silently and slowly as they had come, they stepped away and vanished into the immensity of the savannah. The waterhole was abandoned once again, but my eyes were still so filled with the image of the elephants playing that I kept on seeing them there long after they were gone.

The giraffes came next, two of them with gracious, long necks. They came with small, quick steps and they stopped just in front of the pond, watching all of us up there, hidden on the benches of our observation platform. They probably didn't see us after all: the lodge was very eco-friendly and the observation platforms were well-hidden and built far enough away that the viewing would not disturb the animals. But the two giraffes looked at each other, then they looked around, and as they bowed their heads to drink I realised they flexed their knees as well. Their necks were too rigid to allow them to drink if they didn't flex their legs as well, and this was probably the scientific explanation for the picture I was seeing in front of my eyes; or maybe they were just mocking us, all the silent spectators of this show, and they had bowed to us much like two ballerinas would bow to the audience once their dance is over.

After they drank they left too, with the same quick, small steps, and they vanished into the darkness and the waterhole remained, abandoned once again.

By now I was breathing deeply in the stillness of the night and I realised that I had tears in my eyes and this time they had not come because of thinking of going back home or because of some silly argument or midnight terror. They had come simply because the giraffes had bowed to me.

The next ones to come were the zebras, and they came running in a big herd and they stopped and they drank all at once, nicely aligned on the shores, as if they were an ordered army. They drank silently for a while, quite a short while I thought, and then at a sign from their leader the nicely ordered army left at the same wild gallop with which they had come.

Then the lions came, and I thought that maybe the zebras had been running away for fear that they felt the lions approaching. I did not know then that animals never attack each other near a waterhole, it's a sacred ground and everybody seems to respect the rule. It's a survival instinct, I guess: after all, if the lions eat the zebras by the waterholes then the zebras wouldn't come any longer and they would die of thirst, and the lions would die too since all their prey would have vanished. Or maybe it was not so complicated: maybe it was just simple courtesy and the animals were as capable of courtesy as humans were, and maybe even more so.

The birds came after the lions, and then the squirrels came as well. Then the hole remained empty again for a long time and I thought that maybe it was all over. But no: with shy steps, two hyenas emerged from the bush and they drank too, with quick sideways glances, and then the next time I looked they were there no longer. They had vanished into the night as if they had never been. And the springboks came too, and the gazelles, the big buffalo and the onyxes with their black and white, mask-like faces; and maybe the mice came too, only that they were too small and I probably didn't notice them. One by one the animals entered this silent stage: they bowed to us, the hidden audience, they drank and then they left, as silently and naturally as they arrived.

And late into the night, when the moon came out, I saw the white rhinoceros who came alone and who bowed his head to drink too. And I could see an identical image forming in the water, that of another rhinoceros, upside down this time, and their horns touched as he drank and he looked like he had found his partner, just like maybe one day I would find mine too, and the two animals, one real and the other surreal, were kissing through the surface of the water. And then all of a sudden it became too much and the tears falling down my face told me that I was not prepared to look at this any longer, as if my heart was not yet open enough to contain all this beauty, and I cried silently on my bench. I cried for the sadness of going back home and for the happiness of being there in that moment, witnessing this small miracle, and I let my tears fall freely on to my cheeks until they stopped, all alone, and I understood that this was the Africa of nature that I had not seen, that I had passed by with my eyes shut, and I knew that this was what Chris meant and what was still missing from my experience; what was still left to be discovered, one day, when the time was right. And then and there I made a new promise to myself: I will return to Africa.

EPILOGUE

ELEVEN years have passed. I live in London now, just like Richard and Peter.

Richard came back home from Mozambique and went straight to the Glastonbury Festival. Then he tried various things for a few years and finally decided to settle as a property developer. He has no regrets about giving up the career he started in finance. In memory of our trip he set up a charity – The Georgetown Trust Fund – which sends poor children to school in Gambia and which takes him back to West Africa every year.

Peter continued his trip on his own to Cape Town, then he turned around and drove back on the east coast of Africa until he reached Egypt, where he couldn't enter by car so he used the same trick that got us out of trouble a few times during our trip: he put the car on a boat, crossed the Red Sea into Saudi Arabia, then crossed the Middle East and finally came back home to London some year and a half later. As a tribute to the computer games that kept him company in Pokola and further along the way, he set up a computer business – Computer Angels – whose name probably has something to do with his guardian spirit, the fetish he bought in Congo and which still guards his sleep to this day. His journal and pictures of our trip are available online at **www.camelworld.com**

I have never seen Chris again. We wrote to each other a few times over the years. I know he still takes tourists into the wilderness through his safari company, Living Desert Adventures (**www.livingdesertnamibia.com**) and talks to them about the "courage to become who you are". This book is dedicated to him and the message he passed on to me.

As for me, I still believe in dreams and in the power to make them happen.

After I came back from Windhoek I settled in London but still travelled a lot, working as a management consultant and later for my own company, Value Associates. I went back to Africa and to the desert a few more times. Each time got me closer to the dimension of nature. I followed Chris' advice and kept on searching for answers and opening doors, and realised eventually that he was right: the questions will never go away. The trick is to live with them and be happy at the same time

Africa filled my heart long after the trip was over. I dreamt of it often and used to wake up with the taste of its green bananas on my tongue and the smell of its dust in my nostrils. The memories flooded my brain again and again until one morning I decided to start writing them down in a desperate attempt to set myself free. I wrote this book. I took the demon out.

The more I wrote, the more the trip started to fade away. At first I panicked, but then I made a pledge with myself: I will not fight to keep these memories alive. I will let them go back where they belong: in the past. I will not try to preserve intact in some distant corner of my mind the purple of a sunrise on the African plain and the song of the dunes in the night. I will not stare at an empty dot on the wall and imagine a long, red, dusty, winding road south. I will let all of these go and empty my mind and fill it up again with *here* and *now*, and whatever this *here* and *now* will mean for me. Because not doing so would mean I will be living in the past, and if Africa has taught me anything it's about the power of the everlasting present. *Maintenant.* My life is now.

And by letting them go I will keep them imprinted on my soul forever, and I will not *think* of them but I will *be* them, for they will have sunk deep into my blood and travel through my veins and they will be part of the new me, the me who came back renewed at the end of that trip. And I knew that even if I let those memories go, in some mysterious way, a part of me would still be there, going south, much the same way as a part of Africa is still here, with me, today.

Yes, I have come to know that the only way to keep Africa alive in me is to let it go...

London, August 2014

ACKNOWLEDGEMENTS

My thanks and gratitude to those who helped make this trip and this book happen:

To Chris, for inspiring me to dream.

To Richard and Peter, for travelling together this long, dusty road south.

To my parents, friends and my Bocconi MBA classmates, for supporting me with countless encouraging emails along the way.

To David, for encouraging me to start writing my memories.

To Jill, Bea, Ian and Lisa for feedback, editing, proofreading and very helpful suggestions.

Above all, my gratitude flows to the people of Africa, who shared with us the beauty of their lands and culture. You will be in my heart forever.

9 780993 130908